Munich Studies on Innovation and Competition

Volume 11

Series Editors
Josef Drexl, Germany
Reto M. Hilty, Germany

More information about this series at http://www.springer.com/series/13275

Sunimal Mendis

A Copyright Gambit

On the Need for Exclusive Rights in Digitised Versions of Public Domain Textual Materials in Europe

Springer

Sunimal Mendis
Max Planck Institute for Innovation and Competition
Munich, Germany

ISSN 2199-7462 ISSN 2199-7470 (electronic)
Munich Studies on Innovation and Competition
ISBN 978-3-662-59453-7 ISBN 978-3-662-59454-4 (eBook)
https://doi.org/10.1007/978-3-662-59454-4

This Springer imprint is published by the registered company Springer-Verlag GmbH, DE, part of Springer Nature.
The registered company address is: Heidelberger Platz 3, 14197 Berlin, Germany

This book is dedicated to my parents,
Lakshmi and Ranjan Mendis,
the giants on whose shoulders I stand

Foreword

For almost three decades, digitisation has been a hot topic in copyright. In the focus of discussions lies the quest for an appropriate balance between, on the one hand, measures aiming to secure authors' and other right holders' control over protected content that is disseminated online, and, on the other hand, the individual and societal interests in getting access to such content. In that scenario, protection in the form of copyright (including neighbouring rights) and enhanced possibilities of access appear as antagonisms. In the specific situation investigated in this book, however, the usual scheme is reversed: as postulated and skilfully substantiated by the author, the creation of an exclusive right in the form of a related right in digital copies of rare texts can improve access to such rarities and thus contribute to the conservation of the cultural heritage of mankind. Accepting exclusivity to gain such benefits is the "gambit" to which the title alludes.

What is the problem? While digitisation of texts is constantly ongoing in various forms, gradually creating a virtual library containing the culture and knowledge of the world, the issue poses particular challenges on "rare" texts in the sense that only few original copies exist world-wide. The digitisation of such texts requires particular skills and substantial investment. Such resources are often not readily available at the cultural institutions where they are kept and preserved. Nonetheless, private know-how and investment can only be attracted if something is given in return, such as a license permitting to exploit the results of the investment for a limited time. As the author shows in her comprehensive empirical investigation of the current status quo, such licenses are indeed regularly granted by the cultural institutions in various forms and under various conditions. However, the crux is that until now no secure basis exists for such licenses, as the conditions for copyright protection are rarely fulfilled (if ever), and other intellectual property rights are equally unable to fill the protection gap.

As a member of the International Max-Planck Research School—Competition and Innovation (IMPRS-CI), the author has engaged in thorough field research, interacting with a multitude of cultural institutions in the field, learning about their needs and difficulties, and analysing the strengths and drawbacks of the diverse operation modes chosen. Before that background, she has developed her own proposal for an EU-wide neighbouring right in the digital copies of rare textual material. The proposal is not only innovative because it is the first of its kind in the area concerned, but it is mature, detailed and sophisticated, with a strong emphasis on finding a balanced solution. This part of the book is true pioneer work, showing the profound knowledge of the author of the practical and legal implications of the field. In its other parts, the book likewise conveys valuable information on the empirical background, as well as on (dys)functionalities of intellectual property protection in the area concerned.

Naturally for such a proposal, one may have a number of questions, be it as to details, or on the concept of a new right as such. But such potential scepticism does not detract from the fact that this is a highly interesting, thought-provoking contribution on an issue that forms an important component of contemporary efforts to preserve and secure accessibility of items belonging to the cultural heritage of mankind, for the world of today and for generations to come.

Ludwig Maximilians University
of Munich, Munich, Germany
10 April 2019

Annette Kur

Acknowledgments

This book marks the culmination of a long personal and academic journey. It presents the research I carried out as a doctoral fellow at the International Max Planck Research School for Competition and Innovation (IMPRS-CI), under the supervision of Prof. Josef Drexl. The initial research was carried out between 2011–2014 with revisions and updates effected between 2017–2018.

This journey has been both exciting and arduous, and along the way, many persons have helped to smoothen my path and lighten my load. My sincere gratitude goes out to all of them. Although it is not possible to name every one of these persons, there are a few very special people who deserve particular mention.

My *Doktorvater* Prof. Josef Drexl (Max Planck Institute for Innovation and Competition, Munich, Germany) has been my guide and mentor throughout this journey. Without his able direction, warm-hearted understanding and infinite patience it would not have been possible for me to bring this journey to a successful completion. I am also indebted to Prof. Séverine Dusollier (Sciences Po Law School, Paris) for her steadfast support and encouragement that enabled me to find the time and energy to effect critical updates and revisions to this manuscript while working as a researcher under her supervision. I would also like to extend my sincere appreciation to Prof. Annette Kur (Ludwig Maximilians University of Munich) who, with her characteristic kindness and consideration, agreed to provide a foreword to this publication despite being in the middle of a particularly demanding schedule.

I am grateful to Dr. Sylvie Nérisson (IRDAP-University of Bordeaux) who was the co-ordinator of the IMPRS-CI doctoral program (2011–2014), for her ready assistance and advice on surviving this academic voyage. A warm 'thank you' also goes out to my wonderful colleagues at the IMPRS-CI and Sciences Po, particularly Alina Wernick, Maxime Lambrecht, Martin Husovec, Fabiana Bettini and Veronica Corcodel for their encouragement and friendship. Maxime and Martin provided useful feedback and perceptive insights that were invaluable to me in developing this research—my especial gratitude goes out to them.

I would also like to thank my teachers and colleagues at the Faculty of Law of the University of Colombo, Sri Lanka, where I was first introduced to the fascinating world of legal research. Prof. Sharya Scharenguivel (Professor Emeritus, University of Colombo) was instrumental in developing my skills in research and analysis, and I am grateful to her for inspiring and encouraging me to expand my academic horizons. The foundation for this journey was laid at my *alma mater* Musaeus College, Colombo, Sri Lanka. My sincere appreciation goes out to Mrs. Lilamani Haththotuwegama, my teacher at Musaeus College, who fostered my skills in writing and advocacy, and continues to keenly follow my achievements and successes.

To Kerry, Jarrod and Zaki, I would like to say a heartfelt 'thank you' for keeping me smiling. I am grateful to Vindhya Mahavithana and Nilooshi Eleperuma who have been there for me throughout this journey and have uplifted my spirits with their sincere friendship. I am also indebted to Frau Inge Pfluegel who opened her heart and her home to me, and provided me a haven of comfort in stormy times, and to Johannes for his constant support, encouragement and good advice.

My brother Chinthaka has been my guide and a source of strength since childhood. I am grateful to him, to my lovely sister (in-law) Uthpala and (most importantly) to my little nephew and niece Pramod and Syona, for the boundless joy and affection they bring to my life.

My parents Lakshmi and Ranjan Mendis have worked hard all their lives and sacrificed much to give me the best. During this entire journey, they have staunchly stood by me and made sure that I never falter. This book is dedicated to them, and rightly so, for it is their unfailing love and support that made this wonderful journey possible.

Munich, Germany
15 April 2019

Sunimal Mendis

Contents

Chapter 1
Introduction

1.1 The Digitisation of Rare Documents

Digitisation has become a buzz-word in recent times. Across the world, there is growing awareness as to the potential of digitisation to transform the way in which literary, artistic and scientific content can be accessed, experienced, and enjoyed by users. Digitisation is a technological innovation that enables the conversion of a text, picture, or sound into digital form that can be processed by a computer.[1] This could be achieved using a scanner, digital camera or any other mechanism that enables a process of analogue to digital conversion.[2] Thus, digitisation allows for the creation of exact and faithful reproductions of existing textual, visual, or audio-visual content in digital form.

With the advancements in information technology and the proliferation of the Internet, these digital reproductions (digitised versions), can be speedily and easily reproduced and distributed in electronic format (as computer data files) to users across the world. Therefore, digitisation offers a means by which the public accessibility of scientific and cultural material held by memory institutions (i.e., galleries, libraries, archives, and museums) can be improved and enhanced to a significant level.

Digitisation constitutes a particularly significant innovation as regards rare materials that record textual, visual, or audio-visual content belonging to the public

---

[1] 'Digitisation', *Oxford Dictionaries* (OUP April 2017) <https://en.oxforddictionaries.com/definition/digitization> accessed 31 January 2019.

[2] For example, sound files are converted into digital format by repeatedly measuring the amplitude (volume) of an incoming electrical pressure soundwave (an electrical voltage), and outputting these measurements as a long list of binary bytes. In this way, a mathematical 'picture' of the shape of the wave is created.

Matt Ottewill, 'How Do Audio Analogue to Digital Converters Work?' *Planet of tunes* <www.planetoftunes.com/digital-audio/how-do-analogue-to-digital-converters-work.html#.XFL5NGNCeUk> accessed 31 January 2019.

S. Mendis, *A Copyright Gambit*, Munich Studies on Innovation and Competition 11,
https://doi.org/10.1007/978-3-662-59454-4_1

domain. Examples of such rare materials include Sumerian clay tablets recording *cuneiform* script, ancient Chinese maps drawn on silk, the *Magna Carta* manuscript written in 1215 C.E., rare visual footage of World War I battles, etc. As per the United Nations Educational, Scientific and Cultural Organization (UNESCO), such materials constitute the documentary heritage of the peoples of the world and represent a large proportion of the world's cultural heritage.[3] Accordingly, UNESCO considers such rare materials to constitute the common moral property of all humankind.[4]

However, because of their rarity, antiquity and the need to preserve them for posterity, these materials are often stored in the dark-archives or secure storage spaces of memory institutions to which members of the public either have restricted access or no access at all. When access is allowed, it is subject to strict controls and only granted in exceptional circumstances to select individuals who can provide adequate justification for such access.

Thus, the content recorded upon materials stored in dark-archives have been referred to as the 'unknown-knowns' or repositories of human knowledge to which the public no longer have operational access.[5] In effect, much of the public domain intellectual or informational content recorded upon rare materials stored in dark-archives often constitute 'forgotten-knowledge' that in terms of copyright law are available for the use of humankind, but are unavailable to them in practice.

Even when these materials are exhibited to the public (e.g., Da Vinci's *Mona Lisa* is exhibited to the public at the Louvre Museum in Paris) the format of a public exhibition often does not provide the conditions[6] that are conducive to making a close study of the content recorded upon those materials. Certain memory institutions prohibit visitors from photographing their exhibits or charge substantial fees to grant permission to make photographs, notwithstanding the fact that the content recorded upon them fall within the public domain as per copyright law.[7]

---

[3] *See* Ray Edmondson, 'Memory of the World: General Guidelines to Safeguard Documentary Heritage CII-95/WS-11rev' para 1.1.1. <http://unesdoc.unesco.org/images/0012/001256/125637e.pdf> accessed 31 January 2019. The 'Memory of the World' programme launched by UNESCO in 1992 seeks to preserve endangered documentary heritage and to facilitate its public accessibility. For the purposes of the programme, a document is defined as that which records something by deliberate intellectual intent and encompasses textual, visual and audio-visual content ibid. para 2.6.1–2.6.3.

[4] ibid para 4.3.1.

[5] Tim Maly, 'Dark Archives' (*Contents* 2013) <http://contentsmagazine.com/articles/dark-archives/> accessed 31 January 2019. Maly explains his terminology of 'unknown-knowns' by observing that the documents and records stored in dark-archives hold information that is technically available—and therefore 'known'-to the public, but are yet 'unknown' as the public does not realise they exist.

[6] For example, in the public exhibition, the time allowed to each visitor to view an artefact is limited. Furthermore, the distance that is maintained between the visitors and the artefact, lighting conditions, etc. may not furnish the conditions necessary for a close study of the artefact or the material recorded upon it.

[7] For example, the Louvre Museum in Paris usually permits the photography of art works that are included in its permanent exhibition. However, as was recently reported by *Le Nouvel Observateur*, it sometimes prohibits the photography of public domain paintings that form part of its temporary

Access to exhibitions of rare materials also involves transaction costs (e.g., entrance fees to enter the physical space where the exhibition is held, transport to the location of the exhibition, etc.). When the public domain content recorded upon rare materials is reproduced in books, newspapers or other publications, the entirety of the content may not be reproduced but merely particular extracts or details that are considered relevant to that publication by its author. Furthermore, publications that incorporate accurate high-quality photographic reproductions of rare documents and artefacts are often expensive and would be unaffordable to an average member of the public.

Memory institutions control access to and use of rare materials by means of exercising their ownership rights over the physical document or artefact upon which the textual visual or audio-visual content is recorded (e.g., the clay tablet upon which the *cuneiform* script is inscribed, the canvas upon which the *Mona Lisa* is painted and the film reel upon which footage of the World War I battle is recorded). Furthermore, laws relating to trespass can be invoked to prevent unauthorised persons from entering the dark-archive or exhibition space where the physical document or artefact is kept.

Thus, although the textual, visual or audio-visual content that is recorded upon the document or artefact belongs to the public domain and is available for use and re-use by the public free of restrictions, the restrictions placed upon the access and use of the physical artefact upon which that content is recorded impedes the ability of the public to benefit from its public domain status. In brief, the exercise of exclusive property rights over the physical artefact serves to exclude members of the public from accessing and using the public domain content recorded upon it, notwithstanding the categorisation of that content as being the common cultural heritage of humankind.[8]

Digitisation provides a means by which the public domain intellectual and/or informational content can be separated from its physical carrier and reproduced in digital form. For example, a digitised version of a Sumerian clay tablet will reproduce a digital image of the *cuneiform* script inscribed upon it that is free of its physical medium i.e., the clay tablet. Similarly, a digitised version of the *Mona Lisa* painting will reproduce a digital image of the painting free of its canvas and a

exhibitions. Juliette Montilly, 'Guillaume, Jeté Du Louvre Pour Avoir Pris Des Photos : "C'est Un Mépris Du Visiteur"' (*Rue89-Le Nouvel Observateur,* 2017) <http://tempsreel.nouvelobs.com/rue89/20170310.OBS6400/guillaume-jete-du-louvre-pour-avoir-pris-des-photos-c-est-un-mepris-du-visiteur.html> accessed 31 January 2019. *See also* Alain Marciano and Nathalie Moreau, 'Museums, Property Rights, and Photographs of Works of Art. Why Reproduction through Photograph Should Be Free.' (2016) 13 Review of Economic Research on Copyright Issues 1.

[8]Edmondson (n 3). Under the UNESCO guidelines, a document can be considered to have two major components: firstly, the information content and secondly, the carrier (i.e., surface or medium) on which the information content resides (para 2.6.3). Furthermore, the significance of the documentary heritage is considered to be enhanced if it is rare (para 4.2.6). Accordingly, the intellectual and/or informational content recorded upon rare documents that is the object of this study would qualify as documentary heritage under the guidelines issued by UNESCO.

digitised version of visual footage from World War I will be free of the film reel upon which it is recorded.

The exclusive property rights held over the physical artefact do not automatically extend to a reproduction of that artefact in digital form. Therefore, in the absence of a legal rule to the contrary, restrictions imposed on the access and use of the physical artefact (based on exclusive rights held over the tangible property) will not apply to the digitised version. Furthermore, while the physical artefacts characterise tangible rival goods, the digitised versions of these materials typify intangible digital-goods that are both non-rival[9] and potentially non-excludable[10] and can be infinitely multiplied (i.e., reproduced in the form of electronic computer files) at marginal costs that are so negligible they approach zero.[11] Hence, they can be reproduced and distributed over the Internet much quicker and at substantially lower transaction costs than analogue copies (e.g., photocopies, prints).

Therefore, digitisation offers the possibility of enhancing and improving the public accessibility and availability of public domain content recorded upon rare

---

[9]Foster explains the non-rivalry of digital goods both in consumption and production through the following illustration:

> One person's reading of an e-book does not necessarily diminish the capacity of a second person to read the same text. My reading of the *Complete Works of William Shakespeare* in digital form does not necessarily diminish the capacity of another reader to read the same text. Additionally my digital copy of the *Complete Works* is also non-rival in a secondary sense in that, once the initial digital copy is created further copies of the same text can be created at negligible cost. This is in contrast to the resources needed to produce additional items of tangible physical goods.

Jonathan Foster, 'Valorising the Cultural Content of the Commodity: On Immaterial Labour and New Forms of Informational Work' in Angela Lin, Jonathan Foster and Paul Scifleet (eds), *Consumer Information Systems and Relationship Management: Design, Implementation and Use.* (IGI Global 2013) 190. Ricolfi sets forth another dimension of the non-rival nature of digital copies as being their complementarity in re-use, that is described in terms of their amenability to being used as inputs for the production of an infinite number of downstream goods and services. Marco Ricolfi, 'The New Paradigm of Creativity and Innovation and Its Corollaries for the Law of Obligations' in Peter Drahos, Gustavo Ghidini and Hans Ullrich (eds), *Kritika: Essays on Intellectual Property* (Edward Elgar 2015) 147.

[10]Rayna observes that, while the first unit produced of a digital good is actually excludable, as the producer remains the sole supplier of that good; as the number of consumers owning the good grows, the number of potential suppliers increases and the number of consumers able to obtain the good from other consumers instead of the producer rises. He notes that the rate of consumers who are in a position to supply the good is likely to grow exponentially with time, up to the point where every consumer can potentially obtain the good without having to purchase it from the producer. Therefore, the excludability of the digital good decreases rapidly until the good becomes virtually non-excludable. Thus, according to Rayna, although the producer always remains able to directly exclude consumers from the consumption of the good, his inability to exclude consumers indirectly is such that the digital goods become *de facto* non-excludable when the number of the consumers owning the good becomes large. Thierry Rayna, 'Understanding the Challenges of the Digital Economy: The Nature of Digital Goods' (2008) 71 Communications & Strategies 13, 18–19.

[11]Richard B McKenzie and Dwight R Lee, *In Defense of Monopoly* (University of Michigan Press 2008) 78.

documents and artefacts that was hitherto largely inaccessible to an average member of the public. Consider the following comment published on an online forum regarding the digitisation of public domain paintings:

> Museums have collected and preserved much of the world's cultural heritage. But at the same time they severely limit the public[']s enjoyment of the art and art[e]facts they seek to preserve. I enjoy visiting a museum on occasion, but entry prices are usually extremely high and in the time that I have available I can usually only browse the highlights (from a respectful distance that hurts my eyes and blurs any details). Quick browses of paintings that their authors have spen[t] weeks, or months on. You can often buy (expensive) books with again the same highlights of the collection, but not on a 1:1 scale. High res[olution] scans would make all of this available to a much wider audience; worldwide, 24-7. Let them store that fragile 400+ year old painting in a secure bunker. It[']s the painting I am interested in, not the canvas.[12]

The Comité des Sages Reflection Group on Bringing Europe's Cultural Heritage Online,[13] opined that the enhanced accessibility and availability of cultural heritage material in digital form would assist in the democratisation of culture and knowledge.[14] Thus, the Comité des Sages hails digitisation as the harbinger of a new digital renaissance.[15] In the context of rare materials over which copyright protection has expired (and which therefore belong to the public domain), digitisation has the potential to open up to public use a large body of content that can serve as raw material in the creation of new innovative works.

Furthermore, digitisation has the potential to bring about economic growth, especially in the creative and cultural industries (such as the film, music, and tourism industries) by making available to them a large body of content that is capable of commercial exploitation.[16] As noted by the Comité des Sages, '[d]igitisation breathes new life into material from the past, and turns it into a formidable asset for the individual user and an important building block of the digital economy.'[17] Thus, digitisation has the potential to make a positive impact not only on the

---

[12] martijnd, 'Music Movies, Books...Museums Next' *Slashdot* 17 July 2009 <https://news.slashdot.org/story/09/07/17/085244/new-developments-in-npgwikipedia-lawsuit-threat> accessed 31 January 2019.

[13] Elisabeth Niggemann, Jacques De Decker and Maurice Lévy, *The New Renaissance: Report of the Comité des Sages on Bringing Europe's Cultural Heritage Online* (European Commission 2011) <https://ec.europa.eu/digital-single-market/sites/digital-agenda/files/final_report_cds_0.pdf> accessed 31 January 2019.

[14] ibid 8.

[15] ibid 12.

[16] *See* European Commission Recommendation of 27 October 2011 on the digitisation and online accessibility of cultural material and digital preservation [2011] OJ L283/39, para 7:

> The digitised material can be reused – for both commercial and non-commercial purposes – for uses such as developing learning and educational content, documentaries, tourism applications, games, animations and design tools, provided that this is done with full respect for copyright and related rights.

[17] Report of the Comité des Sages (n 13) 8.

advancement of the social, cultural, and educational spheres but also on economic and industrial growth and expansion.

Therefore, the advancement and sustenance of the digitisation process within the European Union (EU) becomes a priority in the context of the modern knowledge-based society. Europe as a repository of a vast amount of the world's literary, artistic, and scientific patrimony has demonstrated enthusiasm in harnessing the educational, cultural, and economic benefits of digitisation. At both regional and national levels, governments and policy-making bodies have affirmed the need to nurture and sustain the digitisation process with the objective of achieving greater accessibility of public domain materials.

During the past decade, as digitisation moved past its experimental stage and evolved into a structural and continuous activity,[18] memory institutions across the EU embarked upon mass-digitisation projects for the digitisation of their collections and making them available over the Internet. The majority of digitised material constitutes public domain content (possibly because the digitisation of public domain content enables memory institutions to dispense with costly and time-consuming copyright clearance requirements associated with the digitisation of copyright protected content[19]). The European public has also responded positively to the enhanced availability of public domain content in digital form, and has been quick in recognising its potential as a source of raw material for the creation of new cultural content.[20]

---

[18]Edwin Klijn, 'The Current State of Art in Newspaper Digitization: A Market Perspective' (2008) 14 D-Lib Magazine <www.dlib.org/dlib/january08/klijn/01klijn.html#1> accessed 30 January 2019. *See also* S Puglia and E Rhodes, 'Digital Imaging-How Far Have We Come and What Still Needs to Be Done' (2007) 11 RLG DigiNews. <http://worldcat.org/arcviewer/2/OCC/2009/07/29/H1248893457622/viewer/file2.html#pubinfo> accessed 31 January 2019.

[19]For example, Gomez and Keller attribute the diminished availability of in-copyright digitised versions and born-digital content over the Europeana Platform to difficulties associated with copyright clearance. Pablo Uceda Gómez and Paul Keller, 'The Missing Decades: The 20th Century Black Hole in Europeana' *Europeana* 13 November 2015 <http://pro.europeana.eu/blogpost/the-missing-decades-the-20th-century-black-hole-in-europeana> accessed 31 January 2019.

[20]The positive public response to the access and re-use of public domain content in digitised form is reflected in the success of initiatives such as 'Europeana Labs' (launched by *Europeana*) that encourages members of the public to re-use cultural content and meta-data in the development of new products and services (more information available from <https://pro.europeana.eu/what-we-do/creative-industries> accessed 31 January 2019) and crowd-sourcing projects for the development of digitised content such as the Georeferencer project launched by the British Library in 2011 (more information available from <www.bl.uk/georeferencer/georefabout.html> accessed 31 January 2019).

1.2 The Problem: An Overview

However, the process of digitisation has become the subject of controversy. One major factor that has contributed to this controversy is a practice adopted by certain producers (and distributors) of digitised versions of documents and artefacts that reproduce public domain content, to impose restrictions and limitations on the way in which these digitised versions can be accessed and used by the public. These restrictions are usually imposed through copyright claims that reserve exclusive rights over the digitised version to the producer (or distributor); the application of digital-rights-management software (DRM) including the use of technological-protection-measures (TPM) that restrict the ways in which the digitised version can be accessed and used; contractual provisions that require the user to agree to certain terms and conditions of use or by imprinting a non-removable trade mark upon the digitised version that allows the owner of the trade mark to control the ways in which the digitised version can be used and re-used.

The following examples illustrate this point.

Example 1

A first-edition copy of Jane Austen's celebrated novel *Emma*, published in London in 1816, is held by the Bodleian Libraries of the University of Oxford. This book was digitised by Google Inc. under the Oxford-Google Books Project and can now be viewed on the Google Books website by any user with an Internet connection in any part of the world.[21] Copyright over the novel has long since expired and it is a work in the public domain.[22] The publication holds immense interest to scholars of English literature, as well as to readers around the world, who have the intellectual curiosity to access, view, and re-use the first edition of one of Austen's seminal works. The digitised version can be accessed free-of-charge. It can also be downloaded, in PDF, EPUB formats. However, the Google Books 'usage guidelines' request that the digitised version be used only for personal, non-commercial purposes.[23] These usage guidelines automatically appear on the digitised version (either on the first or last page) once it is downloaded in PDF or EPUB formats. The relevant portion of the 'usage-guidelines' is cited below:

---

[21] Jane Austen, *Emma* (John Murray 1816) <https://books.google.de/books?id=rTYJAAAAQAAJ&dq=emma+by+jane+austen+first+edition+google+books&pg=PP13&hl=de#v=onepage&q&f=false> accessed 31 January 2019.

[22] It is noted that even assuming that copyright could have been claimed over the particular published edition by the publisher and his successors under English law (although this is highly unlikely given that protection for typographical arrangements of published works were only protected in the UK following the 1956 Copyright Act) this would also have expired a long time ago.

[23] Complete version of 'usage guidelines' available at <https://fr.wikisource.org/wiki/Page:Rod_-_Les_Id%C3%A9es_morales_du_temps_pr%C3%A9sent,_1891.djvu/1> accessed 31 January 2019.

> Google is proud to partner with libraries to digitize public domain materials and make them widely accessible. Public domain books belong to the public and we are merely their custodians. *Nevertheless, this work is expensive, so in order to keep providing this resource, we have taken steps to prevent abuse by commercial parties,* including placing technical restrictions on automated querying. We also ask that you (. . .) *[m]ake non-commercial use of the files (. . .) [w]e designed Google Book Search for use by individuals, and we request that you use these files for personal, non-commercial purposes.*[24]

Hence, Google Inc. appears to justify the restriction imposed on the ability to use of the digitised version for commercial purposes based on the need to protect the investment made by them in producing the digitised version. Google Inc. also includes a watermark on each page of the work along with instructions to refrain from its removal as it is, 'essential for informing people about [the Google Books] project and helping them to find additional materials through Google Books'.[25] Responding to a query from a user[26] regarding the legal nature of the above usage guidelines Google Inc. provided the following answer:

> The front matter of our PDF books is not a EULA [end user license agreement]. *We make some requests, but we are not trying to legally bind users to those requests.* We've spent (and will continue to spend) a lot of time and money on Book Search, and we hope users will respect that effort and not use these files in ways that make it harder for us to justify that expense (for example, by setting up the ACME Public Domain PDF Download service that charges users a buck a book and includes malware in the download). *Rather than using the front matter to convey legal restrictions, we are attempting to use it to convey what we hope to be the proper netiquette for the use of these files.*[27]

As per the elaboration provided above, it is clear that Google Inc. is not trying to use its usage guidelines to impose legally binding contractual obligations that the user is considered to have accepted through tacit consent. The usage guidelines comprise a mere request from the user to make use of the digitised version in ways that are deemed appropriate by Google Inc. and are designed to serve their best-interests in the distribution of digitised versions of public domain content. Accordingly, there is no legal obligation placed on a user to restrict his use of the digitised version to non-commercial purposes or to refrain from removing the watermark.

However, in the absence of a clear statement as to the exact legal nature of these 'usage guidelines' (i.e., whether they are mere guidelines or binding contractual terms) it is possible that many users would prefer to err on the side of caution and to refrain from any form of contrary use. This creates an uncertainty that is not healthy

---

[24]Reproduced from the 'usage guidelines' appearing on the PDF or EPUB version of digitised version of *Emma* created and made available by Google Books (emphasis added).

[25]ibid.

[26]Philipp Lenssen, 'Freeing Google Books from Google' *Blogscope* January 10 2007 <http://blogoscoped.com/archive/2007-01-10-n14.html> accessed 31 January 2019.

[27]Danny Sullivan, 'Authorama: Testing If Google Can Restrict Public Domain Books It Offers For Download' *Search Engine Land,* January 10 2007 <http://searchengineland.com/authorama-testing-if-google-can-restrict-public-domain-books-it-offers-for-download-10232> accessed 31 January 2019 (emphasis added).

for the efficient operation of the legal framework and could hamper the optimal use of these digitised versions.

Example 2
In 2012, the Ministry of Culture and Communication in France and the National Library of France (BnF) announced the conclusion of a new Partnership Agreement between the BnF Partenariats and the US based electronic publishing Company ProQuest LLC for the digitisation of 70,000 rare books (recording public domain content) in the Library's collection.[28] This Agreement was concluded as a part of ProQuest's Early European Books Programme. As per the terms of the Partnership Agreement, all digitised versions will be freely available to users within the premises of the BnF. However, only 5% of these digitised versions will be made available on the Internet upon open access terms, free of use restrictions. The rest of the digitised versions will be made available subject to exploitation privileges granted to ProQuest by the BnF Partenariats for a period of 10 years (presumably based not on copyright law but rather time-income privileges that are binding on the parties to the contract[29]). During this period, ProQuest has the right to reproduce, market and distribute the digitised material and to sub-license it to ProQuest's customers on a subscription basis. It is only after the expiration of this term that the public will be able to access and use the material over the internet free of restriction.

Example 3
The Musée des Lettres et Manuscrits, in Paris, which is a private sector institution with a collection of rare documents recording public domain textual content, uses DRM software to prevent unauthorised use of the digitised versions displayed on its website. The technological-protection-measures (TPM) that form a part of the DRM system, allow users to access the digitised materials online, but prevent the unauthorised copying or downloading of the materials.[30]

Example 4
The British Library entered into a partnership with BrightSolid to digitise its collection of historic newspapers (recording public domain content) in 2010. As per the agreement, all digitised materials will be available free of charge to users on-site at the British Library.[31] However, on the webpage of the British Newspaper

[28] Aurélie Filippetti, Louis Gallois and Bruno Racine, 'Investing in the Future: Two Major Partnerships Have Been Concluded to Digitize and Make Available Collections Held by the BnF' <http://www.bnf.fr/documents/cp_accords_proquest-believe_eng.pdf> accessed 31 January 2019.

[29] As per the opinion expressed by Phillipe Aigrain « J'utilise à dessein le mot « privilège » car il n'est pas sûr que l'exclusivité soit basée ici sur le droit d'auteur, on en est probablement revenu au temps des privilèges d'imprimeur, à un échange de bon services entre l'Etat et des acteurs privés. » Philippe Aigrain, 'Nous Devons Empêcher La Privatisation Du Domaine Public' *Communs* 16 January 2013 <http://paigrain.debatpublic.net/?p=6333> accessed 31 January 2019.

[30] Interview with Jean-Pierre Guéno Director of Culture, Musée des Lettres et Manuscrits held on 2 April 2014 (transcript in possession of the author).

[31] 'British Library and Brightsolid Partnership to Digitise Upto 40 Million Pages of Historic Newspapers' *British Library* 19 May 2010 <https://www.bl.uk/press-releases/2010/may/british-

Archive is a copyright statement which reserves copyright in the digitised material to BrightSolid in the following terms:

> © brightsolid Newspaper Archive Limited. The material on this website is copyright and is owned by brightsolid Newspaper Archive Limited and its licensors. Use by you of content on this site is subject to our Terms and Conditions.

The Terms and Conditions of the website require that digitised versions of the newspapers made available through the website be used only for personal, academic, or non-commercial purposes.[32] Unlike the Google Books 'usage guidelines', these are clearly indicated as terms and conditions of use that are made under English law and therefore intended to impose legal obligations on the users. Users of the website and the digitised content made available through it are required to agree to these terms and conditions as a pre-condition to use.[33]

These are but some of the more prominent examples of a phenomena that can be observed in varying degrees throughout Europe. As made evident by the Google Book 'usage guidelines' cited above, the placing of restrictions is often justified based on the need to protect the investment made in the digitisation process and to recoup that investment. This is especially the case where a private partner has invested in the digitisation process (although restrictions and controls may also be evident in the case of digitised works produced exclusively using public funds as well). As will be discussed in more detail in Chap. 3, public sector memory institutions often opt to enter into partnership agreements with private sector entities to obtain the requisite investment for the digitisation of their collections. However, these partnership agreements frequently contain clauses that allow the private sector entity to control and limit the way in which the digitised versions are used and accessed by members of the public.

1.3 Do Restrictions Result in Exclusivity?

It is argued that the imposition of restrictions and controls over the way in which a digitised version can be accessed and used by the public amounts to an assertion of exclusivity over that digitised version.

---

library-and-brightsolid-partnership-to-digitise-up-to-40-million-pages-of-historic-newspaper> accessed 31 January 2019.

[32]The British Newspaper Archive, 'Terms and Conditions: How You Can Use Our Service' <www.britishnewspaperarchive.co.uk/content/terms_and_conditions> accessed 31 January 2019.

[33]ibid 'If you use our services you must agree to these conditions. If you do not agree with them, you must not use our services.'

Cornu defines the legal term 'exclusive' as that which precludes any person other than the owner of the right of enjoyment thereof.[34] West's Encyclopedia of American Law defines exclusive as that which is vested in one person alone, apart from all others without the admission of others to participation.[35] According to Dusollier, exclusivity generates the outcomes of 'exclusion' (i.e., a right to exclude others from the use of the owned thing) and 'individuality' (i.e., a right being generally held by one person only).[36]

Therefore, it appears that the entitlement held by the producer or distributor of a digitised version to prevent a user from accessing or making a specific use of that digitised version translates into an assertion of exclusivity over the digitised version, whereby the producer or distributor reserves the ability to authorise or prevent specific uses of the digitised version. The copyright claim, application of a DRM system, imposition of contractual provision or the inclusion of a trademark constitutes the mechanisms by which that exclusivity is claimed and enforced. Copyright and trade mark give rise to an exclusive right that is capable of being enforced against everybody (i.e., *in rem*), while contractual provisions give rise to rights that are enforceable between the parties to the contract (i.e., *in personam*). Article 6 of the Directive on the harmonisation of certain aspects of copyright and related rights in the information society Directive (InfoSoc Directive)[37] require Member States to provide legal protection against the circumvention of DRM systems (including TPM) and the unauthorised removal or alteration of DRM software in a manner that could lead to the infringement of copyright in the DRM protected content. These provisions have been implemented by all EU Member States. Accordingly, the (United Kingdom) UK,[38] Germany[39] and France[40] provide statutory protection against the circumvention of DRM systems.

As noted above, before the advent of digitisation technology, memory institutions sought to exercise exclusivity over rare materials by asserting their property rights over the tangible object (i.e., document or artefact) upon which the public domain

[34]*« De ce qui écarte de la jouissance d'un droit toute autre personne que la titulaire. »* [Translated into English by the author].Gérard Cornu, 'Exclusif,Ive'. *Vocabulaire juridique* (11th edn. PUF 2016) 430.

[35]Jeffrey Lehmann and Shirelle Phelps, 'Exclusive', *West's encyclopedia of American law* (2nd Edition, The Gale Group 2008) <http://legal-dictionary.thefreedictionary.com/exclusive> accessed 31 January 2019.

[36]Séverine Dusollier, 'ERC INCLUSIVE: Research Project Context and Methodology' (SciencesPo, Paris 2016) 2 [Unpublished].

[37]Directive 2001/29/EC of the European Parliament and of the Council of 22 May 2001 on the harmonisation of certain aspects of copyright and related rights in the information society [2001] OJ L167/10 (InfoSoc Directive).

[38]Copyright, Designs and Patents Act 1988 (UK) s.296ZA-D and s.296ZG, grants copyright owners, persons issuing copies to the public or communicating to the public the work to which TPM or DRM has been applied the right to bring an action against the circumventing party.

[39]Urheberrechtsgesetz 1965 BGBl. I S. 1273 (Copyright Act of Germany) Article 95a and Article 95(c).

[40]Code de la propriété intellectuelle (Copyright Code of France) L335-3 and L335-4.

content is recorded. Such exercise of exclusivity over the tangible object can be justified in terms of the necessity to prevent damage to the rare physical document or artefact through negligent use or even over-use.

However, digitisation makes it possible to separate the tangible object from the public domain intellectual and/or informational content. An infinite number of users can access, use and re-use the digital surrogate without affecting the physical document or artefact. As noted above, ownership or custody of the tangible artefact or document does not in itself enable the exercise of exclusivity over its digital surrogate.[41] It is noted here that, the argument against allowing exclusive property rights held over the tangible object to extend to a digital surrogate of that object is further strengthened when the intellectual and/or informational content recorded upon it belongs to the public domain. Thus, an assertion of copyright over the digitised version usually requires separate legal justification that is independent of the property right over the physical document or artefact.

The practical implications of the assertion of exclusive rights over digitised versions is highlighted by the controversy that arose over the unauthorised use by a member of the public of digitised images of portrait paintings produced by the National Portrait Gallery (NPG) of London. The NPG through its digitisation programme produced digital images (digitised versions) of portrait paintings in its collection. The portrait paintings were in the public domain under UK law. The images were made available to the public over the NPG's website. In 2009, a contributor based in the United States (US) named Derrick Coetzee, uploaded 3300 of the high-resolution images of portrait paintings from the NPG website to the Wikimedia Commons platform, without the authorisation of the NPG.

Unsurprisingly, the NPG objected to the unauthorised reproduction and use of its digitised versions. In a letter of demand sent to Coetzee the NPG claimed that these digitised images were copyrighted works in their own right and that the uploading of the images infringed NPG's copyright and database rights. In later statements the NPG claimed that, the unauthorised use of digital images jeopardised its ability to sustain the digitisation initiative that is dependent on the NPG's own self-generated funds.[42] In a statement issued to Wikinews the NPG stated that digitisation involves huge costs including research, cataloguing, conservation and highly-skilled photography,[43] and noted their concern that the potential loss of licensing income resulting from the unauthorised uploading of their high-resolution digitised images onto

---

[41]However, see the decision of delivered by the Higher Regional Court of Stuttgart (Germany), OLG Stuttgart 31.05.2017, 4 U 204/16—*Reiss Engelhorn Museum II (Appeal)* where the court held that the owner of a tangible object that has not been made fully accessible to the public (e.g., the public access of which is subject to control by the owner) has the ability to prevent the use of unauthorised photographic reproductions of the object.

[42]Rory Cellan-Jones, 'Wikipedia Painting Row Escalates' *BBC News* 17 July 2009 <http://news.bbc.co.uk/2/hi/technology/8156268.stm> accessed 31 January 2019.

[43]'U.K. National Portrait Gallery Threatens U.S. Citizen with Legal Action over Wikimedia Images' *Wikinews* 14 July 2009 <https://en.wikinews.org/wiki/U.K._National_Portrait_Gallery_threatens_U.S._citizen_with_legal_action_over_Wikimedia_images> accessed 31 January 2019.

Wikipedia would threaten the NPG's ability to reinvest in its digitisation programme and to make more digitised versions of their paintings available. It further claimed that UK law granted protection to skilfully executed photographs of out-of-copyright (public domain) works.[44] The British Association of Picture Libraries and Agencies (BAPLA) supported the NPG's position. The BAPLA took the stance that the creation of copies of original works intended for commercial use, required skill, expertise, and financial investment on the part of the producer and could thus be considered derivative works that would be protected by copyright under the CDPA.[45] The BAPLA observed that, if owners of out-of-copyright material are not able to protect derivative works based upon those materials created by them, they would cease to invest in digitisation, and everyone would be the poorer.[46] It emphasised that the need to protect derivative works was not induced by the desire to restrict access to those works, but was required to protect those derivative works from being commercially exploited by those who have not invested in their creation (i.e., free-riders).[47]

The statements issued by the NPG and the BAPLA, suggest that the advocacy for copyright protection of digitised versions recording public domain content is based on the need to protect and recoup the investment made in the creation of digitised versions. As pointed out by the NPG, the ability to recoup the investment made in the digitisation process could be an operative factor regarding a memory institution's ability to sustain its digitisation programme, particularly when the digitisation programme is self-funded. Thus, the inability to recoup the investment through the successful commercialisation of the digitised versions could halt further digitisation efforts thereby depriving the public of the opportunity to access further materials held by the memory institution, in digitised form.

The Wikimedia Foundation defended Coetzee's acts mainly on public policy grounds. Erik Moeller (the deputy director of the Wikimedia Foundation) outlining the Foundation's stance through a blog post stated that, locking up and severely limiting access to educational materials to maintain revenue streams ran counter to the educational mission of a cultural institution.[48] He cited Peter Hirtle (President of the Society of American Archivists), who observed as follows:

> The conclusion we must draw is inescapable. Efforts to try to monopolize our holdings and generate revenue by exploiting our physical ownership of public domain works should not

---

[44]ibid.

[45]Based on comments made by Simon Cliffe, Executive Director of the BAPLA (2008–2011) *reported by* 'NPG and BAPLA at War with Wikipedia' *The British Journal of Photography* 22 July 2009 <https://web.archive.org/web/20090805101606/http://www.bjp-online.com/public/showPage.html?page=866109> accessed 31 January 2019.

[46]ibid.

[47]ibid.

[48]Erik Moeller, 'Protecting the Public Domain and Sharing Our Cultural Heritage' *Wikimedia Blog* 16 July 2009 <https://blog.wikimedia.org/2009/07/16/protecting-the-public-domain-and-sharing-our-cultural-heritage/> accessed 31 January 2019.

succeed. Such efforts make a mockery of the copyright balance between the interests of the copyright creator and the public.[49]

The matter never reached the courts and the legal community was deprived of a judicial determination on the legal issues that arose through the controversy; one of the primary issues being the ability of a digitised version of a public domain painting to obtain copyright protection. In 2012, the NPG released 53,000 low-resolution versions of digitised images under a CC-BY-NC-ND (Creative Commons Attribution-NonCommercial-NoDerivatives) license, through its website. A further 87,000 high resolution images were made available for academic use under the NPG's own license that invites donations in return for use.[50]

Nonetheless, the above controversy serves to demonstrate that restrictions placed upon the access and use of digitised versions are not mere paper-tigers, and that the producers of digitised versions can and do tend to take measures for the practical enforcement of their claims of exclusivity. The enforcement of exclusivity over digitised versions could have a substantial impact on the ability of members of the public to access and use the public domain content incorporated within those digitised versions. In this particular instance, it had the effect of precluding members of the public from the unfettered use and enjoyment of high-resolution digital images of portrait paintings in the public domain.

1.4 The Debate: An Overview

To date, there has been considerable discussion within the EU on the issue of claiming exclusivity over digitised versions of documents and artefacts that record public domain content, both at the European level and at the level of EU Member States.[51] However, developments within the region have been characterised by an

[49]Peter Hirtle, 'Archives or Assets?' (67th Annual Meeting of the Society of American Archivists, Los Angeles, USA, 21 August 2003) <https://core.ac.uk/download/pdf/4900558.pdf> accessed 31 January 2019. For an abbreviated version of this address see Peter Hirtle, 'Archives or Assets?' (2003) 66 The American Archivist 235.

[50]Wikipedia, 'National Portrait Gallery and Wikimedia Foundation Copyright Dispute', *Wikipedia* <https://en.wikipedia.org/wiki/National_Portrait_Gallery_and_Wikimedia_Foundation_copyright_dispute> accessed 11 May 2019.

[51]A notable development arising from this discussion is the establishment of Europeana (also referred to as the European Digital Library) in 2008. Europeana provides a common access point to digital cultural resources made available by separate cultural heritage institutions. The catalyst for the establishment of the Europeana platform was a letter sent by the heads of state and government of six EU Member States; France, Germany, Spain, Italy, Poland and Hungary, to the President of the European Commission in April 2005, emphasising the importance of making the cultural patrimony held by European libraries, accessible online in digital format. This letter was a reaction to Google's announcement of the launch of its book digitisation project that gave rise to fears that digitisation by commercial profit-seeking entities such as Google would result in public domain cultural content being appropriated into the private sphere. Thus, the need was felt for a European

overall absence of a concerted policy in determining whether exclusivity is in fact necessary and if so, the nature and scope of the exclusivity that is required, and the legal and economic framework within which it should be exercised.

In 2011, the European Commission issued a Recommendation on the digitisation and online accessibility of cultural material and digital preservation.[52] This Recommendation built upon an earlier Recommendation of the Commission[53] and incorporated some of the proposals put forward by the Comité des Sages on bringing Europe's cultural heritage online.[54] The Recommendation acknowledges that the cost of digitising Europe's cultural heritage is high and cannot be covered by public funding alone. It therefore proposes that, private sector sponsoring or partnerships between public and private sector institutions should be encouraged.[55] As a means of resolving the conflict between producer and user interests, the Recommendation notes that where such public private partnerships are in effect:

> A period of preferential commercial use or preferential commercial exploitation may be necessary in order to give the private partner the possibility to recoup its investment. This period should be limited in time and as short as possible, in order to respect the principle that public domain material should stay in the public domain once it is digitised. The period of preferential use should not be longer than 7 years.[56]

However, the 2011 Recommendation fails to define with any certainty the parameters within which such preferential commercial exploitation may be exercised and the legal basis on which the preferential commercial exploitation is to be founded (i.e., whether it is to be based on contract law in which case it would be binding only on the parties to the contract or an alternative doctrine such as copyright law which would make it binding on third parties as well). It also fails to put forward concrete proposals as to how preferential commercial exploitation rights may be exercised in a way that would assist in resolving the existing conflict between user and producer interests.

The 2011 Recommendation has been complemented by other European policy initiatives such as the final report of the High Level Expert Group (HLEG) on Digital Libraries,[57] which also emphasises the need for a European digitisation strategy that

---

initiative to digitise European cultural heritage and to make it available to the public on open-access, non-exclusive terms. See Jon Purday, 'Think culture: Europeana.eu from concept to construction' (2009) 4 Digitalia 105, 105–6 <https://doi.org/10.1108/02640470911004039> accessed 31 January 2019.

[52]Recommendation on digitisation, 2011 (n 16).

[53]Recommendation 2006/585/EC of the European Commission of 24 August 2006 on the digitisation and online accessibility of cultural material and digital preservation [2006] OJ L236/28.

[54]Comité des Sages Report (n 13).

[55]Recommendation on digitisation, 2011 (n 16) recital 9.

[56]ibid Annex I para 2.

[57]High Level Expert Group on Digital Libraries, 'Final Report: Digital Libraries: Recommendations and Challenges for the Future.' (i2010 European Digital Libraries Initiative 2009) <www.dlorg.eu/uploads/External%20Publications/HLG%20Final%20Report%202009%20clean.pdf> accessed 31 January 2019.

is capable of striking an equilibrium between the need to generate sufficient incentives for investment and the need to preserve user interests.[58] For instance, the advisory report of the HLEG's sub-group on public-private partnerships for the digitisation of Europe's cultural heritage[59] recommends that, legislation aimed at supporting the financing of cultural heritage through the provision of fiscal benefits to private partners, should be more extensively applied to digitisation projects.[60] The sub-group also recommends that content which belongs to the public domain in the analogue world should remain in the public domain in the digital environment but concedes that, if restrictions to users' access and use are necessary to make the digital content available to the public such restrictions may be imposed, although they should only apply for a limited time-period.[61] Thus, these instruments concede the need to maintain exclusivity over digitised versions of documents and artefacts recording public domain content, where such exclusivity is necessary to secure the wider availability of the documents in digital form.

Incentivising investment in the digitisation process by granting preferential commercial exploitation rights for a limited duration is opposed by other policy instruments that resist claims of exclusivity over the use and access of digitised versions of public domain content. This opposition is centred upon two main objections. Firstly, it has been argued that claims of exclusivity over digitised versions has the effect of restoring exclusive rights over the public domain content that is reproduced by the digitised version and of transferring that content to the private sphere, thereby resulting in an enclosure of the public domain. Secondly, the legal validity of copyright claims over digitised versions has been questioned because the digitised versions do not fulfil the standard of originality that is required to qualify them for copyright protection. While the latter issue of copyrightability will be analysed in Chap. 7, the former issue of public domain enclosure will be discussed in Sect. 1.5 below.

The general principles of the Public Domain Manifesto[62] developed within the Communia network[63] enunciate the following postulates:

---

[58] ibid 6–9.

[59] High Level Expert Group on Digital Libraries: Subgroup on Public Private Partnerships, *Final Report on Public Private Partnerships for the Digitisation and Online Accessibility of Europe's Cultural Heritage* (i2010 European Digital Libraries Initiative 2008) <https://www.google.com/url?sa=t&rct=j&q=&esrc=s&source=web&cd=2&ved=2ahUKEwiR_uTRqZjgAhXE2OAKHV_YBqgQFjABegQICRAC&url=http%3A%2F%2Fwww.europeanwriterscouncil.eu%2Fimages%2Fpdf%2Fdigitallibraries%2F1ppp_final.pdf&usg=AOvVaw2yakysL8qhvPfrSjcjzJIh> accessed 31 January 2019.

[60] ibid 2.

[61] ibid 2.

[62] Communia, 'The Public Domain Manifesto' (2010) <www.publicdomainmanifesto.org/manifesto> accessed 30 January 2019.

[63] Communia: The European Thematic Network on the Public Domain was a project funded by the European Commission within its eContentplus programme. The Network was in operation from 2007 to 2011 and aimed at providing a European point of reference for theoretical analysis and strategic policy discussion relating to issues concerning the public domain within the digital

> What is in the Public Domain must remain in the Public Domain. Exclusive control over Public Domain works must not be re-established by claiming exclusive rights in technical reproductions of the works, or using technical protection measures to limit access to technical reproductions of such works.[64]
>
> The lawful user of a digital copy of a Public Domain work should be free to (re) use, copy and modify such work. The Public Domain status of a work does not necessarily mean that it must be made accessible to the public. The owners of physical works that are in the Public Domain are free to restrict access to such works. However, once access to a work has been granted, then there ought not be legal restrictions on the re-use, modification or reproduction of these works.[65]
>
> Contracts or technical protection measures that restrict access to and re-use of Public Domain works must not be enforced. The Public Domain status of a work guarantees the right to re-use, modify and reproduce. This also includes user prerogatives arising from exceptions and limitations, fair use and fair dealing, ensuring that these cannot be limited by contractual or technological means.[66]

The Europeana Public Domain Charter, launched by Europeana[67] in 2010, provides further support to the principles enunciated in the Public Domain Manifesto by emphasising that:

> Exclusive control over Public Domain works cannot be re-established by claiming exclusive rights in technical reproductions of the works, or by using technical and or contractual measures to limit access to technical reproductions of such works. Works that are in the Public Domain in analogue form continue to be in the Public Domain once they have been digitized.[68]

Copyright claims over digitised versions of public domain content have also been denounced as instances of 'copyfraud'. The term 'copyfraud' was coined by Jason Mazzone to describe false claims of copyright over a public domain work.[69] Mazzone alleges that such false copyright claims, which are often accompanied by threats of litigation for reproducing a work without the putative "owner's"

---

environment. *See* Sunimal Mendis, 'Manifeste Pour Le Domaine Public' in Marie Cornu, Fabienne Orsi and Judith Rochfeld (eds), *Dictionnaire des Biens communs* (PUF 2017).

[64]The Public Domain Manifesto (n 62) General Principle 3.

[65]ibid General Principle 4.

[66]ibid. General Principle 5.

[67]Europeana (also referred to as Europe's digital library), is an internet portal that provides a common access point to digital cultural resources (both copyright protected and public domain content) made available by European cultural heritage institutions. It is owned and managed by the Europeana Foundation a private, non-profit entity incorporated in the Netherlands. *See* Sunimal Mendis, 'Europeana' in Marie Cornu, Fabienne Orsi and Judith Rochfeld (eds), *Dictionnaire des Biens communs* (PUF 2017).

[68]Europeana, 'The Europeana Public Domain Charter' (Europeana 2010) <http://pro.europeana.eu/files/Europeana_Professional/Publications/Public%20Domain%20Charter%20-%20EN.pdf> accessed 31 January 2019.

[69]As clarified by Mazzone, 'Under the law, the word fraud is used to describe a false claim by one person to another. Copyfraud is therefore the term I use to refer to the act of falsely claiming a copyright in a public domain work.' Jason Mazzone, *Copyfraud and Other Abuses of Intellectual Property Law* (Stanford University Press 2011) 2.

permission, result in users seeking licences and paying fees to reproduce works that are free for everyone to use, or altering their creative projects to excise the uncopyrighted material. As stated by Mazzone:

> The digital explosion of the past years has increased the incidence of copyfraud. Providers of digitally repackaged public domain materials take the position that because they have digitised or otherwise made available a public domain work, they own the copyright in it. Not so. *Scanning an old newspaper or broadside is not an act of creation. It is copying pure and simple. Copyright is not renewed just because somebody puts the work on film or a CD-ROM or posts it online* and sells it to researchers. Yet compilers of public domain works frequently claim copyrights in these works.[70]

He further argues that 'copyfraud' can have serious consequences in the form of stifling valid forms of reproduction and creativity and in undermining free speech.[71]

It is also interesting to note that, in certain instances even where memory institutions have a policy of maintaining control over the use and access of digitised versions of public domain material (either through copyright claims or the use of other legal and non-legal mechanisms), officials of these institutions who are responsible for the implementation of these policies are themselves to an extent confused as to their legal right and ability to do so. In the survey of European digitisation initiatives undertaken by the author, there were several occasions where officials of memory institutions that had a policy of claiming exclusivity over digitised versions of documents recording public domain content, voiced their scepticism as to the legality of the policies implemented by them. However, with the claiming of exclusivity over digitised versions of documents and artefacts steadily becoming a standard practice among European memory institutions, combined with the perceived necessity to maintain a measure of control over digital surrogates, memory institutions are increasingly inspired to follow the existing trend.

This phenomenon is also noted by the Comité des Sages who report that:

> Many cultural institutions from across Europe claim rights on digitised material that is in the public domain. In other words, they assert new rights that would have been created by the digitisation of the material. The basis for such claims is, however, not always solid (. . .).[72]

1.5 Will Exclusive Rights Lead to Enclosure?

Before proceeding further, it is necessary to determine whether claims of exclusivity over digitised versions, could result in an enclosure of the public domain content that is reproduced by the digitised version.

The term 'public domain enclosure' as used here, denotes a situation where there is a re-establishment of exclusive rights over public domain content with the effect of

---

[70]ibid 11 (emphasis added).

[71]ibid 3.

[72]Comité des Sages Report (n 13) para 4.1.5.

transferring that content from the public domain to the private sphere.[73] It does not include within its scope, practices that do not result in the transfer of public domain content into the private sphere, but only form an impediment to the way in which public domain content can be used and enjoyed. For example, instances of copyfraud would not change the legal status of the content over which the fraudulent or illegitimate copyright is claimed. However, such copyright claims could still impede the use and re-use of the content by the public by creating a false impression of exclusive rights. Thus, as the term enclosure is used in this study, copyfraud would not result in an enclosure of the public domain.

In copyright law, the public domain is viewed as a sphere that is essentially free of claims of exclusivity.[74] The intellectual content that is contained in works such as novels and paintings could belong to the public domain because these works pre-dated the modern copyright law system or because of the expiration of the term of copyright protection over that content. The informational content recorded upon documents such as data, statistics, etc. will fall into the public domain because they are outside the scope of copyright protection. In both instances, the absence of copyright protection results in the intellectual and/or informational content being relegated to the public domain, and thereby enables any person to make free use of that content.[75]

However, if claiming exclusive rights over the digitised version of a cultural artefact has the effort of restoring (or resurrecting) exclusive rights over the public domain content recorded therein, this would result in the intellectual or informational content being re-appropriated into the private sphere and thereby lead to an enclosure of the public domain. It is noted that such an enclosure will arise regardless as to whether the instrument used for claiming exclusivity is copyright law, trademark

[73] For the use of the term 'enclosure' to denote the re-establishment of exclusive rights over intellectual content in the public domain content *see* James Boyle, 'The Second Enclosure Movement and the Construction of the Public Domain' (2003) 66 Law and Contemporary Problems 33, 37; David Bollier, 'Why We Must Talk about the Information Commons' (2004) 96 Law Library Journal 267, 276–280.

[74] Benkler observes that, information is in the public domain to the extent that no person has the right to exclude anyone else from using the specified information in a particular way, resulting in all users being equally privileged to use it. Yochai Benkler, 'Free as the Air to Common Use: First Amendment Constraints on Enclosure of the Public Domain' (1999) 74 New York University Law Review 354, 360. Litman describes the public domain as a commons which includes those aspects of copyrighted works which copyright does not protect. Jessica Litman, 'The Public Domain' (1990) 39 Emory Law Journal 965, 968. *See also* Tyler T Ochoa, 'Origins and Meanings of the Public Domain' (2002) 28 University of Dayton Law Review 215. For an affirmative definition of the public domain as a sphere of resources to which legal rights of access and use are held by the public *see* Anupam Chander and Madhavi Sunder, 'The Romance of the Public Domain' (2004) 92 California Law Review 1331; Christopher M Toula and Gregory C Lisby, 'Towards an Affirmative Public Domain' (2014) 28 Cultural Studies 997.

[75] For a comprehensive mapping of the public domain and its classification *see* Séverine Dusollier, 'Scoping Study on Copyright and the Related Rights and the Public Domain' (WIPO 2011) CDIP/7/INF/2, 20–36 <www.wipo.int/edocs/mdocs/mdocs/en/cdip_7/cdip_7_inf_2.pdf> accessed 31 January 2019.

law, contract law, or DRM systems. If exclusive claims over digitised versions do result in an enclosure of the public domain then the next question to be answered is whether such enclosure can be justified on legal and/or public policy grounds.

In this regard, a distinction must be made between intellectual and/or informational content in the public domain, the medium through which that intellectual content has been conveyed to the user and the tangible artefact upon which it has been recorded. Intellectual and/or informational content is essentially intangible. Therefore, creators of such content utilise different media such as words, colours, sounds, or movement to convey their intellectual expression or information to others. In many instances, these words, colours, sounds, and movements are recorded upon tangible artefacts to preserve the content they convey and to facilitate its wider public dissemination. Thus, for example, in the case of the 1816 first-edition copy of Jane Austen's novel *Emma*, the intellectual expression of the author is conveyed to the reader through the medium of written words and is presented to the public as a specific textual work i.e., the novel *Emma*. This textual work is printed upon a series of tangible artefacts (i.e., papers that are then bound together to form the pages of a book), to facilitate its distribution to the public.

Accordingly, it is argued here that, the first-edition copy of the novel *Emma* is made up of three different constitutive elements. Firstly, the intellectual content, which is the author's expression, secondly, the written words (i.e., text), which are the medium in which the author chooses to convey that expression to others and thirdly, the printed pages of the book that record that text and make it available to the public.[76] Similarly, in the case of Da Vinci's *Mona Lisa,* the intellectual expression of Da Vinci is conveyed to others in the form of a combination of colours and forms, which we refer to as the painting. The painting itself is fixated upon the canvas which is currently placed in the Louvre Museum in Paris, France.

When a book or painting is digitised, the surface of the tangible document or artefact upon which the words or colours conveying the intellectual expression of the author have been recorded is scanned, and a digital photographic image of that surface is created. Thus, digitisation creates a visual representation of the surface of the artefact upon which the intellectual and/or informational content is recorded (e.g., the pages of a book, the surface of a canvas) in digital form. In the case of a book (or any other artefact that records textual content), it is also possible to digitise the writing (i.e., text) that is recorded upon the pages of the book through the use of technologies such as optical-character-recognition (OCR) and intelligent-word-

[76]This distinction reflects Fichte's differentiation of the physical and ideal aspects of a book. According to Fichte, the printed pages of a book constitute its physical aspect, while the ideas presented by it and the form in which those ideas are presented (i.e., the phrasing and wording) constitute its ideal aspect. It is noted that Fichte's notion of the form in which ideas are presented corresponds to the notion of the expression of a work in modern copyright law. Johann Gottlieb Fichte, Proof of the Unlawfulness of Reprinting: A Rationale and a Parable (1793) 21 Berlinische Monatschrift 443, 447 (Martha Woodmansee tr) in L. Bently and M. Kretschmer (eds), *Primary Sources on Copyright (1450–1900)*. Available at <www.copyrighthistory.org/cam/tools/request/showRepresentation?id=representation_d_1793> accessed 31 January 2019.

recognition (IWR), that convert the writing into machine-readable data that can be processed and understood by a computer.

Thus, where the producer of the digitised version of the 1816 first-edition publication of *Emma*, claims exclusivity over the digitised version, the object of the claim of exclusivity would be the particular visual representations of the pages of the book that are reproduced by the digital images, and (if applicable) the conversion of the text reproduced by the digital images into machine-readable form. However, it is argued here that, the claim of exclusivity would not extend to the intellectual expression of the author, or the actual written words used by Jane Austen to convey that expression. Thus, both the text and the intellectual expression it conveys would remain in the public domain.

Accordingly, the exclusivity claimed over digital photographic images of the pages of the book and the digitised version of the text recorded upon those pages would prevent a member of the public from reproducing or re-using those digital images or the particular digitised version of the text, without the producer's authorisation. However, it would not prevent a member of the public from reproducing or re-using the intellectual expression that is conveyed through the text, as long as this is carried out without infringing the producer's exclusive right over the digital images or the digitised version of the text. Thus, for example, it would be possible for a member of the public to create an audio-book of the text of the novel, to adapt the novel into a television series using Jane Austen's characters, plot, and dialogues and even to publish a new edition of the novel by independently transcribing the text reproduced by the digital images. Accordingly, it is argued here, that the claiming of exclusivity or exclusive rights over digitised versions of textual content in the public domain would not result in an enclosure of the public domain, as it would not alter the public domain status of the intellectual and/or informational content.

The same argument holds true in relation to other categories of works. A digitised version of Da Vinci's *Mona Lisa* would reproduce the surface of the canvas on which the paints have been applied and distributed in the form of a digital photographic image. A copyright claim over the digital image (provided that the digital image fulfils the requirements for copyright protection) would prevent any person from re-producing that image either completely or in part. However, it would not prevent any person from using the digital image as a model for independently reproducing the *Mona Lisa* using his own artistic skills. Similarly, the application of DRM software to a digitised version of a cinematic work that is in the public domain could prevent the unauthorised distribution of that digitised version to the public. However, it would not prevent a user from adapting that cinematic work into a theatre play and performing that play in public.

Most importantly, a claim of exclusivity over a digitised version would not extend to the artefact (i.e., the pages of the book, the canvas of the painting) that was subject to digitisation. For example, a copyright claim over a digitised version of the book containing the 1816 first-edition publication of *Emma* would not prevent any person from creating a separate and independent digitised version of that same book.[77]

Hence, in conclusion, a claim of exclusivity over a digitised version would only extend to the particular digital representation of an existing artefact that it has produced. It would neither extend to the public domain content reproduced by the digitised version nor to the tangible artefact that has been subject to the digitisation process.

Therefore, claims of exclusivity or exclusive rights over digitised versions of artefacts recording public domain content will not, as such, result in an enclosure of the public domain. Nonetheless, it is to be noted that restrictions and limitations imposed upon the access and use of digitised versions, based on such exclusive claims, could impede the ability of members of the public to access, use, re-use, and enjoy public domain content. As noted in the above examples, while an exclusive right over a textual or visual work would not prevent the independent transcription or re-creation of that work, the production of such a transcript or re-creation could be costly in terms of the time and skill that needs to be invested in the transcription or re-creation process. Even then, a transcript or re-creation would not have the same authenticity or utility as an exact and faithful reproduction as is produced by a digitised version. For example, an independent re-creation of the *Mona Lisa* would not have the same value to a student who wishes to study the painting technique used by Da Vinci, the type of paints and canvas used by him, etc. Similarly, a digital photographic image of a page of the novel *Emma* not only allows a user to enjoy the text written by Jane Austen, but to also examine the printing technique used in the early nineteenth century, the typographical layout, the effects of ageing upon the paper and the ink, etc. In brief, a digital photographic image of a document or artefact allows a user to place the intellectual and/or informational content recorded upon it within its cultural and historical context, in a way that a transcription or independent re-creation is not able to do.

Therefore, it appears that a digitised version could also hold value as a cultural resource that conveys valuable cultural and historical information in addition to the public domain content reproduced by it. In such an instance, the exclusivity exercised over the digitised version would indeed impede the access, use, and enjoyment of that cultural resource. However, from a copyright law perspective, the exclusivity exercised over the access, use and re-use of the digital photographic image (digitised version) or the digitised version of the particular text reproduced on that image, will not alter the public domain status of the information or intellectual expression (i.e., content) conveyed by that text.

This study focuses upon the effects of exclusivity on the access, use, and re-use of the public domain content reproduced by a digitised version from a copyright law

[77]However, it must be noted that private arrangements entered into between the memory institution having legal possession of the rare material and the producer of the digitised version could result in contractual provisions that prevent the memory institution from permitting another person or entity from accessing the rare materials to create further digitised versions. Such exclusive contractual arrangements could therefore go beyond the parameters of copyright law.

perspective. Thus, an examination of the effects of exclusivity upon the access and enjoyment of the digitised version as a cultural resource is outside the scope of this study. It is proposed that this issue should be explored in the context of laws relating to access to culture and to the use of cultural objects.[78]

1.6 Effects of Exclusivity on the Use and Access of Rare Materials

As noted in the foregoing discussion, restrictions on the access, use and re-use of a digitised version could form an impediment to the access, use, and enjoyment of the public domain content recorded on that rare document or artefact. This is exacerbated in the case of rare materials that are usually kept in the dark-archives of memory institutions, the public domain content recorded upon which is not easily available to members of the public. For example, Da Vinci's notebook (also known as the *Codex Arundel*) that records his handwritten notes relating to various aspects of mechanics and geometry is currently in the possession of the British Library. The content recorded upon the pages of this notebook is in the public domain. However, there is only one copy of the notebook in existence and the British Library is able to enforce its property rights over the physical notebook to determine who may access it and for what purpose. Therefore, access to the public domain content recorded upon the pages of this notebook is usually limited to scholars and researchers who have a justifiable reason for accessing the notebook.

Imagine that the *Codex Arundel* is digitised. The license to digitise is only granted to one producer (i.e., exclusive license to digitise) because multiple exposure to scanning equipment could damage the notebook. The producer of the digitised version becomes to all practical purposes the sole source from which to access the public domain content recorded upon the notebook as far as the public is concerned. Accordingly, the producer would have very high bargaining power in determining the conditions upon which use and access is allowed. An ordinary user who needs to access the work would have no option but to agree to the terms and conditions imposed by the producer of the digitised version of the notebook as there are no viable alternative means of accessing the public domain content recorded upon it.

Even assuming that the British Library revises its existing policy and makes the notebook available to any person who wishes to use it, for a majority of users the transaction costs associated with accessing the notebook in its original analogue

[78]Nevertheless, the proposed legal model for the regulation of digitised versions presented in Chap. 9, proposes the introduction of certain exceptions and limitations to the proposed related right over digitised versions to prevent the related right from being exercised in a manner that unreasonably prevents members of the public from using the digitised version in socially valuable ways, which do not interfere with the producer's ability to recoup the investment made in the digitisation process. *See* Sect. 9.1. Article 18(3) subsections (b), (d) and (f) limiting the related right *inter alia* to enable digitised versions to be used for criticism, commentary and parody.

form would make such access unfeasible (especially for users who live outside the UK and would need to travel to the British Library to access the work). Thus, in the case of rare documents and artefacts that record public domain content, the claiming of exclusivity over a digitised version and the imposition of terms and conditions upon its use and re-use would in practical terms restrict the ability of members of the public to freely use and exploit the public domain content reproduced by the digital version.

Contrast this with the novel *Emma* by the author Jane Austen, which is also a public domain work. Unlike the text of Da Vinci's notebook, the text of *Emma* has been re-printed by diverse publishers and is therefore widely available to members of the public. Despite the wide variety of editions, the text of the novel as reproduced by each of these publications is essentially identical.[79] These editions can be accessed from libraries or purchased from bookshops at relatively low transaction costs. Imagine that the University of Oxford Library grants Google Inc. an exclusive license to digitise its 1816 first edition of *Emma*, and imagine that Google Inc. decides to impose legally enforceable restrictions and limitations upon the access and use of the digitised version. This would not prejudice the ability of the public to access or use the textual content of the novel, as any person who does not wish to abide by the restrictions and limitations imposed by Google Inc. would be able to access the public domain content of the novel from many other alternative sources (e.g., libraries, bookshops). Furthermore, Google Inc. would not have a high degree of bargaining power in determining the terms and conditions of access and use of the public domain content, as they would face competition from the producers of other digitised versions of the novel (although these may not be digitised versions of the 1816 first edition). It is also possible that those who have access to digitisation technology, such as home-scanners or digital cameras would create their own digitised versions of the novel and make it available over the internet either free of restrictions or subject to less stringent restrictions on use and access.

Thus, the impact of the exclusive claim over the use and access of the public domain content would be very different in the case of the *Codex Arundel* (rare public domain content) and the novel *Emma* (public domain content that is widely available). In the case of public domain content that is widely available, it is difficult for a single entity to maintain a monopoly over the distribution of that content in digital form. Therefore, the exercise of exclusivity over digitised versions of rare documents and artefacts has a greater impact on the use of and access to the public domain content recorded upon them, in comparison with digitised versions of works that are widely available. For this reason, as will be explained in greater detail in Chap. 2, this study will focus upon the digitisation of rare documents that record public domain content.

[79]It is possible that these different editions incorporate annotations, commentaries, biographical sketches of the author, etc. that are unique to each edition and serve to differentiate them from each other. However, the public domain textual content of the novel essentially remains the same across all the different unabridged editions.

1.7 Need for a Comprehensive Policy

The placing of restrictions on the use and access of digitised versions that reproduce public domain content and the resulting controversy as to their legal validity give rise to an uncertainty that is unhealthy for the efficient functioning of the EU legal system. In the absence of a statutory framework to regulate the access and use of digitised versions, producers of digitised version either make *ad hoc* copyright claims that are of questionable legal validity, use contractual claims that are heavily weighted in favour of the producer's interests or use DRM systems that impose strict restrictions on the way the digitised versions can be accessed and used. The absence of a clearly enunciated legal framework on claims of exclusivity gives rise to confusion among users that could result in these digitised versions not being utilised to their full potential.

As the Comité des Sages observes, many cultural institutions across Europe claim rights on digitised material in the public domain, although the basis for such claims are not always solid.[80] For instance, during the controversy between NPG and Wikimedia, the NPG claimed copyright protection over digitised images of paintings in the public domain because the skill, expertise, and financial investment expended in their production qualified it for protection under copyright law.[81] However, a subsequent 'copyright notice'[82] published by the Intellectual Property Office (IPO) of the UK expressed doubt whether a digitised copy of an older image would fulfil the author's own intellectual creation[83] standard of originality established by the Court of Justice of the European Union (CJEU) which also has effect in UK law.[84] Nevertheless, the uncertainty surrounding the copyright protectability of digitised versions of public domain books and paintings in the UK is far from being resolved. Owing to the existence of a flourishing market for the commercial exploitation of digitised versions of cultural and historical content, there appears to be support for granting legal recognition to exclusive claims over digitised versions of public domain works.[85] Meanwhile, the prevailing viewpoint in France takes the opposite stance, and holds that it is not legally and ethically possible for an entity to claim

---

[80]Report of the Comité des Sages (n 13) para 4.1.5.

[81]British Journal of Photography (n 45).

[82]Copyright notices are published by the Intellectual Property Office (IPO) of the UK to help explain specific areas of copyright law. It is not a conclusive view of the law. Intellectual Property Office, *Copyright Notice: digital images, photographs and the internet* (1/2014, updated November 2015) 2 <www.gov.uk/government/uploads/system/uploads/attachment_data/file/481194/c-notice-201401.pdf> accessed 31 January 2019.

[83]The author's own intellectual creation standard of originality was established as a harmonised standard of originality within the EU as a result of the interpretation of EU law by the CJEU. For a comprehensive discussion on this point *see* Sects. 7.2 and 7.3.

[84]Copyright Notice (n 82) 3.

[85]Comment made by Simon Cliffe. British Journal of Photography (n 45).

exclusive rights over a digitised version of a public domain work.[86] Resolving this uncertainty necessitates a comprehensive analysis as to the copyright protectability of digitised versions of rare documents recording public domain content within the EU legal framework.

In view of the significance of digitisation for the democratisation of information, the progress of culture and education, and economic growth, there is a need to consider the issue of the exercise of exclusivity over digitised versions from the perspective of achieving an adequate equilibrium between the interests of producers and users. Hence, a comprehensive and focused study on this issue is required to examine whether there are in fact economic and/or non-economic justifications for the maintenance of exclusivity over digitised versions that reproduce public domain content. If it appears that the exercise of exclusivity is in fact justified, then there is a need to formulate a mechanism that would enable the exercise of exclusive rights over digitised versions within a sound policy framework that would preserve and protect the legitimate interests of the public.

1.8 Summary

Digitisation has considerable potential to nurture social, cultural, and economic progress by enhancing the availability and accessibility of public domain content recorded on materials held by memory institutions to users across the world. Digitisation is a particularly significant innovation concerning rare documents and artefacts that record public domain content, which are usually kept in the dark-archives of memory institutions, as it provides a means by which the public domain content recorded upon these documents and artefacts can be speedily and easily distributed to users across the world.

However, the phenomenon of mass-digitisation has been marred by claims of exclusivity over digitised versions made by their producers. While such claims of exclusivity do not in principle extend to the public domain content that is reproduced by the digitised versions, and therefore does not result in an enclosure of the public domain, they could have the practical effect of impeding the ability of members of the public to access, use, and enjoy the public domain content.

[86]For example, the organisations Communia, Open Knowledge Foundation France, La Quadrature du Net, Framasoft and SavoirsCom1 published a communiqué in January 2013 denouncing Agreements concluded between the French Government, the French National Library (BnF) and several private sector entities for the digitisation of materials recording public domain content held by the BnF, on the basis that the preferential commercial exploitation rights over the resulting digitised versions granted to the private sector organisations under that Agreement amounted to the privatisation of an important part of French cultural patrimony. *See* Nicholas Gary 'Refuser La Privatisation Du Domaine Public Par La BnF' *ActuaLitté* 20 January 2013 <https://www.actualitte.com/usages/refuser-la-privatisation-du-domaine-public-par-la-bnf-39680.htm> accessed 31 January 2019. *See also* Jean-Noël Jeanneney, *Google and the Myth of Universal Knowledge: A View from Europe* (Teresa Lavender Fagan tr, University of Chicago Press 2006).

At present, there is a strong body of opinion that challenges the legitimacy of these claims of exclusivity on legal and public policy grounds. Nevertheless, producers of digitised versions justify their claims of exclusivity based on the need to recoup the investment made in the creation of digitised versions. While there has been considerable discussion on this issue at the EU level and at the level of EU Member States, there has been no comprehensive analysis of the necessity to maintain exclusivity over digitised versions. Therefore, there is a need for a focused and in-depth analysis on this issue from the perspective of achieving an adequate equilibrium between the interests of users and producers of digitised versions.

Chapter 2
Objectives and Methodology

2.1 Objectives of the Study

The goal of the study is to find a means of achieving an adequate balance between the conflicting interests of producers and users of digitised versions of rare documents that record public domain content within the EU. The study examines claims of exclusivity made in respect of digitised versions that reproduce public domain content and attempts to formulate a legal model that could bring about a more equitable balance between the competing interests of users and producers within the existing institutional capacities and the conceptual parameters of the EU law framework.

The study seeks to fulfil the following objectives.

1. Examine whether there are economic or non-economic factors that justify the maintenance of exclusivity over digitised versions of rare documents that record public domain content.
2. Consider whether there is a need to regulate the nature and scope of exclusive claims over digitised versions through a statutory framework of regulation, as opposed to the current regulatory framework that is based on private-ordering.
3. Analyse whether there is a need to review existing legal rules to bring about a more equitable balance between the interests of users and producers compared to the *status quo*.
4. Propose a model for EU-wide regulation of digitised versions of rare documents that record public domain content.

S. Mendis, *A Copyright Gambit*, Munich Studies on Innovation and Competition 11,
https://doi.org/10.1007/978-3-662-59454-4_2

2.2 Scope and Definitions

The study limits itself to an examination of exclusive claims over digitised versions of rare documents that record public domain content. It further constrains itself by concentrating upon rare documents that record public domain content in textual form.

Its focus is limited to two dimensional digital photographic reproductions of rare documents, created through the use of scanning hardware such as flatbed scanners and digital cameras, with the objective of producing faithful and exact digital reproductions that are capable of serving as digital surrogates to the original documents (hereinafter referred to as 'digitised versions'), with the objective of enhancing the public availability of these documents. Thus, digitisation processes that reproduce rare documents in three-dimensional form, or have the objective of creating modified digital reproductions of existing rare documents for artistic or creative purposes do not come within the scope of this study.

As noted in Sect. 1.5 above, in the case of a rare document recording textual content, digitisation can operate at two levels. Firstly, the creation of a two dimensional digital photographic image of the rare document will result in the digitisation of the visual information provided by the rare document. Secondly, the textual content that is reproduced in the digital image (i.e., the writing recorded upon the document) can itself be digitised by converting it into machine readable form through the use of technologies such as optical-character-recognition software (OCR). The study focuses upon the digital photographic image that reproduces the visual information provided by a rare document, as this is the first and most important step towards improving the accessibility and available of rare documents. The digitisation of the text reproduced by the digital image is considered as an important value-added-feature that could enhance and improve the user experience.

2.2.1 *Focus on Textual Content*

A rare document is defined as a two-dimensional (planar) physical surface of which there are no more than twenty-five original copies in existence in the world and upon which intellectual and/or informational content is recorded, predominantly in textual form. Examples of such documents include ancient Sumerian clay tablets recording *cuneiform* script, Egyptian papyri, medieval manuscripts, incunables,[1] broadsheets, books, newspapers, ships' passenger lists, census records, etc. By limiting our study to two-dimensional surfaces, we exclude textual content that is recorded upon

[1]An incunable is defined as an early printed book, especially one printed before 1501. 'Incunable' *Oxford Dictionaries* (OUP March 2018) <https://en.oxforddictionaries.com/definition/incunabulum> accessed 31 January 2019.

non-planar, three-dimensional surfaces (ex: conical or spherical surfaces) such as, words written upon a pottery item or upon the spherical base of a sculpture.[2]

Public domain content is defined as intellectual and/or informational content that is not subject to copyright protection. The term 'textual form' refers to public domain content being recorded upon the rare document in the form of writing. The term 'recorded' refers to the textual content being written, printed or inscribed upon the physical surface of the rare document.

Because of its focus on textual content, the study excludes from its scope rare documents that mainly incorporate visual material such as paintings, photographs and maps. It is noted that documents which predominantly incorporate textual material may also incorporate non-textual material to a certain degree. For example, Da Vinci's handwritten notebook *(Codex Arundel)* includes drawings of various mechanical devices. A nineteenth century newspaper may contain photographs and a medieval manuscript may contain illuminations. However, the incorporation of such non-textual elements would not disqualify these documents from the scope of our research, as the character of the material recorded upon these documents is primarily textual.

It is necessary to distinguish the digitisation of textual content from visual, audio or audio-visual content because the market for digitised versions of textual content is different to that for visual, audio and audio-visual content. In the case of visual, audio and audio-visual content, the market for commercial re-use which requires high-resolution digitised versions is larger than in the case of textual works (possibly because there is greater demand for digitised versions of visual, audio and audio-visual works in the creative and cultural industries such as film and television). Consequently, there is greater opportunity for the exercise of price discrimination between low-resolution and high-resolution digitised versions in the case of visual, audio and audio-visual content than in the case of textual content. The revenue that could be earned by selling the high-resolution version would in some instances be sufficient to recoup the investment made in the production of the digitised version. In such an instance, it would be possible for the producer to make the low-resolution

---

[2]This is because from a copyright law perspective, the legal issues surrounding the digitisation of three-dimensional non-planar surfaces can be different from the digitisation of two-dimensional planar surfaces. For example, the digitisation of a two-dimensional surface such as a manuscript or a papyrus are usually automated but yet involve the exercise of personal, creative judgement on the part of the person carrying out the digitisation to varying degrees, depending on the document being digitised (*see* Chap. 7, Sect. 7.1). Meanwhile, the creation of a two-dimensional digital reproduction of a three-dimensional surface such as the conical surface of a pottery artefact usually requires the exercise of a substantial degree of personal, creative judgement on the part of the person carrying out the digitisation. Thus, while the copyright protectability of a two-dimensional digital image of a two-dimensional surface is subject to some debate (in terms of whether the resulting digital image is a mere reproduction or incorporates sufficient originality to attract copyright protection), a two-dimensional digital image of a three-dimensional surface is more likely to incorporate sufficient originality to qualify for copyright protection. For this reason, a distinction is made between the digitisation of two-dimensional and three-dimensional surfaces, and the study limits its focus to the digitisation of two-dimensional surfaces.

copy available free of restrictions or on open access terms to users who wish to access and use the work for non-commercial purposes. In contrast, the relatively lower demand for commercial re-use in the case of textual content means that there is less possibility for the producer to recover the costs of production by relying on the market for commercial re-use. Thus, the producer would be compelled to extend exclusivity to the market for non-commercial re-use as well. On the other hand, visual content such as paintings are more likely to be exhibited for public viewing in art galleries and museums. Audio and audio-visual works such as film footage and recordings may also become available to the public because of their incorporation in documentary films, etc. but textual content is more likely to constitute forgotten knowledge and to remain trapped within the dark-archives of memory institutions.

Thus, it is necessary to make a distinction between each of the above categories in analysing the legal and economic consequences of exclusive claims over digitised versions. Textual content forms the largest category of rare public domain content within the EU. However, the discussion relating to the legal validity of exclusive claims over digitised versions tends to centre around visual content, specifically public domain paintings. In comparison, exclusive claims over digitised versions of textual content have received less attention, both in legal literature and in case law. As the scope of this research does not allow for an analysis of different categories of content, it limits itself to an analysis of exclusive claims over digitised versions of rare documents that record public domain content in textual form.

2.2.2 *Definitions*

A list of key terms and the way they have been defined in the study are given below.

1. Digitisation
The conversion of a text, picture, or sound in analogue form to digital form through a technological process of scanning, with the use of scanning hardware (e.g., flatbed scanners, digital cameras).

2. Digitised version
A two-dimensional digital photographic image of an existing rare document that is created with the objective of producing an exact and faithful digital reproduction of that document.

3. Rare document
A two dimensional (planar) physical surface upon which public domain content is recorded, predominantly in textual form and of which (it is generally accepted) there are no more than twenty-five original copies in existence in the world. (e.g., Sumerian clay tablets recording *cuneiform* script, Egyptian papyri, medieval manuscripts, incunables, broadsheets, books, newspapers, ships' passenger lists, census records).

4. Exclusivity
The maintenance of any form of control or restriction over a digitised version regarding its access and/or use, through legal or non-legal mechanisms (e.g., through a copyright claim, the use of a trade mark, contractual provisions or the application of DRM software) which precludes any unauthorised person from enjoying the utilities of the digitised version.

2.3 Methodology

To carry out an analysis that captures both the legal and economic aspects involved in the study the following methodology was used.

(a) An empirical survey of selected digitisation projects in Europe.
(b) A theoretical legal analysis to examine the need to preserve exclusive rights over digitised versions of rare documents.

2.3.1 Empirical Survey

An empirical survey was carried out on ongoing or already completed digitisation projects, involving rare documents recording public domain content in textual form, in fourteen memory institutions in the jurisdictions of the UK, France, Germany, Italy and Spain.

The participating institutions were selected to form a sample of institutions with small, medium and large collections of rare documents and to reflect a diverse range of digitisation business models. Twelve of these institutions belonged to the category of public or semi-public institutions, while only two could be identified as purely private sector institutions. This is because the great majority of memory institutions with rare document collections in Europe are either public sector institutions (that are directly managed by governmental agencies and depend on the government for their funding), or semi-public sector institutions that obtain a certain portion of their funds from the government.

The empirical survey sought to gather both quantitative and qualitative data *inter alia* in relation to the following aspects of the digitisation projects.

- Financial sources and funding structures.
- The business models employed in the production and distribution of the digitised versions and the reasons for adopting those particular models.
- The reasons behind the decision of the memory institution to digitise their collection (ex: dissemination, preservation, revenue generation) and the challenges they faced in the production and distribution of digitised works.
- Mechanisms used by producers and distributors to maintain exclusivity over the digitised versions (if any).

- If exclusive rights are maintained the reasons for doing so, and if they are not, the reasons why exclusive rights are not claimed over digitised versions.
- The memory institution's policy regarding the preservation of exclusivity over digitised versions and the individual attitudes and perceptions of the resource persons (i.e., officials of memory institutions who participated in the survey) in relation to the same.

In addition to the survey of memory institutions an attempt was also made to gather qualitative data from several private and public sector organisations that are involved as stakeholders in the digitisation process. Accordingly, interviews were carried out with officials from 'Europeana'[3] (Europe's Digital Library), 'Proquest LLC'[4] which is at present one of the most active private sector investors in the digitisation of Europe's cultural patrimony and 'The Public Domain Review'[5] which is a non-profit organisation dedicated to the promotion of the accessibility of public domain works. It was hoped that this input would complement the data gathered from the memory institutions and give greater clarity to the interests of investors, distributors and other stakeholders in the digitisation process, thereby enabling the study to take their concerns into account in formulating its conclusions.

The data collected through the empirical survey is not intended to be used for statistical analysis or for drawing statistical generalisations.[6] The empirical survey was undertaken with the object of obtaining an overall understanding of the issues and challenges faced by producers of digitised versions and to bring to light the ground realities of the digitisation process. It was hoped that an empirical inquiry would assist in the formulation of conclusions and proposals that are both relevant

---

[3]More information about Europeana available from <www.europeana.eu/portal/en/about.html> accessed 31 January 2019. *See also* Sunimal Mendis, 'Europeana' in Marie Cornu, Fabienne Orsi and Judith Rochfeld (eds), *Dictionnaire des Biens communs* (PUF 2017).

[4]Proquest LLC is a company based in Michigan, USA. It is active in the digitisation of rare textual public domain materials in Europe both in the capacity of a producer and distributor of digitised versions. More information available from <www.proquest.com/> accessed 31 January 2019.

[5]The Public Domain Review was founded in 2011 and maintains an online journal that provides a platform for the publication of public domain material with particular significance. More information available from <http://publicdomainreview.org/about/> accessed 31 January 2019.

[6]One of the main reasons why this data will not be used for statistical analysis is that there are questions on the representative nature of the sample from which the data was drawn. It was decided at the outset that finding a representative sample and gathering data which would be suitable for statistical analysis would be beyond the scope of this research project considering the constraints on time and resources. In fact, gathering a representative sample may prove impossible as rare documents tend to be heterogeneous as regards social value and market demand and the costs of producing digitised versions of rare documents (even those that belong to the same collection) can widely differ. Furthermore, memory institutions also have their individual perceptions and priorities as to the production and dissemination of digitised versions that are determined by the administrative and funding structure of each institution, the personal viewpoints and attitudes of the administrative officials, as well as the unique cultural values of the jurisdiction where the memory institution is located. Consequently, it may be impossible to draw a representative sample of memory institutions in Europe which could be utilised for the purpose of drawing statistical generalisations.

and pragmatic. A more detailed outline of the survey design and the methodology that was employed is provided in the Annex.

2.3.2 Legal Analysis

As mentioned in Sect. 2.1 above, the goal of the research is to find a means of achieving an adequate balance between the conflicting interests of users and producers of digitised versions. The 'interests' referred to comprise both legal and economic interests. Therefore, the issue in focus presents a complex web of intertwined legal and economic issues. However, the study primarily proceeds upon a theoretical legal analysis that seeks to test legal assumptions and to make normative statements as to how the digitised versions in focus should be regulated within the EU. For this purpose, it engages in a comparative analysis of legal developments taking place within EU law and at the national level in the legal frameworks of the UK, Germany and France. The theoretical legal analysis derives input from concepts in economic theory and profits from data collected through the empirical survey.

2.4 Research Questions

The research questions are formulated to be open ended so as to allow the study to consider the empirical and theoretical findings that are reached during each stage of the study. As per the manner in which the questions were structured, the study was carried out in three stages, each stage attempting to answer a particular research question. Accordingly, the structure of the research proceeded in a sequential format with the research question to be answered during each stage of the research being determined by the conclusions that were reached in the previous stage. The research questions are set out in Fig. 2.1.

The term adequacy that is used in the research questions (*see* research questions 2 and 3) in relation to preserving an 'adequate balance' between the interests of users and producers, refers to the ability of the legal/non-legal mechanisms to provide sufficient incentives to producers to invest in the digitisation of rare documents, while at the same time enabling users to use and exploit the digitised versions as much as possible (*see* Sect. 3.2 for an explanation of end-user and re-user markets and Sect. 4.7 for a discussion on market failure).

The term 'reasonable return' is not formally defined, but rather used in an intuitive sense, meaning, a return that would be sufficient to preserve incentives of private sector (for-profit) entities to invest in the digitisation of rare documents. The term reasonable return is further discussed in Sects. 4.7 and 9.2 below.

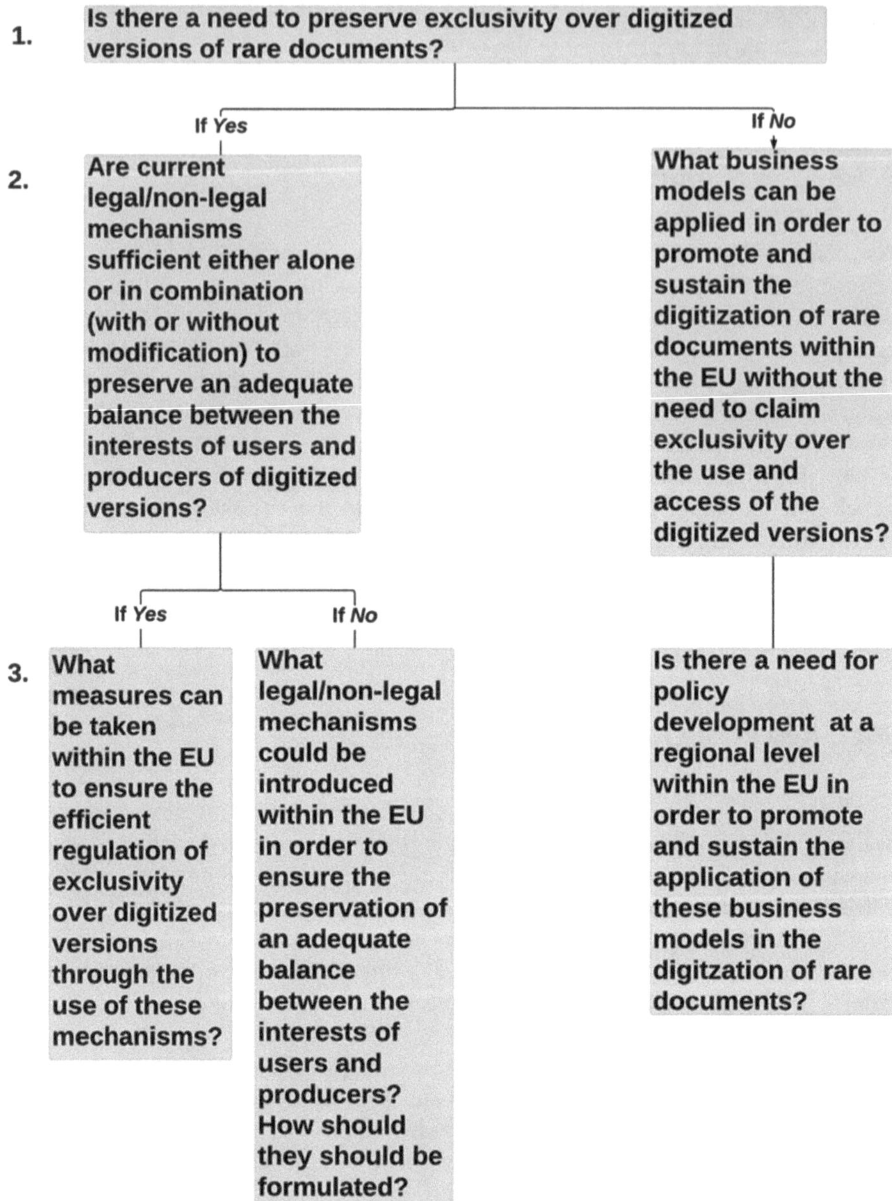

Fig. 2.1 Research questions

2.5 The Title: 'A Copyright Gambit'

In the game of chess, a 'gambit' is an opening move in which a player makes a sacrifice, typically of a pawn for the sake of a compensating advantage.[7] In a wider sense, this term is used to denote a stratagem or manoeuvre that is calculated to gain an advantage especially at the outset of a situation. In its essence, it indicates the sacrificing of a privilege or advantage in real time to secure a relatively greater advantage at a later date.

The reason why this study has been entitled a "Copyright Gambit" is because, in its conclusion, it advocates a legal strategy that involves the sacrifice of user interests in the short-term in order to secure enhanced accessibility to rare public domain textual content in the long-term.

[7]'Gambit', *Oxford Dictionaries* (OUP April 2017) <https://en.oxforddictionaries.com/definition/gambit> accessed 31 January 2019.

Chapter 3
An Overview of Business Models Currently in Use

3.1 A Range of Business Models

At present, a diverse range of business models are employed for the production and distribution of digitised versions of rare documents. The form and structure of each business model is largely determined by the way in which the provision of finances and other responsibilities are divided among entities as regards the following aspects of the digitisation process.

– Production of the digitised version.
– Distribution of the digitised version.
– Ownership of rights over the digitised version.

As the entity that holds the rare documents, a memory institution has the ability to determine the nature and design of the business model it wishes to adopt. The following serves to illustrate the functions that are involved in the digitisation of rare documents and the diverse range of stakeholders who may contribute to the digitisation process.

– *Who selects the materials for digitisation?*

  E.g., is it the memory institution, government, sponsor, donor, not-for-profit partner, for-profit partner?

  The criteria used in the selection process can vary according to the interests of the particular stakeholders. For instance, a memory institution may select rare documents for digitisation *inter alia* based on their value to culture and education. By contrast, a private-sector partner who invests in the production of digitised versions through motives of profit generation (i.e., private sector for-profit partner) would be more likely to base its selection on the perceived market demand for the digitised version of a rare document. Sponsors and donors may choose materials based on their own personal values and interests. It is also possible that a governmental agency funds the digitisation of certain materials that it considers to be of national importance or having substantial social or cultural significance.

S. Mendis, *A Copyright Gambit*, Munich Studies on Innovation and Competition 11,
https://doi.org/10.1007/978-3-662-59454-4_3

- *Who provides the finances?*

  E.g., is it the memory institution, government, sponsor, donor, not-for-profit partner, for-profit partner, fund-raising following public appeal?

  The digitisation process involves considerable fixed costs. These fixed costs may be incurred in the selection and preparation of material for digitisation (e.g., restoration, cataloguing, and transportation to the digitisation centre), the provision of equipment and software, contracting or employing labour for scanning and processing the digitised image, the generation of meta-data, the creation of a distribution network, etc. The financial resources required for covering these costs may be obtained from a single source (e.g., a sponsor, donor, for-profit partner or a government agency who agrees to finance a specific digitisation project), or it may be furnished from a combination of sources. The funding (investment) capacities of different for-profit and not-for-profit sources are considered in Table 3.1.
- *Who provides the technology?*

  E.g., is it the memory institution's in-house digitisation unit, independent contractor, volunteers following the adoption of crowd-sourcing, not-for-profit partner, for-profit partner?

  Technological resources required for digitisation include the hardware and software that is used for scanning and processing the digital image and for incorporating value-added features (e.g., zoom-in, page-turner features[1]). It also includes the technological infrastructure that is used for distributing the digitised version and making it available to the public (e.g., web-hosting, search function).
- *Who provides the human resources?*

  E.g., is it the memory institutions' own staff, independent contractor, volunteers, not-for-profit partner, for-profit partner?

  The digitisation of rare documents is a relatively labour-intensive process. A large portion of these materials may not be in a uniform size or format so as to enable the use of a high level of automation in the digitisation process. Further, their rarity and antiquity require them to be handled by a skilled staff. Expertise is also required at the stage of processing the digitised image and in the inclusion of value-added features. Further, the management of the digitisation work-flow and overall logistics require managerial expertise.
- *Who distributes the digitised version?*

  E.g. is it the memory institution, not-for-profit partner, for-profit partner?

  The distribution of a digitised version requires the creation and maintenance of a distribution network and infrastructure. It may also include the provision of customer service and support.

[1]Page-turner refers to the flip animation function that is applied to digitised versions. The flip function allows a user to view multiple digital images in a way that simulates flipping through the pages of a book, thereby bringing the experience of reading a digitised version of a book closer to the actual experience of reading a book in print form.

Table 3.1 Sources of funding

Funding model	Investment capacity	Focus on social value in the selection of material	Focus on the imposition of controls and restrictions
Self-funding	(---) Public and semi-public sector memory institutions do not have sufficient independent revenue sources that could be channelled into the digitisation process	(+++) Public and semi-public sector memory institutions are driven by their public mission	(+) Memory institution needs to recoup its investment to sustain the digitisation process
Government funding	(++) The majority of officials from memory institutions have low confidence in the government as a reliable source of funding for digitisation projects (*see* Fig. 4.1 in Sect. 4.3 below)	(+++) Funding driven by public interest and the creation of social value	(-) Government and governmental agencies usually not driven by the need to recoup investment. Argument that digitised versions created with tax--payer's money should be freely available to public
Partnership with private sector for-profit entity	(+++) These have a high investment capacity. As their business model is based on the generation of profits, they have sustainable revenue streams that make them a reliable source of funding	(---) Selection driven by potential market-demand for a digitised version of a rare document	(+++) Successful commercial exploitation of digitised version requires exclusivity
Partnership with private sector non-profit organisation	(-) Private sector non-profit organisations are themselves dependent on sponsorships and donations. Thus, their revenue streams tend to be sporadic and they often opt to invest in the distribution of digitised versions as opposed to production (e.g., *Europeana*)	(+++) Funding driven by public interest and the creation of social value	(---) Funding driven by motive to make digitised versions freely accessible and available to the public
Partnership with university or research organisation	(+) Universities and research organisations tend to invest in the digitisation of particular collections of rare documents in which they have an interest.	(+++) Focus on digitisation of rare documents that match the particular interests of the organisation	(-) Educational mission of most universities and research organisations means that there is less focus on recouping costs of investment and

(continued)

Table 3.1 (continued)

Funding model	Investment capacity	Focus on social value in the selection of material	Focus on the imposition of controls and restrictions
	Thus, they cannot be relied upon as a steady source of funding for digitisation in general		greater focus upon making digitised versions freely available to members of the public
Sponsors and donors	(-) Funding tends to be sporadic and unreliable. Furthermore, funding will be provided for collections in which the sponsor or donor has a special interest	(+) Selection based on the interests and values of the individual sponsor or donor	(--) Charitable motive means there is less focus upon recouping investment
Fund-raising following a public appeal	(-) Fund-raising can be a successful source of funding for rare documents that have a strong cultural or social significance. Not reliable as a source of funding for digitisation in general	(+++) Fund-raising model tends to be employed in relation to rare documents that have strong cultural and social significance. The social value of these materials tends to be high	(---) As digitisation is achieved through funding obtained from members of the public, emphasis is placed on the free accessibility and use of digitised versions by members of the public
Volunteers/crowd-sourcing	(---) Can be an indirect source of funding in terms of cutting costs relating to human resources. Not a direct source of funding in the production of digitised versions. More useful in the post-production stage for the development of digitised versions, the creation of meta-data, etc.	(+++) Same as above	(---) Same as above

Indicators: (+++) very high, (++) high, (+) moderately high, (-) moderately low, (--) low, (---) very low

– *Who owns rights over the digitised version?*

E.g. is it the memory institution, not-for-profit partner, for-profit partner?

In the event that exclusive rights are claimed over a digitised version, it is necessary to determine the person or entity that is the owner of those exclusive rights and is therefore entitled to determine the terms according to which a digitised version could be accessed and used by any person.

The memory institution could decide to undertake and carry out all of the above functions on its own. It could finance the digitisation process by using the institution's own funds (or by raising the necessary funds following a public appeal). The technical aspects could be handled by an in-house digitisation unit with a skilled team of staff members or be outsourced to an independent contractor who would carry it out in exchange for payment. On the other hand, the memory institution also has the option of entering into a partnership agreement with an external entity that agrees to take on certain functions and responsibilities.

What follows are brief outlines of three different business models that were observed in the empirical survey of digitisation projects. The outlines are provided in the hope that they would allow the reader to gain a basic understanding of the way in which digitisation business models are structured and the factors that influence their formulation.

Example 1: Bodleian Libraries UK: Digitisation of the John Johnson Collection—An Archive of Printed Ephemera[2]

The *John Johnson Collection of Printed Ephemera* is one of the special collections at the Bodleian Libraries (hereinafter referred to as the 'Library'). It is also one of the largest and most important collections of printed ephemera[3] in the world. It consists of printed documents such as hand-bills, advertisements, play-bills and posters physically arranged under approximately 700 subject headings. The earliest piece dates back to 1508 while the majority is from the eighteenth, nineteenth, and early twentieth centuries. The bulk of the collection is therefore in the public domain.

ProQuest LLC expressed its interest in digitising the collection. ProQuest is a US based private-sector for-profit electronic publishing company. As the Bodleian Library had worked with ProQuest on different types of projects over the years, the Library agreed to work with ProQuest as a partner in the digitisation of this collection. It was agreed that the Library would contribute to the project by providing the raw materials for digitisation (i.e., the documents in their collection) and their expertise in the creation of meta-data. ProQuest contributed their design and interface skills which were considered to be better than what could be provided by the Library's in-house team.

---

[2]The project took place from April 2007 to March 2009. This outline is based primarily upon the views expressed by Michael Popham (Head of Digital Initiatives at the Bodleian Libraries) and Christine Madsen (Manager—Infrastructure and Innovation at the Bodleian Libraries) during an interview held with the author on 2nd September, 2013 (interview transcript in possession of the author). It is to be noted that the views expressed by them are their personal opinions given in their professional capacity and do not represent the official view of the Bodleian Libraries, UK. The outline also incorporates views and data taken from the Bodleian Libraries Website, <www.bodleian.ox.ac.uk/johnson/about> and <www.bodleian.ox.ac.uk/johnson/projects/proquest> accessed 31 January 2019, and from the Final Report published by the Jisc on this project *see David Tomkins, Electronic Ephemera: Digitised Selections from the John Johnson Collection* (JISC 2009).

[3]Ephemera is defined as a class of collectible items not originally intended to last for more than a short time, such as tickets, posters, postcards or labels. 'Ephemera' *Collins English Dictionary* (Collins March 2018) <www.collinsdictionary.com/dictionary/english/ephemera> accessed 31 January 2019.

The Library approached the Jisc,[4] a public sector non-profit company in the UK, for funding. The Jisc had already funded several of the Library's digitisation projects in the past and was especially keen to fund digitisation projects built on collaborations between public sector and private sector entities. They were of the view that the for-profit business model usually adopted under public-private partnership agreements allowed a digitisation project to be more sustainable as the revenue earned from the commercial exploitation of the digitised versions could be used to sustain the preservation of the underlying data. The Jisc agreed to provide 25% of the total cost of the digitisation project on condition that the digitised products would be made freely available to users within the UK. However, it would be possible to charge a fee from users outside the UK.

The finances available for the project were sufficient for the digitisation of about five categories of subject-matter. Thus, a decision had to be made as to which categories would be selected for digitisation. The Library was keen to digitise materials of the collection that were already widely used by visitors and the digitisation of which would therefore have the greatest impact on both access and preservation of the original documents.[5] It was also interested in the digitisation of the 'Entertainment' category (comprising concert and recital programmes, reviews, etc.) that would complement similar material that had previously been digitised by the Library. Meanwhile, ProQuest was interested in the digitisation of the category of material entitled 'Crimes, Murders and Executions' as it was perceived to have a higher potential for commercial exploitation in the end-user and re-user markets. Thus, the selection of material for digitisation involved much debate, discussion and negotiation between the Library and ProQuest. Finally, the following categories were selected for digitisation; '19th Century Entertainment', 'The Booktrade', 'Popular Prints', 'Crimes Murders and Executions' and 'Advertising'.

ProQuest also persuaded the Library to outsource the scanning to an external company named Capita (whose digital imaging centre was less than 10 miles away from the Library) and with whom ProQuest had worked before. The Library possessed an in-house team that was capable of coping with lots of different kinds of material of different degrees of antiquity. However, ProQuest was of the view that outsourcing the digitisation to an independent contractor would result in time and cost efficiency at a scale that could not be provided by the in-house team.

The labour required for digitisation was also provided by Capita while the Library staff dealt with the selection, cataloguing and conservation of the material chosen for scanning. The Library staff was also responsible for overall project management. Of the funding received from the Jisc, approximately three-quarters (¾) were spent on cataloguing the collection and creating the meta-data that enabled the Library to describe and track the images through the entire workflow.

---

[4]Formerly known as the Joint Information Systems Committee, more information available from the Jisc website <www.jisc.ac.uk/> accessed 31 January 2019.

[5]Tomkins (n 2) 4.

The project, at its completion, yielded digitised versions of 67,754 items of printed ephemera that added up to a total of 174,196 high-resolution colour images. Although the quality of the images was sufficient for ProQuest's purposes, they fell below the quality levels normally observed by the Library's in-house team. The Library also assumed responsibility for the preservation of the digital data produced by the project.

Under the terms of the partnership agreement with ProQuest, the Library obtains ownership of the digital images and the associated meta-data created under the project. However, a 5-year exclusive licence has been granted to ProQuest. Following the expiration of the 5-year period, the licence could be renewed for 1-year at a time, at the discretion of the Library. Under the terms of the partnership agreement, the digitised versions are made available free-of-charge to users within the UK. ProQuest recoups its investment made in the digitisation process (primarily infrastructure and design costs) through sales of the digitised versions outside the UK, particularly in the North American market. The Library receives royalties on these sales. Before the royalties are calculated, ProQuest makes a deduction for costs it incurred in the maintenance of their distribution service, etc.

In the event the licence is not renewed, ProQuest would lose their exclusive right to reproduce and distribute the digitised versions. Nonetheless, it must be noted that some of its customers have been provided with copies of the digitised data along with a licence in perpetuity with the consent of the Library. However, this is on the understanding that the product is only used within a particular institution and is not sold or licensed to third parties.

Example 2: Museo Galileo, Florence, Italy: Creation of the 'Digital Library'[6]
The Museo Galileo Library hosts a collection of about 42,000 books published between 1500 and 1899 including approximately 500 works that have been identified as having belonged to the private library of the famous scientist Galileo Galilei. It also maintains an archive consisting of a collection of ancient manuscripts and other printed material.

The Museo Galileo (hereinafter referred to as the 'Museum') is a public sector institution that operates through financial grants from the government and other sponsors. In accordance with the statute under which it was established, the Museum is a non-profit entity and therefore, neither the Museum nor its Library can engage in profit-making activities.

The Digital Library of the Museum was instituted for publishing digital collections on themes relating to the history of science. Under the digitisation project around 1000 rare documents recording public domain content were converted to digital format.

Finances for the creation of the Digital Library were provided by the Italian Ministry of Heritage and Cultural Affairs through its *Biblioteca Digitale Italiana*

[6]This outline is based primarily upon the views expressed by Stefano Casati of the Digital Library, Museo Galileo, Italy during an interview held with the author on 1 February, 2014 (interview transcript in possession of the author).

(Italian Digital Library) project, as well as the Department of Educational Policy and Cultural Affairs of the Region of Tuscany.

In accordance with its status as a non-profit entity, the Museum's ability to enter into partnerships with private sector bodies is constrained. Thus, partnerships with external entities have only taken place within the context of projects financed by the public sector. For instance, the Museum entered into a partnership with the *Biblioteca Europea di Informazione e Cultura* (BEIC) for the digitisation of a collection of works relating to ancient mathematics.[7]

The Museo Galileo claims copyright over the digitised versions of its rare documents. Most of the digitised materials are made available online under open access terms. The Library makes digitised images available in 'jpg' (low-resolution) and 'tiff' (high- resolution) formats. The 'jpg' version of an image can be downloaded free of charge from the website. However, where a 'tiff' version of a work is required, it must be requested from the Library. The relevant digitised image in 'tiff' format will then be supplied upon the payment of a fee.[8] As stated by Stefano Casati of the Digital Library:

> The copyright is limited only to the digitised versions in 'tiff' (high-resolution) format owned by the digital library, since this allows us to recover the costs of digitisation.[9]

Thus, while the Library provides free access and use of its digitised versions in a format that is suitable for non-commercial use (e.g., private use, teaching, etc.), it uses copyright law as a mechanism to facilitate the commercial exploitation of high-resolution images to recover at least a small part of the costs of digitisation.

Example 3: The National Archives, UK: The Licensed Internet Associates Programme (LIA)[10]

The National Archives of the UK (hereinafter referred to as the 'TNA-UK') holds a large collection of unique and original documents (mostly public records) from across the UK, spanning the past 1000 years.[11] It is an executive agency of the

---

[7]Museo Galileo, 'Ancient Mathematics' <www.museogalileo.it/en/explore/libraries/digitallibrary/digitalcollections/en-802.html> 31 January 2019.

[8]The approximate payment being € 1.10 per colour image and € 0.65 for a black and white image. An additional fee is charged for providing a digital image on a CD-Rom *see* Museo Galileo, 'Digital Reproduction' <www.museogalileo.it/en/explore/libraries/library/services/digitalreproduction.html> 31 January 2019.

[9]Reproduced from interview transcript (n 6).

[10]This outline is based primarily upon the views expressed by an Official of The National Archives, UK during an interview held with the author on 3 April, 2013. Participation in the interview was on grounds of anonymity (interview transcript in possession of author).

[11]Nancy L Maron, 'The National Archives (UK): Digitisation with Commercial Partnerships via the Licensed Internet Associates Programmeme.' (Ithaka S+R 2011) <www.google.com/url?sa=t&rct=j&q=&esrc=s&source=web&cd=1&ved=2ahUKEwjxj4rjq7bgAhVRbBoKHSWzD7EQFjAAegQIARAC&url=https%3A%2F%2Fsr.ithaka.org%2Fwp-content%2Fuploads%2F2015%2F08%2FSCA_BMS_CaseStudy_NatArchives.pdf&usg=AOvVaw2ZhpvPFsxrQhWyBddukpvY> accessed 31 January 2019.

Ministry of Justice of the UK (as well as a non-ministerial department) and is the official archive and publisher for the UK government and for England and Wales.[12]

The primary source of funding of the TNA-UK is the government. However, in addition to public funding the TNA-UK generates independent revenue from licensing the use of its documents, co-publishing, operating a bookshop, as well as payments made for digital documents.

The Licensed Internet Associates Programme (hereinafter referred to as the 'LIA') was launched by the TNA-UK with the following objectives:

- to obtain financial resources for digitisation,
- to obtain technological support for digitisation, and
- to preserve original records from wear and tear through usage in physical form.

It was also felt that the formation of partnerships with other organisations would be advantageous in promoting the overall image of the TNA-UK and would allow digitised versions to be made available to the public through a much larger database and across a broader distribution network, thereby improving its public accessibility. Moreover, the LIA programme brings in revenue to the TNA-UK in the form of shares of royalties from sales income generated by the licensees.

The goal of the programme was to improve access and to get as much content online as possible in a financially sustainable manner. The motivation to seek external investment for digitisation came from the realisation that the institution's budget could not sufficiently cope with the costs of digitising its collection (especially in view of the budget cuts the TNA-UK had to undergo during the recent financial downturn). As stated by an official who participated in the survey on the grounds of anonymity:

> Using external investment is the preferred option – this maximises the opportunities for scanning our collection. We only spend public money on digitisation as a last resort. We would always prefer to conserve diminishing public funding for essential operations – onsite public services and information management services – to ensure that records continue to be accessed and kept correctly for the future.[13]

LIA Partnerships are structured as renewable 10-year non-exclusive licences.[14] The licensing team of the TNA-UK arranges materials relating to different categories of information (e.g., ship's passenger lists, military service records, census records, etc.) into collections. Each collection is complemented with an information package that describes the materials and the potential market demand for them.

The TNA-UK calls for tender from entities who are interested in digitising the material. The tender process is regulated by an IFTS[15] accredited scheme to ensure

[12]The National Archives website <www.gov.uk/government/organisations/the-national-archives> accessed 31 January 2019.

[13]Reproduced from interview transcript (n 10).

[14]Maron (n 11) 3.

[15]Refers to the 'Information Fair Trader Scheme' (IFTS) that set and assessed standards for public sector bodies. Since 2017, the IFTS has been superseded by statutory arrangements put in place by

that every bidder gets a fair chance. The winner who secures the LIA licence is required to digitise the relevant collection and to make it available to the public over the Internet. Under the agreement, the TNA-UK retains complete ownership of the intellectual property rights over each digital image and the entity that carries out the digitisation only obtains a non-exclusive licence to commercially exploit the digitised versions it has created and is further required to deposit a copy of each digital image (raw-image) with the TNA-UK. However, it obtains the advantage of having its database of digitised versions linked to the TNA-UK website. Being linked to the TNA-UK website could give the initial licensee a competitive edge over any subsequent licensees by enabling it to attract a greater number of users to its database.

As the owner of the intellectual property rights over the digitised versions, the TNA-UK has the right to grant separate non-exclusive licences for the commercial exploitation of the digitised versions to other entities. This is carried out with the intention of improving the public accessibility of these digital images (as the same image would be available from multiple suppliers), while minimising the damage that could ensue to the original material from multiple exposure to digitisation. The subsequent licensees however, do not receive the right to be linked to the TNA-UK website thereby preserving the incentive for entities to win the bid for digitisation and to become the first non-exclusive licensee of the images that is linked to the TNA-UK website.

While the initial licensee and the subsequent licensees have the ability to commercially exploit the digitised product, the TNA-UK retains control over the prices that can be charged from users of the digital images. These prices are determined with an emphasis on affordability and fair-pricing. The fees charged for access and use by the first licensee and each subsequent licensee must be approved by the TNA-UK, which also sets a maximum-entry level price. Access is provided free-of-charge to onsite users at the TNA-UK building located in Kew, Surrey. As the official from the TNA-UK noted:

> What users are paying when they subscribe to one of our partners is the convenience of being able to do their research in the middle of the night in their own home wherever they are in the world (...) and the price they are paying for that online is very very affordable.[16]

The initial licensee, as well as subsequent licensees, are required to pay royalties to the TNA-UK on their sales of the digitised product that can range from 7% to 14% of the price they charged from users[17] (depending on the type of contract). This

the Re-use of Public Sector Information Regulations n°1415 of 2015 (UK PSI Regulations). For more information *see* The National Archives, 'Closure of the Information Fair Trader Scheme announced' <http://www.nationalarchives.gov.uk/about/news/closure-of-the-information-fair-trader-scheme-announced/> accessed 31 January 2019.

[16]Reproduced from interview transcript (n 10).

[17]ibid.

provides a steady source of revenue that is channelled into the general budget of the TNA-UK and is not solely used for further digitisation efforts.

The LIA programme has succeeded in effecting a quantitative improvement to the digitisation of rare documents held by the TNA and has eased the burden placed on public funding. It has also improved the cost-efficiency of digitisation and has shifted the costs of distribution and customer service from the TNA-UK to its commercial partners.

However, there are several downsides to this business model. Firstly, the LIA programme prioritises the digitisation of rare documents with a high market demand as opposed to documents with high social and cultural value.[18] Secondly, the quality of the digitised images does not always reach the standards that are usually required for long-term digital preservation. Finally, the rights to the meta-data remain with the licensee and without meta-data the value of the digitised versions as a resource for research is diminished.

The TNA-UK attempts to complement the LIA Programme with other digitisation initiatives that focus upon the digitisation of rare documents with social and cultural value that do not hold sufficient appeal to commercial partners. Accordingly, it has launched (and completed) several projects for the digitisation of such documents using the institution's own funding, as well as funding from governmental agencies.

It has also successfully experimented with crowd-sourcing initiatives whereby volunteers are invited to contribute towards the development of digitised versions created through funding obtained from governmental and other non-profit sources. The 'Old Weather Project'[19] is one such example where volunteers were invited to examine digitised versions of ships' log-books, and to analyse and transcribe the information recorded therein to construct a detailed narrative of climate change and marine life. However, such initiatives have so far not been able to match the LIA programme in terms of investment capacity and the sustainability of the digitisation process.

As the above examples illustrate, the structure of a business model for digitisation is fashioned through negotiation and compromise between diverse stakeholders each of whom seeks to promote its individual interests. Public and semi-public sector memory institutions enter into this negotiation process guided by their public mission to make content in their collections freely available to members of the public, but also with an acute awareness of the limited resources available to them to fulfil that mission.

---

[18] ibid.

[19] In the 'Old Weather Project' the TNA-UK partnered with several other institutions in carrying out the crowd-sourced transcription of information from digitised versions of nineteenth century and early twentieth century ships' log-books. More information available from <https://classic.oldweather.org/about> accessed 31 January 2019.

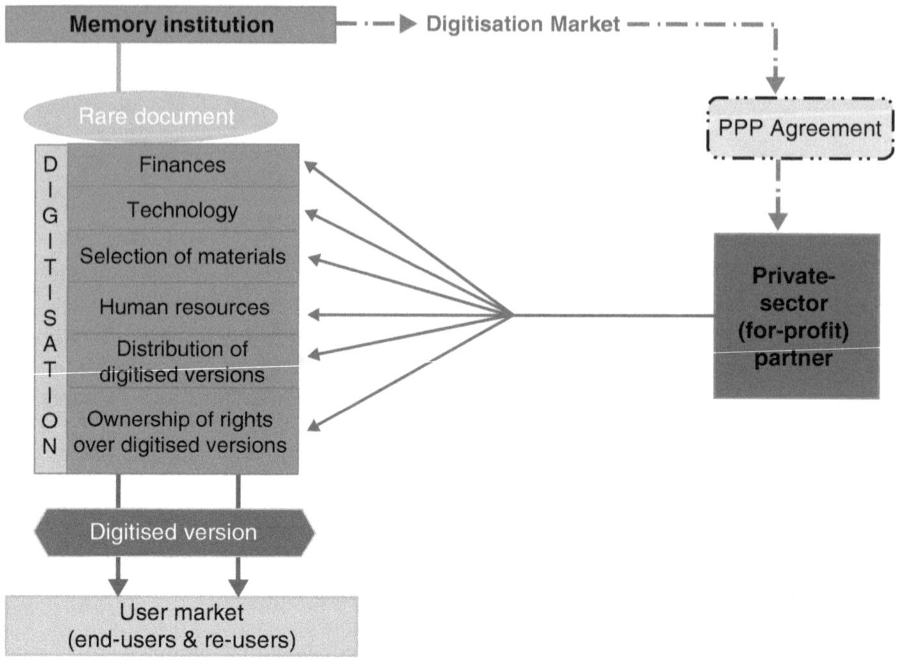

Fig. 3.1 The two markets for digitisation

3.2 A Tale of Two Markets

Presently, two markets have arisen in relation to the digitisation of rare documents. These two markets are mapped in Fig. 3.1.

1. The first is the *user market*. This market is further divided into two categories:
   (a) *the end-user market,* which is comprised of users who seek to make both commercial use and private non-commercial use of the digitised version.
   (b) *the re-user market,* which is comprised of users who seek to re-use the digitised version for both commercial and non-commercial purposes.
2. The second is the *digitisation market*, which is comprised of private sector for-profit entities who agree to carry out the digitisation of rare documents held by a memory institution with the expectation of generating profits through the commercial exploitation of the resulting digitised versions. They often also undertake the task of distributing the resulting digitised versions to the public. In doing so, these entities provide a service to memory institutions by relieving them of the burden of carrying out many (or all) of the functions described in Sect. 3.1 above; particularly that of providing the requisite financial and technological resources. At present, the digitisation market in Europe is dominated by entities such as Google Inc., ProQuest LLC and Brightsolid. These entities

typically use business models that involve the distribution and making available of digitised versions to users and intermediaries (e.g., educational and research institutions, libraries, etc.) in return for payment.

As already noted in Chap. 2[20] above, a great majority (both in a quantitative and qualitative sense) of rare documents within the EU, are held by public sector or semi-public sector memory institutions. These comprise state (including municipal) libraries, archives and museums, as well as university libraries and archives. When a public or semi-public sector memory institution decides to make the rare documents in its collection available to the public in digital format it has a choice between two different strategies. These strategies are discussed below.

3.2.1 Strategy 1: Directly Cater to the User Market

In adopting this strategy, the memory institution carries out the digitisation of rare documents and distributes the digitised versions to the public. A memory institution that follows this strategy needs to furnish the financial, technological, managerial and human resources required for digitisation and the distribution of digitised versions, on its own. Of these, the biggest challenge faced by a memory institution is the provision of finances required for digitisation.

Because of the economic downturn faced by the EU since 2009, many public sector and semi-public sector memory institutions have experienced substantial cuts in their annual budgets and therefore, do not have adequate financial resources to embark on large-scale digitisation projects on their own.

Moreover, these institutions view themselves primarily as educational and cultural establishments with an overarching public mission, and therefore do not place emphasis on the generation of profits. Thus, while they have the potential to generate independent revenue through the services they offer, most of them opt to offer such services free of charge or at-cost. Even when a public or semi-public sector memory institution attempts to generate profits, the profit margin tends to be very slim. Thus, the revenue that is independently generated by these institutions is usually negligible. In any event, many of these public and semi-public sector memory institutions are bound by strict administrative and budgetary rules that restrict their ability to generate independent revenue. Furthermore, the administrative framework and existing infrastructure of memory institutions are ill-adapted to provide the technological and managerial resources and expertise that is required for setting up in-house digitisation facilities. Thus, although a few memory institutions such as the National Archives of the UK have attempted to fund digitisation initiatives

[20] *See* Sect. 2.3.1.

through the institution's own revenue,[21] self-funding does not at present, offer an adequate or sustainable source of funding for the digitisation of rare documents.

A memory institution that wishes to directly cater to the user market needs to rely on external sources of funding. At present, a public or semi-public sector memory institution can appeal to a range of external sources that provide funding based on non-profit motives. Some of the most significant not-for-profit sources of funding for digitisation initiatives within the EU are discussed below.

a. *Government funding*

   This refers to finances obtained from the government of a Member State or from a governmental agency. A good example of government funding in the creation of digitised versions is the funding provided by the Italian Ministry of Heritage and Cultural Affairs in the creation of the Digital Library of the Museo Galileo (Italy).[22] Compared with other external sources of non-profit funding, governments of the EU Member States have a high capacity for financing the digitisation of rare documents. Nonetheless, in view of the many calls on the government purse, the financing of digitisation initiatives understandably obtains minimal priority. As illustrated in Fig. 4.1,[23] at present, officials of EU memory institutions appear to have low confidence in government funding as an adequate or reliable source of external funding for digitisation projects.
b. *Partnership with private sector not-for-profit entity dedicated to providing funding for digitisation.*

   This refers to funding obtained from private sector not-for-profit entities which are dedicated to supporting digitisation initiatives. However, many of these entities are themselves dependent on external sources for obtaining financial resources and therefore do not have a high capacity for providing financial support for digitisation. For example, non-profit organisations such as Europeana,[24] The Public Domain Review[25] and the Internet Archive[26] do not bear the costs of producing digitised versions. However, once digitised versions have been produced, it provides an infrastructure for distributing those digitised versions to the public by permanently storing them on their online digital libraries

---

[21]*See* Sect. 3.1, Example 3 above.

[22]*See* Sect. 3.1, Example 2 above.

[23]*See* Sect. 4.3.

[24]More information about Europeana available from <www.europeana.eu/portal/en/about.html> accessed 31 January 2019. See also Sunimal Mendis, 'Europeana' in Marie Cornu, Fabienne Orsi and Judith Rochfeld (eds), Dictionnaire des Biens communs (PUF 2017).

[25]The Public Domain Review is an online journal and not-for-profit project, that hosts an online platform over which digitised versions of public domain content is made available either free of restrictions or under an open license. More information available from <https://publicdomainreview.org/> accessed 31 January 2019.

[26]The Internet Archive is a non-profit library, based in the United States. More information available from <https://archive.org/about/> accessed 31 January 2019.

and platforms where it can be accessed and used by the public free-of-charge.[27] Thus, at present, private sector not-for-profit partners do not have a lot of capacity to invest in the production of digitised versions.

c. *Partnership with university or research organisation*

Universities and research organisations sometimes provide finances for digitisation initiatives, especially concerning rare documents that align with their particular research interests. For example, the University of Padova (Italy) funded the digitisation of photographic plates belonging to the Asiago Observatory, through a collaborative initiative between the University's department of astronomy and the Asiago Observatory.[28] Partnerships with universities and research organisations have the added benefit of allowing the technological resources and human expertise held by these organisations to be channelled into the digitisation process. However, attracting funding from universities and research organisations will only be feasible when those organisations have sufficient interest in a particular collection of rare documents. Therefore, these sources cannot be relied upon as a steady source of funding for digitisation initiatives.

d. *Sponsors and donors*

This refers to organisations and individuals who provide finances for digitisation from charitable motives or for obtaining publicity or advertising value. An example is the £2 million award provided by the Polonsky Foundation for the digitisation of Hebrew manuscripts, Greek manuscripts, and incunabula held by the Bodleian Libraries (UK) and the Biblioteca Apostolica Vaticana (Vatican Library, Italy).[29] Funding from sponsors and donors tend to be random and sporadic and as such do not constitute a stable or reliable source of funding.

e. *Fund-raising*

Fund-raising refers to raising finances for digitisation through donations received from individuals and organisations, including crowd-funding initiatives. The *Sprint for Shakespeare* project launched by the Bodleian Libraries (UK) is an example of the successful use of fund-raising for digitisation. The *Sprint for Shakespeare* project[30] made a public appeal for donations to raise the finances required for conserving, digitising and making available online *Shakespeare's First Folio* of plays. The fund-raising appeal was also supported and championed

---

[27]The online library includes digitised versions of rare documents from several European memory institutions including the National Library of Scotland, Institut National de la Recherche Agronomique (French National Institute for Agricultural Research) and the Biblioteca Nazionale Centrale di Firenze (National Central Library of Florence). The Internet Archive, European Libraries <https://archive.org/details/europeanlibraries> accessed 31 January 2019.

[28]For more information on the digitisation project *see* C Barbieri, A Omizzolo and F Rampazzi, 'Digitisation of the Archive of Plates of the Asiago Observatory and of the Specola Vaticana' (2003) 74 Memorie della Società Astronomica Italiana 430.

[29]More information available at 'Polonsky Foundation Digitisation Project' <http://bav.bodleian.ox.ac.uk/> accessed 31 January 2019.

[30]More information available from, Sprint for Shakespeare, 'The Project' <http://shakespeare.bodleian.ox.ac.uk/the-project/> accessed 31 January 2019.

by prominent public personalities in the UK. Raising finances for digitisation through public fund-raising initiatives give the opportunity for members of the public to get directly involved in the digitisation of cultural heritage content and to raise public awareness as to the importance of making rare documents accessible to the public in digital form. However, fund-raising cannot be relied upon as a sustainable form of funding for digitisation. As noted by Christine Madsen of the Bodleian Libraries, over-use of the fund-raising model could result in a loss of public enthusiasm for funding digitisation initiatives.[31] Furthermore, while fund-raising could be a successful means of obtaining finances for the digitisation of rare documents holding a high degree of national or cultural significance such as *Shakespeare's First Folio* of plays, it may not have the same measure of success in relation to less significant documents that are unable to capture similar levels of public enthusiasm.

f. *Volunteers and crowd-sourcing*

This refers to the use of volunteers for obtaining human resources and expertise in the development of existing digitised versions, cataloguing them and preparing meta-data. For example, the *Georeferencer* project[32] launched by the British Library (UK) used crowd-sourcing to geo-reference digitised versions of its collection of historical maps in order to make them geographically searchable and viewable through popular online geo-technologies. Although volunteers and crowd-sourcing could be used in the actual digitisation process (e.g., preparing the documents, operating the scanning equipment, etc.) where ordinary printed-matter is concerned, this is not feasible in the context of rare documents because of the specialised care required in the handling of these documents and the sophisticated technology that needs to be used in the digitisation process. Thus, the use of volunteers and crowd-sourcing is usually limited to the post-production phase (e.g., transcribing and indexing) and as such does not offer a viable means of obtaining human resources for the production of digitised versions.

The foregoing discussion demonstrates that, although external sources of not-for-profit funding can be valuable for supplementing a memory institution's resources in achieving the digitisation of its rare documents, the aforementioned sources do not, on their own, constitute reliable, sustainable or adequate sources of funding. At the moment, there is a steady trend on the part of public and semi-public sector memory institutions to cater to the digitisation market instead of directly catering to the user market. Thus, the digitisation market becomes the predominant channel through which digitised versions of rare documents are made available to the user market. Therefore, the dynamics of the digitisation market directly affects end-users and re-users of digitised versions in terms of the amount of digitised versions that will be

[31]Opinion expressed during interview held with the author on 2 September 2013 (n 2). This is the personal opinion of Christine Madsen and does not necessarily reflect the official view of the Bodleian Libraries, UK.

[32]More information available from, Georeference 'About this project' <https://www.bl.uk/georeferencer/georefabout.html> accessed 31 January 2019.

made available to them, the type of documents that would be digitised and the ways in which these digitised versions can be accessed, used and re-used by them. These dynamics along with the reasons that could motivate a memory institution to cater to the digitisation market are discussed below.

3.2.2 *Strategy 2: Cater to the Digitisation Market*

As noted above, the digitisation market comprises entities who wish to obtain authorisation from a memory institution to create digitised versions of rare documents held by them, for exploiting the resulting digitised versions for commercial gain. Such authorisation is usually granted by means of a public-private partnership (PPP) Agreement that is entered into between the memory institution and the private sector for-profit entity.

As a means of enabling the private sector for-profit partner to commercialise the resulting digitised versions, these PPP Agreements usually include clauses that grant the private sector for-profit partner exclusive[33] or non-exclusive[34] rights or privileges[35] over the commercial exploitation of the digitised versions they produce. Thus, digitised versions created under a PPP Agreement with a private sector for-profit partner are more likely to be made available to the public subject to restrictions and controls as to the manner in which they can be accessed, used and re-used. This is a key difference between digitisation that is achieved through for-profit funding models and digitisation achieved through not-for-profit funding models. The reasons for this difference will be discussed in greater detail in Sects. 4.4.1 and 5.3 below. At present, it suffices to say that, private sector for-profit entities consider that the imposition of restrictions on the access and use of digitised versions is essential in enabling their commercial exploitation at an optimal level and in ensuring a return on the investment made in the digitisation process. However, many memory institutions attempt to minimise the detriment that could be caused to users through the imposition of such restrictions by insisting that the digitised versions are made available free of restriction for viewing (although not for downloading) within the institution's own premises.[36]

[33]For example, the Cooperative Agreement entered into between Google Inc. and the University of Michigan Library (USA) includes a provision that grants Google Inc. ownership of the rights, title and interests over its copy of the digitised version. Clause 4.5 of the 'Cooperative Agreement between Google Inc and the University of Michigan/University Library' <https://www.lib.umich.edu/files/services/mdp/um-google-cooperative-agreement.pdf> accessed 31 January 2019.

[34]*See* Sect. 3.1, Example 3.

[35]*See* Sect. 1.2, Example 2. *See also* Philippe Aigrain, 'Nous Devons Empêcher La Privatisation Du Domaine Public' Communs 16 January 2013 <http://paigrain.debatpublic.net/?p=6333> accessed 31 January 2019.

[36]For example, under the 2012 Partnership Agreement between ProQuest LLC and the National Library of France (BnF) all digitised versions produced by ProQuest are made available to users

Additionally, when funding is provided under a for-profit model there is greater likelihood that the selection of rare documents for digitisation will be primarily based upon the criterion of market demand and the potential for commercial exploitation, as opposed to the social value that could be generated by making it available to the public in digital form. Another issue of concern that was voiced in the survey[37] was the likelihood of the private sector for-profit partner compromising on the quality of the digital images to minimise production costs.[38] In view of these disadvantages, it becomes necessary to consider why a public or semi-public sector memory institution may be motivated to cater to the digitisation market.

3.3 Motivation to Cater to the Digitisation Market

A public or semi-public sector memory institution may opt to cater to the digitisation market for several reasons. Foremost among these is the achievement of the digitisation of rare document collections within a steady and reliable funding model that shifts almost the entire burden of furnishing the requisite financial, technological, managerial and human resources to an external entity. Private sector for-profit entities who are active in the digitisation market have established logistical and infrastructure frameworks that enable them to successfully implement digitisation projects while placing minimal strain on a memory institution's own resources.

Within the EU, private sector for-profit entities demonstrate a greater capacity for financial investment in digitisation than other sources of funding (including government funding). This could, at least in part, be attributed to their focus on profit generation which allows their business models to be more sustainable than those adopted by non-profit entities. As noted above, the foremost challenge faced by public and semi-public sector memory institutions in achieving the digitisation of rare documents held by them is in obtaining a steady and reliable source of financial investment for the digitisation process.[39] Private sector for-profit entities fulfil this need by offering stable financial partnerships.

within the BnF premises free of charge under open access terms. *See* Aurélie Filippetti, Louis Gallois and Bruno Racine, 'Investing in the Future: Two Major Partnerships Have Been Concluded to Digitize and Make Available Collections Held by the BnF' <http://www.bnf.fr/documents/cp_accords_proquest-believe_eng.pdf> accessed 31 January 2019. Similarly, digitised versions produced under the LIA programme launched by the TNA-UK are made available free-of-charge to users within the TNA-UK premises. *See* Sect. 3.1, Example 3 above.

[37] *See* Sect. 2.3.1.

[38] *See* Sect. 3.1, Example 1.

[39] 'The primary objective of public-private partnerships for the public institution is access to funding to digitise their collections.' High Level Expert Group on Digital Libraries: Subgroup on Public Private Partnerships, Final Report on Public Private Partnerships for the Digitisation and Online Accessibility of Europe's Cultural Heritage (i2010 European Digital Libraries Initiative 2008) 11.

Moreover, many PPP Agreements entered into with for-profit entities include clauses that entitle the memory institution to obtain a share of the profits generated through the sale or licensing of the digitised versions. Thus, catering to the digitisation market could have the added benefit of opening up additional sources of revenue to a memory institution. This could serve as an incentive for memory institutions that feel the need to supplement their budgets to enter into PPPs with for-profit entities.

The costs that go into making a digitised version available once it has been produced are often ignored or underestimated. These comprise the costs of setting-up and maintaining distribution channels (e.g., launching and maintaining a dedicated website over which the digitised versions are made available), costs of creating meta-data and incorporating value-added-features that improve the user experience, maintaining a customer support system, etc. Many private sector for-profit entities that invest in the creation of digitised versions also have established distribution channels that are familiar to the public. Therefore, making a digitised version available over an established distribution channel maintained by a private sector partner could enhance the public visibility and accessibility of the digitised version[40] while at the same time, relieving the memory institution of the burden of creating and maintaining their own distribution channels.

Table 3.1 attempts to illustrate the capacity for investment held by different funding sources, their focus on the imposition of restrictions and controls over digitised versions and the significance placed on social value as a criterion in the selection of rare documents for digitisation.

It is noted that the 'measurements' provided for each funding model in Table 3.1 as regards the fields; investment capacity, focus on social value in the selection of material and on the imposition of controls and restrictions are based on the author's individual perception of these models. The author's individual perception has been informed by the qualitative and quantitative data gathered in the empirical survey on digitisation projects. Thus, the measurements are not based upon hard empirical evidence. They are merely intended to provide the reader a basic evaluation of the different funding models in relation to the aforementioned aspects.

<https://www.google.com/url?sa=t&rct=j&q=&esrc=s&source=web&cd=2&ved=2ahUKEwiR_uTRqZjgAhXE2OAKHV_YBqgQFjABegQICRAC&url=http%3A%2F%2Fwww.europeanwriterscouncil.eu%2Fimages%2Fpdf%2Fdigitallibraries%2F1ppp_final.pdf&usg=AOvVaw2yakysL8qhvPfrSjcjzJIh> accessed 31 January 2019.

[40]For instance, entering into a PPP with Google Inc. would mean that a rare book collection held by a memory institution would be accessible to the public over the Google Books platform. This would increase its public visibility and accessibility as users are already familiar with the Google Books platform.

3.4 Summary and Conclusions

At present, a wide range of business models are employed for the production and distribution of digitised versions. The digitisation process has given rise to two different markets. The first is the user market that comprises the end-user and re-user markets for digitised versions. The second is the digitisation market that is made up of private sector for-profit entities that seek to obtain authorisation for the production of digitised versions and their exploitation for commercial gain.

Most public and semi-public sector memory institutions find the financial, technological and managerial burden that is involved in directly catering to the user market too much to bear. Of these, the main challenge faced by public and semi-public sector memory institutions is in obtaining the requisite financial investment required for producing the digitised versions. Private sector for-profit entities have a greater capacity for financial investment than government and other not-for-profit sources of funding. Consequently, there is a steady trend on the part of public and semi-public sector memory institutions to cater to the market for digitisation, by entering into PPP Agreements with private sector for-profit entities.

The market for digitisation holds a lot of potential in channelling private sector investment into the digitisation process, improving the distribution and accessibility of digitised versions of rare documents to the public, allowing the managerial and marketing expertise of the private sector to be harnessed for the digitisation of rare documents and in general to make the digitisation process more efficient and sustainable. However, digitised versions that are produced by for-profit entities are more likely to be subject to claims of exclusivity. The study proceeds to examine why private sector for-profit entities feel the need to claim exclusive rights over digitised versions produced by them. It then considers whether there is a way in which the positive effects of the involvement of private sector for-profit entities in the digitisation process could be preserved and optimised while at the same time balancing the competing interests of the public.

Chapter 4
Is There a Need to Preserve Exclusivity Over Digitised Versions?

4.1 Rare Documents in the EU

As noted in Chap. 2 above, Europe as the bedrock of modern western civilisation holds within its memory institutions substantial collections of rare documents that are of immense significance in understanding and appreciating modern science, culture, and society.[1] The bulk of this material is held by public sector and semi-public sector memory institutions. In comparison, the amount of material that is held by private sector establishments is smaller and of lesser significance in terms of scientific, cultural and historical value (although exceptions do apply).

4.2 Is There a Need for Mass-Digitisation?

It is necessary to consider whether there is a need for a mass-digitisation initiative within the EU that is aimed at securing the digitisation of rare documents held by public and semi-public sector memory institutions. At first glance, the answer to this question may seem intuitive. The benefits of digitisation to the progress of culture, education and commerce seem to advocate a positive response. However, in the interests of following a sound methodological approach, it is necessary to consider the need for large-scale digitisation of rare documents more analytically.

---

[1]Examples of seminal rare documents held in European memory institutions include Da Vinci's notebook (*Codex Arundel*) currently held by the British Library, the Mendoza collection of eighteenth century maps housed in the National Library of Spain, *Epistola de insulis nuper repertis* which is a letter assumed to be written by Christopher Columbus announcing the results of his first voyage held by the University of Bologna library, the original copy of the Code Napoleon of 1807 (prepared for the emperor himself) which is in the custody of the National Library of France as well as the archives of the central civil authorities of the German Reich (1867/71–1945) held by the Federal Archive of Germany.

S. Mendis, *A Copyright Gambit*, Munich Studies on Innovation and Competition 11,
https://doi.org/10.1007/978-3-662-59454-4_4

An official of a European memory institution interviewed during the survey stated that, in his institution a single archival document is, on average, consulted by a user once every 54 years. Therefore, in his opinion, it made no sense to digitise archival documents that had such a low public demand.[2] There are many such rare documents holding considerable scientific, cultural, and historical value that are rarely sought to be accessed by members of the public.

However, it may not be accurate to measure the demand for a digitised version purely based on the existing demand for the original analogue (tangible) document. Digitisation offers a completely new way of accessing, using and experiencing a work. It also has the ability to open up public domain content to whole new groups of users. The user who seeks to access a digitised version of a document can be very different from a user who seeks to access the analogue document.[3]

It is also possible that members of the public are keen to use and access a particular rare document but are prevented from doing so because of high transaction costs associated with the access and use of the document in its original analogue form. Thus, low levels of use and access do not necessarily signal a lack of public interest in accessing and using the public domain content recorded upon a rare document. Rather, it could be the result of the existing public demand being untapped by the memory institution. Imagine a scholar in India or Brazil who would like to access a work that is archived in Berlin. The high costs involved in travelling to Berlin to access the work could preclude these users from requesting access to the document. However, if a digitised version of the document was made available (even behind a pay-wall) the cost of accessing that digitised version would in all probability be considerably lower than in accessing the original analogue version. Thus, digitisation would allow a memory institution to capture this untapped market and to cater to the needs of users who are not considered at present. Therefore, it is wrong to underestimate the social value that could be created by digitisation, merely based on existing levels of access and use of a rare document.

It has been observed that, "[t]he relationship between availability of digital material and demand is axiomatic. As technology increases ease of access to a given resource, its user base inevitably grows correspondingly."[4] There is also a need to consider what has been referred to by Samuelson as the serendipitous value of public domain works, i.e., that an information resource that is of no importance, may become suddenly very socially valuable when someone finds a reason to use it.[5]

---

[2]The interview was granted on the basis of anonymity (interview transcript in possession of the author).

[3]Opinion expressed by Mathieu Andro Project Manager—Scanning and Text Mining at the French National Institute of Agricultural Research, formerly Head of Digitisation at the Bibliothèque Sainte-Geneviève, Paris, France (2008–2012) during an interview held with the author on 8 November 2013 (interview transcript in possession of the author).

[4]JISC, 'Digitisation in the UK: The Case for a UK Framework' (2005) <https://www.rluk.ac.uk/wp-content/uploads/2014/02/Digitisation_in_the_UK.pdf> accessed 31 January 2019.

[5]Pamela Samuelson, 'Challenges in Mapping the Public Domain' in Lucie Guibault and P Bernt Hugenholtz (eds), *The Future of the Public Domain* (Kluwer Law International 2006) 23. *See also*

In fact, of the fourteen memory institutions that were surveyed thirteen stated that, as of 2014, less than 25% of their rare document collections had been digitised.[6] When one considers that the survey included some of the most important memory institutions in the UK, France, Germany, Italy and Spain, it is difficult to believe that less than 25% of the rare documents held by these institutions possess sufficient social value to make their conversion to digital format worthwhile. Considering that the phenomenon of mass-book digitisation has been present in Europe for more than a decade, this points to an underproduction problem with respect to digitised versions of rare documents recording public domain content. Thus, it is argued here that, there is a need to accelerate the digitisation process in Europe and to achieve a quantitative increase in the number of rare documents that are available to the public in digital form.

4.3 Is There a Need to Channel Private Sector (for-Profit) Investment?

At first glance, it may seem that the best means of achieving the digitisation of rare documents within the EU is through funding by not-for-profit models. This would enable the selection of rare documents for digitisation to be based on considerations of social value as opposed to market-demand. It would also allow digitised versions of rare documents to be made available to the public relatively free of restrictions and controls in comparison with for-profit funding models.

However, as discussed in Sect. 3.2.1, at present, not-for-profit funding models on their own, do not have adequate capacity for achieving the digitisation of rare documents within the EU. They also have a propensity to be unsustainable in the long-term as they do not have a means of ensuring a steady and reliable stream of revenue that could be used to support a continuous digitisation initiative.

The largest source of not-for-profit funding within the EU is the government. In most Member States, governments or government agencies provide funding for digitisation projects in public and semi-public sector memory institutions.[7] However, government funding by itself cannot be relied upon to achieve the necessary level of digitisation. Officials of memory institutions who participated in the empirical survey (i.e., resource persons) were asked to rate their general opinion of

---

Ricolfi who notes that "(. . .) the way in which digital resources may be combined to create novel goods or services are ex-ante unpredictable". Thus, digitised versions could be used in ways hitherto unforeseen in relation to their analogue counterparts, and could open up completely new markets. Marco Ricolfi, 'The New Paradigm of Creativity and Innovation and Its Corollaries for the Law of Obligations' in Peter Drahos, Gustavo Ghidini and Hans Ullrich (eds), Kritika: Essays on Intellectual Property (Edward Elgar 2015) 148.

[6]The remaining participant stated that between 25–50% of their collection of rare public domain materials have been digitised (based on statistics as of 2014).

[7]For example, the Deutsche Forschungsgemeinschaft (DFG) in Germany and the Jisc in the UK are government agencies that provide funding for digitisation projects.

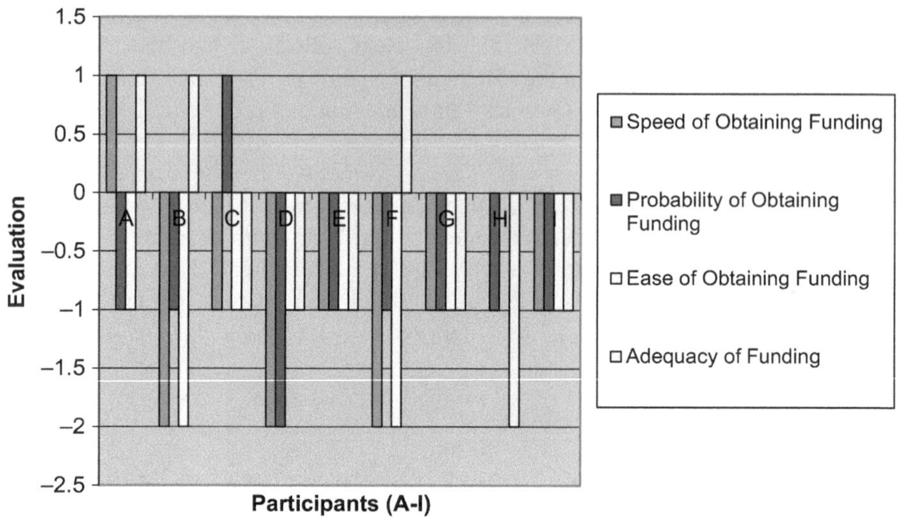

Scale	Speed	Probability	Ease	Adequacy
2	Very Fast	Very High	Very Easy	Very Adequate
1	Fast	High	Easy	Adequate
0	No Opinion	No Opinion	No Opinion	No Opinion
−1	Slow	Low	Difficult	Inadequate
−2	Very Slow	Very Low	Very Difficult	Very Inadequate

Fig. 4.1 Evaluation of government funding for digitisation

securing government funding for digitisation projects in relation to the speed of obtaining funding,[8] the probability of obtaining funding,[9] the ease of obtaining funding,[10] as well as the adequacy of the funding once it has been received.[11] Five participants refrained from responding, as they had no experience in applying for government funding. A summary of the responses given by the remaining nine participants is presented in Fig. 4.1. As some of the resource persons expressed their

[8]Defined in the survey as 'the length of time between making an initial request for funding and obtaining funds'.

[9]Defined in the survey as 'the probability that the funding will be received once a request has been made'.

[10]Defined in the survey as 'the ease of the procedure that needs to be followed in securing funding'.

[11]Defined in the survey as 'how the amount of funding that is received compares with the amount that is in fact necessary for the project'.

opinions of the basis of anonymity, the memory institutions are not identified by name, but are represented by the letters ‘A’ to ‘I’.

Although these scores are based on the perceptions of the individual resource persons who may be influenced by the unique social, cultural and economic conditions that prevail in the different Member States, they still seem to indicate that in general, confidence in the government as an efficient source of funding is not very high. Following the economic downturn in Europe, government funding for public and semi-public sector memory institutions and their digitisation initiatives has been reduced to a substantial degree. Hence, while the demand for digitised versions is growing around the world, the amount of government funding available for digitisation within Europe has diminished.

Against this backdrop, private sector for-profit funding constitutes a valuable supplementary source of funding that could be intelligently and strategically used in combination with government and other not-for-profit funding sources to sustain and to accelerate the digitisation process within the EU.[12]

Of the memory institutions that were surveyed, all participants were unanimous in their opinion that a sustainable digitisation model required a combination of different funding models. This becomes evident when one considers that each funding model has its own shortcomings. For example, it is a common perception among officials of memory institutions that in the production of digitised versions, certain private sector for-profit investors tend to compromise on the quality of the digitised version in the interests of digitising a greater number of rare documents.[13] It is true that, in many instances, private sector investors tend to design their digitisation projects giving priority to cost and time efficiency over the production of high-quality digital images. However, this does have the advantage of making a greater number of rare documents available to the public within a shorter space of time (even if it means that the resulting digital images are of a lower quality, than if it was carried out under

---

[12]The Comité des Sages also agrees on this point. As noted by the Comité:

> Even if the Comité des Sages is firmly convinced that digitisation is mainly a task for public authorities, this does not mean that the private sector should not be involved. Going back to our main objective to enlarge access to our cultural heritage, partnering with the private sector can be a good option to speed up the digitisation of works and collections from the public domain, at a time when public funding is scarce. Moreover, digitisation can also be taken as an opportunity to nurture and develop a whole new range of private activities and initiatives, through the new technologies and processes that have been (and will be) developed, and contribute to job creation.

Elisabeth Niggemann, Jacques De Decker and Maurice Lévy, The New Renaissance: Report of the Comité des Sages on Bringing Europe's Cultural Heritage Online (European Commission 2011) para 2.4.1. <https://ec.europa.eu/digital-single-market/sites/digital-agenda/files/final_report_cds_0.pdf> accessed 30 January 2019.

[13]As noted by André Welters of the University and State Library of Cologne, Germany, "In my opinion under a public private partnership you could digitise a larger quantity of works than with government funding. However, it is debatable whether under such a partnership we could provide the same level of quality as we now do." Opinion expressed in the interview held with the author on 28 January 2014 (interview transcript in possession of the author).

a not-for-profit funding model). Furthermore, the strategic use of private sector for-profit funding in the digitisation process means that, memory institutions have the ability to reserve not-for-profit funding for the digitisation of documents that necessitate high-quality digital reproductions[14] while, channelling private sector for-profit funding towards the digitisation of documents that do not necessarily require such high-quality reproduction.[15]

Thus, although the use of private sector for-profit funding could result in a compromise between quantity and quality in certain cases (although not necessarily in all), private sector for-profit funding is a necessary and valuable source of funding in sustaining a smooth and efficient digitisation initiative within the EU.[16] As such, a decline in private sector for-profit investment in the digitisation process could result in the exacerbation of the underproduction problem that currently prevails within the EU.[17] Conversely, strengthening the incentives of private sector for-profit entities to invest in the digitisation of rare documents could result in a quantitative increase in the number of rare documents that are available to the public in digital form. Thus, it is argued here that, at present, there is a need to incentivise greater private sector for-profit investment in the digitisation of rare documents.

4.4 Is There a Need for Control?

In this discussion, 'control' refers to the ability of the producer of the digitised version (or an authorised entity) to restrict and to limit the ways in which the digitised version can be accessed, the persons who may access it, and the purposes for which it may be used.

[14]For example, in the case of an Egyptian papyri or a medieval manuscript that has undergone damage and in which the writing has faded or become difficult to read, a high quality digital reproduction may be required to reproduce the writing with sufficient clarity. Moreover, documents of special scientific, cultural, or historical significance may merit high quality digital reproductions in view of their importance to education and research.

[15]For example, regarding rare documents such as early twentieth century newspapers in which the printed writing is clear, there may not be a need for a high quality digital reproduction, as the textual content will be reproduced with sufficient clarity upon an average quality digitised version.

[16]The final report of the High Level Expert Group on Digital Libraries states that, public-private partnerships are essential for digitising and enhancing online access to cultural heritage and that the investment made by private partners need to be appropriately compensated. The report acknowledges that the question is how this can be achieved while fully respecting rightholders and guaranteeing the value of public assets held by cultural institutions, and maximising access to content. High Level Expert Group on Digital Libraries, 'Final Report: Digital Libraries: Recommendations and Challenges for the Future.' (i2010 European Digital Libraries Initiative 2009) 8. <www.dlorg.eu/uploads/External%20Publications/HLG%20Final%20Report%202009%20clean.pdf> accessed 31 January 2019.

[17]*See* discussion in Sect. 4.7.

This study argues that, there is a need to enable producers of digitised versions of rare documents to maintain control over the ways in which these digitised versions can be used and accessed by the public. This is exemplified in relation to the reasons given below.

4.4.1 Create Investment Incentives

Private sector for-profit entities are motivated to invest in the digitisation process because of the possibility afforded to them to generate profits through the commercial exploitation of the resulting digitised versions. To preserve the incentives of private sector for-profit entities to invest in the digitisation of rare documents, these entities should (at the very minimum), be afforded the possibility of recouping their investment along with a reasonable profit.

As will be discussed more comprehensively in Chap. 5, digitised versions constitute digital informational goods that are highly susceptible to piracy (particularly in the end-user-market that distributes directly to the public[18]) and free-riding by competitors. Thus, to obtain a return on the investment made in the digitisation process, producers of digitised versions must have the ability to prevent free-riding by competitors[19] (who would otherwise be able to reproduce and distribute the digitised versions at marginal costs approaching zero) and to maintain their position as the sole-source of a particular digitised version in the user market. This denotes an ability to maintain control over the access and use of the digitised version and to ensure that such access and use can only be made by authorised persons. Without the ability to maintain control, competition by free-riders and high-levels of piracy will weaken the ability of a producer to recoup the investment made in the digitisation process and make the prospect of obtaining a reasonable return on that investment uncertain. In such an environment, there will be less incentive for private sector for-profit entities to invest in the digitisation of rare documents. Thus, the ability to maintain control over digitised versions becomes an essential pre-requisite in creating incentives for private sector for-profit investment in the digitisation process.

4.4.2 Ensure Sustainability of the Digitisation Process

In economic terms at least, it makes sense to encourage digitisation initiatives to become financially independent in the long-term by allowing them to generate their

[18]The threat of piracy may not be so high in the end-user market that caters to industry needs because in this market it is possible to exercise more control over the distribution and use of the digitised product.

[19]*See* discussion on incentive theory at Sect. 5.3.

own sources of revenue that could be used to support further digitisation. This would serve to improve the sustainability of digitisation initiatives and to make the digitisation process in Europe less susceptible to effects wrought by changing economic cycles and cuts in government funding for public and semi-public sector memory institutions.[20]

The Jisc[21] in the UK is a non-profit charitable institution which provides funding for digitisation projects. However, it is particularly keen to support sustainable project designs that allow for independent revenue generation. The underlying rationale is that the proceeding income could be used to help sustain the preservation of the digitised data, which is a primary concern in the light of changing innovation cycles. Thus, regardless as to the type of funding that is used, the sustainability of a long-term digitisation initiative can profit from a business model that allows for the recoupment of the costs of production and distribution, if not a reasonable profit.

Thus, the ability to maintain control over digitised versions of rare documents and to commercially exploit these in the user market with the objective of obtaining a reasonable return on the investment (or at a minimum the recoupment of that investment) would enable public and semi-public sector memory institutions to develop sustainable digitisation projects, even in the absence of the involvement of a private sector for-profit partner.

4.4.3 Maintain Relevance of Memory Institutions

Several memory institutions stated that, economic conditions permitting, they would be agreeable to making digitised versions of documents in their collections available free-of-charge for both non-commercial, as well as commercial use. However, they emphasised the importance of having the ability to require acknowledgment of their institution as the source of the original rare documents in the use and re-use of the digitised versions. Thus, the ability of a memory institution to compel users of a digitised version to acknowledge it as the source of the original analogue document could constitute a possible non-economic justification for the maintenance of control over the use and re-use of digitised versions.

According to the opinions expressed during the survey, the acknowledgement of the memory institution as the source of a rare document fulfils two purposes. Firstly, it enables the users of the digitised version to find out where the rare document is held, so that those who have an interest in accessing it (in its original analogue form) are able to do so with relative ease. Secondly, it helps to maintain the relevance of the memory institution by emphasising its importance as a centre for scholarship and the role it fulfils in preserving cultural content for posterity. The acknowledgement of

---

[20] *See* Sect. 3.1, Example 1.

[21] Formerly known as the Joint Information Systems Committee, more information available from the Jisc website <www.jisc.ac.uk/> accessed 31 January 2019.

the memory institution as the source of the original document serves as an indirect form of advertisement and publicity that allow memory institutions to strengthen their reputation and thereby enhance their ability to attract funding from government and charitable sources.

Memory institutions are increasingly concerned that, with the proliferation of digital technology and the ability to access and use cultural and educational material in digital form, their function as centres of culture and education may be undermined. As stated by Michael Popham and Christine Madsen of the Bodleian Libraries, if digitised versions of rare documents in their collection were made available to the public without the library having the ability to control the ways in which the digitised versions could be used and re-used:

> It might not damage the library per se, but it might damage scholarship and thus affect the long-term interests of the library indirectly. The greater ease-of-access outweighs concerns about the future of the library, *but it is difficult to imagine who would maintain that ease-of-access and also the original collections of rare public domain materials, and how these aspects would be managed if not by the library.*[22]

It is important to note that, memory institutions are not mere repositories of information but also provide physical spaces for learning and interacting with cultural content in their full historical and cultural context in a way that may be difficult to achieve within a purely virtual online-setting. For example, in providing access to a rare document, a memory institution is able to certify the authenticity of that document, provide background information as to the purpose for which it was created and to place it within a broader cultural and social context. In the absence of regulation, such vital information could easily be lost or distorted along the chain of re-use of digitised versions. Thus, the identification of the memory institution as the source of the original document and as a potential source for obtaining accurate information about that rare document gains importance.

Therefore, the need to grant memory institutions the right to acknowledgement as the original source of rare documents made available in digital form, merits consideration.[23]

---

[22]Reproduced from transcript of interview held with Michael Popham (Head of Digital Initiatives at the Bodleian Libraries) and Christine Madsen (Manager—Infrastructure and Innovation at the Bodleian Libraries) on 2nd September, 2013 (emphasis added) (interview transcript in possession of the author). It is to be noted that the views expressed are the personal opinions of Michael Popham and Christine Madsen, given in their professional capacity and not necessarily the official view of the Bodleian Libraries, UK.

[23]Testing this hypothesis is not within the scope of this research. However, it has been mentioned here to make the reader aware that apart from economic reasons there may also be non-economic reasons for the preservation of exclusivity over digitised versions of rare documents. In this particular case, it may be necessary to grant memory institutions a right to acknowledgment in respect of digitised versions of rare documents held by them.

4.5 Does the Maintenance of Control Require Exclusive Rights?

As already stated in Sect. 1.3, the maintenance of control essentially translates into an exercise of exclusivity through the claiming of exclusive rights. In the absence of exclusivity, the digitised version of a rare document would belong to the public domain and members of the public would be able to use it without restrictions or limitations.[24]

The following discussion argues that, in the absence of protection under an exclusive copyright or a related right even technological measures, such as digital-rights-management (DRM) systems[25] and technological-protection-measures (TPM),[26] which are applied to digitised versions to protect them against piracy, free-riding and other forms of unauthorised use, would fail to obtain protection against circumvention, under EU law.

The WIPO Copyright Treaty (WCT)[27] and the WIPO Performances and Phonograms Treaty (WPPT)[28] both envision the legal protection against the circumvention of TPM and DRM systems to be limited to instances where the TPM or DRM system

---

[24]Except through the application of other complementary legal regimes such as national laws which prohibit material from being used in a way that would harm the racial or religious sentiments of a particular community or nation, or even contract law and digital rights management (the ability of the two former regimes to override the limitations envisioned by copyright or related rights is the subject of some controversy).

[25]DRM has been defined as, "[a] term for access control technologies that are used by hardware manufacturers, publishers, copyright holders and individuals to limit the use of digital content. The term is used to describe any technology that inhibits the use of digital content that is not desired or intended by the content provider. The term does not generally refer to other forms of copy protection, which can be circumvented without modifying the file or device, such as serial numbers or keyfiles." 'Digital Rights Management' (Encoding.com) <www.encoding.com/digital-rights-management-drm/> accessed 31 January 2019.

[26]A report published by the Institute for Information Law (IViR), at the University of Amsterdam, explains the difference between DRM technologies and TPMs as follows:

> The fundamental difference between DRM and TPMs is that TPMs generally are designed to impede access or copying. DRM systems do not impede access or copying per se, but rather create an environment in which various types of use, including copying, are only practically possible in compliance with the contractual terms set by the rights holders. DRM is used to manage access to content by combining TPMs with elements such as payment mechanisms, customer management and authorisation schemes.

Lucie Guibault and others, 'Study on the Implementation and Effect in Member States' Laws of Directive 2001/29/EC on the Harmonisation of Certain Aspects of Copyright and Related Rights in the Information Society' (IViR 2007) 14 <https://papers.ssrn.com/sol3/papers.cfm?abstract_id=2006358> accessed 31 January 2019.

[27]WIPO Copyright Treaty Apr. 12, 1997, S. Treaty Doc. No. 105–17 36 ILM 65 (1997) (entry into force March 6, 2002).

[28]WIPO Performances and Phonograms Treaty, Apr. 12, 1997, S. Treaty Doc. No. 105-17 36 ILM 76 (1997) (entry into force May 20, 2002).

is circumvented to carry out an act that is not authorised by the holder of a copyright or related right. Article 11 of the WCT requires contracting parties to provide legal protection and remedies against the circumvention of technological measures that are used by authors in connection with the exercise of their rights granted under the WCT or the Berne Convention. Article 18 of the WPPT requires contracting parties to grant similar protection against the circumvention of technological measures that are used by performers or phonogram producers in connection with the exercise of their rights under the WPPT.[29] By linking the protection granted to TPM and DRM systems to the protection of copyright and related rights, Article 11 of the WCT and Article 18 of the WPPT effectively exclude content that is not protected under any one of these regimes from their scope.

Article 6 of the InfoSoc Directive[30] seeks to implement these provisions within EU law.[31] Article 6(1) requires Member States to grant adequate legal protection against the circumvention of technological measures. The term 'technological measures' is defined under Article 6(3) as, 'any technology, device or component that (...) is designed to prevent or restrict acts, in respect of works or other subject-matter, which are not authorised by the rightholder of any copyright or any right related to copyright as provided for by law or the *sui generis* right provided for in Chapter III of [the Database Directive[32]]'. It is observed that the definition of technological measures as any technology, device or component that is designed to prevent or restrict acts in respect of works or other subject-matter, makes it broad enough to encompass both TPM and DRM systems.[33] Henceforth, the term DRM

[29]Renda, et al. observe that Article 11 of the WCT makes it clear that circumvention torts should be linked to an objective violation of copyright or related rights. As Article 18 of the WPPT is drafted in the same terms as Article 11 of the WCT it is possible to argue that both these provisions envision the legal protection against the circumvention of TPM and DRM systems to be limited to instances where the TPM or DRM system is circumvented for the purposes of an act that infringes upon an author's copyright or a rightholder's related right. Andrea Renda and others, *The Implementation, Application and Effects of the EU Directive on Copyright in the Information Society* (Centre for European Policy Studies 2015) 33.

[30]Directive 2001/29/EC of the European Parliament and of the Council of 22 May 2001 on the harmonisation of certain aspects of copyright and related rights in the information society [2001] OJ L167/10 (InfoSoc Directive).

[31]ibid recital 15. A distinction must be made between the protection of DRM (including TPM) under Article 6 and the protection granted to rights management information under Article 7, which is defined as information provided by rightholders which identifies the work or subject-matter protected under the InfoSoc Directive or the *sui generis* right provided by the Database Directive. Thus, Article 7 only refers to the protection of information as opposed to technological measures that are designed to prevent or restrict acts in relation to protected subject-matter.

[32]Directive 96/9/EC of the European Parliament and of the Council of the European Union of 11 March 1996 on the legal protection of databases [1996] OJ L 77/20 (Database Directive).

[33]The definition captures TPM that are designed to impede unauthorised reproduction of content, as well as aspects of DRM systems that restrict the ways in which content can be used, for example, by limiting the use of content to authorised users who have paid for that use. In fact, there is an implicit acceptance among legal scholars that the term 'technological measures' encompass both TPM and DRM systems. For example, *see* Séverine Dusollier, 'Tipping the Scale in Favour of the Right

system is used here to refer to technological measures in general, including TPM systems.

For this discussion, the critical question is whether the protection provided against the circumvention of DRM systems under Article 6(1) is contingent upon the existence of copyright, a related right or the *sui generis* database right over the subject-matter in respect of which the DRM system is applied.

The 1997 European Commission proposal for the InfoSoc Directive[34] linked the legal protection granted against acts of circumvention to the protection of copyright, related rights and the *sui generis* database right granted under the Database Directive. The proposed Article 6(1) was framed as follows:

> Member States shall provide adequate legal protection against any activities, including the manufacture or distribution of devices or the performances of services, which have only the limited commercially significant purpose or use other than circumvention, and which the person concerned carries out in the knowledge, or with reasonable grounds to know, that they will enable or facilitate without authority the circumvention of any effective *technological measures designed to* protect any *copyright or any rights related to copyright as provided by law or the sui generis right* provided for in [the Database Directive].[35]

Recital 30 to the 1997 proposal noted that, such legal protection should be provided to technological measures that effectively inhibit and/or prevent the infringement of any copyright, related right or sui generis rights provided by law.[36]

Furthermore, the explanatory memorandum to Article 6 of the 1997 proposal presented by the EU Commission[37] emphasised that Article 6:

> prohibits activities aimed at an infringement of copyright, a related right or a sui generis right in databases granted by Community and national law: *this would imply that not any circumvention of technical means of protection should be covered, but only those which constitute an infringement of a right, i.e., which are not authorized by law or by the author.*[38]

Thus, the 1997 proposal clearly intended that legal protection against the circumvention of DRM systems was to be made contingent upon the existence of copyright, a related right or a *sui generis* database right over the subject-matter in respect of which the technological measures were applied. It logically follows that, as envisioned under the 1997 proposal, if the subject-matter protected by the DRM

Holder: The European Anti-Circumvention Provisions' in Eberhard Becker and others (eds), *Digital Rights Management: Technological, Economic, Legal and Political Aspects* (Springer Berlin 2003) 462 and Giuseppe Mazziotti, *EU Digital Copyright Law and the End-User* (Springer Berlin 2008) 179.

[34]Proposal for a European Parliament and Council Directive on the harmonisation of certain aspects of copyright and related rights in the Information Society [1998] OJ C108/03.

[35]Proposal for InfoSoc Directive Article 6 (emphasis added).

[36]Recital 30 of proposal for InfoSoc Directive.

[37]Proposal for a European Parliament and Council Directive on the Harmonization of Certain Aspects of Copyright and Related Rights in the Information Society, 10 December 1997, COM (1997) 628 Final (Presented by the Commission).

[38]Article 6(3) of the explanatory memorandum of the proposal for InfoSoc Directive (emphasis added).

system did not enjoy protection under any one of these exclusive rights it would fail to obtain legal protection against circumvention.

The wording of Article 6(1) as framed by the 1997 proposal was carried over to the amended proposal of 1999.[39] However, Article 6(1) as was finally adopted by the InfoSoc Directive of 2001, differs from the wording of the 1997 and 1999 proposals by omitting to establish an explicit link between the protection granted against the circumvention of DRM and the protection of copyright, related rights or the *sui generis* database right.

Article 6(1) of the 2001 Directive merely states that, "Member States shall provide adequate legal protection against the circumvention of any effective technological measures, which the person concerned carries out in the knowledge (…), that he or she is pursuing that objective." The exact reason why the explicit link established by the 1997 and 1999 proposals between the protection of exclusive rights and the protection against circumvention of technological measures was dismantled by the 2001 Directive is not clear.

However, an implicit link between the legal protection against circumvention granted by the InfoSoc Directive and the protection of copyright, related rights and the *sui generis* database right is drawn in Article 6(3). Article 6(3) states that, for the purposes of the Directive the expression 'technological measures' refers to any technological device or component that is designed to prevent or restrict acts which are not authorised by the rightholder of any copyright or right related to copyright or *sui generis* database right.[40] Under the definition provided in Article 6 (3), the protection granted under Article 6(1) is limited to DRM systems applied in respect of subject-matter protected by copyright, related rights or the *sui generis* database right. Thus, protection under one of these exclusive rights becomes a pre-condition for the application of protection granted under Article 6(1).

Furthermore, the protection granted under Article 6(1) is limited acts of circumvention that are carried out with the knowledge of engaging in an 'act' that has not been authorised by the holder of the exclusive rights. It follows that such unauthorised 'acts' should be interpreted as acts[41] that fall within the scope of that

[39]Amended proposal for a European Parliament and Council Directive on the harmonisation of certain aspects of copyright and related rights in the information society [1999] OJ C180/6, Article 6 (1).

[40]*See* definition of TPM in Article 6(3) of the InfoSoc Directive:

> the expression 'technological protection measures' means any technology, device or component that, in the normal course of its operation, is designed to prevent or restrict acts, in respect of works or other subject-matter, which are not authorized by the rightholder of any copyright or any rights related to copyright as provided by law or the sui generis right provided for in Chapter III of Directive 96/9/EC.

[41]Hoeren notes that the term 'acts' (in the context of 'unauthorised acts') used in Article 6(3) of the InfoSoc Directive, relates to traditional exploitation rights such as the act of reproduction. Thomas Hoeren, 'Copyright Dilemma: Access Right as a Postmodern Symbol of Copyright Deconstruction?' in Eberhard Becker and others (eds), *Digital Rights Management: Technological, Economic, Legal and Political Aspects* (Springer 2003) 576.

rightholder's exclusive rights. Otherwise, there would be no need to obtain the rightholder's authorisation in their commission.[42]

Thus, considering the definition of a technological measure in Article 6(3), the legislative history of Article 6 and the fact that its purpose is to implement Article 11 of the WCT and Article 18 of the WPPT, it is possible to argue that the scope of legal protection granted under Article 6 of the InfoSoc Directive against the circumvention of DRM systems is limited to subject-matter that is protected under copyright, related rights or the sui generis database right.

The decision delivered by the Court of Justice of the European Union (CJEU) in the *Nintendo v PC Box*[43] case supports this interpretation of Article 6. The issue before the CJEU was whether the technological protection measures employed by *Nintendo* on their videogame consoles exceeded that which was envisaged under Article 6, and was therefore beyond the scope of protection provided against circumvention under the InfoSoc Directive. The CJEU held that legal protection against circumvention:

> is granted *only* with regard to technological measures which *pursue the objective of preventing or eliminating, as regards works, acts not authorised by the rightholder* (...). Those measures must be suitable for achieving that objective and *must not go beyond what is necessary for this purpose.*[44]

Thus, the CJEU stressed that the legal protection granted under Article 6 should not go beyond the purpose of preventing or eliminating the commission of acts that

[42]This would mean for example that, if the right to access a work or subject-matter does not come within the scope of the exclusive rights held by the owner of the exclusive rights indicated in Article 6(3), then Article 6 (1) could not be invoked to protect DRM systems against acts of circumvention that are carried out for the mere purpose of obtaining access to that content. *See contra* Ottolia who takes the position that Article 6(1) of the InfoSoc Directive does not distinguish between rights-control or access-control measures, but mandates protection for both measures. Andrea Ottolia, 'Preserving User's Rights in DRM: Dealing with "Judicial Particularism" in the Information Society' (2004) 35 International Review of Intellectual Property and Competition Law 491, 505. Furthermore, Ginsburg argues that an access right (defined as an exclusive right to control the manner in which members of the public apprehend a work) is an integral part of copyright law. Jane C Ginsburg, 'Essay: From Having Copies to Experiencing Works: The Development of an Access Right in U.S. Copyright Law' (2003) 50 Journal of the Copyright Society of the U.S.A. 113, 116.

However, where access is sought to carry out an act that infringes upon any exclusive right belonging to the rightholder, then it would be possible to invoke the protection of Article 6. This is borne out by Article 6(3) which states that, "Technological Measures shall be deemed 'effective' where the use of a protected work or other subject-matter is controlled by rightholders through application of an access control or protection process, (...), which achieves the protection objective." This is also reflected in Heide's opinion that a copyright owner has the right against the gaining of unauthorised access where such access is undertaken to engage in the uses reserved to the author. Thomas Heide, 'Copyright in the EU and US: What "Access-Right"?' (2001) 48 Journal of the Copyright Society of the USA 363, 367.

[43]Judgment of 23 January 2014, *Nintendo and Others,* C-355/12, EU:C:2014:25.

[44]ibid para 31. The CJEU noted that as is apparent from Articles 2 to 4 of the InfoSoc Directive these acts constitute the reproduction, the communication to the public of works and making them available to the public, and the distribution of the original or copies of works. ibid paras 24–25.

are not authorised by a rightsholder.[45] Accordingly, where a subject-matter is not protected under an exclusive copyright, related right or *sui generis* database right, the protection of a DRM system against circumvention would go beyond the purpose of Article 6. Therefore, it is possible to argue that, if a digitised version does not obtain protection under a copyright, a related right or the *sui generis* database right, the producer of the digitised version would not be able to benefit from the legal protection against the circumvention of DRM systems that is granted under Article 6 of the InfoSoc Directive.

It is also noted that open access or copyleft licenses (including *Creative Commons* licenses) rely upon the exclusionary rights granted under the traditional copyright law framework for their legal validity. Although copyleft licenses attempt to subvert the exclusionary nature of traditional exclusive copyright by enabling rightholders to share the utilities of their creations with the public at large, they are dependent upon the existence of an exclusive property right held by the licensor to ensure to the enforceability of the copyleft clause. Thus, in the absence of an exclusive property right over the digitised version it would be meaningless to make it available on open access terms or under a *Creative Commons* license, as there would be no legal compulsion for users to respect or to abide by the terms imposed by these licenses.

4.6 Price Discrimination as an Alternative Model

At this point, it is important to consider the price discrimination model as an alternative to the introduction of an exclusive right over digitised versions of rare documents. The price discrimination model is employed by many memory institutions across Europe in making available to the public, digitised versions of textual, visual and audio-visual content. Under this model, usually, two editions of a digitised version—a high-resolution and low-resolution edition—are made available to the public. The lower-resolution edition is typically made available free-of-charge and under an open public license such as a *Creative Commons* (CC) license. Therefore, it is subject to relatively less restrictions and controls than the higher-resolution edition which would be placed behind a pay-wall. The lower-resolution edition would be suitable for non-commercial uses such as teaching, although its quality may not be sufficient for commercial use.

The underlying concept is that those who wish to use the digitised version for non-commercial purposes will be able to make use of the lower-resolution edition free-of-charge and relatively free of restrictions (although limitations may apply as to reproduction and dissemination). The investment made in the production of the digitised version is sought to be recouped through the sale and licensing of the higher-resolution edition. Contractual provisions and DRM systems are used to

[45]Renda, et al. (n 29).

impose and to enforce the restrictions placed on the use and access of the high-resolution edition.

For the price discrimination model to be a feasible means of recouping the investment made in digitisation, it is necessary that an adequate market demand exists for the use and re-use of the higher-resolution edition as would enable the producer to recoup his investment solely through the commercialisation of these editions. This is usually true in the case of content with a high visual appeal such as paintings, photographs, and film footage for which a high market demand for commercial re-use exists, particularly in the entertainment and publishing industries.

However, views expressed during the empirical survey indicate that a comparable market demand does not exist for higher-resolution editions of digitised versions of rare documents that record textual content. Representatives of memory institutions that followed a price discrimination model in the commercialisation of digitised versions were unanimous in their opinion that regarding textual content, the revenue generated from the licensing (or sale) of higher-resolution editions is negligible in relation to the costs of digitisation.[46] Compared with visual and audio-visual works, there is much less demand for high-quality images of textual works because the value of a textual work lies more in the content expressed in the text rather than in its visual appeal. Of course, there are exceptions, for example, Da Vinci's notebook (*Codex Arundel)* is primarily a textual work but contains many sketches and drawings, the fact that it contains Da Vinci's own handwriting also adds to its visual appeal. However, rare documents recording textual content that also hold visual appeal are not common. Thus, in the case of textual works, the price discrimination model does not hold much potential for success.

From the discussion in Sect. 4.5 above, the price discrimination model is also dependent on the maintenance of an exclusive property right over the higher-resolution edition for its proper functioning. Without the protection afforded by an exclusive right, it would not be possible for the producer to commercially exploit the higher-resolution edition to secure an adequate financial return that would enable him to make the lower-resolution version available to the public free-of-charge.

4.7 Absence of Exclusivity Could Lead to Market Failure

In economic terms, the market failure referred to here, stems from the public good characteristics of digitised versions in that they are inherently non-rival and potentially non-excludable.[47] As reiterated above, because of their character as public goods, digitised versions are particularly susceptible to piracy and free-riding. Thus,

[46]Although one participant (speaking on confidentiality) stated that, however negligible, during a time where "every penny counts" this revenue is also important.

[47]*See* Sect. 5.1 below for a comprehensive discussion on the public goods character of digitised versions.

the ability to exercise exclusivity and exclusive rights over a digitised version is required to restrict the use and access of a digitised version solely to authorised persons. In the absence of exclusivity, free riding by competitors and high levels of piracy would make it difficult for a producer to recoup the investment made in the digitisation process[48] and, consequently, private-sector for-profit entities would lose their incentives to invest in the digitisation process.

As noted in Sect. 4.3 above, private sector for-profit investment is necessary to sustain the digitisation of rare documents within the EU. Accordingly, it is argued here that, the failure to secure private sector for-profit investment for the digitisation process would lead to a perpetuation of the existing underproduction problem of digitised versions of rare documents. This is notwithstanding the potential demand for digitised versions in the end-user and re-user markets.

For the purposes of digitisation, rare documents recording textual content in the public domain can be categorised according to,

- the social value that would result from making the rare document available to the public in digital form (i.e., value for culture, education, and scientific research).
- the (projected) market demand for the rare document in digital form.

Figure 4.2 categorises the digitised versions of different types of rare documents according to their social value and market demand, and analyses the type of external funding model(s) that the digitisation of these rare documents is likely to attract. It is noted that our primary concern is to ensure that, rare documents with a high social value are made available to the public in digital form, regardless of the market demand that exists for them.

(High, High) E.g., *The Magna Carta, The Gutenberg Bible* called *'the treasures'* because their availability as digitised versions has a high social value coupled with a high market demand. Governments and private sector not-for -profit partners are likely to be keen to invest in the digitisation of these documents because of their value to cultural heritage and their national and historical importance. Private sector for-profit entities also have an incentive to fund the digitisation of these documents by virtue of the positive publicity and advertising[49] value that would ensue, which may adequately compensate the investment, even if they are not able to exploit the digitised versions for commercial profit.

(Low, High) *E.g., Lists of persons executed at a certain point in time, accounts of ordinary crimes, murders, scandals, and gossip in popular newspapers.* Digitised versions of such content will have high market demand, but relatively low social value in terms of significance for culture, education, or scientific research. Private

[48]For a more comprehensive discussion on this point, *see* Sect. 5.3.

[49]Advertising value that results from being associated with the digitisation of the *'treasure'*.

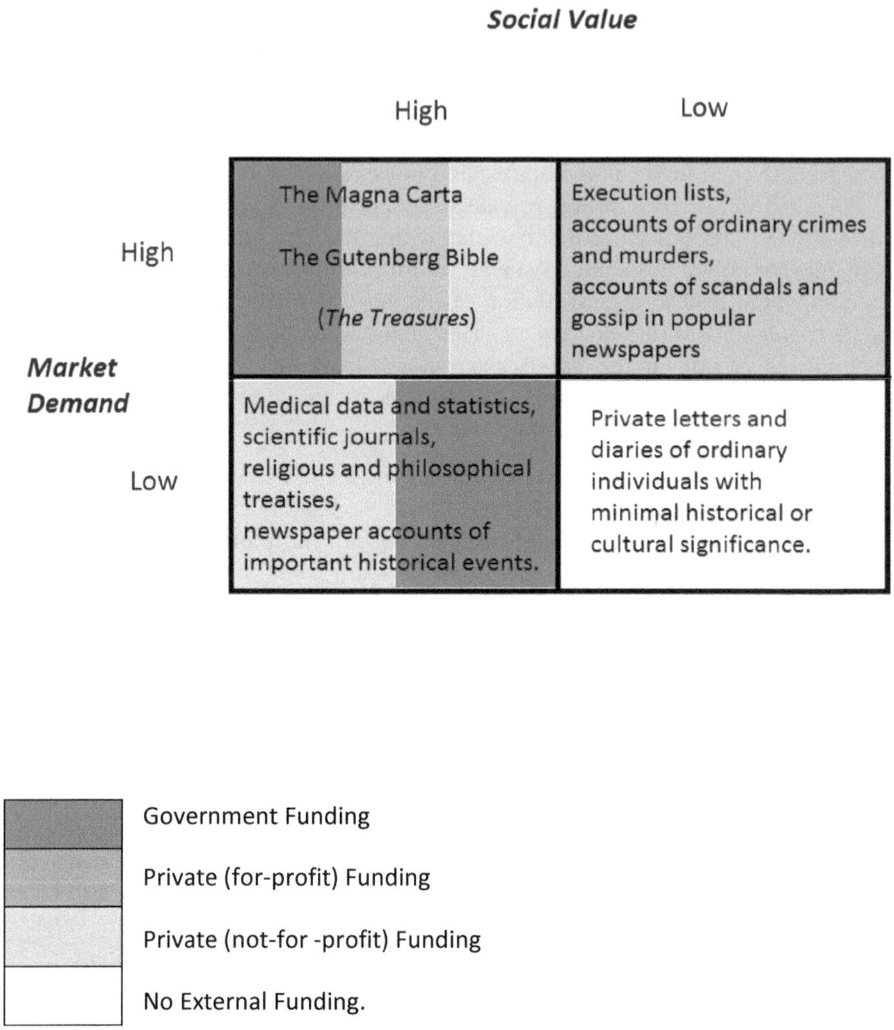

Fig. 4.2 Classification of rare documents

sector for-profit entities will be keen to invest in the digitisation of these documents because of the high market demand for the resulting digitised versions and their potential for commercial exploitation.

(High, Low) *E.g., Medical data and statistics, scientific journals, religious and philosophical treatises and newspaper accounts of historical events.*

The public availability of these documents in digital form can generate social value through the potential held by them for fuelling research and learning. But the market demand for digitised versions of these documents is relatively low as they largely cater to a niche market of scientific researchers and scholars. However, unlike *'the treasures'*, they do not hold palpable cultural or historical significance and as such do not obtain priority under government and non-profit funding. Thus, the underproduction problem of digitised versions of rare documents is particularly acute in relation to documents falling within this category. Accordingly, private sector for-profit investment would prove especially valuable in the digitisation of these documents. However, incentivising greater private sector for-profit investment in the digitisation of these documents would require providing private sector for-profit entities a strong assurance of their ability to commercially exploit the digitised versions in the niche markets to obtain a reasonable return on their investment.

(Low, Low) *E.g., Private diaries of individuals with minimal cultural or historical significance.* There is very little social value in making these available to the public in digital form coupled with very low market demand for their access and use. This study does not concern itself with this category of rare documents, in view of the minimal social or economic value that can be derived from making these available to the public in digital form.

From the foregoing discussion, the following conclusions are made.

1. Rare documents that have high social value and high market demand *(High, High: 'the treasures')* find it relatively easy to attract funding for digitisation. Governments and private sector not-for-profit partners give priority to the digitisation of these documents in allocating their funds. Similarly, the positive publicity and advertising value they could receive from funding the digitisation of *'the treasures'* provide adequate incentives for private sector for-profit entities to invest in the digitisation of these documents, even if they are not able to engage in the commercial exploitation of the digitised versions.
2. In comparison, rare documents with high social value but low market demand *(High, Low)* such as scientific journals and religious treatises, are at a higher risk of not being able to secure adequate funding for digitisation from government and non-profit sources. The failure to obtain sufficient funding for the digitisation of these documents would result in the perpetuation of the existing underproduction problem of digitised versions of these documents within the EU.[50]

[50] *See* discussion in Sect. 4.2 on whether there is a need for mass-digitisation of rare documents within the EU.

3. Therefore, funding from private sector for-profit entities would be particularly useful in achieving greater public availability of these documents in digital form. Accordingly, there is at present a need to channel greater private sector for-profit funding for the digitisation of rare documents with a high social value but a low market demand *(High, Low)* to secure a quantitative increase for documents that are available in digital form.
4. Channelling greater private sector for-profit funding into the digitisation of these rare documents require strengthening the incentives of private sector for-profit entities to invest in the production of digitised versions of these rare documents. Considering the relatively low market demand for digitised versions, it becomes crucial to provide these entities with the ability to obtain a reasonable return on their investment through the commercial exploitation of the digitised versions in the niche markets.
5. To ensure a reasonable return on the investment made in the digitisation process, it is necessary that the private sector for-profit entity is provided with a means by which to control the access and use of the digitised versions by members of the public to minimise the risks of piracy and free-riding by competitors. Thus, as discussed in Sect. 1.3 it is necessary to enable the exercise of exclusivity over digitised versions to enhance the availability of these rare documents in digital form.

In conclusion, strengthening the incentives of private sector for-profit entities to invest in the digitisation of rare documents with high social value but low market demand requires enabling the exercise of exclusivity over the digitised versions of these documents. In the absence of an ability to exercise exclusivity, private sector for-profit funding will not be channelled towards the digitisation of these rare documents and the existing problem of underproduction will continue (and possibly exacerbate in the long-term). This would result in a market failure in the end-user and re-user markets and deprive potential users from accessing and using the public domain content recorded upon these documents in socially valuable ways. Consequently, society as a whole would be deprived of the social benefits that would accrue from the availability of the public domain content recorded upon these rare documents in digital form.

From the foregoing discussion, the following proposals are made.

(a) Memory institutions should categorise the rare documents in their custody according to the degree of social value that could be generated by making them available to the public in digital form.
(b) Government and private sector not-for-profit funding should be given preference over private sector for-profit funding in the digitisation of rare documents that have high social value, regardless of the potential market demand. Digitised versions produced through not-for-profit funding models should be made available to the public on open access terms that impose minimal restrictions on their access, use and re-use.

(c) Where government and other not-for-profit funding is not available or is inadequate for the digitisation of rare documents that have high social value, private sector for-profit funding should be harnessed to achieve their digitisation.

Thus, if intelligently and strategically used, private sector for-profit funding could supplement existing not-for-profit sources of funding, in bringing about a quantitative increase in the amount of rare documents with a high social value that are available to the public in digital form. It would thereby accelerate the digitisation process of these documents and enable members of the public to access the public domain content recorded upon them at an earlier point in time than what would have been possible under a digitisation process that was solely dependent on government and other non-profit sources of funding.

4.8 The Nature and Scope of the Exclusivity That Is Required

If exclusivity is in fact needed, then what should be the nature and scope of the exclusive right that should be granted over a digitised version? As noted at the outset, the goal of this study is to find a means of balancing the conflicting interests of producers and users of digitised versions of rare documents with the objective of maximising the social value that would accrue from the availability of rare documents in digital form.

As observed in Sect. 4.7 above, the inability to exercise exclusive rights over digitised versions would act as a disincentive for private sector for-profit investors to invest in the production of digitised versions and would result in social losses resulting from the underproduction of digitised versions.

The exercise of exclusive rights over digitised versions could also give rise to social losses. These social losses arise from the exclusive rights impeding the public's ability to access, use, and re-use the digitised versions to an optimal level in social and cultural discourse. They can be categorised as follows; firstly, social losses that result from the public being prevented from accessing and using digitised versions to an optimal level and secondly, social losses that result from the exercise of exclusive rights impeding (or acting as a disincentive to) the use of digitised versions in the creation of new works.

It is proposed that, to maximise the social value that would accrue from rare documents being made available to the public in digital form, the exclusive right over digitised versions should be designed in a way that minimises social losses arising from the underproduction of digitised versions and the social losses arising from the exercise of exclusive rights over digitised versions.

A cost-benefit analysis based on empirical evidence is beyond the scope of this study. On the one hand, it is difficult to accurately project the costs and benefits resulting from the recognition of an exclusive right over digitised versions, until such exclusive right and the corresponding legal framework is in application. On the other hand, it is uncertain whether a cost-benefit analysis that is based on empirical evidence would allow us to draw precise conclusions as to what the exact scope and parameters of the exclusive right should be. As noted in Sect. 2.3.1[51] above, the heterogeneity of rare documents means that the social value and market demand of individual documents can widely differ. Therefore, it would be difficult to draw a representative sample of digitised versions so as to engage in a statistical analysis that leads to conclusions which could be generalised in relation to all digitised versions. Thus, an effort is made to identify the general factors that are involved, in order to discern the broader issues relating to the effects of exclusivity.

Nevertheless, it is argued here that, the minimisation of social losses could be achieved by calibrating the scope and strength of the exclusive right so that it allows private sector for-profit entities that invest in the digitisation process to obtain a 'reasonable return' on their investment while at the same time, granting to users the maximum possible freedom to access, use and re-use the digitised version in socially valuable ways. The term 'reasonable return' refers to a return on the investment that would be able to provide and to sustain adequate incentives for private sector for-profit entities to invest in the digitisation process. Thus, the strength and scope of the exclusive right should not over-compensate the private sector investor by allowing him to obtain a return on the investment that would exceed what is necessary to grant him an incentive to invest in the digitisation process.

Limiting the duration of the exclusive right to a fixed time-period would serve to achieve the twin objectives of enabling investors to obtain a reasonable return on their investment during the period of protection while ensuring that after the expiration of the period of protection, the digitised version would fall into the public domain and be available for free and unrestricted use by the public. Nonetheless, it is proposed that the introduction of mandatory exceptions and limitations to the exclusive right to authorise uses that generate significant social value but do not cause substantial prejudice to the investor's ability to obtain a reasonable return on his investment, would serve to minimise the social costs that would result from the exercise of exclusive rights.

In conclusion, an effective calibration of the exclusive right over digitised version, could serve to ensure that the short-term social losses that accrue to society through the exercise of exclusive rights during the term of protection, would be off-set by the long-term social value that accrues to society from the enhanced availability of public domain content recorded upon rare documents in digital form.

---

[51] *See* Chap. 2 (n 6) above, discussing why the data collected during the empirical survey will not be used for drawing statistical generalisations.

4.9 Who Should Be the Owner of the Exclusive Right?

The creation of a digitised version is a process that could involve a variety of stakeholders. Thus, if an exclusive right is granted to the 'producer' of the digitised version, it needs to be determined who is to be considered as the 'producer' of the digitised version for the purpose of exercising these exclusive rights. Should a digitised version be treated similar to a work of joint authorship[52] that is created through the co-operative efforts of a multiplicity of persons; thereby granting rights of ownership over the exclusive rights to all persons in common,[53] or should the ownership of exclusive rights be granted to a single stakeholder?

The creation of a digitised version could involve all or several of the following stakeholders. The primary stakeholder in this exercise is without doubt the person or entity who has possession of the original rare document. Next, there could be investors, technology providers (including software providers) and human resource providers, persons who manage the digitisation process (i.e., in charge of designing and supervising the work-flow), persons who scan the rare document and convert it into digital format, perform quality control of the digital image, etc. and finally persons who distribute and market the final digitised version.

Unlike traditional works of joint authorship that are protected by copyright law (for example, movies and musical works), the creation of a digitised version involves very little creative or original input from any of these stakeholders.[54] Their input is more a contribution of resources and expertise in the creation of a copy of an existing analogue document in a different (digital) medium. Therefore, none of these persons can make a moral or ethical claim to the ownership of exclusive rights over the digitised version. Hence, it is possible to determine the ownership of the exclusive right based on the objective of achieving a balance between user and producer interests.

---

[52]In the UK under s. 10(1) of the Copyright, Designs and Patents Act (CDPA) 1988, a work produced by the collaboration of two or more authors in which the contribution of each author is not distinct from that of the other(s) is known as a work of joint authorship. In France, such a work is referred to as an *oeuvre de collaboration* under Art. L113-2 of the Code de la propriété intellectuelle (Intellectual Property Code of France). In Germany, the same concept in captured by the term 'Miturheber' (joint author) in s. 8 of the Urheberrechtsgesetz 1965 BGBl. I S. 1273 (German Copyright Act).

[53]For example, as established in the case of *Powell v Head* [1879] 12 Ch D 686, within the copyright law system of the UK, co-authors of a work of joint authorship own the copyright over their work as tenants in common. Accordingly, all co-authors have equal shares in the copyright (unless otherwise agreed). In France, the common work forms a whole, over which each co-author has an indivisible right, a right that bears upon the work and is indivisible in this respect Frédéric Pollaud-Dulian, *Le Droit D'Auteur* (2nd Ed, Economica 2014) 350. In Germany under s. 8(2) of the German Copyright Act, the right of publication and of exploitation of the work accrues jointly to the joint authors.

[54]*See* Chap. 7 for a discussion as to why a digitised version of a rare document would probably not qualify as an original work under copyright law within the EU law framework.

Accordingly, it is proposed that, the person or entity that has ownership of the original rare document should be considered the owner of the exclusive right over the digitised version, notwithstanding other entities who may have contributed towards its production and dissemination. As observed above, within the EU, the bulk of rare documents recording public domain content are in the custody of public or semi-public sector memory institutions. Thus, granting ownership of the exclusive right to the person or entity that has ownership of the original document would mean that, in most instances, the ownership of the exclusive right over digitised versions of rare documents would be vested in public and semi-public sector entities. This would result in the following advantages.

4.9.1 Preservation of the Interests of the Public

A notable observation made during the survey was the genuine commitment demonstrated by public and semi-public sector memory institutions towards their public mission in the promotion of culture and education and contribution to overall public welfare. Fulfilling this mission is a primary objective of these institutions and they are guided by it in the creation and execution of their policies. Many institutions operate upon a not-for-profit basis, usually seeking to merely cover their costs. A considerable number of memory institutions have already adopted mechanisms such as price-discrimination schemes and open-access licensing in the distribution of digitised versions to enhance their public accessibility and to facilitate their use by members of the public.

Thus, it is expected that granting ownership of the exclusive right to public and semi-public sector memory institutions would lead to it being exercised and enforced in accordance with the public mission of these institutions and in a manner that would seek to optimise public welfare. Additionally, it would also result in the exercise of the exclusive right being made susceptible to public policy and administrative guidelines, thereby making it subject to a greater degree of institutional regulation and supervision. Such institutional regulation and supervision would assist in ensuring that the exclusive right over digitised versions is exercised in a manner that gives primacy to the interests of the public.

4.9.2 Single Ownership to Prevent Fragmentation of Rights

Granting ownership of the exclusive right to the entity that has ownership of the rare document would also prevent the exclusive right from being fragmented between multiple co-owners.

One of the main problems associated with works of joint authorship is the fragmentation of ownership among a multiplicity of co-owners (or ‘co-authors’). In many jurisdictions, including the UK, Germany, and France, the exploitation of a work of joint authorship, either by an individual co-owner or by a third party, must have the unanimous consent of all co-owners.[55] This could give rise to two problems. Firstly, by requiring a potential licensee to obtain the consent and authorisation of every co-owner, it could result in a substantial increase of the transaction costs associated with the licensing procedure. These transaction costs would *inter alia* include the search costs of correctly identifying all co-owners, communicating with them and negotiating the terms of license. Furthermore, it would be possible for a single co-owner to impede the re-use of the digitised version by refusing to grant his consent to a license even when all other co-owners have given their consent.[56] When the rights-clearance procedure involves high transaction costs, potential users would be discouraged from obtaining licenses over the work. This could result in the sub-optimal use and re-use of the digitised version, and thus negate the very objective of introducing an exclusive right, which is to improve the accessibility and availability of rare documents for use, re-use, and exploitation by the public.

Granting ownership over the exclusive right to a single entity would provide potential users with an identifiable person or entity to approach to obtain a license, thereby lowering the transaction costs associated with the licensing process by obviating the need to negotiate with multiple persons and entities.[57] The licensing market for the commercial re-use of digitised versions has considerable financial potential. Hence, it is in the interests of the Member States to ensure that this market is kept free of obstructions and that transaction costs are kept at a reasonable level. Accordingly, maintaining clarity concerning the entity that owns the exclusive right over a digitised version and preventing the fragmentation of the exclusive right is an important consideration.

It is necessary to consider how vesting the ownership of the exclusive right over a digitised version in the entity that has ownership of the rare document would affect the incentives of private sector for-profit entities to invest in the digitisation process. Although private sector investors would naturally prefer to obtain ownership of

---

[55]For example, in the UK the cases of *Powell* (n 53), *Cescinsky v George Routledge and Sons* [1916]2KB 325 and *Robin Ray v Classic FM* [1988] FSR 622. In France, "*Morris et autres v Goscinny*" Cass 1er civ, 27 nov 2001. In Germany, s. 8(2) of the German Copyright Act.

[56]It is noted that certain legal frameworks include rules that prevent a co-owner of a work of joint-authorship from refusing consent to a license, other than in good-faith or for justifiable cause. For example, s. 8(2) of the German Copyright Act states that a joint author may not refuse his consent to publication, exploitation, or alteration contrary to the principles of good faith. In France, Art. L113-3 of the Intellectual Property Code provides that in the event of a failure on the part of co-owners to reach a common accord as to the exercise of their rights over the common work, the courts are able to intervene. Nevertheless, it is noted that challenging the decision of a single co-owner to deny his consent to a license over the digitised version in court, would not serve as a practical solution to most licensees, as this would in itself involve substantial costs.

[57]Gordon categorises transaction costs as a type of market-barrier. She argues that as long as the cost of reaching and enforcing bargains is lower than anticipated benefits from the bargains, markets will form. However, if transaction costs exceed anticipated benefits, no transactions will occur. Wendy J Gordon, 'Fair Use as Market Failure: A Structural and Economic Analysis of the Betamax Case and Its Predecessors' (1982) 82 Columbia Law Review 1600, 1628.

the exclusive right in a digitised version produced by them, it is unlikely that vesting ownership of the exclusive right with the entity that has possession of the analogue document would serve as a disincentive to invest in the digitisation process.

The Licensed Internet Associates (LIA) programme launched by the The National Archives of the UK (TNA-UK),[58] grants a 10-year (renewable) non-exclusive license to producers of digitised versions of documents in its collection. However, TNA-UK retains ownership of the intellectual property rights in the digitised versions. This enables the TNA-UK to grant further non-exclusive licenses for the commercial exploitation of the digitised versions to other entities, thereby enabling the digitised versions to be distributed and exploited through a multiplicity of sources and through a variety of business models.

The success of the LIA programme and the large number of documents that have been digitised under it, indicates that the retention of exclusive property rights over digitised versions by a memory institution does not necessarily discourage private sector entities from investing in the digitisation process, as long as they are able to obtain a license for the commercial exploitation of the digitised version and to obtain an adequate return on their investment. It appears that, if the potential for commercial exploitation of a digitised version is sufficiently high, even the prospect of obtaining a mere non-exclusive license, would not discourage private sector entities from investing in the production of the digitised version.

Private sector investors would be able to negotiate the terms of the initial license for digitisation with the memory institution that holds the rare document and to obtain certain privileges regarding the commercial exploitation of the resulting digitised version, as would allow them a competitive advantage over subsequent licensees in the market for end-use and re-use.[59]

When the market demand for the commercial exploitation of a digitised version is sufficiently high, memory institutions would be able to negotiate terms and conditions of use and access that are more favourable to users. Allowing public and semi-public sector memory institutions to be the arbiters of the terms and conditions that are imposed upon the use and access of a digitised version, would serve to ensure that those terms and conditions are necessary and proportionate for allowing a private-sector partner to secure a reasonable return on his investment.

---

[58] *See* Sect. 3.1, Example 3 for an outline of the *LIA* programme of The National Archives (UK).

[59] For example, under the *LIA* programme the producer of the digitised version (who is also the first licensee) is allowed to link his database of digitised versions to the TNA-UK webpage, which gives him a competitive advantage over subsequent licensees in terms of attracting users to his database. ibid.

4.10 Summary and Conclusions

It is necessary to grant exclusive rights over digitised versions of rare documents in order to create incentives for private-sector investment in the digitisation process, and to preserve the long-term sustainability of the digitisation process. Granting a right of acknowledgement over digitised versions to memory institutions may also assist in maintaining the relevance of memory institutions as centres of scholarship in the digital age. However, the latter is merely a hypothesis and testing this hypothesis is not within the scope of this study.

The nature and scope of the exclusive right must be determined with reference to the overall objective of the study which is the maintenance of an adequate balance between user and producer interests. Vesting ownership of the exclusive right in the person or entity that has ownership of the original rare document would mean that in a majority of instances public and semi-public sector memory institutions would obtain ownership of the exclusive right over digitised versions within the EU.[60] This has the advantage of allowing the exercise and enforcement of the exclusive right to be brought within the framework of the public mission of these institutions. It also makes it more probably that the exclusive right would be exercised and enforced in a manner that optimises public welfare. Furthermore, it would prevent the exclusive right from being fragmented among a multiplicity of co-owners. It is also argued here that, granting the exclusive right to the entity that has ownership over the rare document would not serve as a disincentive to private sector investment in the digitisation of rare documents. In fact, it would enable public and semi-public memory institutions to exercise control over the terms and conditions imposed upon the use and access of digitised versions by members of the public, and to ensure that they are necessary and proportionate for enabling the investor to recoup a reasonable return on his investment.

[60]In instances where the ownership of a rare document or a collection of rare documents is held by a private person or private-sector entity, such private persons or entities would own the exclusive right over the digital version.

Chapter 5
A Conceptual Basis for Justifying the Grant of an Exclusive Right

Is it possible to identify a conceptual basis that would support the granting of an exclusive right over digitised versions within the EU legal framework? This chapter proceeds to argue that the utilitarian doctrine of intellectual property law (and the incentive theory in particular), provides a conceptual basis that can justify the granting of exclusive rights over digitised versions. The discussion will focus upon the incentive theory as it has been developed in relation to copyright law. This is because copyright law provides the closest analogy for an exclusive right over a digitised version of a rare document, in the sense that both concern themselves with the protection of cultural content and informational goods. The discussion also explores the ability of the social planning theory of copyright law, to be a normative influence in the formulation of the proposed exclusive right.

5.1 The Objective of the Proposed Exclusive Right

To recapitulate the economic argument made in the preceding chapters, a digitised version is an informational good in digital form.[1] It has the characteristics of a public good[2] in that it is inherently non-rival and potentially non-excludable. A digitised version is non-rival in the sense that the marginal cost of creating and delivering a perfect reproduction of a digitised version to an extra consumer is close to zero.[3] It is

[1]Paul Belleflamme, 'The Economics of Digital Goods: A Progress Report' (2016) 13 Review of Economic Research on Copyright 1, 1.

[2]ibid. *see also* Jonathan Foster, 'Valorising the Cultural Content of the Commodity: On Immaterial Labour and New Forms of Informational Work' in Angela Lin, Jonathan Foster and Paul Scifleet (eds), *Consumer Information Systems and Relationship Management: Design, Implementation and Use*. (IGI Global 2013) 190.

[3]Thierry Rayna, 'Understanding the Challenges of the Digital Economy: The Nature of Digital Goods' (2008) 71 Communications & Strategies 13, 18–19.

S. Mendis, *A Copyright Gambit*, Munich Studies on Innovation and Competition 11,
https://doi.org/10.1007/978-3-662-59454-4_5

potentially non-excludable as the negligible costs of reproducing a digitised version and distributing it to the public means that each consumer of a digitised version can also be a potential supplier of unauthorised copies of the digitised version to the market.[4] Therefore, absent policy intervention, it would become very difficult for the producer of a digitised version to restrict the supply of the digitised version solely to authorised buyers or licensees. The non-rivalrous nature of a digitised version means that it is capable of being used and exploited by a multiplicity of users at the same time and highlights its ability to contribute to a participatory culture. However, as noted in the preceding chapters, its potential non-excludability places at risk the ability of the producer to recoup the costs incurred in the creation of the digitised version.

The proposed exclusive right over digitised versions of rare documents has the dual objectives of protecting the producer's investment in the digitisation process while seeking to ensure to users the enhanced accessibility and availability of public domain content recorded upon rare documents. The identification of a conceptual framework within which the exclusive right could be located and built upon would assist in the formulation of the exclusive right and the determination of its scope and parameters.

5.2 An Overview of the Principle Conceptual Foundations for Copyright

Within the EU, copyright law and its continental counterpart the author's rights and related rights systems have been explained and justified in relation to many theoretical doctrines. In the following discussion, some of the prevalent theories of copyright law, namely, the personality theory, the labour theory, the incentive theory, and the social planning theory, are discussed to examine their ability to justify the introduction of an exclusive right over digitised versions of rare documents. Although these theories are explored for the purposes of providing a comprehensive overview of the possible conceptual framework within which the proposed exclusive right could be located, the analysis proceeds upon the intuition that the incentive theory of copyright law provides the most suitable conceptual basis for justifying the grant of an exclusive right over digitised versions of rare documents.

The personhood theory[5] of copyright law is loosely derived from the writings of Kant[6] and Hegel.[7] Its basic premise is that an intellectual creation is so closely intertwined with its author's personal identity that its protection under copyright law

---

[4]Belleflamme (n 1).

[5]For a general discussion of the theory of personhood *see* Margaret Jane Radin, 'Property and Personhood' (1982) 34 Stanford Law Review 957.

[6]Immanuel Kant, *The Philosophy of Law* (W Hastie tr, Clarke 1887).

[7]GWF Hegel, *The Philosophy of Right* (SW Dyde tr, G Bell 1896).

can be justified as a means of protecting the personality of its author.[8] The theory of personhood has long figured prominently in the European copyright law discourse[9] and its influence is reflected in the strong moral rights enjoyed by authors over their intellectual works within continental copyright law systems.[10] However, the theory of personhood is unsuitable for providing a conceptual basis for the granting of exclusive rights over digitised versions for the reason that, a faithful and accurate reproduction of an existing rare document produced through a process of scanning cannot be considered to reflect its creator's personality or to be intimately intertwined with it. Furthermore, locating the exclusive right over digitised versions within the conceptual framework of the theory of personhood would require ownership of the exclusive right to be granted to the person who is directly responsible for its creation (i.e., to the person who operated the scanner or to the person who processed the scanned image) as opposed to the memory institution or the entity that invested in the digitisation process. For this reason, the personhood theory does not offer a suitable conceptual basis for the justification of an exclusive right over digitised versions.

The labour theory is derived from the writings of Locke[11] that deal with real property and tangible goods. It has been developed in the context of intellectual property rights and informational goods through the writings of contemporary authors such as Becker,[12] Gordon,[13] and Hughes.[14] Under Locke's labour theory, a person who labours upon resources that are either unowned or held in common[15] has a natural property right to the fruits of his efforts[16] if his appropriation satisfies

[8]William Fisher, 'Theories of Intellectual Property', in Stephen R Munzer (ed), *New Essays in the Legal and Political Theory of Property,* (Cambridge, 2001) 168, 171 and Justin Hughes, 'The Philosophy of Intellectual Property' (1988) 77 The Georgetown Law Journal 287, 330.

[9]Fisher (n 8) 9.

[10]Radin (n 5) 1014 note 3.

[11]*See* John Locke, 'Second Treatise of Government', *The Works of John Locke* (Rev ed, Thomas Tegg 1823) <http://socserv2.socsci.mcmaster.ca/econ/ugcm/3ll3/locke/government.pdf> accessed 31 January 2019.

[12]Lawrence C Becker, 'Deserving to Own Intellectual Property' (1993) 68 Chicago-Kent Law Review 609.

[13]Wendy J Gordon, 'A Property Right in Self-Expression: Equality and Individualism in the Natural Law of Intellectual Property' (1993) 102 Yale Law Journal 1533. Wendy J Gordon, 'On Owning Information: Intellectual Property and the Restitutionary Impulse' (1992) 78 Virginia Law Review 149.

[14]Hughes (n 8) 296–330.

[15]"When there is some land that has the status of a *common*—being held in common by the community by agreement among them—taking any part of what is common and removing it from the state nature leaves it in creates ownership (...)." Locke (n 11) chapter 5 s. 28. In the context of our discussion, the common property would be the rare documents and the public domain content recorded upon them.

[16]ibid chap 5 s 27.

the so-called 'no-harm' proviso (also known as the Lockean proviso)[17] which requires that his appropriation leaves enough and as good of the resources for others.[18] The labour theory offers an attractive conceptual justification for the granting of an exclusive right over a digitised version. The 'added-value' interpretation[19] of the labour theory, which holds that when a person's labour produces something that is of value to society, then that labour deserves to be rewarded with property rights, seems particularly suitable for justifying an exclusive property right over digitised versions.[20] Based on the added-value interpretation, it is possible to argue that the creator of a digitised version of a rare document transforms or develops it in a way that enhances its social value and therefore deserves to be rewarded with an exclusive property right. It is also possible to argue that this exclusive right would satisfy the conditions of the 'no-harm' proviso, as the exclusive property right over the digitised version would not diminish the ability of others to make use of the original rare document.[21] The object of the exclusive right would be the digitised version as opposed to the rare document held by the memory institution. Accordingly, the exclusive right over the digitised version would not make the public worse-off in terms of their ability to consult the rare document, to use the public domain content recorded upon it or to create their own digitised versions of that document. However, the main problem in locating the proposed exclusive right within the labour theory is that, the labour theory fails to offer a cogent basis for limiting the strength or scope of the exclusive right to achieve a balance between the competing interests of the producer and users of the digitised version.[22] The labour theory argues in favour of granting an absolute exclusive right to the person who has laboured in the creation of a digitised version. Thus, locating the exclusive right within the conceptual framework of the labour theory would make it difficult to justify the imposition of exceptions and limitations on that right in balancing user interests. Accordingly, it is concluded that the labour theory does not offer a suitable conceptual framework for the justification of an exclusive right that is limited to achieve an adequate balance between producer and user interests.

---

[17]Gordon (1993) (n 13) 1560–1561. Robert Nozick, *Anarchy, State and Utopia* (Basic Books 1974) 178–182.

[18]Fisher (n 8) 170.

[19]Hughes (n 8) 305–310.

[20]ibid. See also Nozick (n 17) 175, who interprets Locke's theory to mean that labouring on something improves it and makes it more valuable and the person who has laboured is entitled to own a thing, the value of which has been created by him.

[21]This in accordance with Gordon's interpretation of the 'no-harm' proviso to mean that, 'creators should have property in their original works, only provided that such grant of property does no harm to other persons' equal abilities to create or to draw upon the pre-existing cultural matrix and scientific heritage.' Gordon (1993) (n 13) 1563–1564.

[22]Gordon attempts to interpret the 'no-harm' proviso to mean that exclusive rights granted over the intellectual creations (such as a patents or copyrighted works) should be limited to allow the public to benefit from new creations and cultural tools. Although interesting, this interpretation does not offer a coherent conceptual basis for the achievement of a balance between user and producer interests in relation to digitised versions. ibid 1572–1605.

Under the utilitarian theory, copyright law is perceived as an instrument for the maximisation of social welfare.[23] Therefore, the institution of private property can only be justified if it is seen to assist in the maximisation of the total satisfaction obtained from resources.[24] Although the utilitarian justification as it is currently applied has been greatly influenced by US copyright law, Lambrecht points out that the utilitarian justification is not totally unknown within the continental European copyright law discourse. For instance, it gains support in the writings of the nineteenth century, French economists Jules Dupuit[25] (in relation to property rights in general), and Léon Walras[26] (in relation to intellectual property rights).[27]

Presently, it is possible to identify two main strands of utilitarian theory that provide a conceptual framework for copyright law, both of which adopt a market-oriented economic approach to welfare maximisation. The first of these is the incentive theory, in which copyright is conceptualised as a mechanism for providing incentives for the production of informational goods.[28] The second is what is termed by Netanel as the neo-classicist approach[29] that is associated with the Chicago School of Law and Economics.[30] The neo-classicist approach conceptualises copyright as a mechanism for market facilitation and for moving existing creative works to their highest socially valued uses.[31] As Lambrecht explains, while the incentive theory focuses upon the benefits of a property right from the point of view of a dynamic analysis on incentivising the creation of new works, the neoclassical approach focuses upon the benefits of a property right from the perspective of a

[23]Fisher (n 8) 169; Maxime Lambrecht, 'Droit d'auteur et Ouverture de l'environnement Numérique : Responsabilité Sociale Contre Législation ?' (Université catholique de Louvain 2015) 85. <https://dial.uclouvain.be/pr/boreal/fr/object/boreal%3A157582> accessed 31 January 2019.

[24]William Dibble, 'Justifying Intellectual Property' (1994) 59 UCL Jurisprudence Review 74, 81.

[25]Jules Dupuit, 'Du Principe de Propriété: Le Juste-l'utile' (1861) 30 Journal des Economistes 28, "Le principe de l'utilité publique donne seul la solution de tous les problèmes si nombreux de la question de la propriété de la richesses et de beaucoup d'autres questions économiques." [Only the principle of public utility offers the solution for all the numerous problems relating to property of wealth and many other economic question] translated by the author. ibid 52–53.

[26]Léon Walras, 'De La Propriété Intellectuelle' 24 *Journal des économistes* 392 (1859) *cited in* Jérôme Lallement, 'La Propriété Intellectuelle Selon Walras : Entre Monautopole et Majorat Littéraire' (2011) 1 Oeconomia 393. <https://journals.openedition.org/oeconomia/1527> accessed 31 January 2019.

[27]Lambrecht (n 23) 87.

[28]According to Netanel, the incentive approach seeks to explicate copyright's traditional incentive rationale in economic terms. Neil Weinstock Netanel, 'Copyright and a Democratic Civil Society' (1996) 106 Yale Law Journal 283.

[29]Netanel defines the neo-classicist approach as being based on a blend of neoclassical and new institutional economic property theory, and as corresponding to the 'property rights theory' in economic literature. ibid 306–307, 313.

[30]Maxime Lambrecht, 'The Time Limit on Copyright: An Unlikely Tragedy of the Intellectual Commons' (2017) 43 European Journal of Law and Economics 475, 478–479.

[31]Netanel (n 28) 309.

static analysis by seeking to ensure the optimal social exploitation of existing works.[32] Netanel observes that "[f]or neo-classicists, copyright enables owners to charge users for access to creative work public goods not so much to preserve author incentives as to determine what creative works are worth and thus to create a guide for resource allocation."[33]

Proponents of the neo-classicist approach, while acknowledging the validity and utility of the incentive theory, criticise it as a crude oversimplification of the function of intellectual property rights.[34] However, it is argued here that, in comparison with the neo-classicist approach, the incentive theory holds particular relevance to our discussion as it is more accommodative of the notion that the scope and strength of the exclusive copyright requires calibration to provide adequate incentives for creation, while at the same time minimising social costs arising from restrictions placed upon the access to and use of copyrighted content. For example, Sterk notes that expanded copyright protection increases the costs to authors by requiring them to obtain permission when they seek to build upon an existing work. Thus, he argues that, at some point the expansion of copyright protection will result in a reduction in the supply of new works because the number of authors deterred from creation as a result of the high cost of source material will exceed the number of persons incentivised to create new work as a result of copyright protection.[35] As Lunney notes, in the context of the incentive theory, defining copyright's proper scope has become a matter of balancing the benefits of broader protection, in the form of preserving incentives to create new works, against its costs, in the form of lost access to those works.[36] In contrast to the incentive theory, the neo-classicist approach propounds that to reap the optimal social utility of literary and artistic works, the owner's exclusive property right (copyright) should extend to all uses that could be derived from the work at present, as well as potential uses that could be derived from the work in the future.[37] It argues in favour of a broad and absolute copyright that would allow the copyright owner to exploit creative works to their optimal social value, and is less open to the notion of calibrating the scope and strength of exclusive rights to protect user interests. However, the extension of the neo-classical approach

[32]Lambrecht (n 23) 87.

[33]Netanel (n 28) 309.

[34]William M Landes and Richard A Posner, *The Economic Structure of Intellectual Property Law* (Harvard University Press 2003) 11. Merges notes that the economic justification for copyright has progressed beyond the point where a crude "incentive" story passes for analysis in every case. Robert P Merges, 'Are You Making Fun of Me? Notes on Market Failure and the Parody Defense in Copyright.' (1993) 21 AIPLA QJ 305, 306.

[35]Stewart E Sterk, 'Rhetoric and Reality in Copyright Law' (1996) 94 Michigan Law Review 1197, 1207.

[36]Glynn S Lunney Jr, 'Reexamining Copyright's Incentives-Access Paradigm' (1996) 49 Vanderbilt Law Review 483.

[37]Paul Goldstein, *Copyright's Highway: From Gutenberg to the Celestial Jukebox* (Rev ed, Stanford University Press 2003) 17; Netanel (n 28) 315.

to copyright law has been criticised by authors such as Lemley[38] and Frischmann[39] *inter alia,* on the grounds that empirical evidence does not support the argument that broad property rights will lead to increased incentives for investment in the efficient distribution of copyright protected works. Thus, from the two strands of utilitarian theory discussed above, the incentive theory of copyright law is more suited to provide a conceptual framework for the formulation of an exclusive right over digitised versions that could achieve an equilibrium between providing adequate incentives for investment in the creation of digitised versions of rare documents and allowing members of the public to access, use, and re-use them.

In comparison with the three theoretical doctrines discussed above, the social planning theory (as it has been labelled by Fisher[40]) is of more recent origin. In the context of copyright law, the social planning theory presents an ideological approach rooted in the proposition that copyright can and should be shaped to help foster a just and attractive democratic culture.[41] It makes the assumption that human nature flourishes through self-expression, communication and social dialogue and that these elements are facilitated through opportunities to freely access and interact with a rich and diverse body of cultural and artistic content.[42] Therefore, copyright law should be designed to secure consumer welfare and social enrichment by sustaining the production and dissemination of a rich and diverse body of cultural works that are open to being shared, used and re-used by members of the public. This is to be achieved *inter alia* by sustaining a rich artistic tradition, equalising access to content and promoting a participatory culture.[43] The social planning theory finds expression in the writings of Netanel,[44] Fisher,[45] and Elkin-Koren,[46] who stress the need for copyright law to be redesigned to facilitate and promote greater public

[38]MA Lemley, 'Ex Ante versus Ex Post Justifications for Intellectual Property' (2004) 71 The University of Chicago Law Review 129.

[39]Brett M Frischmann, 'Evaluating the Demsetzian Trend in Copyright Law' (2007) 3 Review of Law and Economics 649.

[40]Fisher (n 8) 173.

[41]ibid 172. 'Copyright is in essence a state measure that uses market institutions to enhance the democratic character of civil society.' Netanel (n 28) 288.

[42]William Fisher, 'Reconstructing the Fair Use Doctrine' (1988) 101 Harvard Law Review 1744.

[43]Fisher (n 8) 192–193.

[44]Netanel (n 28).

[45]Fisher (n 8); (n 42).

[46]Niva Elkin-Koren, 'Copyright and Social Dialogue on the Information Super Highway: The Case Against Copyright Liability of Bulletin Board Operators' (1995) 13 Cardozo Arts & Entertainment Law Journal 346.

engagement with cultural content. It also profits from the writings of scholars such as Madow[47] and Coombe.[48]

Rather than rejecting the granting of exclusive rights over creative content and informational goods, the social planning theory affirms the need for exclusive rights in order to preserve the incentives of creators and to prevent the underproduction or inadequate distribution of content. Thus, it acknowledges and upholds the incentive function of copyright law.[49] The social planning theory diverges from the incentive theory by relocating copyright from a purely-market oriented perspective (i.e., as a mechanism to prevent market-failure) to a social enrichment oriented perspective.[50] As Fisher notes, the social planning theory is similar to utilitarianism in its teleological orientation, but dissimilar in its willingness to deploy visions of a desirable society richer than the conceptions of 'social welfare' deployed by utilitarians.[51] Proponents of the social planning theory discuss ways in which existing copyright law could be calibrated by adjusting its scope and strength to minimise impediments to the public's ability to engage with creative content in socially and culturally valuable ways while at the same time preserving adequate incentives for creation.[52] For instance, Fisher explores how the fair-use privilege in US law could be redesigned to advance the realisation of a just and attractive intellectual culture.[53] Madow (discussing the adverse impact of publicity rights granted under US law in fostering a participatory culture) raises the possibility of introducing a compulsory licensing scheme or a more generous fair-use privilege to facilitate the use of cultural and social content in social criticism and satire.[54] It is argued here that, the social planning theory is able to provide valuable normative guidance in formulating the

---

[47]Madow criticises a purely economic analysis of publicity rights on the grounds that it takes people's existing preferences as given and does not question or evaluate them from a normative perspective. Michael Madow, 'Private Ownership of Public Image: Popular Culture and Publicity Rights' (1993) 81 California Law Review 125, 225.

[48]Rosemary J Coombe, 'Objects of Property and Subjects of Politics: Intellectual Property Laws and Democratic Dialogue.' (1991) 69 Texas Law Review 1853.

[49]Netanel (n 28) 292.

> Copyright protection is necessary because, in its absence, unbridled competition from free riders who are able to copy and distribute without paying copyright royalties would drive the price for user access near-zero marginal cost. This free rider problem, in turn, would greatly impair author and publisher ability to recover their fixed production costs. In a world without copyright, only authors unconcerned with monetary remuneration would produce creative expression and *only publishers with no need for financial return would invest in selecting, packaging, marketing, and making such expression available to the public.* Without copyright, creative expression would likely be both underproduced, and, no less importantly, underdisseminated. (emphasis added).

[50]ibid 288.

[51]Fisher (n 8) 172.

[52]"[Copyright] must be designed to underwrite a vital and independent expressive sector without unduly hampering access and the free exchange of ideas." Netanel (n 28) 365.

[53]Fisher (n 42).

[54]Madow (n 47) 240.

parameters of an exclusive right over digitised versions within the EU legal framework. This aspect of the social planning theory will be explored in Sect. 5.4 below.

5.3 Applying the Incentive Theory to Digitisation

The incentive theory recognises the public good characteristic of informational goods. It acknowledges that, although the creation of informational goods may incur considerable fixed costs, once created they can be reproduced and disseminated at marginal costs approaching zero. As Bollinger observes, if left to an open market without government regulation or special legal protection, investment in public goods would be uniquely risky and unappealing, and few producers would have the incentive to invest in its production.[55] Within a competitive market-place, the creator of an informational good would be exposed to competition from free-riders who are able to reproduce and distribute it at marginal costs (which in the case of digital goods would be close to zero).[56] Thus, competition from free-riders would make it more difficult for the original creator to recoup the investment made in the production of the informational good, and would undermine his incentives to continue to engage in the production activity.[57] This would result in the underproduction of informational goods gradually leading to a market failure.[58] Under the incentive theory, copyright law provides a legal mechanism by which the creator of an informational good is able to control its unauthorised exploitation. Thus, copyright law preserves incentives for creation by granting to the creator of an informational good the exclusive right to determine the ways in which it could be used, re-used, and distributed to the public.[59] The essence of the incentive theory is succinctly encapsulated by Bentham who notes that an exclusive privilege is absolutely necessary with respect to a great number of inventions in the arts as otherwise, 'he who has no hope that he shall reap, will not take the trouble to sow'.[60]

[55]Lee Bollinger, 'Book Review: Protect This Work of Expression: Clarifying the Unique Economics of Intellectual Property Rights' (2004) 44 Santa Clara Law Review 1287, 1291.

[56]Netanel (n 28) 292, Landes and Posner (n 34) 11, Kenneth J Arrow, 'Economic Welfare and the Allocation of Resources for Invention' in Universities-National Bureau Committee for Economic Research, Committee on Economic Growth of the Social Science Research Council (ed), *The Rate and Direction of Inventive Activity: Economic and Social Factors* (Princeton University Press 1962) 609, 617.

[57]Landes and Posner (n 34) 11.

[58]Gillian K Hadfield, 'The Economics of Copyright: An Historical Perspective' (1988) 38 Copyright Law Symposium 1, 5.

[59]*See* Shyamkrishna Balganesh, 'Debunking Blackstonian Copyright (Reviewing Neil Weinstock Netanel, Copyright's Paradox (2008))' (2009) 118 Yale Law Journal 1126, 1137.

[60]Jeremy Bentham, 'The Works of Jeremy Bentham', in John Bowring (ed), *The Works of Jeremy Bentham*, vol 3 (William Tait 1838), 71.

Exclusive rights enable the creator of a copyright protected work to exploit his creation without competition from free-riders, and therefore assists in sustaining his incentive to engage in the creation process. An absence of exclusive rights would benefit users in the short-term by making available to them cheap, unauthorised copies of an informational good. However, in the long-term, as the incentives for creators to engage in the creation process gradually erode, users would be adversely affected as a result of the supply of informational goods drying up.[61]

The problem of free-riding is exacerbated in the case of digital informational goods. In the face of technology that enables the creation of perfect reproductions and their distribution to the public at negligible costs approaching zero, digital informational goods are particularly susceptible to piracy. Unlike creators of traditional publications who in some instances could profit from the first-mover advantage (i.e., the lead-time gained by being the first provider of a particular informational good on the market until free-riders catch up), in the case of digitised versions the reproduction process is so quick that the producer cannot hope to benefit from the advantage of lead-time to recoup of the costs of his investment.

It is observed that, the proposed exclusive right is not aimed at creative activity leading to the production of new intellectual content—such as would be the case in the creation of a novel, song or film—but is aimed at the presentation of existing intellectual and/or informational content in a new form that enhances and improves its public availability and accessibility.[62] As emphasised in Sect. 1.5, the exclusive right granted over a digitised version (i.e., the digital photographic image) would not apply to the public domain intellectual and/or informational content that is reproduced by that digitised version. Nevertheless, the following arguments that have been made in support of granting exclusive rights over public domain works as a means of incentivising investment in their development or dissemination, are relevant to our discussion. Abramowicz contends that, where a work in the public domain requires some form of development which no one will have sufficient incentive to provide if the work remains in the public domain, social welfare would benefit from transferring intellectual property rights over that work from the public domain back into the private domain.[63]

Landes and Posner make a case for re-granting exclusive rights to persons who invest in the dissemination of obscure or forgotten public domain works and thereby re-introduce them to the public. They state as follows.

[61]Ruth Towse, Christian Handke and Paul Stepan, 'The Economics of Copyright Law: A Stocktake of the Literature' (2008) 5 Review of Economic Research on Copyright Issues 1, 11. Hadfield explains market failure as the failure of the market to supply such quantities of a good as are socially justified by cost. Hadfield (n 58) 33–34.

[62]Thus, the argument that production of creative content will continue to flourish in the absence of exclusive rights because of the intrinsic motivations of the creator who obtains satisfaction from the mere fact of creative expression cannot be maintained in the context of digitised versions.

[63]Michael Abramowicz, 'Privatizing the Public Domain', in F. Scott Kieff, Troy A. Paredes (eds), *Perspectives on Commercializing Innovation* (Cambridge, 2012) 146.

> Imagine a novel published many years ago in which copyright has expired. The novelist is rediscovered and there is a surge in demand for his novels. As no publisher could establish a property right in them, the incentives of publishers to publish and promote them might well be inadequate from a social standpoint.[64]

They go on to argue that:

> The need to invest in intellectual property to maximize its value is not exhausted in the initial creation of the property. Investment is necessary to maintain the value of the property as well, and also to resurrect abandoned or otherwise unexploited intellectual property.[65]

The case for re-granting exclusive rights to incentivise investment in the development or dissemination of public domain works is also captured in the following comment by Rappaport:

> For a work to be commercially successful, it requires effort and investment, which while not 'creative', is still necessary to generate value. For example authors employ literary agents, publishers advertise etc. Arguably, none of these activities will be pursued vigorously on behalf of public domain works as they are for works with ownership rights. And from an economic point of view, these activities 'create' real value.[66]

As noted in Sect. 4.8 above, the problem with the granting of exclusive rights is that, along with the social value gleaned from the creation and distribution of a greater number of digitised versions, their exercise also creates social costs. These social costs can be categorised as social costs that result from restrictions on accessing the digitised version, social costs resulting from restrictions placed upon the use and exploitation of the digitised version, social costs arising from restrictions placed upon the modification and development of the digitised version (e.g., the addition of value-added-features, software applications) and finally the social costs that result from restrictions placed upon the ability to use the digitised version in the creation of new original works (i.e., derivative works). A digitised version of a rare document, has a high potential to serve as raw material in the creation of new works (e.g., the digital photographic images of old books and newspapers being used in the creation of a textual collage, a page from an old newspaper being used to create a parody or satire of a modern day political scandal). It is therefore necessary to consider the social costs incurred through the introduction of an exclusive right over digitised versions that may make it more difficult and/or more expensive for members of the public to use the digitised version or portions thereof, in the creation of new content.

However, it needs to be kept in mind that in the case of digitised versions, the social costs arising from the exclusive right do not result in members of the public being made worse-off than their situation before the introduction of the exclusive right. Without the incentive for private sector entities to invest in the digitisation

---

[64]Richard A Posner and William M Landes, 'Indefinitely Renewable Copyright' (2003) 70 University of Chicago Law Review 471, 488–489.

[65]ibid 491.

[66]Edward B Rappaport, 'Copyright Term Extension: Estimating the Economic Values' (Congressional Research Service 11 May 1998) 4.

process through the granting of exclusive rights it is likely that the public would not obtain access to the rare document in digital form and consequently to the public domain content recorded upon it, at a particular point in time.[67] Nonetheless, the digitised version does not effect any change to the ability of a user to access and use the original rare document in analogue form. It merely, provides an additional option to the user of accessing it in digital form.

Additionally, although the digitised version will come under an exclusive right, the exclusive right would not prevent the use or re-use of the public domain textual content recorded upon it. In comparison to visual or audio-visual content, the prejudice caused to the public because of restrictions upon the use and re-use of a digitised version recording textual content would be minimal because of the relative ease with which the textual content can be extracted from the digital photographic image of the rare document that forms the subject matter of the exclusive right.

The incentive theory of copyright law posits that the social welfare created through the introduction of a copyright can be maximised by finding an optimal balance between the social benefits and the social costs created by the introduction of exclusive copyright.[68] In accordance with prevailing economic theory, the balance between costs and benefits will be optimised at the point at which the monopoly costs created by the existence of the exclusive right will be outweighed by the social benefits resulting from its incentivising effects.[69]

It has been argued that, this optimal balance between the cost-benefit trade-off could be achieved by calibrating the scope and strength of exclusive rights granted over a copyright protected work.[70] In fact, copyright law attempts to carry out this calibration process *inter alia* through the imposition of exceptions and limitations on the exclusive rights enjoyed by the holder of copyright and the establishment of a term of protection that is limited by duration.

Carrying out a precise cost-benefit analysis would prove particularly difficult in the context of an exclusive right over digitised versions considering the heterogeneity of the rare documents subject to the digitisation process and the social value and market demand that attaches to each of them. Nevertheless, the cost-benefit approach can provide guidance in designing the exclusive right in a manner that would assist in balancing the incentives granted to producers against the ability of users to access and use the digitised version.[71] The practical means by which this

[67]It is possible that within a more gradual process of digitisation purely financed by public funds, a rare document would be digitised at some indeterminate point in the future, but it can be argued that without the impetus provided by the channelling of private sector investment, a particular rare document may not be available to the public in digital form at the present time.

[68]*See* Peter Drahos, *A Philosophy of Intellectual Property Law* (Australian National University eText 2016) 144 <www.researchgate.net/publication/304514536_A_Philosophy_of_Intellectual_Property> accessed 31 January 2019.

[69]Balganesh (n 59) 1138; *see also* Lunney (n 36) 498.

[70]Balganesh (n 59) 1138.

[71]To be discussed further in Chap. 9 outlining the proposed model for an exclusive right over digitised versions.

balance could be achieved will be discussed more fully in Chap. 9. For the moment, it is noted that, under the incentive theory, the proposed exclusive right should be formulated with the following objectives in mind:

(a) it should create adequate incentives for the production and dissemination of digitised versions, where no adequate incentive exists at present.
(b) it should aim to achieve an optimal balance between the social costs and benefits resulting from the introduction of an exclusive right over digitised versions.
(c) the scope, strength, and duration of the exclusive right should not be more than what is necessary to provide the producer the ability to recoup an adequate and reasonable return on his investment.

5.4 The Social Planning Theory as a Normative Influence

Fisher underlines the need to select a combination of rules that could maximise consumer welfare by balancing incentives for creativity with incentives for dissemination and use.[72] However, he cautions that this goal must be tempered by other aspirations such as the sustenance of a rich artistic tradition, distributive justice, and semiotic democracy.[73] These goals could be achieved by ensuring that copyright protection is designed in a manner that allows members of the public to access cultural content and to participate in its creation.[74] The need for copyright law to be re-formulated to allow members of the public to freely engage and interact with cultural content is also reflected in Coombe's discussion on intellectual property and democratic dialogue.[75]

As per the democratic paradigm of copyright law presented by Netanel, copyright serves two democracy enhancing functions.[76] Firstly, by supporting a market for creative content it serves to incentivise the production of creative expression and investment in the dissemination of creative expression, thereby bolstering the discursive foundations of democratic culture and civic association.[77] Netanel identifies this as copyright's production function. Secondly, Netanel argues that copyright fulfils a structural function by supporting a sector of creative and communicative activity that is relatively free from reliance upon state subsidy, elite patronage, and cultural hierarchy.[78] It is assumed that the degree of independence afforded to

[72]Fisher (n 8) 192.

[73]ibid 192–193.

[74]ibid.

[75]*See* Coombe (n 48) 1861–1866.

[76]Netanel (n 28) 288.

[77]ibid. "Absent massive government or private subsidy, some measure of copyright protection is necessary to support a viable sector of authors and publishers engaged in the creation and dissemination of original expression."

[78]ibid.

creative and communicative activity by locating it within a free market would enable the creative content generated through it to be politically and socially neutral, and to cater to a wider public interest rather than simply promoting the interests of specific groups of political or social elite. Netanel observes that the democratic paradigm requires that copyright protection is sufficiently strong to support the production and structural functions, while at the same time sustaining public discourse and a participatory culture.[79] Netanel argues that copyright must not only aim towards enabling authors and publishers to appropriate a somewhat larger share of consumer surplus than that which would merely support a minimally adequate quantity of creative production[80] but should also allow substantial room for risk taking.[81] Nevertheless, he makes it clear that while copyright may operate in the market, its overall aim is to support a robust democracy-enhancing civil society through the maximisation of consumer welfare by advancing individual autonomy, social enrichment, and expressive diversity.

The foregoing discussion demonstrates that, similar to the incentive theory, the social planning theory seeks to achieve an optimal balance between the social benefits offered by copyright (in terms of greater levels of production and dissemination of creative content and the sustenance of the creative autonomy of authors), and the social costs arising from restrictions placed upon the public's ability to engage with creative content at an optimal level from the exercise of exclusive rights. It identifies certain specific types of use and re-use of copyright protected content that are critical to the sustenance of a participatory culture and a robust public discourse, and therefore need to be facilitated and encouraged. These are transformative use,[82] educational use[83] and use for public discourse and debate.[84]

Additionally, Fisher emphasises the need to ensure equitable public access to copyrighted content.[85] Netanel advocates the necessity to circumscribe copyright both in scope, as well as in duration,[86] and to prevent standard-form contracts from being used to expand a copyright holder's control over his content.[87] Elkin-Koren

[79]ibid 347.

[80]ibid 339.

[81]ibid 335–336. This is especially relevant in the case of digitised versions as the potential market demand for the digitised version of a rare document (or a collection of rare documents) may be difficult to accurately predict in advance. Thus, an element of risk taking is involved in investing in the creation of digitised versions of rare documents, and the proposed exclusive right should provide adequate incentives for such risk-taking by investors.

[82]Fisher identifies transformative use as a particularly important and socially valuable way of interacting with cultural content. Fisher (n 42) 1768. *See also* Netanel (n 28) 301–305; 376–382 and Coombe (n 48) 1879.

[83]Netanel (n 28) 345; Fisher (n 42) 1754, 1770.

[84]Netanel (n 28) 349; Coombe's concept of dialogic interaction (n 48); Elkin-Koren (n 46) 399–401.

[85]Fisher (n 8) 193.

[86]Netanel (n 28) 366–371.

[87]ibid 384–385.

opines that when access and use of copyrighted content do not substantially damage the ability of the copyright owner to recoup his investment in the creation of a work, such use and access should be allowed.[88]

It is argued here that, the integration of the proposals and guidelines presented by the social planning theory in the formulation of the proposed exclusive right would assist in achieving our goal of bringing about an equilibrium between the competing interests of users and producers. Therefore, we proceed to briefly discuss the ways in which these proposals could be incorporated into the design of the proposed exclusive right.

5.4.1 Transformative Use

Netanel argues that, from a democratic perspective, a broad derivative right poses an unacceptable burden on expressive diversity and that copyright owners' expansive control over transformative uses unduly stifles the creative reformulation of existing expression.[89] It is noted that, as rare documents are considered the cultural heritage of all humankind and as the intellectual and/or informational content recorded upon them belong to the public domain, there is a strong argument in favour of allowing users a broad scope of freedom on transformative uses such as the creation of new creative or artistic content (e.g., textual collages, graphic art) and especially in the creation of parody and satire. It is proposed therefore that, the exclusive right granted to the producer of a digitised version should not include an exclusive right over the creation of derivative works, especially when such a derivative works transform the underlying digitised version to the extent that it is not able to act as a substitute for the digitised version. Meanwhile, most private sector for-profit entities who are engaged in the creation of digitised versions of rare documents do not usually engage in the production of creative and artistic derivative creations based on the digitised versions produced by them. Their business models focus upon the commercial exploitation of the digitised versions along with the requisite meta-data. Therefore, it is argued here that use of a digitised version in the creation of a new creative or artistic work that does not constitute a substitute for the initial digitised version, is unlikely to damage the ability of the producer to recoup his investment. Furthermore, a broad exception to the exclusive right should be introduced to enable the use of digitised versions for the purposes of social commentary including use in parody and satire.[90]

---

[88]Elkin-Koren (n 46) 369–371. *See also* Fisher (n 42) 1781.

[89]Netanel (n 28) 378.

[90]*See* Madow (n 47) 240. "[W]e need to consider carefully whether there are measures short of abolition (a compulsory licensing scheme, or a generous 'fair use' privilege to protect social criticism and satire, for example) that can reduce the impact of the right of publicity on popular cultural practices."

5.4.2 Use for Educational Purposes and Use in Public Communication and Debate

Proponents of the social planning theory underline the importance of securing the broad availability of copyright protected content for educational contemplation and deliberation, as well as in social communication and public debate.[91] Thus, it is proposed that, an exclusive right over digitised versions should include an exception for use in education and scientific research including teaching within the classroom. Exceptions should also be introduced to enable use of digitised versions in news reporting, social commentary, and criticism in order to foster a broad public discussion and deliberation on these documents and the public domain content recorded upon them.

5.4.3 Reproduction for Personal Non-commercial Purposes

Should an exception be introduced to allow reproduction of a digitised version for personal non-commercial purposes? Unlike in the case of traditional analogue works such as paper-based books and newspapers, individual users have the ability to make perfect copies of digitised versions and to disseminate them to the public at negligible costs approaching zero.[92] Thus, each copy made by a user has the potential to compete with the digitised versions marketed by the producer within the same market. Furthermore, as sale or licensing to individual users constitutes a substantial portion of the market for digitised versions, non-commercial uses such as peer-to-peer sharing could have a substantial impact on the ability of a producer to commercially exploit the digitised versions. As Netanel observes, if left unchecked, massive consumer copying could undermine publisher markets no less than could infringing competitors.[93] However, the ability to make at least a limited number of copies for one's personal use would facilitate the optimal use and enjoyment of a digitised version by a buyer or a licensee. It is therefore argued here that, the proposed exclusive right should incorporate an exception that allows a legitimate buyer or a licensee the ability to make at least a limited number of reproductions subject to suitable limitations and restrictions that would prevent any significant erosion to the producer's ability to commercially exploit the digitised version.

---

[91]Netanel (n 28) 345; Fisher (n 42) 1754, 1770.

[92]Elkin-Koren (n 46) 383–384.

[93]Netanel (n 28) 299–300. As Ginsburg points out, much copying in cyberspace will be private as intermediaries such as traditional booksellers and publishers who reproduce, package and distribute copies to end-users will no longer be necessary and as a consequence the market for the work will by and large be the private copying market. Jane C Ginsburg, 'Putting Cars on the "Information Superhighway": Authors, Exploiters and Copyright in Cyberspace' 95 Columbia Law Review 1466, 1477–1478.

5.4.4 Price Discrimination

Fisher propounds that, to the greatest extent practicable, all persons should have access to informational and artistic resources.[94] Equalising access to digitised versions is important because of their status as cultural heritage materials. Proponents of the social planning theory support price discrimination as a mechanism that serves to minimise the deadweight loss to users while enabling the producer to capture a larger share of the consumer surplus.[95] As Fisher points out, these two effects sharply increase the ratio between incentives for creativity and welfare loss.[96] It has been emphasised that digital technology significantly enhances the ability of copyright owners to engage in price discrimination *inter alia* by enabling users to be charged for each individual discreet use[97] through the employment of digital-rights-management systems (DRM) that enable the tracking of different uses and reproductions. If carefully designed, price discrimination could allow producers to commercialise customised editions of digitised versions that could cater to the specific needs of different groups of users and thereby maximise their revenue. Regulation of pricing and licensing fees for digitised versions could also serve to ensure that the sale or licensing of the digitised version allows the holder of the exclusive rights to recoup a reasonable return without the possibility to engage in the creation of excessive profits to the detriment of users.

5.4.5 Duration of the Proposed Exclusive Right

Netanel notes that copyright duration should be limited to what is necessary to provide incentives for production and for supporting the creative autonomy of producers, so that, once the production and structural functions of copyright law have been served, the content can fall into the public domain to be freely used by any member of the public.[98] Netanel concedes that, given the variegation and fluidity of copyright markets it would be difficult if not impossible to determine the exact duration of copyright to effect an optimal balance between creator and user interests.[99] However, in determining the duration of the exclusive right over digitised versions it is necessary to keep in mind the fundamental objective of providing sufficient incentives for producers to invest in the digitisation process while ensuring that the digitised versions (i.e., the digital photographic images of the rare documents) would fall into the public domain at the earliest possible point in time. It is

[94] Fisher (n 8) 193.
[95] ibid.
[96] Fisher (n 8) 197.
[97] Netanel (n 28) 293.
[98] Netanel (n 28) 368–369.
[99] ibid 369.

interesting that, already in 1996, Netanel proposes the granting of a limited 'copyright-like' protection for those who publish public domain works in digital format, as a means of encouraging the initial production and storage of digital versions of public domain works that require a material amount of time to produce but, as digital goods, are particularly vulnerable to free-rider problems.[100]

5.4.6 *Preventing Contractual Provisions and DRM from Being Used to Bypass Exceptions and Limitations*

One of the major challenges facing copyright law at present is the application of digital-rights-management (DRM) systems and contractual provisions (especially standard-form contracts) to expand the scope and strength of the copyright owner's exclusive rights over the copyright protected content. In most instances, the application of contractual provisions and DRM systems result in users being denied the ability to benefit from the legally provided exceptions and limitations to the copyright owner's exclusive rights.

Netanel stresses that, attempts to use standard-form contracts to expand exclusive copyright should not be allowed,[101] but does not offer any concrete proposals as to how the law could prevent contractual provisions from being used to override copyright limitations and exceptions. However, under Article 6(4) of the InfoSoc Directive[102] Member States are required to take appropriate measures to ensure that, users who have legal access to content subject to DRM protection are able to benefit from certain exceptions and limitations that are specified by that Article. However, Article 6(4) limits itself to certain specific limitations and exceptions and does not impose upon Member States a blanket requirement to ensure that the application of DRM systems does not impede users from benefitting from all exceptions and limitations to copyright as provided by law.[103] Furthermore, it also enables copyright owners to bypass the application of Article 6(4) by entering into private

[100]ibid 370–371.

[101]"The democratic paradigm (. . .) would affirmatively disallow attempts to use standard contracts to expand copyright owner or content provider control over works that are made available to the public." ibid 385.

[102]Directive 2001/29/EC of the European Parliament and of the Council of 22 May 2001 on the harmonisation of certain aspects of copyright and related rights in the information society [2001] OJ L167/10 (InfoSoc Directive).

[103]The exceptions and limitations specified by Article 6(4) of the InfoSoc Directive include reproductions on paper or similar medium effected by the use of any photographic technique [Art 5(2)(a)], specific acts of reproduction made by publicly accessible libraries, educational establishments, museums or archives that is not for direct or indirect economic or commercial advantage [Art 5(2)(c)], use for the sole purpose of illustration for teaching or scientific research [Art 5(3)(a)], uses for benefit of people with a disability which are directly related to the disability and of a non-commercial nature to the extent required by the disability [Art 5(3)(e)].

contractual agreements with users. However, as will be discussed in greater detail in Sect. 6.1.1 below, there is reason to be sceptical as to the ability of private contractual arrangements to bring about an equilibrium between the interests of producers and users of digitised versions.

In formulating a model for the introduction of an exclusive right over digitised versions, it is necessary to consider if Article 6(4) is adequate to prevent the application of DRM systems in a manner that impedes the ability of users to benefit from the exceptions and limitations to the proposed exclusive right. Furthermore, it is necessary to explore ways of preventing contractual provisions (particularly standard-form contracts) from being used to override exceptions and limitations to the exclusive right.

5.5 Summary and Conclusions

The incentive theory of copyright law that flows from the utilitarian doctrine provides a conceptual framework for the introduction and formulation of an exclusive right over digitised versions. It offers an economic and market-oriented justification for the introduction of an exclusive right of limited strength and scope that would sustain adequate incentives for investment in the creation of digitised versions of rare documents while maximising social welfare.

The social planning theory of copyright, which is of more recent origin, provides a valuable normative framework for the calibration of the exclusive right to achieve an equilibrium between user and producer interests. While affirming the incentive function of copyright law, the social planning theory perceives the ultimate goal of copyright as being the achievement of social enrichment by fostering the creation of a rich and diverse body of creative and cultural content that is open to public interaction and engagement. Proposals for re-shaping copyright law (and the strength and scope of exclusive rights granted to authors) that have been advanced within the framework of the social planning theory have the potential to serve as guidelines in the formulation of an exclusive right over digitised versions that is capable of balancing the competing interests of users and producers.

Chapter 6
Adequacy and Suitability of Existing Protection Mechanisms

At present copyright claims, contractual provisions and digital-rights-management (DRM) systems are commonly used to control the ways in which members of the public are able to access and use digitised versions. Other mechanisms such as trade mark law, database rights and equitable remuneration schemes have the potential to be used for the maintenance of exclusivity over digitised versions, although they are not commonly employed for that purpose at present.

This chapter examines these mechanisms to determine their suitability[1] and adequacy[2] for the protection of digitised versions within the EU law framework.

6.1 Commonly Used Mechanisms

6.1.1 Copyright Law

The question whether a digitised version of a rare document could in fact qualify for copyright protection within the EU law framework will be discussed in the following chapter (Chap. 7). However, for the moment, we consider whether copyright law offers a suitable and adequate mechanism for the protection of digitised versions, based on the assumption that digitised versions would in fact qualify for copyright protection.

---

[1]Suitability refers to the appropriateness of a particular mechanism for protecting digitised versions e.g., the nature and scope of the protection offered, the efficiency of its enforcement within the digital environment, etc.

[2]Adequacy refers to the ability of the mechanism to achieve an adequate balance between the competing interests of users and producers of digitised versions by providing sufficient incentives to producers to invest in the digitisation of rare documents, while at the same time enabling users to use and exploit the digitised versions as much as possible (*see* Sect. 2.4 above).

S. Mendis, *A Copyright Gambit*, Munich Studies on Innovation and Competition 11,
https://doi.org/10.1007/978-3-662-59454-4_6

Copyright protection (or its continental counterpart author's rights) is commonly used for the protection of digitised versions. From the point of view of the producer, copyright law offers an established legal framework that grants protection *in rem* and affords to the copyright holder a 'bundle' of exclusive rights (e.g., exclusive rights to reproduce,[3] communicate to the public[4] and to distribute[5]) that would enable the producer to exercise a substantial degree of control over the distribution, use, and re-use of a digitised version. Copyright is also a relatively inexpensive tool by which to obtain protection as it does not require the fulfilment of formalities (e.g., there is no registration requirement) and arises automatically upon creation. Hence, it is a very 'accessible' protection mechanism that can be easily employed by any producer. Furthermore, under Article 6 of the InfoSoc Directive, DRM systems applied in respect of copyright protected works are themselves protected against acts of circumvention that are intended to carry out an act of copyright infringement.[6] This serves to improve the effectiveness of copyright protection and enforcement within the digital environment.[7]

As noted in the preceding discussion on the incentive theory of copyright,[8] the achievement of an adequate balance between the competing interests of creators and users of intellectual expression can be considered ingrained in the structure and design of the copyright law system. This is primarily reflected in the range of limitations and exceptions that apply to exclusive rights granted to a copyright holder. Foremost among these is the limitation placed upon the duration of protection whereby the copyright protected work falls into the public domain upon the expiration of the term of protection. Further, the limitations and exceptions placed upon the rightholder's exclusive right to control the distribution and use of copyright protected content, enable members of the public to use the content in certain specified ways, without the need to obtain the authorisation of the copyright owner.[9]

However, is copyright law able to achieve an adequate balance between the interests of users and producers of digitised versions in practice? As discussed in Chap. 5 above,[10] the indiscriminate use of DRM systems could prevent users from benefitting from legally established exceptions and limitations. Article 6(4) of the InfoSoc Directive requires Member States to take appropriate measures to ensure that beneficiaries of specified exceptions and limitations who have legal access to

---

[3]Article 2 of the Directive 2001/29/EC of the European Parliament and of the Council of 22 May 2001 on the harmonisation of certain aspects of copyright and related rights in the information society [2001] OJ L167/10 (InfoSoc Directive).

[4]ibid Article 3.

[5]ibid Article 4.

[6]*See* discussion in Sect. 4.5.

[7]*See* Sect. 6.1.3 below.

[8]*See* Sect. 5.3.

[9]These exceptions and limitations are provided in Article 5 of the InfoSoc Directive.

[10]*See* Sect. 5.4.6 for discussion on preventing contractual provisions and DRM from being used to bypass exceptions and limitations to copyright.

DRM protected content are able to benefit from those exceptions and limitations. However, Article 6(4) restricts itself to certain specified exceptions and limitations and does not stipulate a general requirement to prevent DRM systems from being used to override the exceptions and limitations provided under Article 5 of the InfoSoc Directive. For example, it does not include the exception provided under Article 5(3)(k) of the InfoSoc Directive that authorises the use of a copyright protected work for purposes of caricature, parody or pastiche, which as we noted in our discussion on the social planning theory is an important aspect of social discourse and commentary.

Rightholders are also able to bypass the application of Article 6(4) through the use of contractual arrangements.[11] In doing so, Article 6(4) only requires rightholders to afford users the means of benefitting from the specified exceptions and limitations to the extent 'necessary to benefit from that exception and limitation'. Thus, the rightholder is granted a wide discretion in determining the extent of use that is considered necessary in allowing a user to benefit from a particular exception or limitation. It is argued here that, there is a high likelihood that in making this determination the rightholder will be guided by his own interests and that the scope afforded to a user to benefit from an exceptions or limitation will be narrow and inadequate. Nevertheless, within the present EU copyright law framework, rightholders are generally not prevented from employing contractual provisions to override exceptions and limitations to copyright.[12] The absence of an effective and established mechanism to prevent the use of DRM systems and contractual provisions from being employed in denying users the ability to benefit from statutorily granted exceptions and limitations, is a major weakness of the EU copyright law framework that renders it an inadequate mechanism for the maintenance of a satisfactory balance between the interests of producers and users of digitised versions.

---

[11]Article 6(4) is triggered in the absence of voluntary measures (including agreements) between rightholders and the parties concerned that enable those parties to benefit from exceptions and limitations set out in Article 5(2)(a), (2)(c), (2)(d), (2)(e), (3)(a), (3)(b) and (3)(e), to the "extent necessary to benefit from that exception or limitation". The meaning of this term 'extent necessary to benefit' is not defined by the Directive. Thus, Article 6(4) allows discretion to rightholders in determining the freedom of use that should be accorded to users to benefit from the specified exceptions and limitations. For a more detailed discussion on the shortcomings of Article 6(4) *see* Christophe Geiger and others, 'The Information Society Directive' in Irini Stamatoudi and Paul Torremans (eds), *EU Copyright Law: A Commentary* (Edward Elgar 2014) 467–470. *See also* Martin Kretschmer and others, 'The Relationship between Copyright and Contract Law' (Strategic Advisory Board for Intellectual Property and Policy (SABIP) 2010), 138–140 <http://eprints.bournemouth.ac.uk/16091/1/_contractlaw-report.pdf> accessed 31 January 2019.

[12]This is contrasted with Article 8 paragraph 2 of the Directive 2009/24/EC of the European Parliament and of the Council of 23 April 2009 on the legal protection of computer programmes [2009] OJ L 111/16 (Computer Programmes Directive), and Article 15 of the Directive 96/9/EC of the European Parliament and of the Council of the European Union of 11 March 1996 on the legal protection of databases [1996] OJ L 77/20 (Database Directive), that explicitly prevent contractual provisions from being used to override certain specific exceptions and limitations to the exclusive rights granted by those Directives.

In the absence of its combination with complementary protection mechanisms such as DRM systems, copyright enforcement is usually expensive and time consuming. Thus, while a copyright claim over a digitised version may have a deterrent effect on piracy it does not offer an efficient means of preventing it. As observed by André Welters of the University and State Library of Cologne, Germany:

> We have a lot to do here in this Library. We do not have as much staff as we would wish to have to do all the work. We do not at the moment have the capacity to check online if anyone has used our public domain material in a way we object to. Even if we were made aware of this use, we would not consider suing anyone a sensible option (. . .) considering the financial resources we would have to spend and the indefinite nature of the outcome of the case (since there is no guarantee we would be successful). So our rights in these instances are mere 'paper tigers' since we would not always necessarily have the means to enforce the rights.[13]

Although the use of DRM and tracking systems provide a means of effectively preventing unauthorised use of copyright protected works, the application of DRM systems can also be expensive as they would have to be bought or licensed from a third party.[14]

Furthermore, the current 70 years *post mortem auctoris* (p.m.a.) period[15] of copyright protection would be excessive in the case of digitised versions. The Comité des Sages Report recommends a maximum 7-year period of preferential commercial use or preferential commercial exploitation to be granted to a private sector investor in the digitisation process in order to enable it to recoup its investment.[16] It is noted that, if 7 years is considered sufficient for recouping the investment made in the digitisation process, granting exclusive rights for a duration of 70 years p.m.a. goes far beyond what is necessary to create incentives for private sector investment. Meanwhile, with rapid changes in technology it is likely that the economic life span of a digitised version would expire long before the 70 years p.m.a. protection period ends, and would therefore be redundant in the case of digitised versions. Thus, applying the current copyright protection period to a digitised version would result in social costs which far outweigh the social benefits that accrue from the introduction of an exclusive right.

Thus, although the conceptual structure and scope of copyright protection makes it an appropriate mechanism for the protection of digitised versions, in its practical application it would not be able to achieve an adequate balance between the interests of producers and users, especially due to the excessive period of protection and the ability of producers to employ DRM systems in precluding users from benefitting from exceptions and limitations granted under the copyright law framework.

---

[13]Opinion expressed by André Welters of the University and State Library of Cologne, Germany (Universitäts und Stadtbibliothek Köln) during an interview held with the author on 18 February 2014 (interview transcript in possession of the author).

[14]For a more comprehensive discussion on the adequacy and suitability of DRM protection *see* Sect. 6.1.3 below.

[15]Article 1 of Directive 2006/116/EC of the European Parliament and of the Council of 12 December 2006 on the term of protection of copyright and certain related rights [2006] OJ L372/12 (Term Directive).

[16]Comité des Sages (Chap. 1, n 13) Annex I para 2.

6.1.2 Contract Law

Contractual provisions hold greater flexibility than other mechanisms, as they can be tailored to suit the particular needs of individual producers and users. Contractual provisions also have the ability to define with a greater degree of clarity the actual nature and scope of the protection that is claimed. This enables users to have more certainty as to the ways in which a digitised version can be used and accessed, although the drafting of contractual provisions tailored to the specific needs of particular situations can be a cumbersome and expensive process.

Nevertheless, contract law only provides protection *in personam*. This means that the restrictions imposed through contractual provisions can only be enforced against parties to the contract. Thus, it would not provide a remedy for unauthorised access and use carried out by third parties. Contractual provisions that regulate the use of digitised versions are often unfairly tilted in favour of the producer. Considering that the producer of the digitised version is usually the sole-source of a rare document in digital form, the user of a digitised version would have very little bargaining power in negotiating the terms of the contract. In most instances, producers and distributors use standard-form contracts the terms of which cannot be easily negotiated and are presented to the user on a 'take-it or leave-it' basis. Furthermore, the exclusive rights granted through a contractual provision is not limited by duration and can exist in perpetuity. The shortcomings of a regulatory framework based on private ordering will be discussed in more detail in Chap. 8[17] below. For the moment it is sufficient to note that, in the absence of strict regulation,[18] contract law would not provide an adequate legal mechanism for achieving a satisfactory balance between user and producer interests.

6.1.3 Digital-Rights-Management (DRM) Systems

The use of DRM systems is considered one of the most effective ways of protecting digital content against piracy although the application of a DRM system can be relatively expensive as the DRM software needs to be either created by the producer or distributor of the digitised version, or bought or licensed from an external source. DRM systems use technological-protection-measures (TPM) supported by a network of usage contracts and technology license agreements to prevent unauthorised reproduction, use, and re-use of digital content.[19] They create an environment in

[17] *See* discussion in Sect. 8.2.1.

[18] It is noted that the discussion or formulation of a strict regulatory framework that could model contract law into a suitable and adequate mechanism for the protection of digitised versions is beyond the scope of this thesis.

[19] Stefan Bechtold, 'Digital Rights Management in the United States and Europe' (2004) 52 The American Journal of Comparative Law 323, 325.

which various types of use, including copying, are only practically possible in compliance with the terms set out by the content provider.[20] Within the EU law framework, DRM systems including TPM are protected against circumvention under Article 6(1) of the InfoSoc Directive.

While the efficiency and suitability of DRM systems in providing protection to digitised versions against unauthorised access, use, and re-use is not disputed, its ability to bring about an equilibrium between the interests of producers and users of digitised versions is questionable. As discussed in Sect. 6.1.1 above, at present, the EU law framework does not offer an efficient mechanism to prevent DRM systems from being used to override exceptions and limitations to copyright protection.[21]

Nevertheless, as discussed in Sect. 4.5 above, it is possible to argue that legal protection against the circumvention of DRM granted under Article 6(1) of the InfoSoc Directive, is limited to instances where content to which the DRM system is applied is protected under a copyright, a related right or the *sui generis* database right. If this argument is correct, a DRM system that is applied over a digitised version that does not enjoy copyright or related rights protection would not be protected against circumvention under Article 6(1).[22]

Furthermore, assuming that protection against circumvention is limited to content that is protected under one of the specified exclusive rights, and that the protection against circumvention would cease once the duration of these exclusive rights have expired, this only means that following the expiration of the exclusive rights the DRM systems would not be protected against circumvention. It does not mean that the DRM system would automatically cease to have effect or that the content would be free of the restrictions imposed by the DRM system. Thus, the restrictions on use and access imposed by a DRM system could continue for an indefinite period following the expiration of the exclusive rights and users would be prevented from freely accessing, using, and re-using content that in fact belongs to the public domain. Thus, for the reasons given above it is argued here that, the application of DRM systems is not an adequate mechanism for the protection of digitised versions as the protection it grants, unless properly regulated, could be abused by a producer of a digitised version to extend the scope and strength of the exclusive claim beyond the limits stipulated under legally granted exclusive rights.

[20] Institute for Information Law (IViR) (Chap. 4, n 26) 14. *See also* Encoding (Chap. 4, n 25).

[21] *See* discussion on the scope of Article 6(4) of the InfoSoc Directive in Sect. 6.1.1 above (n 11).

[22] This is notwithstanding the fact that the contractual restrictions imposed upon users by the DRM system would continue to be valid and could also be applied to produce third party effects.

6.2 Potential Mechanisms

6.2.1 Trade Mark Law

Trade mark law can be used for the protection of digitised versions by imprinting a trade mark upon a digitised version either as a logo (that is placed on a corner of the digitised version) or by incorporating it within a visible watermark that is embedded upon the digitised version. While the Comité des Sages recommendation advises against the use of intrusive watermarks there does not seem to be much opposition to the insertion of subtle non-intrusive logos or watermarks on a digital image in a way that does not substantially detract from its value for research and education.

The use of a trade mark is inexpensive and allows the source of the image to be easily identified. A watermark embedded upon a digital image is difficult to remove, and even when removal is possible, is a process that requires considerable time and patience. Therefore, the inclusion of a trademark upon a digital image by embedding it within a watermark can deter piracy and enable the producer to easily identify unauthorised uses of a digitised version.

However, protection granted under trade mark law is not limited in time. Thus, where a trademark is imprinted upon a digitised version, the digitised version would be protected against unauthorised use, so long as the trademark remains valid. Hence, the use of a trademark for the protection of a digitised version would enable the owner of the trademark to exercise control over the use and re-use of the digitised version almost in perpetuity.

The inclusion of a trademark could detract from the utility of a digitised version to users. Even if the trade mark is incorporated into a subtle and non-intrusive watermark that is embedded upon the digitised version, this would make it more difficult to use the digitised version in the creation of derivative works.

Thus, trade mark protection does not enable the maintenance of a sufficient equilibrium between the interests of producers and users. The unlimited duration of protection and its potential to impede the re-use of digitised versions in the creation of new derivative works renders it an inadequate mechanism for the protection of digitised versions.

6.2.2 Database Protection

The EU Database Directive[23] grants protection to original databases under copyright law and to non-original databases under a *sui generis* regime. Databases are granted copyright protection if they are considered to be original in the sense that they, "by reason of the selection or arrangement of their contents, constitute the author's own

[23]Database Directive (n 12).

intellectual creation."[24] Non-original databases are protected under a *sui generis* regime if it can be shown that, "there has been quantitatively and/or qualitatively a substantial investment in either the obtaining, verification or presentation of contents" of the database.[25]

In a majority of instances, digitised versions are distributed and made available to the public in the form of archival collections (arranged thematically, chronologically, etc.), or in other words as 'databases' that are indexed and searchable.[26] The creation of the database is normally carried out by the same private sector for-profit entity that invested in the creation of the digitised versions, as the distribution and making available of the digitised versions in the form of a searchable database constitutes an important component of the business model commonly used by these entities.

It is possible that, some databases of digitised versions may obtain protection under copyright law when the originality demonstrated in the selection and arrangement of digitised versions (i.e., digital photographic images) within an archival collection qualifies the database as its author's own intellectual creation. However, the creation of a database of digitised versions more often tends to be a technical process as opposed to a creative or intellectual exercise. It aims to present the digitised versions of rare documents to the user in a coherent and accessible manner and in many instances, the arrangement of digitised versions in the database closely follows or is inspired by the way in which the original rare documents are arranged within the memory institution's archives. Thus, it is more likely that a database of digitised versions would qualify for protection under the *sui generis* regime under Article 7(1) on the basis that the creator of the database has made a qualitatively and/or quantitatively substantial investment in the presentation and/or verification of the digitised versions incorporated in the database.[27]

The decision of the CJEU in the case of *British Horseracing Board v William Hill*[28] affirms that the investment made in the production of the digitised versions cannot be considered in assessing whether the investment made in the creation of the database is substantial.[29] However, it is argued here that, in many instances the investment made in the selection of digitised versions to be included within the database, in the creation of the meta-data that allows the digitised versions to be

[24]ibid Article 3(1).

[25]ibid Article 7(1).

[26]For example, ProQuest's database entitled 'Early English Books Online' presents a collection of digitised versions of early printed works in English <www.proquest.com/products-services/databases/eebo.html> accessed 31 January 2019; The Digital Vatican Library gives online access to its database of digitised versions of manuscripts digitised through the Polonsky Project <http://digi.vatlib.it/mss/> accessed 31 January 2019; the British Library makes available its British Newspaper Archive that includes digitised versions of newspapers printed in Britain dating back to the sixteenth century <www.britishnewspaperarchive.co.uk> 31 January 2019.

[27]Article 7(1) of the Database Directive.

[28]Case C-203/02 *British Horseracing Board* [2004] ECR I-10415.

[29]ibid paras 32 and 33.

arranged in a systematic manner, in the cataloguing and indexing of each digitised version and finally in verifying the contents of the database and the associated metadata would be adequate for establishing a substantial investment to obtain protection under Article 7(1). As noted by the CJEU in the *British Horseracing case,* although obtaining the data to be included in the database may not require any particular investment (as that data has already been produced and is therefore available to the creator of the database), the investment made by the creator in collecting the data, arranging it systematically, organising the individual accessibility of each item of data and verifying their accuracy throughout the operation of the database would be relevant factors in determining a substantial investment for the purposes of Article 7 (1).

Both the *sui generis* and copyright regimes, grant protection against the unauthorised extraction and/or re-utilisation of the whole or substantial part of the contents of a database (the substantiality being evaluated qualitatively and/or quantitatively).[30] Protection is also granted against the repeated and systematic extraction and/or reutilisation of insubstantial parts of the database that conflict with its normal exploitation or unreasonably prejudice the legitimate interests of its creator. However, the critical point is that both regimes seek to protect the arrangement and presentation of the data as a collection or compilation and do not grant protection to the individual items of data themselves. As emphasised in recitals 45 and 46 to the Database Directive, the right to prevent unauthorised extraction and/or re-utilisation does not result in the extension of copyright protection to unprotected items of data, neither does it create a new right in the individual data items. Thus, protection of the database under copyright law or the *sui generis* regime would not have the effect of bestowing copyright or other exclusive rights over the individual digitised versions. Nor would it grant protection against the unauthorised reproduction or use of individual digitised versions incorporated within the database as long as those digitised versions do not constitute a quantitatively or qualitatively substantial part of the contents of the database, and the unauthorised use does not amount to a systematic extraction or re-utilisation of the contents of the database.

The protection granted under the Database Directive may be sufficient for databases that include collections of information, where each individual item of information taken on its own does not have significant economic value. For example, in the case of a telephone directory the value of the database lies in the collection and arrangement of individual informational elements within a single compilation. Thus, the reproduction and use of individual names, addresses and telephone numbers by members of the public would not prejudice the ability of the creator of the telephone directory to recoup his investment. However, in the case of a database of digitised versions, there is economic value both in the database (i.e., the arrangement and presentation of individual digitised versions as a compilation of searchable data), as well as in each individual digitised version itself. The unauthorised reproduction and use of individual digitised versions could cause substantial prejudice to the ability of

[30] Article 7(1) of the Database Directive (n 12).

the producer of digitised versions to obtain an adequate return on his investment. For this reason, it is argued that the protection afforded under the Database Directive is not a suitable mechanism for providing incentives to private sector entities to invest in the digitisation process.

6.2.3 Equitable Remuneration (Fair Compensation)

The right to equitable remuneration is increasingly being adopted in legal systems as an alternative to exclusive rights. It refers to an obligation on the part of the user to pay a reasonable fee to the author or producer of a work for its use or re-use. The amount of the payment is determined either statutorily (by the legislature or an entity nominated by the legislature for that purpose) or by a judge (i.e., courts). The right to equitable remuneration has been referred to as a 'minimum standard', a right to money in place of a full exclusive right[31] and is usually enforced by means of statutory or compulsory licensing schemes. The essence of equitable remuneration is that it compensates authors for the use of their works while dispensing with their ability to prevent such use through the exercise of exclusive rights. Thus, introducing an equitable remuneration regime over digitised versions of rare documents would serve to facilitate their use by members of the public and prevent producers from imposing discriminatory terms upon the use and re-use of digitised versions. It would also diminish the transaction costs associated with the negotiation of individual licences.

The question is whether an equitable remuneration right could be a suitable means of ensuring a fair return on the investment made by the producer. The first problem is that, to introduce a right to equitable remuneration, it is necessary to establish that the author or producer holds an intellectual property right over the work with regard to which equitable remuneration is to be levied. Thus, in the absence of an established intellectual property right over a digitised version it would be difficult to justify the grant of a right to fair compensation. However, if for example, a digitised version is eligible for protection under copyright law then, the problem arises as to how the amount of remuneration (i.e., the fee that is to be paid by a user) is to be determined. As reiterated many times, digitised versions are heterogeneous goods and it would be difficult to determine a uniform fee that is suitable and reasonable for all digitised versions. It is argued that the imposition of a uniform fee for identical uses of digitised versions that involve very different costs to produce and have different social and economic value is not satisfactory.

Furthermore, if a right to equitable remuneration is introduced in relation to digitised versions, the scope of the remuneration right would need careful calibration to ensure the maintenance of a fair balance of interests. For example, if a right to

[31] David Brennan, 'What Is Equitable Remuneration for Intellectual Property Use?' Paper Prepared for a Seminar at Oxford Intellectual Property Research Centre (25 January 2005) 4.

remuneration is introduced in relation to the reproduction of digitised versions for private non-commercial purposes, the scope of the right would still need to be limited to a certain amount of reproductions, as a broad right that enables the creation of an unlimited number of reproductions against the payment of a fee could prejudice the ability of the producer to commercialise the digitised version in the end-user market.

Thus, it is argued here that, an equitable remuneration right is not a protection mechanism in itself, but a mechanism for enforcing intellectual property rights that have already been established through some other legal framework such as copyright or related rights law. Therefore, to give effect to a system of equitable remuneration rights, it would be necessary to first introduce an intellectual property right over digitised versions.

6.3 Summary and Conclusions

The advantages and disadvantages of the above mechanisms as tools for the protection of digitised versions are summarised in Table 6.1.

In the light of the foregoing analysis, it appears that none of the legal and non-legal mechanisms discussed above are able to protect or regulate the use and access of digitised versions in a manner that could adequately balance user and producer interests. Copyright law provides an established and entrenched legal framework that is capable of balancing the interests of copyright owners and users of copyright protected content. However, in the context of digitised versions, copyright law does not offer a suitable or adequate framework. This is due to certain shortcomings of the existing copyright law framework within the EU, particularly the excessive period of protection and the ability to override exceptions and limitations to exclusive copyright through the application of DRM systems and contractual provisions.

It appears therefore that, there is a need to develop an alternative legal mechanism for the protection and regulation of digitised versions within the EU legal framework. However, if digitised versions do in fact fulfil the requirements for copyright protection within the EU law framework, copyright protection would arise automatically and digitised versions of rare documents would be protected under copyright law. Therefore, before considering alternative legal mechanisms that could be introduced for the protection of digitised versions, it is necessary to determine whether digitised versions could qualify for copyright protection within the EU.

Table 6.1 Advantages and disadvantages of different legal and non-legal mechanisms

Mechanism	Advantages	Disadvantages
Copyright law	– *In rem* protection – Established framework of legal rules – No formalities – Limited duration of protection – Limitations and exceptions on the exercise of exclusive rights	– Duration of protection too long – Limitations and exceptions can be overridden by contract and in some instances by DRM [in situations where Art 6(4) of EU InfoSoc Directive does not apply] – Enforcement is expensive and time consuming
Contract law	– Flexibility to be adapted to different user and producer needs – Clarity as to exact scope of protection claimed	– *In personam* protection – Duration of protection not limited in time – Drafting contractual terms can be an expensive and cumbersome process – Inequality of bargaining power between the user and producer that is unfairly tilted in producer's favour – Private ordering as opposed to an established statutory framework of regulation
Digital-rights-management (DRM) systems	– Effective enforcement mechanism – Protection against circumvention under Art. 6 of the EU InfoSoc Directive	– Protection not limited in time – Relatively expensive mechanism as DRM software must be bought or licensed – Protection against circumvention may be dependent upon the existence of a copyright or related right over the digitised version – Limitations and exceptions can be overridden by contract and in some instances by DRM [in situations where Art 6(4) of EU InfoSoc Directive does not apply]
Trade mark law	– *In rem* protection – Established framework of legal rules	– Duration of protection not limited in time – Incorporation of trade mark could detract from utility of digitised version, especially for the creation of derivative works
Database protection	– *In rem* protection – Limited duration of protection – Established statutory framework with well-defined parameters	– No protection for digitised versions individually, only for database. Does not provide protection against unauthorised extraction and/or re-utilisation of individual digitised versions
Equitable remuneration (fair compensation)	– No exercise of exclusivity only a right to reasonable remuneration	– The operation of an equitable remuneration scheme requires the existence of an intellectual property right over the

(continued)

Table 6.1 (continued)

Mechanism	Advantages	Disadvantages
	– Allows more widespread and equitable use of and access to, digitised versions	subject-matter. Thus, it is more a limitation on existing exclusive rights rather than a protection mechanism – As digitised versions are heterogeneous goods, it may be difficult to determine upon a remuneration fee that is fair and reasonable for all digitised versions

Chapter 7
Can a Digitised Version Obtain Copyright Protection Within the EU?

As noted in Chap. 2 above, the study deals with digitised versions of rare documents that are created through a process of digital scanning.[1] It focuses upon two-dimensional digital photographic reproductions of existing two-dimensional planar surfaces (i.e., rare documents) that are created by using scanning hardware such as flatbed scanners[2] and digital cameras.[3]

This research does not deal with digitisation processes that are aimed towards creative or artistic expression. It focuses solely upon digitisation that is carried out to enhance the public availability of rare documents and the content recorded upon

[1]According to Lee, "scanning involves conversion of specifically image-based analogue material into digital form. Digitisation, on the other hand, means the conversion of any analogue material to electronic storage, including sound and video. In other words, all scanning is digitisation, but not all digitisation is scanning". Stuart D Lee, *Digital Imaging: A Practical Handbook* (1st Ed, Neal-Schuman Publishers 2001) 36.

[2]"Flatbed scanners have become the most commonplace method for capturing images or text. Their name comes from the fact that the scanner is literally a flat glass bed, quite similar to a copy machine, on which the image is placed face down and covered. The scanner then passes light-sensitive sensors over the illuminated page, breaking it into groups of pixel-sized boxes." Alan Morrison, Michael Popham and Karen Wikander, *Creating and Documenting Electronic Texts: A Guide to Good Practice* (AHDS 1999) <https://ota.ox.ac.uk/documents/creating/cdet/chap3.html#2> accessed 31 January 2019.

[3]Morrison, Popham, and Wikander note that, the flatbed scanner requires that the document must be placed completely flat on the scanning bed. In the digitisation of books this poses a problem because, the way in which a book is bound does not allow it to be placed completely flat upon the scanning bed and the only way to accomplish this would be to bend the spine of the book to breaking-point. They point out that the problem is exacerbated when dealing with texts with very fragile pages such as early printed books and manuscripts, as the inversion and pressure can cause the pages to flake away or rip, and that a solution to this problem is to digitise such material with a stand-alone digital camera. ibid.

S. Mendis, *A Copyright Gambit*, Munich Studies on Innovation and Competition 11,
https://doi.org/10.1007/978-3-662-59454-4_7

them.[4] Accordingly, these digitisation processes are carried out with the objective of creating faithful and exact digital reproductions of rare documents that can serve as digital surrogates to the original analogue documents. Thus, the study focuses upon digital photographic reproductions of rare documents that are intended to fulfil a utilitarian purpose as opposed to an artistic or creative function.

This chapter considers whether a faithful and exact digital photographic reproduction of an existing rare document that records public domain content (hereinafter referred to as a 'digitised version'), could qualify for copyright protection within the existing EU legal framework. Section 7.1 of the chapter provides a brief overview of the digitisation process, particularly focusing on the nature and extent of the human involvement in the creation of a digitised version. Section 7.2 gives a brief overview of the EU legal framework on copyright law and considers the (alleged) introduction of the author's own intellectual creation standard as the uniformly applicable, harmonised standard of originality in EU copyright law. Section 7.3 examines whether a digitised version could qualify for copyright protection under the harmonised European standard of originality. Section 7.4 analyses whether a digitised version could obtain copyright protection in the United Kingdom (UK), Germany and France, both under the traditional copyright law frameworks of these EU Member States and in the light of the developments that have taken place following the introduction of the harmonised European standard of originality. These three jurisdictions have been selected because their legal systems represent the main copyright law traditions that prevail within the EU namely, the English common law copyright law tradition (UK) and the continental civil law author's rights tradition (Germany and France). For convenience, the term 'copyright' will be used in referring to both the English copyright system and the continental author's rights system. Section 7.5 summarises the findings of the chapter and presents conclusions.

7.1 An Overview of the Digitisation Process

A basic understanding of the digitisation process is useful to our discussion. Issues such as the nature and extent of human input that is involved in the production of a digitised version and the level to which that human involvement is dictated and governed by technical and/or functional considerations is relevant in determining whether the final digitised version will come within the framework of copyright protection.[5]

[4]It is noted that most of these digitisation initiatives also have the objective of preserving these rare documents for posterity in digital format. This also requires that the digitised version represents an exact and faithful digital reproduction of the rare document.

[5]As defined by Gervais, "a creative choice is one made by the author that is not dictated by the function of the work, the method of technique used or by applicable standards or relevant good practice (...) a conscious human choice must have been made, even though it may be irrational".

Digital scanners operate by shining a light on the object or document that is being digitised and then directing the reflected light (usually through a series of mirrors and lenses) onto a photosensitive element (usually an electronic light-sensor) thereby converting levels of brightness into electronic signals that are then processed into a digital image.[6] Commonly used light-sensors include CCD,[7] CIS,[8] and PMT[9] light-sensors. Similarly, digital cameras use CCD or CMOS[10] light sensors in the creation of a digital photographic image.[11] Therefore, both scanners and cameras create digital images through a photographic process, i.e., a process in which light and light-sensitive components are used to record an image of an existing object or document. Thus, a digital image has been described as an 'electronic photograph' mapped as a set of picture elements (pixels) and arranged according to a predefined ratio of columns and rows.[12]

Thus, the degree of freedom allowed for the exercise of independent human choice within the digitisation process becomes a relevant consideration in the determination of the originality of a digitised version and thereby its possibility of qualifying for copyright protection. Daniel Gervais, 'Feist Goes Global: A Comparative Analysis of the Notion of Originality in Copyright Law' [2002] 49 Journal of the Copyright Society of the USA 949, 976–977. *See also* André Lucas, Agnès Lucas-Schloetter and Carine Bernault, *Traité de la propriété littéraire et artistique* (5th edn, Lexis Nexis 2017) 121, "La forme dans laquelle doit s'incarner l'œuvre de l'esprit ne lui permet pas d'accéder à la protection du droit d'auteur si elle est purement fonctionnelle". ("The intellectual work will not qualify for authors' rights protection if it is in a form that is purely functional".) (Translated into English by the author). In Germany, works that are produced under fully automated processes without the presence of human intervention is excluded from copyright protection. Löwenheim (n 222) § 2 para 11. Similarly, in France, the conception of a work as an extension of its author's personality implies that subject-matter created through fully automated processes, without human intervention would not qualify for copyright protection. On the other hand, in the UK [s 9(3) of the Copyright, Designs and Patents Act (CDPA) 1988 (UK)] and Ireland [s 21(f) Copyright and Related Rights Act n°28 of 2000 (Ireland)] computer generated works can qualify for copyright protection in which case the person by whom the arrangements necessary for the creation of the work are undertaken will be designated as its author. S178 of the CDPA defines computer generated works as, works that are generated by a computer in circumstances such that there is no human author of the work. However, as will be discussed below, it is unlikely that a digitised version of a rare document would qualify as a computer generated work under this definition, as the process used for the digitisation of rare documents is usually not fully automated, and involves a certain degree of human involvement.

[6]Cornell University Library/Research Department, 'Moving Theory into Practice: Digital Imaging Tutorial' <http://preservationtutorial.library.cornell.edu/contents.html> accessed 31 January 2019.

[7]Charged Coupled Device.

[8]Contact Image Sensor.

[9]Photomultiplier Tube.

[10]Complementary Metal Oxide Semiconductor.

[11]Chris Woodford, 'Digital Cameras', *Explain That Stuff* (2016) <www.explainthatstuff.com/digitalcameras.html> accessed 31 January 2019.

[12]National Mission for Manuscripts 'Guidelines for Digitisation of Manuscripts' <https://fr.scribd.com/document/376803180/Guidelines-for-Digitization-of-Manuscripts> accessed 31 January 2019.

Software programmes and tools are also used during the digitisation process often in combination with the digital hardware. In the digitisation of textual content, it is possible that text-scanning software such as optical-character-recognition (OCR) software is used to digitise the text that is recorded upon the digital image. OCR software converts the text appearing upon the digital image into computer-readable text that *inter alia* enables computer-searchability of words, phrases, and characters. Image-editing software can be used to edit images after they have been created (i.e., in the post-production phase). Software can also be used to incorporate value-added features such as 'zoom-in'[13] and 'page-turner'.[14]

Margoni[15] observes that, the level of automation that is employed in digitisation processes can range from automated to semi-automated and finally to 'human digitisation'.[16] He describes automated digitisation as digitisation that is realised in the absence (or negligible presence) of human intervention (e.g., Google Inc. automatically scanning all the books in an entire collection) and semi-automated digitisation as automated digitisation realised by a human operator (e.g., human operator taking pictures or manually photocopying collections for inventory or classification purposes).[17] Human digitisation is described as digitisation carried out by a person with professional expertise with the objective of realising high quality outputs (e.g., a photographer taking different shots in different light conditions to create high-resolution digital images).[18] Margoni admits that these three scenarios of digitisation are an over-simplification of the complex and idiosyncratic dynamics that digitisation processes usually follow. Nevertheless, Margoni's categorisation is useful to our analysis in highlighting the different degrees of human intervention that can be perceived in different digitisation initiatives.

The importance attached to the protection and preservation of rare documents means that, as at present, rare documents are usually not digitised through fully automated processes (e.g., digitisation that is entirely carried out by robotic book scanners). Thus, the creation of digitised versions of rare documents requires a certain degree of direct human intervention. Accordingly, it is argued here that the digitisation of rare documents and would fall within the categories of semi-automated or human digitisation under Margoni's classification.

[13]The zoom-in feature allows users to obtain an enlarged view of the image or particular portions of the image.

[14]'Page-turner' refers to the flip animation function that is used by many distributors of digitised products. The flip function allows a user to view multiple digital images in a way that simulates flipping through the pages of a book, thereby bringing the experience of reading a digitised version of a book closer to the actual experience of reading a book in print form.

[15]Thomas Margoni, 'The Digitisation of Cultural Heritage: Originality, Derivative Works and (Non) Original Photographs' (IVIR University of Amsterdam 2014) <https://papers.ssrn.com/sol3/papers.cfm?abstract_id=2573104> accessed 31 January 2019.

[16]ibid 5–6.

[17]ibid.

[18]ibid 6.

Meanwhile, the exact degree of human intervention can differ between different digitisation initiatives depending *inter alia* on the type of scanning hardware that is used (some scanning hardware can be automated to a higher level than others) and the type of rare document that is being digitised. When the rare document is very fragile or damaged, there would be a greater need for human involvement in the digitisation process. In such cases, human involvement and expertise is required to manipulate the settings on the scanner or camera to produce a clear and exact reproduction of the original document. Furthermore, human involvement may be required in the post-production phase to correct and modify an image that reproduces distortions or damage present in the original document to create a clear reproduction of the textual content. Similarly, although the digitisation of textual content through the application of software such as OCR is almost fully automated, such software cannot be relied upon to produce a completely accurate digitised version of the text. Especially in the case of old documents, the reduced visibility levels of the text in the digital reproduction can lead the software to make mistakes in digitising the text. Thus, human intervention is critical to check and correct the digitised text, which can be a painstaking and labour-intensive task.

However, it is argued here that, notwithstanding differences in the degree of human intervention as regards different initiatives for the digitisation of rare documents, in each of them, the human intervention will be directed by the overall objective of creating a faithful and exact digital photographic reproduction of an existing rare document. It is observed that, the objective of producing an exact visual representation of the underlying document will act as a functional constraint that would preclude the human actor from exercising his personal aesthetic choices or creative preferences in determining the final form of the digitised version. Thus, while the degree of human intervention may vary depending on the type of document that is being digitised and the purpose for which the digitised version is intended (i.e., whether it is a low-resolution version that is intended for non-commercial use or a high-resolution version that is intended for commercial exploitation), there will be little variation on the scope afforded within the digitisation process for the exercise of free and creative choices on the part of the human actor.

The digitisation of a rare document usually involves the following stages. These stages belong to three different phases of the digitisation process, i.e., the pre-production phase, the production phase, and the post-production phase.

Pre-production phase;

(1) selection of content,
(2) preparation of content for scanning.

Production phase;

(3) conversion to digital format (including image capture and processing of image).

Post-production phase;

(4) quality control of digitised image,[19]
(5) database management (including the creation of meta-data),
(6) distribution of digitised product,
(7) preservation of digitised product (including the management of innovation cycles).

Of these, stages 3 and 4, i.e., the conversion stage (production-phase) and the quality control stage (post-production phase) allow for direct human intervention in the creation of the digitised version.

The conversion to digital format (in the production phase) involves two steps; firstly, capturing the raw image by means of the scanning hardware (image capture) and, secondly, processing the raw image. Image capture is automated to a high degree. Nevertheless, it may require the human actor to determine the appropriate light, exposure, resolution, and temperature settings to ensure that the document is not damaged during the image capture process and that a clear and faithful photographic reproduction of the document is produced. The image capture process may also include electronic text creation, through the application of text-scanning software such as OCR software.[20] At the stage of processing, the raw image that has been captured by the scanning hardware, human involvement may be needed to orient the image (by cropping, rotation, etc.), to adjust the tone and colour of the digital image (including correction for fading and exposure, gamma correction, sharpening, and blurring), and to clean and repair flaws that have occurred during the digitisation process such as shadow, skew or other distortions such as damages, stains, fading, etc., that are present in the original document and have been reproduced in the digital image.[21] Correction of the digitised version of the text that is produced through the application of text-scanning software could also take place at this stage. Human intervention is also required for compressing the image, which refers to the reduction of file size to facilitate storage and distribution, through methods such as the reduction of redundancy[22] and irrelevancy.[23]

The post-production quality control phase involves an evaluation of the digital image *inter alia* for colour calibration, spatial resolution, and tonal reproduction.[24] This requires that the person who carries out the quality control has the ability to

[19]National Mission for Manuscripts (n 12).

[20]Morrison, Popham and Wikander (n 2) 3.3.2.

[21]*See* Dipti S Tripathi 'Guidelines for Digitisation of Archival Material' 26–27. <https://namami.gov.in/downloads> accessed 31 January 2019.

[22]Redundancy reduction is often used during 'lossless' encoding (which refers to a compression technique in which no information from the original image is lost or removed). It looks for patterns and repetitions that can be expressed more efficiently. *See* Jisc Digital Media, 'Digital File Formats: Redundancy and irrelevancy' <https://edu.hioa.no/ark2200/h18/pensum/jisc/infokit/file_formats/redundancy-and-irrelevancy.html> accessed 31 January 2019.

[23]Irrelevancy reduction aims to remove or alter information that makes little or no difference to the perception of the file content. ibid.

[24]Tripathi (n 21) 30.

visually evaluate the image and to spot potential elements of the photographic reproduction that need to be modified or corrected.[25] Colour calibration refers to the use of a calibrated chart to evaluate both greyscale, as well as colour reproduction. The object of the calibration process is to ensure that the colours of the digitised image correspond as nearly as possible to that of the original document. Typically, a human actor sits in front of a colour calibrated monitor with the actual rare document before him and manually adjusts the colours in the digital image to match those of the original document as exactly as possible.[26] Some scanning hardware also offer automated colour calibration facilities, whereby the scanner perceives and automatically adjusts elements such as colour and contrast.

It is noted that in each of the stages discussed above, there is space for the exercise of human skill, labour, and judgement in determining the final representation of the digital image. However, as noted before, in the exercise of such choice and judgement the human actor is constrained by the need to ensure that the final representation of the digital image corresponds as exactly as possible to the original rare document. For example, in carrying out the colour calibration process, the exercise of skill and judgement on the part of the human actor is limited by the functional requirement of choosing the colours that correspond as closely as possible to the original colours of the rare document. Hence, the human actor is not able to exercise his personal aesthetic choices or creative preferences in determining the final visual appearance of the digitised version. The same is true as regards the correction of the digitised text that has been created through text-scanning software, as the proofreader is required to ensure that the text correctly reproduces the text that is recorded upon the original document. It is interesting therefore to consider whether the exercise of human intervention within the functional and technical constraints that apply to the digitisation process, could prevent a digitised version from obtaining copyright protection within the EU law framework.

[25]"Even when digitisation equipment is assessed (. . .) it is still necessary to have knowledgeable and experienced staff to evaluate images visually. At this time, it is not possible to rely entirely on the objective test measurements to ensure optimum image quality. It is still necessary to have staff with the visual literacy and technical expertise to do a good job with digitisation and to perform quality control for digital images." Steven Puglia, Jeffrey Reed and Erin Rhodes, 'Technical Guidelines for Digitizing Archival Materials for Electronic Access: Creation of Production Master Files-Raster Images.' <www.archives.gov/files/preservation/technical/guidelines.pdf> accessed 31 January 2019.

[26]*See* comments made by Kimber Wiegand, Digitisation Specialist *in* National Endowment for the Humanities, US, *Digitizing Illuminated Manuscripts at the Walters Art Museum, Maryland* (video) <www.youtube.com/watch?v=umOc5nXmO_U> accessed 31 January 2019.

7.2 Can a Digitised Version Be Protected Under Copyright Law Within the EU Law Framework?

As the foregoing discussion illustrates, digitisation—whether it is carried out by means of a scanner or digital camera—is not something that can be achieved by the mere clicking of a button as is often argued to be the case in the creation of photocopies by means of a photocopier machine. This is especially true in the case of old, fragile, or otherwise damaged documents. Nevertheless, as reiterated above, regardless of the degree of human intervention that is involved, the human actor is necessarily constrained by the functional objective of creating an exact digital reproduction of an existing rare document, and is therefore not able to exercise his own personal choices as regards the visual appearance or textual content of the digitised version. Therefore, a digitised version falls into what may be referred to as the gray-zone of copyright protection, meaning that the copyright protection of a digitised version can only be determined following a comprehensive analysis of the criteria for copyright protection within EU law.

Unlike patent or trademark law, copyright law has not been the subject of full harmonisation within the EU law framework. Legislative harmonisation of copyright law has been piece-meal in the sense that it has been directed at specific subject-matter that have been considered as having particular significance for the smooth-functioning of the EU common market and intra-Community trade.[27] Thus, the 1991 Directive on computer programmes[28] (meanwhile consolidated by the 2009 Directive on the legal protection of computer programmes[29]) harmonised the copyright protection of computer programmes. The Term Directive of 1993[30] (codified by the Term Directive of 2006[31]) harmonised the copyright protection of original photographs and the Database Directive of 1996[32] granted a harmonised standard of

[27]Thomas Margoni, 'The Harmonisation of EU Copyright Law: The Originality Standard' in Mark Perry (ed), *Global Governance of Intellectual Property in the 21st Century* (Springer International Publishing 2016) 88–90. The need to harmonise intellectual property law to facilitate intra-Community trade is reflected in the 1985 White Paper of the European Commission, which states that, "[d]ifferences in intellectual property laws have a direct and negative impact on intra-Community trade and on the ability of enterprises to treat the common market as a single environment for their economic activities." Completing the Internal Market: White paper to the Commission from the European Council 1985, COM (85) 310 final 37 para 145.

[28]Council Directive 91/250 of 14 May 1991 on the Legal Protection of Computer Programmes [1991] OJ L122/42.

[29]Directive 2009/24/EC of The European Parliament and of the Council of 23 April 2009 on the legal protection of computer programmes [2009] OJ L 111/16 (Computer Programmes Directive).

[30]Council Directive 93/98/EEC of 29th October 1993 harmonizing the term of protection of copyright and related rights [1993] OJ L 290/9.

[31]Directive 2006/116/EC of the European Parliament and of the Council of 12 December 2006 on the term of protection of copyright and certain related rights [2006] OJ L372/12 (Term Directive).

[32]Article 3(1) of the Directive 96/9/EC of the European Parliament and of the Council of the European Union of 11 March 1996 on the legal protection of databases [1996] OJ L 77/20 (Database Directive).

copyright protection to original databases within the EU. Although the concept of originality which is the fundamental criterion that needs to be fulfilled by a subject-matter to obtain copyright protection, had not been the subject of legislative harmonisation, these three Directives set out a harmonised level of originality for the protection of the specific subject-matter they deal with. Thus, the Directives expound that computer programmes, photographs and databases are to be protected by copyright under EU law if they are original in the sense that they are their author's own intellectual creation[33] and emphasise that no other criteria shall be applied to determine their eligibility for copyright protection.

Therefore, under Article 6 of the Term Directive, the copyright protection of a digital image produced during scanning would be determined under the author's own intellectual creation standard and no other criteria could be applied to determine its eligibility for copyright protection. A digitised version could incorporate several other features apart from the photographic image. As noted earlier, it could include a digitised version of the text reproduced by the digital image, as well as value-added features such as 'zoom-in', 'page-turner', etc. However, the application of software features for 'zoom-in' and 'page-turner' is almost completely automated and does not require a high degree of human intervention. Nor do they allow space for the exercise of personal choice on the part of the human actor. Similarly, while text-digitisation (through software applications such as OCR) requires a greater level of human intervention, the task of the human actor is that of a proof-reader who mechanically makes changes and modifications to the digitised text so that it correctly represents the original textual content reproduced by the digital image. Thus, it is unlikely that the addition of value-added features or the digitisation of textual content would be relevant to the determination of the originality of a digitised version. Accordingly, the discussion is likely to focus upon the originality of the digital photographic reproduction of the rare document. Therefore, we proceed to consider the ability of a digital photographic reproduction to obtain copyright protection as an original work within the EU.

There is widespread opinion that, as a result of the interpretation of EU law by the Court of Justice of the European Union (CJEU), the author's own intellectual creation standard has now been established as the harmonised standard of originality within the EU copyright law framework. According to Margoni, the vertical harmonisation (i.e., harmonisation in respect of specific subject-matter through legislative intervention) of the author's own intellectual creation standard of originality has now been horizontally extended to all kinds of works covered by EU copyright law by the CJEU.[34] Although the uniform applicability of this standard of

---

[33] *See* Article 1(3) of Computer Programmes Directive (n 29); Article 6 of Term Directive (n 31); Article 3(1) of Database Directive ibid.

[34] Margoni (n 27) 91.

originality has not been unchallenged,[35] it appears that the majority opinion[36] accepts that the standard of originality in EU law has been harmonised through judicial intervention. As van Eechoud observes:

> Commentators are in broad agreement that the [CJEU] holds it a matter of European law that there is such a thing as a generalized work concept ('the author's own intellectual creation') (. . .) the conclusion seems inescapable: no freedom remains for Member States to condition which subject-matter warrants copyright protection.[37]

Indeed, national courts in the UK[38] and Germany[39] have applied the author's own intellectual creation standard in determining the copyright protection of subject-matter other than computer programmes, photographs, or databases. In the *Premier League*[40] decision, the CJEU applied the author's own intellectual creation in determining whether a football match could obtain copyright protection as an original work under the InfoSoc Directive. Hence, it is anticipated that even if a digitised version is not considered as a photograph within the meaning of Article 6 of the Term Directive, its copyright protectability would still be determined under the 'author's own intellectual creation' standard.

The CJEU's interpretation and elaboration of the author's own intellectual creation standard does not allow one to derive a clear understanding of the exact criteria that needs to be fulfilled by subject-matter to obtain copyright protection under the harmonised EU standard. For example, in the *Premier League*[41] decision, the CJEU indicates that the fulfilment of the author's own intellectual creation standard requires an effort on the part of the author that goes beyond 'mere skill

[35]For example, Rahmatian argues that the author's own intellectual creation standard can only apply to subject-matter that is protected by EU Directives and that the development of a rule that is of uniform application would exceed the proper role of the CJEU. Andreas Rahmatian, 'Originality in UK Copyright Law: The Old "Skill and Labour" Doctrine Under Pressure' (2013) 44 IIC 4. Silke von Lewinski, 'Introduction: The Notion of a Work under EU Law' (2014) 63 GRUR Int 1098.

[36]*See* Valérie-Laure Benabou, 'Jurisprudence Infopaq: Que Reste-T-Il Au Juge National Pour Dire Le Droit D'auteur' (2009) 37 Revue du Droit des Technologies de l'Information 71; Christian Handig, 'The Copyright Term "Work" – European Harmonisation at an Unknown Level' (2009) 40 IIC 665; Stef Van Gompel and Erlend Lavik, 'Quality, Merit Aesthetics and Purpose: An Inquiry into EU Copyright Law's Eschewal of Other Criteria than Originality' (2013) 236 RIDA 100; Estelle Derclaye, 'Assessing the Impact and Reception of the Court of Justice of the European Union Case Law on UK Copyright Law: What Does The Future Hold?' (2014) 240 RIDA 5.

[37]Mireille Van Eechoud, 'Along the Road to Uniformity – Diverse Readings of the Court of Justice Judgements on Copyright Work' (2012) 3 JIPITEC 60, 70.

[38]*The Newspaper Licensing Agency and others v Meltwater Holding BV and others* [2010] EWHC 3099 (Decision of the High Court of Justice Chancery Division); *Temple Island Collections Ltd v New English Teas Ltd* [2011] EWPCC 21 (Red Bus case).

[39]BGH 13.11.2013 – I ZR 143/12, GRUR 2014, 175 – *Geburtstagszug*.

[40]Judgement of 4 October 2011, *Football Association Premier League and Others*, C-403/08 and C-429/08, EU:C:2011:631 (Premier League case).

[41]ibid.

and labour'. In the *Football Dataco v Yahoo! UK*[42] decision, the CJEU requires an author to express his creative abilities in an original manner by making free and creative choices. Furthermore, under the *BSA*[43] decision, it is necessary that these choices were not dictated by functional requirements. Nevertheless, under the CJEU dicta in the *Painer*[44] decision, the rather banal choices made by a photographer in terms of light, background, angle, etc., in creating a realistic portrait photograph of a child would be sufficient to stamp the photograph with the author's personal touch to qualify for protection. Benabou observes that, the CJEU jurisprudence leaves open the possibility for judges of national courts, to draw from a range of different criteria set out in successive decisions in determining the originality of a particular subject-matter.[45] On that basis, she argues that the CJEU jurisprudence allows the judges of national courts a margin of discretion in the interpretation of the author's own intellectual creation standard which could result in the application of different standards of originality as opposed to a single harmonised standard.[46] In fact, the national courts of different Member States have interpreted the substantive requirements of this standard and its parameters in different ways. It is alleged that in doing so, they have been guided by the traditional standards of originality that exist in their individual copyright law frameworks.[47] Therefore, even if one accepts that the standard of originality in EU law has been harmonised, the diverse ways in which this standard has been interpreted and applied by the national courts of EU Member States, could result in different criteria being applied by these national courts in determining whether a digitised version could qualify for copyright protection. As Margoni succinctly notes, it will be a matter for the national courts to establish whether a specific work meets the 'author's own intellectual creation' definition and it is safe to assume that in applying this definition national courts will be guided—consciously or unconsciously—by their own traditional legal constructions that are deeply rooted in the minds of legal practitioners and interpreters.[48]

Therefore, in the interests of presenting a thorough legal prognosis as to whether a digitised version would be able to obtain copyright protection within the EU, the following discussion will first explore the establishment of the author's own intellectual creation standard as a harmonised standard of originality within the EU

---

[42]Judgement of 1 March 2012, *Football Dataco v Yahoo! UK*, C-604/10, EU:C:2012:115.

[43]Judgement of 22 December 2010, *Bezpečnostní softwarová asociace*, C-393/09, EU:C:2010:816 (BSA case).

[44]Judgement of 1 December 2011, *Painer*, C-145/10, EU:C:2011:798.

[45]Valérie-Laure Benabou, 'Originalité? Vous Avez Dit Originalités' (2014) 53 LEGICOM 5, 9–12.

[46]ibid.

[47]ibid 9. "[C]ette définition avait été en quelque sorte oubliée par les Etats membres qui continuait gaiement à appliquer leurs propres critères, présumant une sorte d'euro-compatibilité de leur originalité avec l'originalité communautaire. [T]his definition had been somewhat forgotten by the Member States who continued to apply their own criteria, presuming a sort of Euro-compatibility of their originality standard with the EU originality standard". (Translated into English by the author).

[48]Margoni (n 27) 101.

through CJEU interpretation. It will then examine the ability of a digitised version to obtain copyright protection under the author's own intellectual creation standard as it has been interpreted in relation to diverse subject-matter by the CJEU. Finally, it will analyse the possibility for a digitised version to obtain copyright protection under the traditional originality standards of the UK, Germany and France, and consider whether the introduction of the harmonised standard of originality would effect a change on the ability of a digitised version to obtain copyright protection in these jurisdictions.

7.3 The 'Author's Own Intellectual Creation' Standard as a Harmonised Standard of Originality

7.3.1 CJEU Case Law

In the *Infopaq* case,[49] the question before the CJEU was whether the storing and subsequent printing of an eleven-word text extract from a newspaper article could constitute a 'reproduction in part' under Article 2(a) of the InfoSoc Directive.[50] In reaching its determination, the CJEU observed that the InfoSoc Directive defined neither the concept of 'reproduction' nor that of 'reproduction in part'. In the circumstances, it was necessary to define these terms in the light of the overall objectives of the Directive and international law,[51] specifically the provisions of the Berne Convention,[52] which the EU was bound to follow because of the EU's adherence to the TRIPS Agreement.[53]

The CJEU noted that as Article 2(a) of the InfoSoc Directive upheld the exclusive right of authors to authorise or prohibit the reproduction—either in whole or in part—of their works, the author's right to reproduction under Article 2(a) was clearly intended to cover a 'work'. The CJEU opined that under the general scheme of the Berne Convention, the protection of subject-matter as literary or artistic works was

---

[49]Judgement of 16 July 2009, *Infopaq*, C-5/08, EU:C:2009:465, para 30.

[50]Directive 2001/29/EC of the European Parliament and of the Council of 22 May 2001 on the harmonisation of certain aspects of copyright and related rights in the information society [2001] OJ L167/10 (InfoSoc Directive).

[51](n 49) para 30. *See also* Stephen Vousden, 'Infopaq and the Europeanisation of Copyright Law' (2010) 1 The WIPO Journal 197 who argues that the critical analysis of the reasoning reveals that this reasoning does not rest on international copyright law or EU law but rather the German originality standard of personal intellectual creation.

[52]Berne Convention for the Protection of Literary and Artistic Works S. Treaty Doc. No. 99-27 (1986) 1161 UNTS 3.

[53]Agreement on Trade-Related Aspects of Intellectual Property Rights, Apr. 15, 1994, Marrakesh Agreement Establishing the World Trade Organization, Annex 1C, Legal Instruments – Results of the Uruguay Round vol 31; 33 ILM 81 (1994).

based upon the pre-supposition that these were 'intellectual works'.[54] Moreover, the CJEU remarked that under the EU *acquis* (specifically the Computer Programmes Directive, Term Directive, and the Database Directive) works are protected only if they are original in the sense that they are their author's own intellectual creation.[55] The CJEU reasoned that, as the InfoSoc Directive was based on the same principle of the need for a harmonised legal framework on copyright as these other Directives (as evidenced by recitals 4, 9–11 and 20 of the InfoSoc Directive), copyright protection within the meaning of Article 2(a) of the Directive can only apply in relation to subject-matter which is original in the sense that it is its author's own intellectual creation.[56]

The CJEU observed that, while words considered in isolation are not as such, an intellectual creation of the author who employs them, the author may express his creativity in an original manner through the choice, sequence, and combination of those words and thereby achieve a result which is an intellectual creation. Accordingly, the CJEU held that, the reproduction of an eleven-word extract from a newspaper article could constitute a 'reproduction in part' under Article 2(a) of the InfoSoc Directive if it contained, 'an element of the work which, as such, expresses the author's own intellectual creation'.[57] Thus, in the *Infopaq* case, the CJEU applied the author's own intellectual creation standard during the determination whether the author's right to reproduction under the InfoSoc Directive had been infringed by the reproduction of the eleven-word extract. It has been argued that, as a matter of strict precedent, it may be possible to regard the CJEU dicta in the *Infopaq* case as being limited in its application to matters of copyright infringement rather than of copyright subsistence.[58] However, in the subsequent determination delivered in the *BSA* case,[59] the CJEU applied the 'author's own intellectual creation' standard in determining the copyright protectability of a graphic user interface (GUI) under the InfoSoc Directive, which was an issue of copyright subsistence. Thereby the CJEU arguably interpreted the standard of an 'author's own intellectual creation' as

---

[54]Judgement of 16 July 2009, *Infopaq*, C-5/08, EU:C:2009:465, para 34.

[55]ibid, para 35.

[56]ibid, para 37, "[i]n those circumstances, copyright within the meaning of Article 2(a) of [of the InfoSoc Directive] is liable to apply only in relation to a subject-matter which is original in the sense that it is its author's own intellectual creation."

[57]ibid, para 48. The CJEU left it to the referring national court to determine whether the particular text extract which was reproduced contained elements which are the expression of the author's own intellectual creation to amount to an unauthorised reproduction in part, under Article 2(a) of the InfoSoc Directive.

[58]*See* Thomas Höppner, 'Reproduction in Part of Online Articles in the Aftermath of Infopaq (C-5/08): Newspaper Licensing Agency Ltd v. Meltwater Holdings BV' [2011] EIPR 331, 332.

[59]Judgement of 22 December 2010, *Bezpečnostní softwarová asociace,* C-393/09, EU:C:2010:816 (BSA case).

a general test for determining the copyright protection of subject-matter under EU law.[60]

The question before the CJEU was whether a GUI could be protected as a computer programme under the Computer Programmes Directive. The CJEU determined that the GUI did not constitute a form of expression of a computer programme within the meaning of Article 1(2) of the Computer Programmes Directive and therefore could not be protected under that Directive. Nevertheless, the CJEU referred to its determination in the *Infopaq* case and interpreted the dicta given in that case to mean that, 'copyright within the meaning of [the InfoSoc Directive] is liable to apply *only in relation to a subject-matter* which is original in the sense that it is its *author's own intellectual creation*'.[61] Accordingly, the CJEU held that, a GUI could be protected as a work under the InfoSoc Directive if it is its author's own intellectual creation.[62] The CJEU noted that, in carrying out this assessment of originality, the national court must consider *inter alia* the specific arrangement or configuration of all the components that form part of the GUI to determine which of these meet the criterion of originality. The CJEU emphasised that, the criterion of originality would not be met by components of the GUI which are differentiated only by their technical function.[63] Its determination was based on the reasoning that, where the expression of the components is dictated by their technical function the author would not be permitted to express his creativity in an original manner to achieve a result which is his own intellectual creation.[64] Accordingly, the CJEU observed that, in such a situation the criterion of originality will not be met, as the different methods of implementing an idea are so limited that the idea and expression become indissociable.[65] As observed by Griffiths, the decision in the *BSA* case demonstrates the beginning of the CJEU's attempt to flesh out the meaning of the author's own intellectual creation in EU law.[66]

[60]Jonathan Griffiths, 'Infopaq, BSA and the "Europeanisation" of United Kingdom Copyright Law' [2011] 16 Media & Arts Law Review, available at <https://papers.ssrn.com/sol3/papers2.cfm?abstract_id=1777027> accessed 31 January 2019.

[61]Judgement of 22 December 2010, Bezpečnostní softwarová asociace, C-393/09, EU:C:2010:816 (BSA case), para 45 (emphasis added). Griffiths notes that this appears to suggest that the question of whether a particular subject-matter is the author's own intellectual creation is the sole precondition for a particular subject-matter to be recognised as a copyright work and that if this its correct reading then it goes well beyond the dicta of the *Infopaq* case. ibid, 8.

[62]ibid, BSA case, para 46.

[63]ibid, para 48.

[64]ibid, para 50.

[65]ibid, para 49.

[66]Jonathan Griffiths, 'The Role of the Court of Justice in the Development of European Union Copyright Law' in Irini Stamatoudi and Paul Torremans (eds), *EU Copyright Law: A Commentary* (Edward Elgar 2014) 1103.

Further insight into the interpretation of the term 'intellectual creation' is provided by the CJEU's decision in the *Premier League*[67] case. The case involved *inter alia* the question as to whether football matches could be protected by copyright. The CJEU held that the Football Association Premier League could not claim copyright in the football matches themselves because they failed to qualify as 'works' under the InfoSoc Directive for the reason that they did not fulfil the criterion of originality under the author's own intellectual creation standard.[68] This determination was based on the observation that sporting events (and football matches in particular), by reason of being subject to the rules of the game leave, 'no room for creative freedom for the purposes of copyright'.[69] However, the CJEU failed to elaborate the exact nature and scope of the creative freedom that was required to render a subject-matter an intellectual creation that could be protected by copyright.

This interpretation was cited with approval and further elaborated by the CJEU in the determination given in the *Painer*[70] case. This case is of particular relevance to the present study as it involves a discussion as to the requirements which need to be fulfilled by a realistic photograph (in this case a portrait photograph) to obtain copyright protection under the author's own intellectual creation standard. The CJEU noted that, under Article 6 of the Term Directive,[71] the originality test for a photograph is whether it qualifies as its 'author's own intellectual creation'. Citing its determination in the *Premier League* case the CJEU held that, an intellectual creation will be its author's own if its reflects the personality of the author which would be the case if the author was able to express his creative abilities by making free and creative choices.[72] The CJEU noted that, as regards portrait photography, the photographer is able to make free and creative choices in several ways and at various points in the production. For example, in the preparation phase, he can choose the background, the subject's pose, and the lighting. When taking the photograph, he can choose the framing, the angle of view and the atmosphere created. Finally, when selecting the snapshot, he may adopt a development technique of his choice from amongst a variety of choices.[73] The CJEU held that, by making these various choices, the author of a portrait photograph can stamp the work created with his personal touch.[74] Interestingly, therefore, the CJEU elaborated upon the notion of the creative freedom of the author (applied in the *Premier League*

[67]Judgement of 4 October 2011, *Football Association Premier League*, C-403/08 and C-429/08, EU:C:2011:631.

[68]ibid, para 98, "[h]owever, sporting events cannot be regarded as intellectual creations classifiable as works within the meaning of the [InfoSoc] Directive. That applies in particular to football matches, which are subject to rules of the game, leaving no room for creative freedom for the purposes of copyright."

[69]ibid, paras 96–99.

[70]Judgement of 1 December 2011, *Painer*, C-145/10, EU:C:2011:798.

[71]Term Directive (n 31).

[72]Judgement of 1 December 2011, *Painer*, C-145/10, EU:C:2011:798, paras 88–89.

[73]ibid, paras 90–91.

[74]ibid, para 92.

determination) to develop the idea that in using the creative freedom afforded by the creation process, the creator can exercise his creative judgement in such a way as to stamp the work with his personal touch. Thus, the CJEU seems to suggest that the author's expression of his creative abilities by making free and creative choices would result in his personality being reflected in the intellectual creation.

The notion of the author's ability to make free and creative choices as the central criterion of the author's own intellectual creation standard was further developed in the succeeding determination delivered in the *Football Dataco v Yahoo! UK*[75] case. The case arose regarding the copyrightability of a football league fixture list as a database under Article 3 of the Database Directive.[76] It is recalled that Article 3(1) of the Database Directive grants copyright protection to databases that, by reason of the selection or arrangement of their contents, constitute the author's own intellectual creation. One of the questions before the CJEU was whether the notion of author's intellectual creation required more than significant labour and skill from the author and, if so, what that additional requirement was. The CJEU noted that under recital 16 of the Database Directive, the notion of the author's own intellectual creation referred to the criterion of originality.[77] The CJEU determined that, regarding the setting up of a database, that criterion of originality was satisfied when, through the selection or arrangement of the data it contains, its author expressed his creative ability in an original manner by making free and creative choices and thereby stamped the database with his personal touch.[78] By contrast, that criterion was not satisfied when the setting up of the database was dictated by technical considerations, rules, or constraints, which left no room for creative freedom. Accordingly, the CJEU determined that, where the selection and arrangement of the data incorporated within the database was an original expression of the author's creativity, the database would obtain copyright protection under Article 3. The CJEU further held that the originality criterion would not be satisfied by the mere expenditure of skill and labour on the part of its author if that labour and skill did not express any originality in the selection or arrangement of the data.[79] The CJEU emphasised that, the fact that the creation of the database involved the expenditure of significant skill and labour on the part of its author, 'cannot *as such* justify protection by copyright under Article 3 of the Database Directive'.[80] The primary significance of the CJEU's determination in the *Football Dataco v Yahoo! UK* case lies in its rejection of the English law 'sweat of the brow' standard as a criterion of originality in the context of EU copyright law. It re-emphasises the expression of the author's creative abilities through the making of free and creative choices as the core element of the author's

[75]Judgement of 1 March 2012, *Football Dataco*, C-604/10, EU:C:2012:115.

[76]Database Directive (n 32).

[77]Judgement of 1 March 2012, *Football Dataco*, C-604/10, EU:C:2012:115, para 37.

[78]ibid, para 38.

[79]ibid, para 39 citing Judgement of 1 December 2011, *Painer*, C-145/10, EU:C:2011:798 and Judgement of 4 October 2011, *Football Association Premier League and Others*, C-403/08 and C-429/08, EU:C:2011:631 (Premier League case).

[80]ibid, para 42 (emphasis added).

own intellectual creation standard and further elucidates that this element will not be present when the creation of the subject-matter is dictated by functional or technical considerations that leave no room for creative freedom.

The dicta of the CJEU on the author's own intellectual creation standard can be summarised as follows. The notion of the 'author's own intellectual creation' refers to the criterion of originality under EU copyright law (*Football Dataco*). The term 'intellectual creation' refers to the expression of an author's creative abilities in an original manner (*Infopaq*). An author expresses his creative abilities in an original manner by making free and creative choices (*Premier League, Painer, Football Dataco*). By doing so, an author is able to stamp the intellectual creation with his personal touch (*Painer, Football Dataco*) and consequently, the intellectual creation will reflect the author's personality thereby making it the 'author's own' (*Painer*). By contrast, where the subject-matter is dictated by its technical function (i.e., where the parameters of a task are constrained by the need to satisfy a particular technical function[81]), rules or constraints, an author will be left without the creative freedom that is required for him to express his creativity in an original manner to achieve a result which is an intellectual creation (*BSA, Premier League, Football Dataco*). Furthermore, contrary to the traditional 'skill and labour' standard of originality in the UK, the expenditure of skill and labour as such will not satisfy the criterion of author's own intellectual creation when that skill and labour does not express any originality (*Football Dataco*).

7.3.2 *Analysis of the CJEU Case Law and Its Application to Digitised Versions*

The author's own intellectual creation standard has been interpreted in various ways by legal scholars. Lucas and others interpret it as giving rise to an objective test of originality[82] and others as giving rise to a subjective test.[83] This difference in

[81]*See* Griffiths (n 60) 11.

[82]As per the objective notion of originality, a work will be original if it is the independent creation of its author in the sense it is not copied. Thus, under the interpretation of the author's own intellectual creation standard as an objective test, a work will be considered original if it originates from the author and is not copied. Lucas, Lucas-Schloetter and Bernault (n 5) 143, are of the view that the harmonised standard of originality reflects an objective approach. "Pour nous, la Cour a creusé le même sillon que la directive de 1991, et c'est bien une définition objective de l'originalité qui est retenue." ("For us, the [CJEU] has dug the same furrow as the computer programmes Directive, and it is very much an objective definition of originality that has been retained"). (Translated into English by the author). Lucas, et al. further argue that, the personal touch stamp test applied in the *Painer* case is in perfect harmony with the objective notion of originality as the CJEU considered it as being fulfilled if the author was able to express his creative capacities in the realisation of the work by making free and creative choices. ibid.

[83]As per the subjective notion of originality, a work will be original if it reflects its author's personality. Thus, under the interpretation of the author's own intellectual creation standard as a subjective test, a work will be considered original if the author's personality is reflected in the work.

interpretation is also perceptible in the interpretations delivered by the national courts of different jurisdictions.[84]

The requirement that the subject-matter must be stamped with the author's personal touch has been widely discussed. It has been questioned whether this requirement is only applicable to photographs (as the requirement was introduced by the CJEU in the context of the originality of a portrait photograph in the *Painer*[85] case) or if it is to be interpreted as being uniformly applicable to all works.[86]

Nevertheless it is argued here that, based on the elaboration provided by the CJEU, the central criterion of the author's own intellectual creation standard is that the subject-matter must express the creative abilities of the author ('intellectual creation') as a result of the author's utilisation of the freedom afforded to him by the creation process for making free and creative choices ('author's own').[87] Thus, the essence of the author's own intellectual creation standard lies in the expression of an author's creativity through the making of free and creative choices.[88] This

---

Hence, the ability of the author to exercise his personal creative choices and to thereby imprint his personality upon the work is of critical importance to the subjective test, as it is through the exercise of such personal creative choices that the author is able to imprint his personality on the work. Proponents of the subjective interpretation include Derclaye who opined that the decision of the CJEU in the *Infopaq* case shows that creativity is the criterion of originality. Estelle Derclaye, 'Wonderful or Worrisome? The Impact of the ECJ Ruling in Infopaq on UK Copyright Law' [2010] EIPR 247, 248; Michaux who notes that the CJEU's application of the author's own intellectual creation standard in the Infopaq case inclines it towards a subjective notion than an objective notion. Benoît Michaux, 'L'originalité en droit d'auteur, une notion davantage communautaire après l'arrêt *Infopaq*' (2009) 5 Auteurs & Media 473; Pollaud-Dulian who opined that in the *Painer* decision, the CJEU elaborated the author's own intellectual creation standard in a way that is closer to the civil law subjective notion. Pollaud-Dulian (n 53) 158–159.

[84]For example, while courts in the UK tend to interpret it as an objective test (*see The Newspaper Licensing Agency v Meltwater* [2010] EWHC 3099, n 38). Courts in France (*see TGI Paris, 3eme Ch 1, 21 mai 2015 [Jimmy Hendrix case]*, n 359) and *Cour de Cassation Ch civ, 15 mai 2015, 13-27391 [Glamour case]*, n 360) and in Belgium have interpreted it as a subjective test (*see* Belgium Supreme Court decision in *M-Design Benelux SPRL [2013] SC C120263 N/1*, which overturned the previous Supreme Court decision in *Artessuto v B&T Textilia [2012] SC C1101018N* to hold that a work would be original if it is the intellectual creation of the author that bears his personal stamp).

[85]Judgement of 1 December 2011, *Painer*, C-145/10, EU:C:2011:798.

[86]Derclaye opined that the 'personal touch stamp' requirement is uniformly applicable to all works and not only to photographs. Derclaye (n 36) 10.

[87]It is observed that this formulation is under the sub-standards of 'intellectual labour' and 'freedom of choice', which Waisman argue are used to facilitate the practical application of 'intellectual originality standards', i.e., the creativity standard and the personality standard. Thus, it is possible to argue that the author's own intellectual creation standard is more on the side of the line of an intellectual originality standard than a sweat of the brow or skill and labour standard. Agustin Waisman, 'Revisiting Originality' (2009) 31 EIPR 370, 370–374.

[88]*Cf.* The interpretation of an intellectual creation given by the CJEU in the SAS case, "It is only through the choice, sequence and combination of those words, figures or mathematical concepts that the author may express his creativity in an original manner and achieve a result, namely the user manual for the computer programme, which is an intellectual creation (see, to that effect, Infopaq International, paragraph 45)." Judgement of 2 May 2012, *SAS Institute,* C-406/10, EU:C:2012:259.

argument is supported by Vivant and Bruguière who state that, the notion of choice is the key reflection of the creative freedom afforded by the creation process.[89] Although, the CJEU does not provide any elaboration of the exact parameters of the concept of creativity that is deemed to be so crucial in establishing the originality of a work, the *Infopaq*[90] case indicates that, the creativity expressed in the work is not required to be of a high standard and that the creativity that is expressed in determining the choice, sequence or combination of eleven words in a newspaper article would be sufficient for achieving copyright protection. Furthermore, the *Painer* decision demonstrates that even a realistic portrait photograph would be able to fulfil the originality requirement based on the choices made during the entire creation process; including the choice of the background during the preparatory stage and the choice of developing techniques during the stage at which the photograph is processed and printed. Therefore, in the case of a digitised version it would be possible to consider all choices made by the human actor during the pre-production, production, and post-production phases, in determining the originality of the digitised version. The choice of light and exposure settings at the point of capturing the raw image, the choices made in processing that image (e.g., adjustment of tone and colour, cleaning, and repairing) and the choices made in carrying out colour calibration during the quality control stage would all be relevant to this determination.

The issue however remains whether, in making these various choices, the creator of the digitised version is afforded sufficient freedom to express his creative abilities to qualify the digitised version as his own intellectual creation. The *BSA* decision holds that, the requisite freedom for expressing that creativity will not exist when the creation process is dictated by the technical function of the subject-matter or constrained by rules, as any choices made by the author would be determined by the functional requirements or pre-established rules (*Premier League, Football Dataco*). As reiterated above, it is argued here that, the overarching functional objective of the digitisation process (i.e., to produce a faithful and exact reproduction of an existing rare document) which dictates the entire digitisation process, precludes the human actor from making personal creative choices. In fact, the making of such personal creative choices by individual creators would be prejudicial in maintaining the accuracy of the digital reproduction of the original rare document. The choices made by human actors in the creation of a digitised version would be guided by the features and appearance of the existing rare document as opposed to their own creative or aesthetic sensibilities. Thus, it is argued here that, the resulting digitised version would not qualify as an 'intellectual creation' as it would not constitute an expression of its producer's creative abilities and therefore would not be stamped with its creator's personal touch (*Premier League, Painer, Football Dataco*). The rather considerable amount of labour and skill that is expended by a creator would

[89]Michel Vivant and Jean-Michel Bruguière, *Le Droit d'auteur et Droits Voisins* (3rd Edition, Dalloz 2016) 249.

[90]Judgement of 16 July 2009, *Infopaq International*, C-5/08, EU:C:2009:465.

not be considered a relevant factor in qualifying a digitised version for copyright protection (*Football Dataco*).

Therefore, it appears that, under the interpretation of the author's own intellectual creation standard in CJEU jurisprudence, a digitised version would not qualify for copyright protection either as a photograph under Article 6 of the Term Directive or under EU copyright law in general. However, as noted above, national courts of EU Member States have also contributed their own interpretations of the harmonised originality standard. Therefore, in the following discussion we consider the copyrightability of a digitised version under the traditional legal frameworks (i.e., the originality standard that was applied in these jurisdictions before the introduction of the harmonised EU standard) of the UK, Germany and France, as well as following the introduction of the harmonised standard of originality.

7.4 Protection Within the Legal Frameworks of the UK, Germany, and France

7.4.1 UK

7.4.1.1 The Traditional Copyright Law Framework

Under the traditional copyright law framework of the UK, for a work to come under copyright protection, it needs to fulfil two main requirements.[91]

Closed-List of 'Works' Firstly, under section 1 of the Copyright Designs and Patents Act (CDPA),[92] for a work to qualify for copyright protection, it needs to come within one of the 'closed-list' of categories of works that are stipulated by the Act. Any subject-matter that fails to come under any one of these categories would be excluded from copyright protection. It is argued here that, a digitised version of a rare document would come within the category of an artistic work under section 4(1) (a) for being a photographic work. A photographic work is defined under section 4 (2)(b) as, 'a recording of light or other radiation on any medium on which an image is produced or from which an image may by any means be produced'.[93] It is

[91]Bently and Sherman, indicate four characteristics that are required to be fulfilled by a literary, dramatic, or artistic work, to come within copyright protection. These are (1) that the work is recorded in material form; (2) its originality; (3) that the work is sufficiently connected to the UK to qualify for protection under UK law and (4) that the work is not excluded from protection under public policy grounds. However, as (1), (3) and (4) are not relevant to our discussion, we shall not consider those. Lionel Bently and Brad Sherman, *Intellectual Property Law* (4th Edition, Oxford University Press 2014) 91.

[92]Copyright, Designs and Patents Act 1988 (UK).

[93]ibid, CDPA s 4(2), "photograph means a recording of light or other radiation on any medium on which an image is produced or from which an image may be any means be produced and which is not part of a film".

observed that this definition is broad enough to encompass a digital reproduction of a rare document that is created using scanning technology.

Originality: 'Sweat of the Brow' Standard The second requirement under section 1(1) of the CDPA is that the digitised version satisfies the requisite standard of originality as an artistic work. The standard of originality in UK law is not statutorily defined. It is a concept that has evolved through case-law over a long period of time. Its exact nature or scope remains unclear; primarily because of the inconsistent standards that have been applied by UK Courts in testing the originality of subject-matter. Bently and Sherman note that, as a result, it is very difficult to explain the traditional British approach to originality in terms of any overarching principles.[94] However, they observe that the originality standard in UK copyright law tends to be explained in relation to two characterisations. Firstly, that a work originates with the author in the sense that it is not copied and secondly, that the author has exercised the requisite skill, labour or judgement in producing the work.[95] Copinger and Skone James view these two characterisations of originality as two interconnecting strands suggesting that both must be considered in determining the originality of an artistic work such as a digitised version.[96]

In the *University of London Press* case,[97] Petersen J exemplified the first characterisation of originality by stating that:

> The originality which is required relates to the expression of the thought. The Act does not require that the expression must be in original or novel form, but that the work must not be copied from another work – *that it should originate from the author.*[98]

This principle was reiterated by Atkinson J in the case of *Macmillan and Company Ltd. v K and J Cooper*[99] when he observed that, a product would qualify as the claimant's own original work, although it may be neither novel nor ingenious in that it is originated by him, emanates from him, and is not copied.[100]

---

[94]Bently and Sherman (n 91) 96–97.

[95]ibid.

[96]Kevin Garnett, Gillian Davies and Gwilym Harbottle, *Copinger and Skone James on Copyright* (15th ed, Sweet & Maxwell 2005) 119 citing *Ultra Marketing (UK) Ltd v Universal Components Ltd* [2004] EWHC 468 (Ch), para 51, where the question of originality was broken down to consist of these two characterisations.

> The question is whether his drawing was an original drawing. In the sense that the drawing originated with him, and that he did not copy it from a pre-existing source, it was, in my judgement, original. It is also the product of skill and labour, so that in principle it is entitled to copyright protection as an artistic work.

[97]*University of London Press v University Tutorial Press* [1916] 2 Ch 601. (University of London Press case).

[98]ibid 608–609 (emphasis added).

[99]*Macmillan And Company Ltd v K and J Cooper* (1924) 26 BOMLR 292.

[100]ibid para 19, citing *Frederick Emerson v. Chas. Davies* (1843) 3 Story Under Section Rep. 708.

Therefore, notwithstanding the fact that a digitised version is a digital photographic image that reproduces or depicts an existing rare document in digital form, it would satisfy this strand of the originality test if it can be shown that the digital photographic image was created by a particular person and therefore emanates from him.

The second characterisation of originality as arising from the author's expenditure of skill, labour or judgement in the creation of the work (generally referred to as the 'skill and labour' standard) is not capable of being precisely defined. Courts tend to be inconsistent in the application of this standard sometimes using it disjunctively; as 'labour, skill, or judgement' and sometimes cumulatively as 'labour, skill, and judgement'.[101] Derclaye notes that, in recent years the cumulative construction appears to have gained favour.[102] Furthermore, the exact nature and degree of the labour, skill, and/or judgement that needs to be invested in the creation of a work to qualify for copyright protection is unclear.[103] In the decision delivered by the Supreme Court of Canada—a jurisdiction that follows the Anglo-American copyright tradition—in *The Law Society of Upper Canada v CCH Canadian Ltd*[104] case, the element of skill was defined to refer to the use of one's knowledge, developed aptitude or practiced ability in producing a work.[105] The element of judgement was defined as the use of one's capacity for discernment or ability to form an opinion or evaluation by comparing different possible options in producing the work.[106] The Supreme Court of Canada noted that, the exercise of skill and judgement will necessarily involve intellectual effort and while creativity is not required to make a work original, the skill and judgement that is required to produce an original work must not be so trivial that it could be characterised as a purely mechanical exercise.[107] Craig argues that, considering the application of the cumulative construction of the standard (i.e., skill, labour, *and* judgement) by UK courts, it is not possible to reduce the threshold of originality in UK law to a mere sweat of the brow standard or pure industriousness test.[108] In the words of Davison, the UK position would be best described as coupling sweat of the brow with a small amount of skill and/or judgement.[109]

---

[101]Bently and Sherman (n 91) 97.

[102]Derclaye (n 36) 3.

[103]Copinger and Skone James note that it is almost impossible to state in any precise terms the amount of labour, skill and/or judgement that the author of a work must bestow on his creation for the work to acquire copyright. Copinger and Skone James (n 96) 119.

[104]*The Law Society of Upper Canada v CCH Canadian Ltd* [2004] SCC 13.

[105]ibid para 16.

[106]ibid.

[107]ibid.

[108]Carys J Craig, *Copyright, Communication and Culture: Towards a Relational Theory of Copyright Law* (Edward Elgar Publishing 2011) 125–126.

[109]Mark J. Davison, The legal protection of databases (Cambridge University Press, 2003) 144.

It is generally accepted that the precise amount of skill, labour, and/or judgement that the author of a work must bestow upon his/her composition to acquire copyright in it, would largely depend on the particular facts of each individual case, and is very much a question of degree.[110] The inexactitude of the skill and labour standard and the inconsistent manner in which it has been defined and applied by UK Courts means that, the dividing line between original (and therefore protected) works and unoriginal (and therefore unprotected) works in UK law remains an uncertain and shifting one.[111]

In the case of *Walter v Lane*[112] a verbatim transcription of a public speech by a newspaper reporter was judged to satisfy the requisite standard of originality because of the skill and labour expended by the reporter in recording the public speech, and on the basis that the written report originated from the reporter in the sense that it was not copied.[113] Lord James held that a mere copyist of written matter or a person to whom words are dictated to write down would not be considered an author, but observed that the reporter's art in recording a live public speech was different from a process of mere transcription or writing from dictation.[114] The decision in *Walter v Lane* is also significant for the exposition of the British concept of originality as a mechanism that safeguards skill, labour, and capital invested by an author in the creation of a work and prevents another person from appropriating and profiting from that investment without the author's permission.[115] This view is echoed by Cornish and Llewelyn who observe that, this rather low threshold of originality can be explained as, on the one hand, reducing to a minimum the element of subjective judgement in deciding what qualifies for copyright protection and on the other hand,

---

[110]Macmillan and Company Ltd v K and J Cooper (1924) 26 BOMLR 292, para 36 per Atkinson J.

[111]*See* Sam Ricketson, 'The Concept of Originality in Anglo-Australian Copyright Law' (1991) 39 Journal, Copyright Society of the USA 265, 280.

[112]*Walter and Another v Lane* [1900] AC 539.

[113]*Contra* see Lord Halsbury, ibid 548,

> My Lords, if I have not insisted upon the skill and accuracy of those who produce in writing or print spoken words, it is not because I think the less of those qualities, but because, as I have endeavoured to point out, neither the one nor the other are conditions precedent to the right created by the statute. That right, in my view, is given by the statute to the first producer of a book, whether that book be wise or foolish, accurate or inaccurate, of literary merit or of no merit whatever.

[114]ibid 553 per Lord James of Hereford.

[115]ibid 545, per Lord Halsbury:

> I should very much regret it if I were compelled to come to the conclusion that the state of the law permitted one man to make profit and to appropriate to himself the labour, skill, and capital of another. And it is not denied that in this case the defendant seeks to appropriate to himself what has been produced by the skill, labour, and capital of others. In the view I take of this case I think the law is strong enough to restrain what to my mind would be a grievous injustice. The law which I think restrains it is to be found in the Copyright Act (...).

See also ibid 552 per Lord Davey, "it is a sound principle that a man shall not avail himself of another's skill, labour, and expense by copying the written product thereof".

allowing for the protection of the investment of labour and capital that results in the production of a literary result.[116]

The case of *Ladbroke v William Hill*[117] concerned the copyrightability of the design and layout of betting coupons (specifically football pools coupons). In this case, it was held that, the skill, labour and judgement displayed in the way the information conveyed by the coupons was expressed and presented to the eye of the customer qualified these coupons for copyright protection. Thus, it appears that, notwithstanding the minimal amount of creativity or intellect that had gone into its creation even something as commonplace as a football coupon could be protected as an original work under the skill, labour and/or judgement standard.

7.4.1.1.1 Originality of a Reproductive Work[118]

The term reproductive work is used here to denote subject-matter that reproduce existing works either in whole or in part. In more simple terms, it refers to subject-matter that copy existing works. In comparison with non-reproductive works, case law demonstrates a tendency to carry out a more rigorous inquiry into the existence of labour and skill in determining the originality of a reproductive work. A close examination of the case-law also suggests that judges often (either implicitly or explicitly) require the exercise of intellect on the part of the creator in determining the originality of a reproductive work. The difference in the approach taken by judges in establishing the originality of reproductive and non-reproductive works can be attributed to the need to prevent subject-matter that merely produce slavish or mechanical reproductions of existing materials from obtaining copyright protection.

The judgement delivered by the Privy Council in the case of *Macmillan and Company Ltd. v K. and J. Cooper*[119] involved the copyrightability of a textbook that extracted and reproduced passages taken from another book (namely, 'Plutarch's Life of Alexander, translated by Sir Thomas North') which was in the public domain.

---

[116]William Cornish and David Llewelyn, *Intellectual Property: Patents, Copyright, Trade Marks and Allied Rights* (6th Edition, Sweet & Maxwell 2007) 422. Drassinower opined that Lord Halsbury's affirmation of the normative significance of the sweat of the author's brow generates a vision of copyright law as a remedy for the misappropriation of labour. Abraham Drassinower, 'Sweat of the Brow, Creativity, and Authorship: On Originality in Canadian Copyright Law' (2003) 1 University of Ottawa Law & Technology Journal 105.

[117]*Ladbroke (Football) Ltd v William Hill (Football) Ltd* [1964] 1 WLR 273.

[118]We avoid the use of the term 'derivative work' to identify works that reproduce existing works, because especially in the US, there has been doubt expressed as to whether a digitised version can be identified as a derivative work, or whether it is an independent work that depicts an existing work [*see SHL Imaging Inc v Artisan House Inc [2000] 117 F Supp 2d 301 (SDNY).*]. This discussion is beyond the scope of this analysis. Therefore, to maintain neutrality, the term 'derivative work' is not used. For further discussion *see also* William Patry, 'Photographs and Derivative Works' <http://williampatry.blogspot.com/2008/02/photographs-and-derivative-works.html> accessed 31 January 2019.

[119]*Macmillan and Company Ltd v K and J Cooper* (1924) 26 BOMLR 292.

The textbook reproduced detached passages from the public domain work sometimes introducing words so that the text could as far as possible represent an unbroken narrative. Atkinson J citing the earlier case of *Fredrick Emerson v Chas. Davies*[120] stated that a new and original plan, arrangement or combination of materials will entitle its author to copyright, whether the material themselves are old or new. However, he noted that, to secure copyright for such a product, the labour, skill, and capital expended should be sufficient to impart to the product some quality or character which the raw material did not possess, and which differentiates the product from the raw material. Thus, Atkinson J emphasised the distinction between the pre-existing product and the new work that comes into being as a result of the author applying his skill, labour and capital to that pre-existing product. In his opinion, the new work would be the subject of copyright protection as it would be the claimant's original work in that it is originated by him, emanates from him, and is not copied. Atkinson J observed that the selection and combination of passages from an existing work of authorship and reprinting them for use by students may require labour, scientific knowledge, literary skill, and sound judgement, which would qualify the reprinted selection of passages for copyright protection. However, in this case the Privy Council denied copyright protection for the reprinted text because there was no evidence that sufficient labour, skill, or judgement had been expended in reprinting passages from the public domain work.

The 1944 case of *GA Cramp Sons Ltd v Frank Smythson Ltd*[121] involved the question whether a compilation of seven tables containing factual information (such as a calendar, inland postal rates, tables of weights and measures, etc.) included in a pocket diary could be protected by copyright, based upon the knowledge, skill and labour expended by the publishers of the diary in the selection of the tables. The House of Lords held that it could not. As stated by Viscount Simon LC:

> One of the essential qualities of such tables is that they should be accurate, so there is no question of variation in what is stated (...) and the utmost that a table can do on such a subject is to state the result accurately. *There is so far no room for taste or judgement.* There remains I agree, the element of choice as to what information should be given (...) but the bundle of information furnished in the respondent's diary is commonplace information, commonly found prefixed to diaries. *There was no feature of them which could be pointed out as novel or specially meritorious or ingenious from the point of view of the judgement of the compiler.*[122]

Lord Macmillan added that the collection is of an obvious and commonplace character and observed that the inclusion or exclusion of one or more of the tables constituting the ordinary stock material of the diary-compiler seemed to involve a minimum of labour and judgement.[123]

---

[120] *Fredrick Emerson v Chas Davies* [1843] 3 Story Under Section Rep 708.

[121] *GA Cramp Sons Ltd v Frank Smythson Ltd* [1944] AC 329.

[122] ibid 335–336 (emphasis added). It is to be noted that this decision pre-dates the 1996 EU Database Directive (n 32).

[123] ibid 338.

The need for the expenditure of independent skill, labour, and judgement on the part of the creator is further emphasised in several decisions that deny copyright protection for works that were considered slavish copies of pre-existing works. Laddie, et al. note that, in general, a work which is a slavish copy of an earlier written work will not enjoy copyright but observe that a work which is an independent re-creation produced with the expenditure of sufficient skill, useful labour, knowledge, taste or judgement will qualify for copyright protection.[124]

The case of *Sawkins v Hyperion Records Ltd*[125] concerned restored editions of musical scores in the public domain that had been prepared by Sawkins, with corrections and additions and modern musical notation, in a way that made them capable of being performed by present-day musicians. The question before the Court of Appeal was whether the restored editions could qualify as original musical works to obtain copyright protection.

It was generally accepted that, in creating the restored editions Sawkins' objective was as far as possible, to reproduce faithfully the pre-existing musical scores in the form of an accurate edition that would be close to the intentions of its original composer. The Court of Appeal also observed that Sawkins' work in general did not involve a re-composition of the musical scores in the public domain or making an arrangement of it in the copyright sense. Nevertheless, the Court of Appeal stated that, while mere servile copying such as tracing or photocopying would not give rise to copyright protection, copying that involved adequate skill and labour would obtain copyright protection. As Jacob LJ noted, "the true position is that one has to consider the extent to which the 'copyist' is a mere copyist—merely performing an easy mechanical function. The more that is, the less is his contribution likely to be taken as original."[126] Thus, in the opinion of the Court of Appeal the actual test of originality in the context of a reproductive work involved a question as to the degree of skill and labour that is required to make the reproductive work an original work as opposed to a mere servile copy. Accordingly, the Court of Appeal held:

> This was not a case of servile copying. It had the practical value (unchallenged) of making the work playable. [The author] *re-created* [the pre-existing] *work using a considerable amount of personal judgement.* [The author's] *re-creative work was such as to create something really new using his own original (not merely copied) work.*[127]

The Court of Appeal also cited the view expressed by the trial judge that, "the process of editing undertaken by [the author] combines the scholarship and knowledge derived from a long and detailed study of the composer's music with a certain amount of *artistic inventiveness*".[128]

---

[124]Hugh Laddie, Peter Prescott and Mary Vitoria, *The Modern Law of Copyright and Designs* (LexisNexis, 4th Ed, 2011) 87.

[125]*Sawkins v Hyperion* [2005] 1 WLR 3281.

[126]ibid para 83 per Jacob LJ.

[127]ibid para 86 (emphasis added).

[128]ibid para 23 per Mummery LJ (emphasis added).

The Court of Appeal therefore made a clear distinction between mere servile copying by performing a mechanical function and the creation of a new work through the exercise of personal judgement. It appears that the Court of Appeal determination was influenced by the fact that, Sawkins' editorial intervention involved the contribution of expertise and artistic inventiveness in making music that could not be performed, capable of performance. As the Court of Appeal pointed out, it was accepted that none of the original music could have been performed using only the existing musical scores that were in the public domain. As observed by Bently and Sherman, what seemed to be pertinent here was that the labour and skill exerted by Sawkins affected the manner in which the totality of sound was produced by musicians.[129] Hence, the contribution made by Sawkins had a transformative effect on the pre-existing work by allowing it to be experienced aurally as opposed to being experienced as a textual work of written music.

An objection to a finding of copyright in the performing edition was raised by Hyperion because this would hamper the public interest in the availability of ancient music. Hyperion cited the *Interlego*[130] case in arguing that, granting copyright protection to editorial work of the kind that was carried out by Sawkins would expand the proper limits of intellectual property protection by extending the life of the copyright and even creating a perpetual monopoly. However, this argument was rejected by the Court of Appeal that justified its decision based on the public policy interest in encouraging the re-creation of near lost works. The Court of Appeal further emphasised that the granting of copyright over re-creations of existing works did not have the effect of creating a monopoly over those works. The copyright granted over the restored version merely had the effect that a person who wished to use that particular version would require the permission of Sawkins. In effect, there would be no revival of copyright over the pre-existing work, but solely over the particular restored version created by Sawkins.

Torremans cites this view with approval and discusses the public policy implications of granting copyright protection to restorations of works in the public domain.[131] In his view, copyright in a restored or reconstituted version of an out-of-copyright (public domain) work will only protect the expression of the restored or reconstituted version. Everyone remains free to use the public domain material itself. Torremans observes that while it has been argued that granting copyright in a restored version of a public domain work would hinder access to the public domain work itself, the case of *Sawkins v Hyperion* offers a unique opportunity to dispel that myth, and that:

---

[129]Lionel Bently and Brad Sherman, *Intellectual Property Law* (3rd edn, Oxford University Press 2009) 103.

[130]*Interlego v Tyco* [1989] AC 217.

[131]Paul Torremans, 'Legal Issues Pertaining to the Restoration and Reconstitution of Manuscripts, Sheet Music, Paintings and Films for Marketing Purposes', *Copyright Law: A Handbook of Contemporary Research* (Edward Elgar Publishing 2009) 31.

> [g]ranting [Sawkins] copyright in the performing editions will not [prevent] anyone from copying [the public domain] music or from making their own performing editions. *All they cannot do is to use the short cut offered by the existence of the Sawkins performing editions by copying these without his consent.* The latter point is the most basic expression of the public policy of copyright i.e. to prevent the unauthorised copying of certain *material forms of expression.*[132]

Accordingly, for a restored or reconstituted version of a public domain work to obtain copyright protection, it must incorporate the original expression of its creator. The original expression forms the substance of copyright protection.

It is interesting to compare the decision in *Sawkins v Hyperion* and the decision delivered by the Supreme Court of Israel[133] in the case of *Eisenmann v. Qimron,*[134] which involved a similar factual scenario. The *Eisenmann* case involved the reconstitution of the famous Dead Sea scrolls. When the scrolls were discovered they were in fragments and the task of reconstituting these fragments and deciphering them was mainly carried out by Qimron who not only physically matched and put the fragments together but also used his extensive linguistic expertise to decipher the text and to reconstruct missing parts of the text. The case before the Supreme Court involved the question as to whether Qimron could claim copyright in his version of the deciphered text. The Supreme Court held that:

> [e]xamining the work, with its various phases, as one whole work, reveals undoubtedly originality and creativity. Qimron's work was not technical, 'mechanical', like simple labour which result is pre-known.[135]

Analysing the possible outcome of the *Eisenmann* case under English law, MacQueen[136] notes that, within the British copyright tradition, skill and labour in producing an independent form of expression would be sufficient to attract copyright protection, at any rate if it is skill and labour of the right kind.[137] This is contrasted with the 'spark of creativity' that is required in US copyright law following the *Feist*[138] decision.[139] MacQueen opines that the editorial activity that is required to

---

[132]ibid.

[133]This case was decided under Israeli Copyright law that at the time was based on the British Copyright Act of 1911. According to Hilty and Nerisson, "Although, throughout the years certain amendments were made to the Israeli Copyright Act (. . .) most of this legislation remained identical to the British Copyright Act, 1911." Reto M Hilty and Sylvie Nerisson, *Balancing Copyright – A Survey of National Approaches* (Springer 2012) 533.

[134]*Eisenmann v Qimron, 54[3] PD 817.* Unofficial English translation by David Birnhack available at <www.tau.ac.il/law/members/birnhack/DSStransaltion.pdf> accessed 31 January 2019.

[135]ibid para 14.

[136]Hector Lewis MacQueen, 'Copyright Law and the Dead Sea Scrolls: A British Perspective' (Social Science Research Network 2014) SSRN Scholarly Paper ID 2430794 <https://papers.ssrn.com/abstract=2430794> accessed 31 January 2019.

[137]Ibid 1, citing *Interlego v Tyco* [1989] AC 217.

[138]*Feist Publications Inc v Rural Telephone Service Co* [1991] 499 US 340.

[139]MacQueen (n 136) 1, referring to Carson's argument that the reconstituted version of the Dead Sea Scrolls would fall outside the scope of copyright protection under US law as it would lack the

produce scholarly editions of such intractable and difficult material as the Dead Sea scrolls would evidently involve appropriate skill and labour of the kind meriting copyright protection.[140] Citing the *Interlego*[141] case, MacQueen observes that the mere expenditure of skill and labour is not enough to create a copyright and that the skill and labour must be of a relevant kind. MacQueen argues that, the literary skill and labour expended by an editor of an ancient or medieval manuscript—even when it survives in its entirety—is neither a slavish imitation of another's work nor a purely mechanical process and the end result cannot be taken as a merely unoriginal reproduction of what the original author wrote.[142]

The decision delivered by the Privy Council in the *Interlego* case further elaborates this viewpoint. The case which originated in Hong Kong, involved the question whether revised engineering drawings of toy building-bricks that made minor alterations (of technical significance) to earlier drawings over which intellectual property protection (design protection) had already lapsed could be considered significantly different in their visual image to merit copyright protection.

It was contended on behalf of Interlego that the technical skill of the draftswoman, the time taken by her in the production of these drawings and the inclusion of additional design information of technical importance, had invested these drawings with sufficient originality to qualify them for copyright protection. This argument was accepted by the Court of Appeal of Hong Kong. As stated by Clough J.A., "the degree of skill, labour, and judgement was, in my judgement, not only more than negligible but substantial".[143] He went on to state that, in view of the expertise, skill and experience that had gone into the drawings with the objective of improving the functional capacity of the toy building-bricks, the revised drawings did not represent an act of slavish copying.[144] The Privy Council disagreed with this view and overturned the determination of the Court of Appeal Hong Kong. In its decision, the Privy Council articulated two important points.

Firstly, it held that, on a work that is a reproduction of an existing work, skill, labour and judgement merely in the process of copying could not confer originality. Lord Oliver noted that there is no statutory definition of the word originality, but observed that, the definition given in the *University of London Press* judgement was not altogether complete because it did not sufficiently describe the originality of works that make use of material obtained by the author from pre-existing sources.[145] Thus, Lord Oliver indicated the possibility of a different standard of originality for

---

requisite 'spark of creativity' required for a work to qualify for copyright protection following the *Feist* decision. Cindy Alberts Carson, 'Raiders of the Lost Scrolls: The Right of Scholarly Access to the Content of Historic Documents' (1995) 16 Mich. J. Int'l L. 298, 325–326.

[140]MacQueen (n 136) 4–12.

[141]*Interlego v Tyco* [1989] AC 217.

[142]MacQueen (n 136) 5.

[143]*Interlego v Tyco* [1989] AC 217, 259.

[144]ibid.

[145]ibid 260.

works that are copies of existing works from that voiced in the *University of London Press* judgement. He distinguished the decision delivered by the House of Lords in the case of *LB (Plastics) Ltd. v Swish Products Limited*[146] where it was held that a drawing of a three-dimensional prototype, not itself produced from the drawing and not being a work of artistic craftsmanship, would qualify as an original work. Lord Oliver stated as follows:

> It by no means follows, however that, that *which is an exact and literal reproduction in two dimensional form of an existing two dimensional work* becomes an original work simply because the process of copying it involves the application of skill and labour. There must in addition be some element of *material alteration or embellishment* that suffices to make the totality of the work an original work. Of course, even a relatively small alteration or addition quantitatively may, if material, suffice to convert that which is substantially copied from an earlier work into an original work. Whether it does so or not is a question of degree having regard to the *quality rather than the quantity of the addition. But copying per se, however much skill or labour may be devoted to the process, cannot make an original work.*[147]

To support his argument Lord Oliver gave the example of a reproduction of a painting or an enlarged photograph of a positive print of a photograph. Lord Oliver noted that although it takes great skill, judgement, and labour to produce a good reproduction of a painting or to produce an enlarged photograph from a positive print, no one would reasonably contend that the copy painting or enlargement was an original artistic work in which the copier is entitled to claim copyright. It appears therefore that, on reproductive works, the Privy Council in the *Interlego* case applied a higher standard of originality than that which is required in the case of works that do not reproduce pre-existing works (non-reproductive works). While in the case of non-reproductive works the traditional skill and labour standard of originality applies, following the dictum in the *Interlego* case, it appears that in the case of a reproductive work one is further required to demonstrate the existence of a qualitative alteration or embellishment to qualify for copyright protection.

Secondly, the Privy Council noted that the essence of an artistic work is that which is visually significant.[148] Thus, in determining the copyright protection of an artistic work (such as a drawing, painting, or photograph) the visual element obtains primacy. While the Privy Council conceded that the amendments introduced to the engineering drawings no doubt embodied valuable technical concepts and improvements, it held that, "there was no alteration of any visual significance such as to entitle the drawing, as a drawing, to be described as original".[149] Under the Privy Council dictum, it appears that the material embellishment introduced by the creator of the reproduction through the expenditure of skill and labour must produce a qualitative transformation that is relevant to an artistic work, which is the category of work to which the drawings belonged. Bently and Sherman attribute this view of the

[146] *LB (Plastics) Ltd v Swish Products Limited* [1979] RPC 551 (Ch).

[147] *Interlego v Tyco* [1989] AC 217, 259, 263 (emphasis added).

[148] ibid 266, citing the dictum of Whitford J, in *Rose Plastics GmbH v William Beckett & Co (Plastics) Ltd* [1989] FSR 113 (Ch).

[149] *Interlego v Tyco* [1989] AC 217, 266.

Privy Council to the traditional approach of British judges to copyright categories (i.e., categorisation as literary, dramatic, musical or artistic works under s. 1(1) of the CDPA) and observe that such a category based enquiry into originality may not take place under the harmonised originality standard in EU law.[150]

Nonetheless, Laddie, et al.[151] interpret the dicta of the decision in *Interlego* to mean that the skill and labour that has been expended in the creation of the second work, must go towards the creation of an original work in the sense that the creator of the second work has space for the individual interpretation of the pre-existing work even where the second work seeks to be a faithful replication of it. They illustrate this point by providing the example of a drafter who sets out to make a faithful reproduction of an engineering drawing. Although the work of reproduction involves a great deal of labour, it would not be difficult for him to succeed in his task because of the mathematical precision of the lines and measurements. They contrast this with a group of persons who set out to create a faithful reproduction of a painting of Vermeer and point out that, in this case only very few persons will succeed in making an exact reproduction because the creation of the reproduction requires the exercise of personal skill and judgement on the part of the creator. It is noted that, this interpretation provides a new meaning to the concept that the labour and skill must be of the right kind, in that it must have not been expended in a merely mechanical manner but must involve the exercise of some judgement on the part of the creator. As Holyoak and Torremans observe, the skill and labour must not be so trivial that it could be characterised as a purely mechanical exercise, but creativity as such is not required either.[152]

Laddie, et al. cite the case of *Reject Shop Plc v Robert Manners*[153] to point out that the mere act of making a standard photocopy would not give rise to an original artistic work for the reason that it does not involve the expenditure of sufficient skill and labour.[154] Thus, although a common (two dimensional) photocopy made on a standard xerographic machine is a photograph within the meaning of the Act it would not qualify for copyright protection because of the automatic process of creation that involves no substantial intervention by way of skill, labour, etc.

The nature of the personal choice and judgement that is required to be exercised by the creator of a reproductive work is elaborated by Copinger and Skone James in relation to the creation of an engraving. They note that, although it is often a copy of an existing work:

> [t]he engraver's work will usually be original in the sense that he has employed skill labour and judgement in its production, even where the engraving is a close copy of an existing

---

[150]Bently and Sherman (n 91) 106.

[151]Hugh Laddie and others, *The Modern Law of Copyright and Designs* (3rd edn, Butterworths 2000) 206–207.

[152]Paul Torremans (ed), *Holyoak and Torremans: Intellectual Property Law* (8th edn, Oxford University Press 2016) 195.

[153]*Reject Shop Plc v Robert Manners* [1995] FSR 870.

[154]Laddie (n 151) 207.

> work such as a painting or drawing. An engraver of the classical kind uses means which are very different from those of the painter or draughtsman whose work he copies, producing his effect by the management of light and shade (the "chiaroscuro"), using different lines and dots which usually requires a high degree of skill and labour involved.[155]

Thus, it is the personal choices made in the management of light and shade, etc., that allows the engraver to create a reproduction of a painting or drawing that can qualify for copyright protection.

In the following section, case law and scholarly opinions that specifically deal with photographic reproductions of existing works will be examined to assess the way in which the originality test has been applied in relation to this particular category of reproductive works.

7.4.1.1.2 Protection of Photographic Reproductions

The seminal case in relation to photographic reproductions (specifically colour transparencies[156]) of public domain works is the case of *Bridgeman Art Library Ltd., v Corel Corporation.* Although it is a case from the Southern District Court of New York (USA), in the first hearing of the case the question as to whether copyright could subsist in the colour transparencies was determined under the UK law; this decision (referred to as '*Bridgeman I*'[157]) was delivered in 1998. Following this decision, objections were raised that the District Court had erred on the choice-of-law issue by applying UK law in determining the subsistence of copyright in the colour transparencies. Accordingly, the District Court of New York reconsidered the copyright protection of the photographs, this time applying US copyright law. This decision (referred to as '*Bridgeman II*')[158] was delivered in 1999. The following discussion will consider both decisions.

The facts of the case were as follows. Bridgeman was an English Company with an office in the US that was involved in the business of acquiring rights to market reproductions of public domain works of art. It maintained a library of such reproductions in the form of large format colour transparencies and digital files. A colour correction slip was attached to each transparency to ensure that the reproduction was as close a representation as possible to the original work of art at the time it was photographed. Bridgeman distributed these transparencies and digital files (on a CD-ROM) to its clients. The low-resolution versions of the images were generally

---

[155]Copinger and Skone James (n 96) 125.

[156]A colour transparency is defined as, "a positive colour image photographically produced on transparent film or glass and viewed by transmitted light, usually by projection". 'Colour transparency', *dictionary.com* <www.dictionary.com/browse/color-transparency> accessed 31 January 2019.

[157]*Bridgeman Art Library Ltd., v Corel Corporation* [1998] 25 F Supp 2d 421 (SDNY) [hereinafter referred to as 'First hearing' – *'Bridgeman I'*].

[158]*Bridgeman Art Library Ltd., v Corel Corporation* [1999] 36 F Supp 2d 191 (SDNY) [hereinafter referred to as 'Rehearing' – *'Bridgeman II'*].

distributed free-of-charge in the form of a digital catalogue of available transparencies while the high-resolution transparencies were commercialised through licensing arrangements.

Corel was a Canadian company engaged in the creation and marketing of computer software products. Corel created and marketed a series of CDs that contained seven hundred digital reproductions of well-known paintings in the public domain. Bridgeman claimed that one hundred and twenty of those images had been reproduced from the colour transparencies they created. While Bridgeman conceded that all of the paintings included in the Corel CD were in the public domain, it claimed that it owned copyright in the colour transparencies and that by reproducing those transparencies without its authorisation Corel had infringed its copyright.[159] Accordingly, Bridgman sued Corel in the Southern District Court of New York, for the infringement of copyright in its transparencies of public domain art works.

As noted above, in *Bridgeman I* the District Court determined the question of the subsistence of copyright in the images reproduced by the colour transparencies under the UK law. The District Court noted that to be original, a work need not be original or novel in form, but must originate with the author and not be copied from another work.[160] The District Court considered the colour transparencies of the public domain paintings to be derivative works and observed that the protection of a derivative work turns on whether the author's skill judgement and labour transforms the underlying work in a relevant way and remarked that, the originality requirement is not met where the work in question is wholly copied from an existing work, without any significant addition, alteration, transformation, or combination with other material.[161] Accordingly, the District Court held that the colour transparencies would not qualify for copyright protection under the UK law as the images reproduced in the colour transparencies were:

> substantially exact reproductions of public domain works, albeit in a different medium. The images were copied from the underlying works without any avoidable addition, alteration or transformation.[162]

The District Court was not persuaded by Bridgman's argument that a mere differentiation in medium could establish sufficient variation from the underlying work to support a finding of originality. The District Court cited the judgement

[159]Bridgeman claimed that the owners of the physical paintings strictly limit access to these works and that Bridgeman's transparencies of those works, from which it prepared its digital images and presumably other reproductions, are the only authorised transparencies of some of these works of art and that by inference and logical conclusion, the images in Corel's CD-ROMs must be copies of Bridgeman's transparencies because they have not proved a legal source. First hearing – '*Bridgeman I*' (n 157), 424.

[160]ibid 426, para 6, citing the decision delivered by the Pricy Council in *Interlego v Tyco* [1989] AC 217.

[161]ibid citing Melville B Nimmer and Paul E Geller, *International Copyright Law and Practice* (Matthew Bender & Co 1998), s. 2[3][b] and s. 2[1][b][ii].

[162]ibid.

delivered by the US Court of Appeals in the case of *L. Batlin & Son, Inc. v. Snyder*[163] where the Court of Appeals held that, '[t]he mere reproduction of a work of art in a different medium should not constitute the required originality for the reason that no one can claim to have independently evolved any particular medium'.[164]

Bridgman further argued that the colour correction bars attached to the colour transparencies imbibed them with sufficient originality to qualify for copyright protection. However, the District Court declined to grant a determination on this point, because it noted that, if the images with the colour bars attached are considered to be protected by copyright, this would be because of the colour correction bars being considered as bringing about a unique variation in the reproductive photograph in comparison with the original painting. Thus, infringement of the reproductive photographic images could only result through the reproduction of the image with the colour correction bars attached. As Corel's images did not include the colour correction bars, the District Court held that their significance for the determination of copyright protection in the colour transparencies was purely academic, and that therefore there was no need for the Court to make a determination as to the copyrightability of the colour transparencies in relation to this feature.[165]

Bridgman's final argument was to the effect that photography required artistic talent and originality, and therefore, the transparencies, which in effect were photographs of the underlying works of art, were original works because of the artistic talent that went into their production. The District Court rejected this argument and Judge Kaplan observed that, while the art of photography is inherently a creative exercise, it was necessary to acknowledge, "that a photograph which is no more than a copy of the work of another *as exact as science and technology permit lack originality*".[166] Judge Kaplan conceded that, the creation of an exact photographic reproduction of an existing work may not be a trivial exercise, but that the non-triviality of the exercise does not mean that such a reproduction could be considered original.

Judge Kaplan drew the analogy of a photocopier noting that, designing technology to produce exact reproductions of documents required much engineering talent but this did not mean that reproductions produced using such technology could qualify for copyright protection. Judge Kaplan cited the Privy Council judgement in *Interlego,* which held that skill, labour, and judgement merely in the process of copying cannot confer originality.[167]

Accordingly, the District Court held that the images of the public domain paintings reproduced by Bridgman's colour transparencies lacked sufficient originality to qualify for copyright protection under UK law as:

---

[163] *L Batlin & Son, Inc v Snyder* [1976] 536 F2d 486 (Court of Appeals 2d Cir).

[164] ibid 491.

[165] First hearing – *Bridgeman I* (n 157) para 6.

[166] ibid (emphasis added).

[167] ibid.

> there has been no independent creation, no distinguishable variation from preexisting works, nothing recognizably the author's own contribution that sets Bridgeman's reproductions apart from the images of the famous works it copied.[168]

Following the *Bridgman I* decision, the District Court was bombarded with additional submissions.[169] It was argued that the District Court had erred in its application of UK law in determining the copyrightability of the colour transparencies, and that this issue should have been determined under the US law.[170] Bridgeman also moved for re-argument and reconsideration arguing *inter alia* that, the District Court had in any event, erred in its application of UK law by failing to follow the *Graves'* case; a decision of the Queen's Bench from the year 1869.[171] Thus, the District Court proceeded to re-determine the issue of the subsistence of copyright in the images reproduced by the colour transparencies, under the copyright law of the US. It also proceeded to consider the relevance of the *Graves'* case to the issue of copyrightability under UK law. Accordingly, the District Court delivered the *Bridgeman II* decision, which is discussed below.

The *Graves'* case involved the copyright protection of three photographs that reproduced certain engravings. It was argued before the Queen's Bench that the photographs were not copyrightable as they were copies of existing engravings. The Queen's Bench rejected this argument and held that, while the distinction between an original painting and its copy is well understood, since all photographs were necessarily copies of some object; a photograph of an engraving would constitute an original photograph so as to render its unauthorised reproduction an infringement of copyright.[172] Bridgeman argued that under the dictum of the *Graves'* case, photographs of public domain paintings could be protected by copyright under UK law. However, the District Court of New York held that the antiquity of the *Graves'* case and subsequent developments that have taken place in the law relating to originality in the UK, resulted in the dictum of the *Graves'* case being no longer good in law.[173] Kaplan J. citing Laddie, et al. noted that under the current law of the UK, originality presupposes the exercise of substantial skill, labour, and judgement. Therefore, a person who makes a photograph merely by placing a drawing or painting on the glass of a photocopying machine and pressing a button would get no copyright at all.[174] The District Court further cited Laddie, et al. in observing that the *Graves'* case does not necessarily take a contrary position to existing law because

---

[168]ibid citing the US decision in *Durham Industries, Inc v Tomy Corp* [1980] 630 F2d 905, 910 (2d Cir).

[169]Rehearing – *Bridgeman II* (n 158) 192.

[170]The District Court received an unsolicited letter from William Patry who argued that the Court had erred on the choice-of-law issue. ibid.

[171]*Graves case* [1869] LR 4 QB 715.

[172]Rehearing – *Bridgeman II* (n 158) 197 at para 3.

[173]ibid 198 at para 3.

[174]Nevertheless, the District Court conceded that a copyright may be obtained if the creator employed skill and labour in assembling the photocopied thing, such as in the creation of a montage. ibid.

at the time the case was decided, the primitive photographic equipment and material that were available to a photographer may have required special skill and labour in the creation of even a simple reproductive photograph. In any event, the District Court maintained the analogy that it drew in the *Bridgeman I* decision between photocopies and photographs of two-dimensional articles (in this case paintings) that reproduce the articles in the photographic medium as precisely as technology permits. The fact that the creation of such a photograph may involve greater skill and labour than the creation of a mere photocopy was considered immaterial, as skill, labour or judgement merely in the process of creating a slavish copy could not confer originality.[175] The District Court emphasised that a change of medium alone is not sufficient to render a copy of an existing work copyrightable but that the copier must also make some 'identifiable original contribution'.[176]

The District Court also considered the copyrightability of the colour transparencies under US law, and held that they would not qualify for copyright protection. The District Court held that following the decision in the *Feist*[177] case, sweat of the brow alone is insufficient for a finding of originality that also requires the demonstration of a creative spark. The District Court noted that as such, slavish copying although doubtless requiring technical skill and effort did not qualify for copyright protection. As Bridgman by its own admission had laboured to create slavish copies with absolute fidelity to the public domain paintings, the colour transparencies were judged to be devoid of a spark of originality, and thus, the District Court held that the colour transparencies did not qualify for copyright protection.[178]

The case of *Antiquesportfolio.com v. Rodney Fitch*[179] involved photographs of three-dimensional antique objects. The question before the High Court of Justice was whether a photograph of a single (three-dimensional) static item, such as a jug, candelabra, or sofa, could be protected by copyright. Neuberger J took the view that there was no direct authority that could offer a resolution to this problem. Neuberger J. proceeded to argue that because section 1(1)(a) of the CDPA provides that copyright subsists in original literary, dramatic, musical or artistic works, in this case, the photographs under review must qualify as original artistic works to obtain copyright protection.[180] Neuberger J cited with approval the opinion of Copinger and Skone James[181] that, on the subsistence of copyright in a photograph, the required level of originality is low and may be satisfied by little more than the

[175]ibid 198 at para 3 citing *Interlego v Tyco* [1989] AC 217.

[176]ibid 199 at para 3.

[177]*Feist Publications Inc., v Rural Telephone Service Company Inc.,* [1991] 499 US 340.

[178]Rehearing – *Bridgeman II,* 197 at para 2. We shall not go into greater details into the application of US law under the Bridgeman II decision, as the study does not concern itself with the US law except as a comparison to the UK law at appropriate points.

[179]*Antiquesportfolio.com v Rodney Fitch* [2001] FSR 345.

[180]ibid para 28.

[181]ibid para 30 citing EP Skone James and others, *Copinger and Skone James on Copyright* (Sweet & Maxwell, 14th Ed, 1999) 3.104.

opportunistic pointing of the camera and pressing the shutter button, if the photographer can demonstrate that he expended some small degree of time, skill and labour in producing the photograph. Copinger and Skone James observe that the requisite time, skill and labour could in turn be established by demonstrating that the photographer exercised judgement on matters such as the angle from which to take the photograph, the lighting, the correct film speed, the type of filter to use, etc., Neuberger J. cited Nimmer's opinion which is to the effect that even a reproductive photograph could obtain copyright protection if the photographer has exercised personal choice on the subject-matter, angle of photograph, lighting, etc., except if the photograph amounts to nothing more than a slavish copy without there being any distinguishable variation of the pre-existing material.[182] Neuberger J noted that, under the foregoing view expressed by Nimmer, the determination made by the District Court of New York in the *Bridgman I* case could be qualified to the effect that a purely representational photograph of a two dimensional object (such as a photograph or a painting) could obtain copyright protection if the photographer could show that he had used some degree of skill and care in taking the photograph.[183] However Neuberger J correctly determined that, as the case concerned photographs of three dimensional objects he was not required to discuss this issue further.[184]

Neuberger J concluded that, in the case of the photographs under review (i.e., reproductive photographs of three dimensional objects) the photographer's selection of the objects, the positioning of the objects for photography, determining the angle, lighting and focus in the creation of the photograph and the fact that the photographs had been taken with a view to exhibit particular details of the objects (e.g., colours and other salient features) could all demonstrate the exercise of skill and judgement (albeit at a very basic level). Accordingly, Neuberger J. determined that the photographs qualified for copyright protection.[185] The judgement delivered in the *Antiquesportfolio.com* case is important because it emphasises that under the traditional skill and labour standard of originality, even a purely representational photograph of a three dimensional object may be able to obtain copyright protection if the photographer has exercised some skill, labour and judgement in its creation, which could be demonstrated through the exercise of personal choice and if the photographic reproduction is not a mere slavish copy of that three dimensional object but incorporates some distinguishable variation to it.

Thus, under traditional UK law the fact that a digitised version seeks to produce a faithful and exact reproduction of an existing rare document in digital form would not necessarily negate its ability to satisfy the skill and labour standard of originality. If the digitisation process affords the human actor space for the individual

[182]ibid para 31.

[183]ibid para 35.

[184]ibid.

[185]ibid para 36–38. *See also* Helen Norman, *Intellectual Property Law: Directions* (2nd Edition, Oxford University Press 2014) 209–210.

interpretation of the existing work, this would allow a digitised version to qualify for copyright protection. As noted in the *CCH Canadian* case, and further emphasised by Holyoak and Torremans, what is required is not creativity but intellectual effort. However, according to the elaboration provided by Laddie, et al., it appears that this intellectual effort requires the exercise of personal choice that goes beyond the mere mechanical application of intellect, and results in some material alteration or addition of visual significance that serves to differentiate the digitised version from the original rare document. As noted in *Bridgman I* a mere differentiation in the medium from analogue to digital would not be sufficient in enabling a substantially exact reproduction of a rare document to obtain copyright protection. Rosati observes that, what copyright law protects is the contribution by the author, the engraver, designer who individualised the subject-matter they worked on or, "put differently what [was] protected was the (...) human element embodied in the resulting product".[186]

It is argued here that, the digitisation process does offer space for the exercise of intellectual effort on the part of the human actor in determining the optimal image settings that can produce a clear and undistorted reproduction of an existing rare document in digital form. However, it is unlikely that in exercising this intellectual effort the human actor is afforded sufficient freedom to engage in the exercise of personal choice, as any decisions made by him would be directed by technical and functional considerations. From the foregoing discussion, it is more likely that a digitised version would be considered as a slavish reproduction of an existing rare document. In the *Antiquesportfolio* case, the photographs under review concerned two dimensional representations of three dimensional objects. Thus, the photographer enjoyed a certain level of creative freedom to make personal choices concerning the positioning of the objects and in determining the camera angle, etc. This creative freedom would not be afforded to a human actor producing a two dimensional representation of a two dimensional rare document. Furthermore, in determining the manner in which to exhibit and highlight certain salient features of a three dimensional object, the photographer in the *Antiquesportfolio* case was also able to engage in an individual interpretation of the underlying object. Such an opportunity is not afforded to the human actor producing a digitised version. Thus, the producer of a digitised version is precluded from exercising his personal creative choices to produce a particular creative visual effect in the resulting digitised version or in engaging in an individual interpretation of the visual representation of the underlying rare document. In any event, as required by the decision delivered in the *Interlego* case it would not be possible to demonstrate that the contribution of the human actor producing the digitised version resulted in a material alteration or addition of visual significance that serves to differentiate the digitised version from the underlying rare document to make it an original work.

---

[186] Eleonora Rosati, 'Originality in US and UK Copyright Experiences as a Springboard for an EU-Wide Reform Debate' [2010] 5 IIC 524, 539 citing Brad Sherman and Lionel Bently, *The Making of Modern Intellectual Property Law. The British Experience* (Cambridge University Press 2008) 46.

The inconsistency in the way the skill and labour standard has been interpreted and applied through case-law makes it difficult to enunciate with certainty whether a digitised version would or would not be granted copyright protection under the traditional skill and labour standard of originality. However, it is argued here that, considering the emphasis that has been placed upon the existence of personal choice and judgement and artistic inventiveness by case-law, as well as the requirement for the existence of a qualitative alteration, a digitised version of a rare document would not be able to obtain copyright protection under the traditional skill and labour standard of originality in UK copyright law.

7.4.1.2 Following CJEU Harmonisation

As observed by Bently and Sherman, although the British legislature has, as yet, not responded to CJEU jurisprudence on the harmonised standard of originality and the courts have been slow to adapt their language, there can be little doubt that UK law must be interpreted in line with CJEU case-law.[187] Thus, it is argued here that, as a result of the CJEU's interpretation, the traditional skill and labour standard of UK law has been replaced with the new harmonised European standard.

It is generally accepted that, as a result of the application of the new harmonised European standard to UK law, copyright protection can no longer be limited to the 'closed-list' of categories of works that come under s. 1 of the CDPA. In the context of the harmonised European standard of originality, a creation obtains copyright protection by consequence of being its author's own intellectual creation and not because it belongs to a specific category of creation, i.e., a literary, dramatic, artistic or scientific work. Thus, a digitised version of a rare document would qualify as a work for the purpose of obtaining copyright protection if it qualifies as its author's own intellectual creation.

What is more interesting is how the UK Courts have interpreted the 'author's own intellectual creation' standard, and if, as a result of such interpretation any difference could be made to the conclusions reached under the traditional legal framework on the ability of a digitised version to obtain copyright protection under UK law. Derclaye notes that, the case-law is very unsettled with judges giving inconsistent interpretations of the harmonised originality standard.[188] The following discussion will consider some of the more relevant and significant of these decisions.

The case of *Meltwater*[189] involved the question whether copyright could be infringed through the reproduction of newspaper headlines and text extracts. The determination given by the High Court of Justice was delivered shortly after the judgement in the *Infopaq* decision. Therefore, as Rosati notes, it provides the first

[187] Bently and Sherman (n 91) 99.

[188] Derclaye (n 36) 18.

[189] *The Newspaper Licensing Agency and others v Meltwater Holding BV and others* [2010] EWHC 3099.

assessment as to how and to what extent the decision in *Infopaq* has affected UK copyright law.[190] In the decision delivered by the High Court, Proudman J held that, subsequent to the *Infopaq* decision, the test of partial infringement of a copyrightable work had now changed. It no longer focuses on the labour and skill that has been expended upon the copied portion, but on whether the relevant portion contained elements, which are the expression of the intellectual creation of the author.[191] Proudman J went on to state that, following *Infopaq*, even a very small portion of a work may be protected by copyright if it demonstrates the stamp of individuality of the author.[192] However, Proudman J observed that following the author's own intellectual creation test *"it is not the completed work as published but the process of creation and the identification of the skill and labour that has gone into it which falls to be assessed"*.[193]

Griffiths notes that the reference to 'skill and labour' demonstrates a preference for retaining the UK's existing jurisprudential framework as far as possible, but observes that this judgement was delivered before the CJEU decision in the *Football Dataco* case where the CJEU unambiguously rejected the skill and labour test as being adequate to fulfil the threshold of originality that is required under the harmonised European standard.[194] However, Griffiths further observes that the emphasis on the process of creation also indicates a movement towards an altered model. On appeal, the Court of Appeal[195] considered the *Infopaq* decision and opined that, under the reasoning of the CJEU in that case, the author's own intellectual creation standard related to the question of the origin of creation (objective test of originality) and was not an inquiry into novelty or merit. Hence, the Court of Appeal held that they did not understand the decision in *Infopaq* to have qualified the long-standing test of originality as established in the decisions given in the cases of *University of London Press* and *Ladbroke v. William Hill*.[196] Therefore, it is noted that the decisions delivered by the High Court of Justice and the Court of Appeal in the *Meltwater* case, did not result in any explicit alteration to the traditional skill and labour standard of originality.

---

[190]Eleonora Rosati, 'Originality in a Work, or a Work of Originality: The Effects of the Infopaq Decision' (2011) 58 Journal Copyright Society of the USA 795.

[191]*The Newspaper Licensing Agency and others v Meltwater Holding BV and others* [2010] EWHC 3099, paras 42–43.

[192]ibid para 83.

[193]ibid para 71 (emphasis added).

[194]Jonathan Griffiths, 'Dematerialization, Pragmatism and the European Copyright Revolution' (2013) 33 Oxford Journal of Legal Studies 767 available at, <https://papers.ssrn.com/sol3/papers.cfm?abstract_id=2291502> accessed 31 January 2019.

[195]*The Newspaper Licensing Agency and others v Meltwater Holding BV and others* [2011] EWCA Civ 890 (Decision of the Court of Appeal).

[196]ibid para 19. *See also* Steven James and Ruth Arkley, 'Euopean Jurisprudence and Its Impact on Copyright Protection' [2013] E-commerce Law & Policy <https://www.lw.com/thoughtLeadership/impact-on-copyright-protection> accessed 27 May 2017.

In the decision delivered by the Patents County Court in the case of *Temple Island Collections Ltd v New English Teas Ltd* (Red Bus case)[197] Judge Birss QC noted that, during the trial it was common ground that the impact of EU law meant that, copyright might subsist in a photograph if it is the author's own intellectual creation.[198] This provides an unambiguous statement that the traditional skill and labour test for determining the copyrightability of photographs had now been usurped by the harmonised European standard. However, what is interesting is how Judge Birss proceeded to interpret the author's own intellectual creation standard. Interestingly he referred to a judgement given by the Austrian Supreme Court in the case of *O (Peter) v F KG*[199] where the Austrian Supreme Court held that photographs would obtain copyright protection if they are the result of the creator's own intellectual creation and that the decisive factor was that the creator's personality is reflected by the arrangements (motif, visual angle, illumination, etc.) selected by him in the creation of the photograph. The Austrian Supreme Court further determined that, even if the photographer's task was to achieve a representation that was as true to nature as possible, this would still leave ample room for an individual arrangement.[200] Judge Birss held that, in effect, there was no difference in substance between the Austrian Supreme Court's test of originality and the test of originality under UK law, as under the UK law too, a photograph of an object found in nature can qualify for copyright protection if the task of taking the photograph leaves ample room for an individual arrangement; the decisive factors being individual arrangements (motif, visual angle, illumination, etc.) selected by the photographer.[201] Judge Birss cited Laddie, et al. who elaborate upon different aspects in the process of photography that provide scope for such individual arrangements, one of which is the specialties of angle of shot, light and shade, exposure and effects achieved with filters, developing techniques and so on.[202] Accordingly, Judge Birss concluded that skill and labour directed towards the composition of a photograph can give rise to copyright protection.[203] Judge Birss proceeded to observe that, in this particular instance, the claimant's photograph was original as:

> [i]t is the result of [the photographer's] own intellectual creation both in terms of his *choices* relating to the basic photograph itself: the precise motif, angle of shot, light and shade, illumination, and exposure and also in terms of his work after the photograph was taken to manipulate the image to *satisfy his own visual aesthetic sense.* (. . .) [p]articular elements worthy of attention in the picture (. . .) derive from and are the expression of the *skill and labour* exercised by [the photographer], or in *Infopaq* terms, they are his intellectual creation.[204]

---

[197] *Temple Island Collections Ltd v New English Teas Ltd* [2011] EWPCC 21 (Red Bus case).

[198] ibid para 18.

[199] *O (Peter) v F KG* [2006] ECDR 9.

[200] ibid para 19 citing *O (Peter) v F KG* [2006] ECDR 9, para 2.1.

[201] ibid.

[202] ibid para 22.

[203] ibid para 27.

[204] ibid paras 51–53.

Thus, as demonstrated above, Judge Birss clearly emphasised the relevance of the individual choices made by the photographer during the process of its creation, as well as during the post-production phase in fulfilling the originality test under the harmonised European standard.

Nevertheless, the decision in the *Red Bus* case recognises that computerised manipulations made by the photographer can have a bearing on the question of originality. Judge Birss held that these manipulations were not just matters affecting the colouring and contrasts in the image but that they also had an effect on the composition itself, as people were removed from the foreground.[205] However, interestingly, in carrying out the infringement test Judge Birss, citing the *Interlego* case held that, in determining the question of infringement and whether the substantial part of the work that had been taken could be considered to be visually significant:

> [w]hat is visually significant in an artistic work is not the skill and labour (or intellectual creative effort) which led up to the work, it is the product of that activity. The fact that the artist may have used *commonplace techniques to produce his work is not the issue*. What is important is that he or she has *used them under the guidance of their own aesthetic sense* to create the visual effect in question.[206]

Thus, Judge Birss appears to be of the view that, even where a commonplace photo editing software such as Photoshop is used for the creation of the final visual appearance of the photograph, if in carrying out that post-production editing process, the photographer had been guided by his own aesthetic sense, the outcome of that editing would nevertheless be protected under copyright.

It has been observed that the frequent use of the term skill and labour in conjunction with the author's own intellectual creation test is an indication that, for Judge Birss, the traditional skill and labour test appears to be akin to the author's own intellectual creation test.[207] It is also necessary to note that this judgement too was delivered a few months before the CJEU decision in *Football Dataco*[208] where the CJEU unambiguously rejected skill and labour as being an adequate measure of originality. Thus, even if Judge Birss did in some way attempt to equate the author's own intellectual creation standard with that of the traditional skill and labour standard, that part of the decision may no longer be valid. Nevertheless, it is significant that the interpretation of the author's own intellectual creation standard in the *Red Bus* case closely follows the test applied under traditional UK law in relation to the originality of representative photographs in terms of the emphasis placed on the individual arrangements made by the photographer during the composition of the photograph and in the post-production phase.

---

[205]ibid para 29.

[206]ibid para 34.

[207]*See also* Eleonora Rosati, *Originality in EU Copyright Full Harmonization through Case Law* (Edward Elgar 2013) 194; Cornish and Llewelyn (n 116) 460.

[208]Judgment of 1 March 2012, *Football Dataco v Yahoo! UK Ltd,* C-604/10, EU:C:2012:115. The Football Dataco decision was delivered on 01 March, 2012, the Red Bus decision was delivered on 12 January, 2012. Thus, it preceded the Football Dataco decision by approximately two months.

In the 2013 decision delivered in the *SAS Institute Inc v World Programming Ltd*[209] case, the Court of Appeal held that the essence of the term intellectual creation is that the person in question has exercised expressive and creative choices in producing the work. The more restricted the choices, the less likely it is that the product will be the intellectual creation (or the expression of the intellectual creation) of the person who produced it.[210] Citing the dicta delivered in the *BSA* case, the Court of Appeal held that mere intellectual effort could not qualify a work for copyright protection because the expression is dictated by technical function. Hence, the criterion of originality would not be satisfied and when the criterion of originality is not satisfied the product would not qualify as the intellectual creation of the author.[211] As the case involved the copyrightability of the functional aspects of a computer programme, the Court of Appeal tested its originality under the 'author's own intellectual creation' standard under Article 1(3) of the Computer Programmes Directive. The Court of Appeal was not called upon to determine whether the author's own intellectual creation standard had changed the traditional test of 'skill and labour'. Nevertheless, Lewison LJ proceeded to observe that, if the InfoSoc Directive had in fact changed the traditional domestic test, it seems to have raised rather than lowered the hurdle to obtain copyright protection.[212] It is interesting however, that he did not refer to the decision in *Football Dataco* where the CJEU clearly held that the skill and labour standard was not applicable in determining the harmonised European originality test. Similarly, in a more recent decision delivered by the Intellectual Property Enterprise Court (IPEC) in the case of *Taylor v Maguire,*[213] District Judge Clarke failed to even refer to the harmonised standard of originality and instead stated that the detailed choices made by the claimant in the creation of certain paper-cuttings qualified the paper-cuttings for copyright protection on the grounds that it brought the claimant's independent skill and labour to the finished work.[214]

It is interesting to note that in 2015, the UK Intellectual Property office (UKIPO) clarified through a copyright notice[215] that under the new harmonised standard of

---

[209] *SAS Institute Inc v World Programming Ltd* [2015] ECDR 17.

[210] ibid para 31. In this case, the Court denied copyright protection to the functionalities of a software programme, holding that the nature of the skill and judgement expended in devising the functionality of a computer programme (which involves making choices) falls on the ideas side of the line. ibid para 46. *See also* decision of the CJEU delivered consequent to the reference for a preliminary ruling by the High Court of Justice Judgment of 2 May 2012, *SAS Institute,* C-406/10, EU:C:2012:259.

[211] ibid para 33.

[212] ibid para 37.

[213] *Taylor v Maguire* [2013] EWHC 3804 (IPEC) (High Court of Justice Chancery Division).

[214] *See also* Kirsten Toft, 'Case Comment: Suzy Taylor v Alison Maguire' (2014) 25 Entertainment Law Review 154.

[215] 'Intellectual Property Office (UK) "Copyright Notice: Digital Images, Photographs and the Internet" 1/2014 (Updated November 2015)' <www.gov.uk/government/uploads/system/uploads/attachment_data/file/481194/c-notice-201401.pdf> accessed 31 January 2019. Copyright notices are published by the Intellectual Property Office (IPO) of the UK to help explain specific areas of copyright law. It is not a conclusive view of the law.

'author's own intellectual creation' it is unlikely that a merely retouched, digital image of an older work can be considered original, even if specialist skills have been used to optimise and improve the images (e.g., by removing blemishes, stains, or creases). According to the UKIPO this is because, "there will generally be minimal scope for a creator to exercise free and creative choices if their aim is simply to make a faithful reproduction of an existing work".[216] Derclaye[217] concurs with this opinion noting that, following the CJEU decisions a work resulting from pure, labour, skill, or judgement will not be original if this labour, skill, or judgement does not result from free and creative choices. She observes that even in instances that the creation process requires the exercise of judgement on the part of the creator, the criterion will not be met if the choices made are either banal or not free, which would be the case if the choices are dictated by technical or functional considerations or constrained by rules. Griffiths observes that following the CJEU's determination in the *BSA* case, it would not be possible for UK law to grant copyright protection to works in which the parameters of the task of creation are constrained by the need to satisfy a particular technical function.[218] He observes that, as a result, the decision in the case of *Sawkins v. Hyperion* can no longer be held valid in law, as "[t]he aim to replicate an original in exact terms is surely just such a functional constraint".[219] Thus, this seems to effectively rule out the copyright protection of digitised versions that aim to replicate as exactly as possible an existing rare document. Accordingly, as per the developments that have taken place in the copyright law of the UK following the introduction of the harmonised European standard, it can be stated with a high degree of certainty that a digitised version of a rare document would not be able to obtain copyright protection under UK law.

7.4.2 *Germany*

7.4.2.1 The Traditional Copyright Law Framework

Under section 2(2) of the German Copyright Act,[220] copyright protection is granted to 'works' that constitute their author's personal intellectual creation (*persönliche geistige Schöpfung*). Accordingly, a photograph (or a work produced by processes similar to photography) that constitutes its authors' personal intellectual creation is granted copyright protection under section 2(1)(5) as a *Lichtbildwerk* (plu.

[216]ibid.

[217]Derclaye (n 36) 12.

[218]Griffiths (n 60) 11.

[219]ibid. *See contra* Derclaye who is of the view that, "the Sawkins case would not be decided differently nowadays. Even if Dr. Sawkins was trying to stick as closely as possible to Lalande's lost or unfinished works he had choices, exercised them and put his personality in the work". (n 36) 13.

[220]Urheberrechtsgesetz 1965 BGBl. I S. 1273 (Copyright Act of Germany).

Lichtbildwerke) or a photographic work. However, a photograph (or a product manufactured in a similar manner to a photograph) that does not constitute its authors' personal intellectual creation (such as those that are routinely produced in the course of a particular trade or business, and ordinary amateur photographs) obtain related rights (*Leistungsschutzrecht*)[221] protection under section 72 as a *Lichtbild* (plu. *Lichtbilder*) or a non-creative photograph. From the three jurisdictions reviewed in this analysis, Germany is the only jurisdiction that offers a two-tiered protection regime for photographs, i.e., protection under the copyright regime for photographic works and protection under a related rights regime for non-creative photographs. Löwenheim notes that, while the definition of a photograph (*Lichtbildwerke* or *Lichtbilder*) in German law is generally constructed with reference to the chemical or physical alteration of a light-sensitive film to form an image, these traditional methods of photography are now equated to digital photographic techniques and as such, the definition of 'photograph' can now be extended to digital photography as well.[222] Thus, it appears that a photographic reproduction of an existing document made by means of a digital scanner would fall within the definition of a photograph under German law.

The following discussion considers whether a digitised version would qualify as a *Lichtbildwerk* under German law in order to obtain copyright protection. If it appears that it would not qualify for copyright protection, it shall proceed to consider whether a digitised version could obtain protection under a related right as a *Lichtbild.*

7.4.2.1.1 A Digitised Version as a Lichtbildwerk Under Section 2(1)(5) of the German Copyright Act

To qualify for protection under section 2(1)(5), it is necessary that a work can be demonstrated to contain elements that stem from its author's distinct personality. Thus, a digitised version would qualify for protection under German law if it can be demonstrated to be the personal intellectual creation (*die persönliche geistige Schöpfung*) of its creator. German copyright law has been traditionally following an individuality test meaning that a work is not merely protected because it originates in the author's efforts but because it shows traits of his personality and individuality (i.e., a subjective test of originality).[223] According to Löwenheim, German law defines a protectable work in relation to four elements: personal creation (*persönliche Schöpfung*), intellectuality (*geistigen Gehalt*), expression (*Formgestaltung*), and individuality (*Individualität*).[224]

[221]The term *Leistungsschutzrecht* is translated in different ways, sometimes as a related right and sometimes as an ancillary copyright. However, for this discussion, the term related right is adopted.

[222]Ulrich Löwenheim in Gerhard Schricker and Ulrich Löwenheim (eds), *Urheberrecht: Kommentar* (4th ed, CH Beck 2010) § 2 para 179.

[223]Karl-Nikolaus Peifer, '"Individualität" or Originality? Core Concepts in German Copyright Law' [2014] 12 GRUR Int. 1100, 1101.

[224]Löwenheim (n 222), § 2 para 9.

The element of personal creation (*persönliche Schöpfung*) refers to the requirement that the work owes its origin to the creative activity of a natural person.[225] Thereby German law excludes from the scope of copyright protection, creations that are produced by machinery, an apparatus, or a computer under a fully automated process.[226] As Dreier, et al. note, where a machine operates independently without human intervention, no copyright protectable work is created because of the absence of a personal human contribution.[227] However, Löwenheim observes that a product that is created through an automated process could nevertheless qualify for copyright protection if sufficient human creative activity has been involved in the pre-production and post-production phases, so that the final formulation of the product is shaped by human activity.[228] Löwenheim gives the example of a computer-generated translation of a text that benefits from corrections and modifications made by a human actor resulting in its final character being influenced by human activity to a sufficient degree.[229] Löwenheim emphasises that, in the case of photographs that are produced by a fully automated process, the ability of the photograph to fulfil the criterion of personal creation depends on whether the formulation of the photographic depiction (*Bildgestaltung*) involves human creative activity.[230] Thus, the use of a machine in the creation process does not as such, exclude the existence of a personal creation if sufficient human influence and creativity can be discerned in the final product. Accordingly, although a digitised version is produced through a largely automated process of scanning, the human involvement in the post-production phase (e.g., adjusting tone and colour) may arguably prove sufficient to qualify the final digital image as a personal creation (*persönliche Schöpfung*).

The second element of intellectuality requires that the copyrightable work must have an intellectual (*geistige*) content. Löwenheim explains this requirement to mean that the work must have something that goes beyond the mere bounds of sensory perception, i.e., it must communicate a statement or message that belongs to the

---

[225] ibid para 11.

[226] ibid para 12.

[227] Gernot Schulze in Thomas Dreier, Gernot Schulze and Louisa Specht (eds), *Urheberrechtsgesetz: Urheberrechtswahrnehmungsgesetz, Kunsturhebergesetz Kommentar* (5th Edition, CH Beck 2015) § 2 para 8:

> Wo hingegen die Maschine selbständig tätig wird wie zum beispiel bei einem Ubersetzungscomputer oder bei Computerprogrammemen, die ausschliesslich und ohne Einwirkung des Menschen von Datenverarbeitungsanlagen geschaffen werden, fehlt ein personlicher Beitrag des Menschen, so dass kein Schutzfähiges Werk entsteht. ("On the other hand, when the machine operates independently, for example a translation computer or computer programmes which are created exclusively by data processing systems without human intervention, there is no personal contribution from the human being, so that no protective work is created"). (Translated into English by the author).

[228] Löwenheim (n 222) §2 para 12.

[229] ibid.

[230] ibid.

domain of human thought or emotion, thereby allowing the human mind to be expressed within the work.[231] Peifer defines it in terms of copyrighted works needing to serve a communicative function in the sense that they express sentiments, ideas and concepts that communicate with the recipient.[232] In the decision delivered by the Federal Supreme Court (*Bundesgerichtshof*) in the *Seilzirkus*[233] case, it was noted that where a design is dictated by technical requirements, there would be no room for artistic creation, and consequently a personal intellectual creation would be excluded. The Supreme Court elaborated its position by stating that copyright protection for an object of daily use (i.e., a functional object) is only possible if its design embodies not only a technical solution but also includes aesthetic content that is brought about through creative effort. Characteristics dictated by technical requirements would be those elements without which an object of applied art could not function. Such elements that are solely based on technical requirements will not attract copyright protection. The Supreme Court noted that a personal intellectual creation is a creation of individual character, the aesthetic content of which has reached a certain degree that those in circles that are familiar with and receptive to art would regard it as having an artistic effort.[234]

It is argued here that, the contributions made to a digitised version by a human actor would be dictated by technical and functional considerations as opposed to his own aesthetic choices. For example, in cleaning the raw image to remove shadow, skew, etc., or in carrying out colour calibration, the human actor would be dictated by the functional requirement of producing a digital reproduction that is faithful to the rare document and therefore would not have the opportunity to express his particular aesthetic or creative choices.

The third element of expression (*Formgestaltung*) requires that the creation has assumed a form which makes it accessible to the perception of human senses.[235] However, fixation in a tangible form is not necessary.[236] It is evident that a digital image produced through a process of photography although intangible can be perceived visually by a human being. Therefore, this element is fulfilled in the case of a digitised version and need not be discussed further.

Individuality (*Individualität*) is a fundamental criterion of copyright protection. To qualify for copyright protection, it is necessary that a work is not only established to originate from the creativity of a human author but that it also contains elements that stem from that human author's distinct personality. The concept of individuality

---

[231]ibid section 2.C.II.2., 101 para 18. "Es muss etwas haben, das über das bloße sinnlich wahrnehmbare Substrat hinausgeht, eine Aussage oder Botschaft, die dem Bereich der Gedanken, des Ästhetischen oder sonstiger menschlicher Regungen und Reaktionsweisen zugehört". (Translated into English by the author).

[232]Peifer (n 223) 1102.

[233]BGH 12.05.2011 – I ZR 53/10, GRUR 2012, 58 – *Seilzirkus.*

[234]ibid para 17.

[235]Löwenheim (n 222) § 2 para 20 citing BGH 09.05.1985 – I ZR 52/83, GRUR 1985, 1041 – *Inkasso Programm*, 1046.

[236]ibid.

in German copyright law is defined in relation to the scope that is available to the author of a work to unfold his personal traits during the creation of the work (referred to as *Spielraum*). Ulmer explains the concept of *Spielraum* in terms of the freedom of choice that is available to an author in the creation of a work.[237] Thus, it can be concluded that individuality refers to an author's exercise of the freedom of choice that is available to him in the creation of a work, to invest the work with his own personal expression.[238] Löwenheim observes that, while the individuality of an author can be so heavily pronounced in the work that it bears the stamp of the personality of the author; this is not necessary to trigger copyright protection. Individuality can also be limited to a minimum as would be the case with regard to works that fall into the so-called 'small coin' (*kleine Münze*) category.[239] Following the rejection of the requirement of a quantitative measurement of individuality by the Supreme Court in the *Geburtstagszug*[240] decision, the concept of the level of creativity (*Gestaltungshohe*) in German law is no longer a requirement for a finding of individuality.[241] Nevertheless, it is evident that to obtain copyright protection a work must be able to demonstrate elements of the author's own personality so as to satisfy the element of individuality. A creation process that is governed by mere technical considerations would not allow the required *Spielraum* for the creator of a work to incorporate his personal expression into the work.

Peifer explains the relationship between the elements of intellectuality and individuality as follows:

> While the opportunity to make choices apart from what is merely functional, offers the chance to work 'intellectually', the use of this chance leads to something strictly personal to the creator. This distinguishes intellectuality (open to all human creation) from individuality (strictly personal).[242]

Therefore, if the judgements made by the human actor within the digitisation process—in terms of making modifications and corrections to the digital image produced by a scanner or digital camera—are dictated by the technical requirement of producing a digital reproduction as faithful to the original document as possible; it follows that human intervention during the image processing stage does not allow for the exercise of freedom of choice on the part of the human actor as could allow him to invest the work with his own individual expression. Similarly, during the post-production phase, in performing the colour calibration, adjusting the spatial resolution, etc., the human actor must constrain his personal preferences in the

---

[237]Eugen Ulmer, *Urheber- Und Verlagsrecht* (3rd edn, Springer Berlin 1980) 131.

[238]*See* Marjut Salokannel, *Ownership of Rights in Audiovisual Productions: A Comparative Study* (Martinus Nijhoff Publishers 1997) 44.

[239]Löwenheim (n 222) § 2 para 24.

[240]BGH 13.11.2013 – I ZR 143/12, GRUR 2014, 175 – *Geburtstagszug*. For a summarised English translation of the Federal Supreme Court decision *see* 'Case Comment: Birthday Train (Geburtstagszug)' (2014) 45 IIC 831.

[241]Löwenheim (n 222) § 2 para 24.

[242]Peifer (n 223) 1103.

interests of ensuring that the visual representation of the digital image is as faithful as possible to the visual appearance of the original document. As observed by Löwenheim, where the design or representation of a work is pre-determined by technical necessities an individual creation will not be possible.[243] He gives the example of the creation of a chemical formula where the intended outcome of the creation process does not allow for the possibility of different variation options. It is argued that, the expected outcome of a process of digitisation is similarly limited by the intended outcome of creating an exact visual reproduction of a particular rare document to prevent any space for the exercise of aesthetic or creative preferences on the part of the human actor.

In the Red Couch (*Rote Couch*) case,[244] the Regional Court (*Landgericht*) in Cologne found that, in a series of photographs taken by the artist Horst Wackerbarth in different settings with the recurring motif of a red couch, only those photographs where there was a conscious staging of the subject-matter by the artist would qualify as *Lichtbildwerke.* The rest of the photographs were considered as *Lichtbilder* for the reason that these did not display a sufficient degree of originality. The Regional Court observed that, the communication of the photographer's individual observation or artistic expression differentiates a *Lichtbildwerk* from a mere *Lichtbild.* A similar view was expressed by the Court of Appeal (*Oberlandgericht*) of Stuttgart in the decision delivered in the *Reiss Engelhorn Museum II*[245] case, where *Lichtbildwerke* were distinguished from ordinary (everyday) photographs because of their individuality, which results from the artistic statement made by the image.[246] Thus, *Lichtbildwerke* convey an individuality that goes beyond mere representational photographs such as photographs that reproduce existing objects as faithfully as possible (*Gegenstandfotografie*), average tourist photos, etc.[247]

Accordingly, Löwenheim postulates that the production of photographic prints by mechanical-reprographic methods would not lead to the creation of a *Lichtbildwerk.*[248] Hence, photocopies, which are reproductions but not creative works, are distinguished from *Lichtbildwerke.* As observed by Löwenheim, *Lichtbildwerke* are characterised in general by the fact that they capture a mood particularly well above the representational image and present a topic in a vividly expressive manner which stimulates the viewer's thought process; the bulk of everyday pictures, images that can be attributed to nothing more than the technical aptitude of the photographer would not qualify as *Lichtbildwerke.*[249]

---

[243]Löwenheim (n 222) § 2 para 29.

[244]LG Köln 12.12.2013, 14 O 613/12 – *Rote Couch.*

[245]OLG Stuttgart 31.05.2017, 4 U 204/16 – *Reiss Engelhorn Museum II* (Appeal).

[246]ibid 55.

[247]Löwenheim (n 222) § 2 para 184.

[248]ibid.

[249]ibid.

This view is supported by a recent decision delivered in the *Reiss Engelhorn Museum I*[250] case by the Regional Court (*Landgericht*) in Berlin. The case involved a determination as to whether photographs of portrait paintings that were in the public domain could be protected as *Lichtbildwerke*. The Reiss Engelhorn Museum in Mannheim, Germany had commissioned a photographer to photograph several public domain portrait paintings held by the Museum. The photographs were taken using an analogue camera and all photographs represented a frontal 1:1 reproduction of each painting at a ninety-degree angle without the inclusion of other figurative elements such as the picture frame. The photographer transferred his intellectual property rights in the photographs to the Museum. The photographs were published by the Museum in several of its publications (including a Museum catalogue). A user uploaded scanned copies of the photographs (taken from the Museum's publications) onto the *Wikimedia Commons* website where they were made available to the public as public domain works. The Museum argued that, the photographs of the paintings qualified as *Lichtbildwerke* under section 2(1)(5) or in any event were protected under section 72 as *Lichtbilder* and brought an action against the Wikimedia Foundation[251] for copyright infringement.

The Regional Court held that the photographs could not qualify as *Lichtbildwerke* under section 2(1)(5) of the German Copyright Act. The Regional Court observed that, photographs are protected as *Lichtbildwerke* when they are the result of their author's own intellectual creation. The Regional Court determined that, in creating these photographs the creative freedom (*Gestaltungsspielraum*) of the photographer had been limited by the objective of the task which was to create faithful reproductions of the paintings. This was evidenced by the directions issued by the Museum to the photographer which stated that the paintings should be photographed frontally, without capturing other figurative elements (such as the picture frame) and that distortions to the photographic representation of the paintings (e.g., through lighting, colour shifts, etc.) should be avoided as much as possible. Although the photographer had room to exercise his personal judgement in relation to resolving issues such as the nature and degree of the lighting and exposure that was to be used in the photography process, the Regional Court held that these involved the exercise of judgement in relation to aspects of pure craftsmanship (*handwerklicher Art*) that related to the general technical process of photographic reproduction. Therefore, it did not allow the photographs to be invested with the element of individuality that was required for them to be protected as *Lichtbildwerke*. However, the Regional Court held that the photographic reproductions would qualify for protection as *Lichtbilder* under section 72. This aspect of the decision will be discussed below.

[250] LG Berlin 03.05.2016, 15 O 428/15 – *Reiss Engelhorn Museum I.*

[251] An action was also brought against Wikipedia Germany but was dismissed by the Regional Court because Wikipedia Germany was not legally responsible for the images that had been held by Wikimedia Commons.

As noted in the decision delivered by the Court of Appeal of Düsseldorf (*Oberlandgericht*) in the *Beuys-Fotografien*[252] case, when it comes to reproducing two dimensional, flat (*flächigen*) works of art as contrasted with three dimensional works of art (*räumlicher Kunstwerke*) as accurately as possible, the photographer is not allowed any appreciable artistic scope (*Gestaltungsspielraum*) as the correct angle for shooting the photograph is pre-determined. The decisions made by a photographer in relation to the lighting, choice of photographic paper, exposure, development technique, etc. are decisions relating to craftsmanship and as such would not be relevant to the qualification of a photograph as a *Lichtibildwerk.*[253] Citing the *Beuys-Fotografien* decision, Talke observes that, faithful digital reproductions of book pages that are produced during mass-digitisation initiatives would not generally qualify as *Lichtbildwerke,* as the creative space (*Gestaltungsspielraum*) afforded to the creator of the digital reproductions, is low.[254]

Thus, it is argued here that, a digitised version of a rare document would not qualify for copyright protection as a *Lichtbildwerk* under German law for the reason that, the process of creating a digitised version does not allow sufficient creative space (*Gestaltungsspielraum*) for the creator of the digitised version to unfold his personal traits or to exercise individual creative choices in a manner that would allow the digitised version to qualify as his personal intellectual creation under section 2(1) (5) of the German Copyright Act.

7.4.2.1.2 Related Rights Protection of a Digitised Version as a Lichtbild Under Section 72 of the German Copyright Act

Unlike a *Lichtbildwerk* that is granted copyright protection (*Urheberrecht*), a *Lichtbild* is protected under a related right (*Leistungsschutzrecht*) under section 72.[255] The subject of protection is not a creative work but a technical

---

[252]OLG Düsseldorf 13.02.1996 – 20 U 115/95, GRUR 1997, 49 – *Beuys-Fotografien.*

[253]ibid 51. However, Talke notes that may be exceptions to the *dictum* expressed in the *Beuys-Fotografien* decision, citing the decision of Supreme Court in the *Stadtplanwerk* case (BGH, 28.05.1998 – I ZR 81/96, GRUR 1998, 916 – *Stadtplanwerk*) where a city map that was produced based on a previously known design concept, can also be protected by copyright law if, in its elaboration, there is nevertheless sufficient scope for individual formative cartographic services. Armin Talke, 'Lichtbildschutz Für Digitale Bilder von zweidimensionalen Vorlagen' (2010) Zeitschrift für Urheber- und Medienrecht 846, 848–49.

[254]Interestingly, Talke makes a distinction in the case of documents that include visual content such as old manuscripts that are embellished with illustrations. He argues that in the digitisation of such material, creative elements may need to be used to specify details and colour schemes, considering the purpose for which the digitised version is to be used and indicates that these creative elements need to be considered in evaluating its protection as a *Lichtbildwerke*. ibid 849.

[255]As at present, *Lichtbilder* obtain protection for a period of 50 years as opposed to the 70 year duration of copyright protection granted to *Lichtbildwerke. See* section 72(3) of German Copyright Act (n 220).

achievement.[256] Vogel notes that the justification for section 72 is found in its protection of all those non-creative photographs produced in scientific spheres (especially in the fields of natural sciences), with considerable financial and technological investment (and sometimes using sophisticated technical knowledge and craftsmanship) against unauthorised access and use by third parties.[257] Dreier and Specht note that the rationale behind the distinction between copyright and related rights is that the subject-matter protected by related rights is not of a creative nature, but rather of a re-creative, organisational, technical or financial nature.[258]

Lichtbilder (which roughly translates as 'light images') refer to photographic images that are produced by means of a photographic device that uses radiant light or energy (*strahlendes Licht oder Energie*) to create a photographic image of an object. It encompasses a broad range of photographic images that are created by means of diverse technological methods and equipment such as cameras (both analogue and digital), digital imaging technologies and technologies such as X-ray and Computertomography (which is for example used in the creation of CT and Ultrasound scans).[259] Most importantly, it captures within its definition images created by digital scanners (such as used in the digitisation of rare documents) that use light sensor technologies such as CIS,[260] CCD[261] or CMOS[262] to create digital reproductions of a physical document.[263] What is required is that the image is produced through the application of a photographic technique by a natural person who operates the photographic device. Whether the creation apparatus is manually operated, automatic, or controlled by a computer,[264] this natural person will be deemed its producer (*Lichtbildner*). Thus, the existence of human involvement in the creation process is a necessity for *Lichtbild* protection. It is unclear whether such human involvement must be present at the point of the creation of the photograph or whether it suffices that the human intervention is made at the post-production stage.

Vogel notes that the criteria for the qualification of an image as a *Lichtbild* under section 72 is a minimum level of intellectual effort (*geistiger Leistung*)[265] on the part

---

[256]As per decisions delivered in the cases of LG Berlin 03.05.2016, 15O 428/15 – *Reiss Engelhorn Museum I* and OLG Stuttgart 31.05.2017, 4 U 204/16 – *Reiss Engelhorn Museum II* (Appeal).

[257]Martin Vogel in Gerhard Schricker and Ulrich Löwenheim (eds), *Urheberrecht: Kommentar* (4th ed, CH Beck 2010) § 72 para 13.

[258]Thomas Dreier and Louisa Specht, 'Germany' in Reto M Hilty and Sylvie Nérisson (eds), *Balancing Copyright – A Survey of National Approaches* (Springer 2012) 431.

[259]Vogel (n 257) § 72 paras 19–21.

[260]Contact Image Sensor.

[261]Charged Coupled Device.

[262]Complementary Metal Oxide Semiconductor.

[263]Vogel (n 257) § 72 para 21.

[264]ibid 1398 at para 20. "Schutzbegründend ist allein der Einsatz der genannten Techniken durch den jeweiligen Lichtbildner als natürlicher Person, gleich, ob er das Bild einer einfachen oder hochkomplexen, einer automatischen, handbetriebenen oder mit einer digitalen computergesteuerten Kamera herstellt." (Translated into English by the author).

[265]*See also* BGH, 03.11.1999 – I ZR 55/97, GRUR 2000, 317 – *Werbefotos*.

of the natural person operating the apparatus, which is imprinted upon the image during the execution of the photographic technique.[266] This is to be contrasted with the requirement of intellectual creativity (*geistiger Schöpfung*) required in obtaining copyright protection as a *Lichtbildwerk*. Thus, the element of individuality that is central to protection as a *Lichtbildwerk* is not required in the case of a *Lichtbild*. However, the mere pressing of a button will not be sufficient to obtain protection under section 72.[267] Although there is no specific definition of the term intellectual effort (*geistiger Leistung*) case law and scholarly opinion seem to presume the existence of intellectual effort in the form of the exercise of choice and judgement that is reflected in the final visual representation of the image. This choice and judgement although not aimed towards investing the image with artistic or creative features may yet contribute towards the fulfilment of a technical objective such as for example the creation of a faithful reproduction of an existing object in photographic form. Thus, case-law has established that a mere mechanical duplication of an existing photograph will not lead to protection as a *Lichtbild*. It is necessary that the photographic image that seeks protection under Article 72 is a prototype photographic image (*Urbild*) that demonstrates a technical achievement in representing an existing object.

For example, in the *Telefonkarte*[268] case, the Federal Supreme Court held that, to be protected under section 72, an image would require to be more than a mere technical reproduction of an existing graphic. The case involved telephone cards produced by the plaintiff that included a background image of a stylised world map with a blue quadrant network that was reproduced upon telephone cards manufactured by a competitor, in black and white and in a reduced size. The Federal Supreme Court noted that, it could not be inferred from the arguments put forward by the plaintiff that the stylised world map was more than a mere technical reproduction of an existing graphic or that a minimum intellectual effort had been expended in its creation to justify protection under Article 72.[269] This decision followed the Supreme Court's earlier decision delivered in the *Bibelreproduktion*[270] case.

The *Bibelreproduktion* case involved photographs of certain engravings. The negatives of these photographs had been reprocessed to produce photographic images for which protection was claimed under Article 72. The Federal Supreme Court rejected protection under Article 72 for the photographic reproductions. It emphasised that the technical reproduction process alone does not justify protection as a *Lichtbild* and that a minimum level of personal intellectual effort would not be

[266]Vogel (n 257) § 72 para 17. "Wohl aber bedarf es notwendigerweise des Einsatzes fotografischer Technik und eines Mindestmaß an geistiger Leistung, die in der oft schwierigen Handhabung der Technik zum Ausdruck kommt." *See also* ibid para 18. "Lichtbilder, die – im Gegensatz zu gestalten Lichtbildwerken – lediglich abbildende Fotografien (Gegenstandfotografien) sind, ohne die Qualität einer persönlichen geistigen Schöpfung (. . .) zu erreichen".

[267]Talke (n 253) 849.

[268]BGH, 07.12.2000 – I ZR 146/98, GRUR 2001, 755 – *Telefonkarte*.

[269]ibid 757.

[270]BGH, 08.11.1989 – I ZR 14/88, GRUR 1990, 669 – *Bibelreproduktion*.

found in cases where a *Lichtbild* (or similarly manufactured product) is a mere reproduction of another *Lichtbild.* Mere insignificant changes, such as changes to the image size, would not serve to change the status of a photograph as a direct reproduction of an existing photographic image. The Supreme Court also pointed out that the German Copyright Act of 1965[271] did not intend to protect purely technical processes through which an image is generated such as photocopies (including micro and macro copies), as well as negative or positive prints of films.[272]

Vogel notes that, the meaning and purpose of section 72 does not allow for the extension of its scope of protection to reproductive photographs, in which a two dimensional picture or textual presentation is mechanically copied *inter alia* through photocopying, or through digital techniques such as scanning. This is because, protection granted under section 72 is based on the notion that the image, as such, is original in the sense that it is a prototype image (*Urbild*),[273] i.e., the first original photographic version of that image. They observe that otherwise, the protection of a light image could be lengthened as desired by repeated photographic reproduction processes. The same applies to prints produced by a picture or text template for printing, and prints which are produced from a photographic prototype. Vogel argues that in this sense, the scope of protection for *Lichtbild* is similar to the protection of audio recordings which, under section 85(1), is not granted to a mere reproduction of a phonogram.[274] This opinion is re-echoed by Heckmann who notes that the mere technical reproduction of an existing graphic or handwriting does not achieve the required minimum level of personal intellectual effort, to qualify for protection as a *Lichtbild.*[275] Schulze concurs with this view by stating that a photographic reproduction will not be protected as a *Lichtbild* if it is produced in an exclusively mechanical way.[276]

However, Talke opines that *Lichtbild* protection can apply to digital photographic images of two dimensional works if the creator of the image has made a technical effort in defining conditions of shooting angle, lighting, exposure, resolution, colour-depth, etc.[277] He proceeds to consider the status of scanned images of book pages created within a mass-digitisation process[278] where the human actor determines and fixes the image settings at the outset, following which the book-pages are automatically flipped and scanned by scan-robots. Talke argues that, in such cases too, it would be possible for the individual images to qualify for protection under section 72 as the technical effort made by the human actor relates to the entire series of

[271]German Copyright Act (n 220).

[272]BGH, 08.11.1989 – I ZR 14/88, GRUR 1990, 669 – *Bibelreproduktion*, 673.

[273]Vogel (n 257) § 72 para 23.

[274]ibid.

[275]Jörn Heckmann, *Die Retrospektive Digitalisierung von Printpublikationen* (Peter Lang 2011) 57.

[276]Schulze (n 227) § 72 para 10.

[277]Talke (n 253) 851.

[278]Eric W Steinhauer, 'Informationskompetenz Und Recht' in Wilfried Sühl-Strohmenger (ed), *Handbuch Informationskompetenz* (Walter de Gruyter 2012) 77–78.

images. In doing so, he draws an analogy between digitised versions produced through mass-digitisation processes and photographic 'stills' produced by computer controlled digital cameras that obtain protection under section 72.[279] Thus, the emphasis seems to be placed upon the determination of the shooting conditions (i.e., the photographic image settings) rather than on the actual pressing of the button. It is therefore argued here that, even if the pressing of the button is done by a scan-robot, the intellectual effort that is usually expended by the human actor in determining the image settings, light, exposure, etc., should enable digitised versions of book pages to qualify as *Lichtbilder* under section 72.

It is interesting to consider the determinations delivered by German courts in a series of cases dealing with the unauthorised reproduction and making available of photographs of public domain paintings held by the Reiss Engelhorn Museum in Mannheim. While these cases were referred to above, in our discussion on *Lichtbildwerke,* the following discussion will focus upon the *dicta* relating to the protection of these photographs as *Lichtbilder* under section 72.

In the *Reiss Engelhorn Museum I*[280] decision, the Regional Court (*Landgericht*) of Berlin held that, the painstaking technical effort expended by the photographer in adjusting the illumination, alignment and exposure to create detailed, faithfully colour-contrasted photographs of the paintings without any disturbing reflections and distortions, succeeded in fulfilling the requirement of the personal intellectual effort (*persönliche geistigen Leistung*) for protection under section 72. The production of these photographic reproductions also involved a high degree of human involvement and expertise as they were created by a professional human photographer who manually photographed the two dimensional paintings by means of an analogue camera. The Regional Court of Berlin noted that, the production of photographic reproductions of paintings, of a quality that enabled them to be published in a Museum catalogue, could not be so easily achieved by spontaneously pressing a button, especially in the case of analogue photography.

Although it was not relevant to the case before it, the Regional Court proceeded to caution that the views expressed above need not be construed to mean that a technical reproduction by means of a scanner, that requires a similar technical effort, would not correspondingly lead to protection as a *Lichtbild*. It appears therefore that the Regional Court did not wish to rule out the possibility that a similar technical effort expended by a human actor operating a scanner (in terms of adjusting the light and exposure settings, etc., to ensure the production of a detailed and faithful digital reproduction devoid of distortions) would enable the scanned image to obtain protection under section 72. As noted above, the production of a digitised version of a rare document (especially in the case of an old and fragile document) would necessarily involve the expenditure of technical effort along these lines by the

[279]Talke (n 253) 851.

[280]LG Berlin 03.05.2016, 15O 428/15 – *Reiss Engelhorn Museum I*. In this case, the Museum brought an action against the *Wikimedia Foundation* who operated the website on which the scanned copies of the photographs were made available.

human actor who operates the scanner. Therefore, notwithstanding its status as *obiter dictum* the Court's opinion does support the argument that the mere fact of utilising a scanning process may not necessarily prevent a digitised version from obtaining protection as a *Lichtbild* under section 72.

The *Reiss Engelhorn Museum II*[281] case saw the Museum bringing an action in the Regional Court (*Landgericht*) of Stuttgart against the user who uploaded scanned copies of the photographs to the Wikimedia Commons website. Similar to the decision delivered by the Regional Court of Berlin, the Regional Court of Stuttgart also held that the photographs were protected under section 72. The Regional Court observed that a minimum of mental performance (as would be present in all simple photographs) was sufficient to bring a photographic reproduction within the scope of section 72. The Regional Court held that, the effort expended by the photographer in the creation of a faithful, colour-accurate reproduction of the photographed object that was as true to the original as possible,[282] was sufficient to satisfy the minimum mental performance needed for protection under section 72.[283] Citing the *Bibelreproduktion*[284] decision, the Regional Court emphasised the nature of these photographs as photographic prototypes (*Urbilder*) and as technically elaborate imitations of works of art as opposed to being mere copies of pre-existing photographic images that would fail to qualify for protection under section 72. An appeal was made against this decision to the Court of Appeal of Stuttgart and the decision delivered by the Court of Appeal (*Oberlandgericht*), (referred to here, as *Reiss Engelhorn Museum II-Appeal*[285]) upheld the decision given by the Regional Court. The Court of Appeal of Stuttgart highlighted that protection as a *Lichtbild* required the existence of a minimum of intellectual effort and that the photographic image should be a prototype image as opposed to being a copy of an existing image.[286]

However Talke argues that, *Lichtbild* protection cannot be obtained in the case of digitised versions of book pages where the textual content has been printed upon the book pages using an image reproduction technique such as reprographic printing, gravure-printing or photographic printing because, in such cases, the book-page already constitutes a *Lichtbild*.[287] Therefore, Talke argues that, a digital photographic image of such a book-page would not qualify as an *Urbild* for the purpose of obtaining protection under section 72.[288] Nevertheless, he notes that, digitised

[281] LG Stuttgart, 27.09.2016 – 17 O 690/15 – *Reiss Engelhorn Museum II.*

[282] ibid 54.

[283] ibid 51. The Court noted that the effort expended by the photographer was demonstrated in the selection of the correct shooting position, optimum exposure of the photographed object and the choice of a suitable camera.

[284] BGH, 08.11.1989 – I ZR 14/88, GRUR 1990, 669 – *Bibelreproduktion.*

[285] OLG Stuttgart 31.05.2017, 4 U 204/16 – *Reiss Engelhorn Museum II* (Appeal).

[286] Ibid 55–57.

[287] Talke (n 253) 850.

[288] ibid.

versions of manuscripts and book-pages that contain handwritten textual content would qualify as *Urbilder.* While photographic printing processes are a more recent invention originating in the mid-twentieth century, reprography and gravure printing have been used in the printing of books and newspapers since the nineteenth century. Therefore, it is possible that the textual content recorded upon rare documents such as nineteenth century books and newspapers have been printed using these techniques. The question therefore arises whether digitised versions of these documents would fail to qualify as photographic prototypes (*Urbilder*) for obtaining protection under section 72.

It is argued here that Talke's opinion requires qualification in the case of digitised versions of old and fragile rare documents and that a digitised version of a page of an old book or newspaper that contains text that has been printed upon the document using an image reproduction technique (e.g., reprography, gravure printing) should not be denied the status of an *Urbild.* The creation of a scanned reproduction of a printed page involves a greater degree of technical effort than the reproduction of a photograph from an existing photographic negative as in the *Bibelreproduktion* case. The printed page although a reproduction of an existing template can, over time, develop characteristics of its own such as fading of the text, distortions and wrinkles. It cannot be denied that the production of a clear and accurate digital photographic image of such a document (that minimises the effects brought on by fading, distortions, wrinkles, etc.), involves substantial technical skill and effort on the part of the human actor who determines the image settings of the scanner (e.g., exposure, brightness, contrast) that goes beyond the mere pressing of a button. Neither can it be denied that, by exercising his judgement in relation to the image settings, the human actor is able to influence the visual representation of the final digital reproduction even if not in a creative or artistic sense.

Denying protection under section 72 to a digitised version merely because it reproduces a text that has been printed upon the document using an image reproduction technique, would go against the purpose of section 72, which is to provide protection to photographs that have been created with considerable financial and technological investment and craftsmanship.[289] Thus, it is noted that, the relevant factor in determining protection under section 72 should be the technical effort (*geistiger Leistung*) that has gone into the production of a digitised version. Although in a general sense, the fact that a photographic image constitutes a reproduction of a pre-existing photographic image gives rise to a presumption that its production does not require a technical effort, this should not be used as a general presumption to deny protection under section 72 to digitised versions of old and fragile documents, the production of which could involve a substantial technical effort.

A further point of interest in the three decisions relating to the photographic reproductions of public domain paintings belonging to the Reiss Engelhorn Museum is that, in all three instances, the courts refused an application made by the defendant

---

[289] *See* Vogel (n 257) § 72 para 13.

to adopt a teleological interpretation of section 72 in order to prevent photographic reproductions of public domain works from being protected as *Lichtbilder*. While an extensive discussion into the grounds on which this application was rejected is not within the scope of this study, it is sufficient to note that the courts held that no exception should be made to protection under section 72 where the subject of the photograph is a two-dimensional work in the public domain. The courts observed that this would result in protection under section 72 being granted based on an assessment of the motif reproduced by the photograph as opposed to the intellectual effort that has been expended in its creation, which would go against the will of the legislature in enacting the provision.[290] In the *Reiss Engelhorn I* decision, the Regional Court of Berlin pointed out that the protection granted to the photographic image of a public domain painting is limited to that particular photographic image and would not extend to the painting itself or affect its public domain status.[291] However, in the *Reiss Engelhorn Museum II-Appeal* decision, the Court of Appeal of Stuttgart emphasised that a public domain painting and its photographic reproduction are different works that can have different legal status. It highlighted that the public domain status only extended to the original painting itself and could not therefore prevent the protection of a photograph that reproduces it.[292]

It is not clear whether post-production activities such as colour calibration, cleaning of the raw image, etc., could be considered in determining whether an intellectual effort is present to determine the ability to protect a digitised version as a *Lichtbild* under section 72. It is argued here that, the decisions made during these activities are not part of the process of creating the digitised version but are aimed towards the modification or improvement of an existing digitised version. Therefore, the intellectual effort expended in the modification and/or improvement of an existing digitised version would be relevant in determining whether the digitised version could qualify as an artistic work under Article 2(1)(4) or (7) of the German Copyright Act. Hence, it could not be considered in determining whether the initial digitised version could obtain protection as a *Lichtbild* under Article 72.[293]

Overall, there is a convincing case to be made in favour of the protection of a digitised version of a rare document as a *Lichtbild* under section 72 of the German Copyright Act. However, in the absence of a specific judicial determination on this point it is not possible to predict with certitude, the position that would be taken by a

---

[290] LG Stuttgart, 27.09.2016 – 17 O 690/15 – *Reiss Engelhorn Museum II*, 54.

[291] LG Berlin 03.05.2016, 15O 428/15 – *Reiss Engelhorn Museum I*, 33.

[292] OLG Stuttgart 31.05.2017, 4 U 204/16 – *Reiss Engelhorn Museum II* (Appeal), 59.

[293] Vogel (n 257) § 72 para 21,

> Fotocomposing, Web designing u.a. digital veranderte bilder [..] begrunden kein Recht nach S.72, weil sie nicht auf der Verarbeitung von Lichtreizen sondern der Wiedergabe und/oder Veranderung gespeicherter Bilder mittels elektronische Befehle beruhen und der Umstanden nach S. 2 Abs 1 Nr. 4 oder Nr. 7 geschutzen Zeichnung naher stehen als der fotografischen Abbildung.

German court if the protection of a digitised version of a rare document is brought before it.

7.4.2.2 Following CJEU Harmonisation

Following the rejection of the higher degree of creativity (*Gestaltungshöhe*) by the Federal Supreme Court in the *Geburtstagszug*[294] case, it is argued here that, there does not appear to be much difference between the author's own intellectual creation standard of originality and the traditional German standard. In the *Geburtstagszug* decision the Federal Supreme Court held that, under Article 6 of the Term Directive, the originality of photographic works (*Lichtbildwerke*) should be determined based on the author's own intellectual creation standard and that no other special protection standards (such as a higher degree of creativity or *Gestaltungshöhe*) could be applied.[295] Thus, it is clear that the correct standard of originality that is to be applied in the case of a *Lichtbildwerk* under German law is the author's own intellectual creation standard.

According to Schulze, the author's own intellectual creation can be interpreted to require that the work originates from its creator and is characterised by his individual intellect.[296] Schulze argues that both the traditional standard of personal intellectual creation (*persönliche geistige Schöpfung*) and the author's own intellectual creation (*eigene geistige Schöpfung*) require the author's individuality to be present in the creation and that as such, there is no fundamental difference between the two standards. Schulze underlines that, in applying the author's own intellectual creation standard to determine the copyrightability of subject-matter, no other criteria; particularly non-qualitative or aesthetic criteria, can be applied.[297]

It is noted that, both under the traditional standard of originality (personal intellectual creation) and the harmonised EU standard, the individuality of the author is considered to be expressed in his work as a result of the exercise of personal creative choices that are not dictated by technical requirements. In the light of the conclusions in Sects. 7.3.2 and 7.4.1.1 above, that the creation of digitised versions does not allow for the exercise of personal creative choices on the part of its creator, it is argued here that, German courts would not be able to extend copyright protection to a digitised version as a *Lichtbildwerk*, because of its inability to fulfil the requirement of individuality.

If the standard of originality has been harmonised through CJEU jurisprudence, the question arises whether it would be possible for German copyright law to continue to maintain the two-tiered system of protection for photographs, i.e., as photographic works (*Lichtbildwerke*) under section 2(5)(1) and as photographic

[294]BGH 13.11.2013 – I ZR 143/12, GRUR 2014, 175 – *Geburtstagszug*.

[295]ibid 14–15 at para 30.

[296]Schulze (n 227) § 2 para 23.

[297]ibid.

images (*Lichtbilder*) under section 72. If the author's own intellectual creation standard is considered to be of uniform applicability to all copyrightable subject-matter, it may be argued that, it is no longer possible to apply a lower threshold of originality based on mere intellectual effort (*geistiger Leistung*) to photographic images that do not demonstrate the individuality of the photographer.

However, in the *Geburtstagszug* decision, the Federal Supreme Court emphasised that, although the originality of computer programmes, databases and photographic works (*Lichtbildwerke*) should be determined according to the author's own intellectual creation standard without any special protection standards (such as an elevated requirement of creativity) being applied, such restrictions are not imposed upon other types of works.[298] This *dictum* could be interpreted as an indication that the Federal Supreme Court did not consider the author's own intellectual creation standard to be of uniform application to all subject-matter that seeks copyright protection, and considered its application to be restricted to subject-matter in respect of which the standard of originality has been explicitly harmonised by EU Directives. Citing this *dictum*, Schulze notes that it remains to be seen whether national courts extend the author's own intellectual creation standard to subject-matter, the originality standard of which has not yet been expressly regulated by EU Directives.[299] These viewpoints call into question whether German scholars and judges do in fact acknowledge the harmonisation of the standard of originality in EU copyright law through CJEU interpretation.

Nevertheless, even if German judges did acknowledge the uniform application of the author's own intellectual creation standard to all copyrightable subject-matter, it is argued here that, there would be no impediment to the maintenance of a lower threshold of originality in relation to subject-matter that are protected under the regime of *Leistungsschutzrecht*. The InfoSoc Directive makes a distinction between copyright protectable 'works' and 'other subject-matter' (i.e., phonograms, broadcasts, fixations of performances, etc.). Thus, Article 2 of the InfoSoc Directive states that Member States shall provide an exclusive right to reproduction for authors of their works[300] and for performers, phonogram producers, film producers and broadcasting organisations in respect of the fixations of performances, phonograms, first fixations of films and broadcasts respectively.[301] This distinction is made further evident in Article 3 of the Directive. Article 3(1) of the InfoSoc Directive grants to authors the exclusive right to prohibit the communication of their 'works' (including the making available of their works) to the public. Article 3(2) grants to performers, phonogram producers, film producers and broadcasting organisations the exclusive right to prohibit the making available of their performances, phonograms, films and broadcasts. It appears that the term 'work' is intended to cover content that comes under the category of author's rights as per the continental tradition while the term

[298]BGH 13.11.2013 – I ZR 143/12, GRUR 2014, 175 – *Geburtstagszug*, 15 at para 31.

[299]Schulze (n 227) § 2 paras 22–23.

[300]InfoSoc Directive (n 50) Article 2(a).

[301]ibid Article 2 subsections (b)–(e).

'other subject-matter' refers to content that would normally fall within the category of related rights. The *Infopaq*[302] decision was concerned with determining the standard of originality that should apply to 'works' under Article 2(a) of the Directive. Accordingly, it is argued here that—if it is in fact to be treated as a standard of uniform applicability—the author's own intellectual creation standard applies to authorial works as distinguished from entrepreneurial subject-matter. For example, the standard should not be applied in determining the copyright protection of a phonogram created by a phonogram producer, under EU law.

In fact, an entrepreneurial subject-matter such as a phonogram would not be able to obtain copyright protection under the author's own intellectual creation standard, as it would not be possible to establish that the phonogram is characterised by its producer's individuality. In fact, it is argued here that, an assessment of originality under the author's own intellectual creation standard does not even arise in the case of entrepreneurial subject-matter, which are inherently devoid of their author's personality or individuality. The protection granted under section 72 to photographic images (*Lichtbilder*) is an entrepreneurial copyright or related right (*Leistungsschutzrecht*) as opposed to an author's right (which is granted over *Lichtbildwerk*). Section 72 grants protection to non-creative photographs that do not display a sufficient degree of originality to satisfy the standard of personal intellectual creation (*persönliche geistige Schöpfung*). Thus, it is argued here that, even if the author's own intellectual creation standard is considered to be harmonised within the EU and therefore to be of uniform applicability to all copyright protected content, this should not impede the intellectual effort (*geistiger Leistung*) standard from being applied to determine the protection of a photograph as a *Lichtbild* under section 72.

It is further noted that, Article 6 of the Term Directive also provides for the maintenance of alternative regimes for the protection of photographic images by allowing Member States to provide protection for non-original photographs under their national laws, notwithstanding the harmonised term of protection granted to original photographs under that Directive. Therefore, if section 72 is deemed to grant protection to non-original photographs, it would be possible to justify the maintenance of a lower threshold of originality in determining the protection of *Lichtbilder* under Article 6 of the Term Directive. Accordingly, it may be possible for digitised versions of rare documents that have been created with sufficient technical effort (*geistiger Leistung*) to obtain protection under section 72 of the German Copyright Act, notwithstanding the application of the harmonised EU originality standard.

[302] Judgment of 16 July 2009, *Infopaq International*, C-5/08, EU:C:2009:465.

7.4.3 *France*

7.4.3.1 The Traditional Copyright Law Framework

The French copyright (authors' rights) system is founded upon the perception that a work is an extension of its author's personality. Copyright law seeks to protect the specific relationship that is deemed to exist between an author and his work.[303] Thus, similar to the traditional German copyright law framework, to qualify for copyright protection under traditional French law, it is necessary that a work is demonstrated to contain elements that stem from its author's distinct personality. Although the standard of originality has not been defined through statute, a work is deemed original if it bears the 'stamp of the author's personality' (*l'empreinte de la personnalité de l'auteur*).[304] Thus, photographs or works that are created with the use of techniques that are analogous to photography will be protected as original works under Article L112-2 subsection 9 of the CPI if they bear the stamp of their authors' personality.[305]

Unfortunately, French law does not offer a stable interpretation of the standard of originality,[306] and the 'stamp of the author's personality' has been explained in many different ways. As Lucas opines, the flexibility of the notion of originality makes it difficult to elaborate the actual operational test of originality.[307] Pollaud-Dulian is of the view that creation implies that the author expresses his personality in the work created by him[308] in the sense that, the works draws its individuality and uniqueness from the individuality and personality of the artist.[309] He goes on to note that, the stamp of the author's personality lies in the individual style of the creator

[303]As Pollaud-Dulian notes, "Dès lors, l'œuvre est unie à l'auteur par un lien indissoluble. Dès lors, il n'y a pas que des intérêts patrimoniaux à protéger à propos de l'œuvre, mais aussi la personnalité qui s'y est exprimée". ("From then on, the work is united to the author by an indissoluble bond. Consequently, it is not only the patrimonial interests in the work that need to be protected, but also the personality that is expressed in it"). (Translated into English by the author). Fréderic Pollaud-Dulian, 'O.Lalignant, La Véritable Condition d'application Du Droit d'auteur: Originalité Ou Création?' (2000) 52 Revue internationale de droit comparé 270, 270.

[304]Vivant and Bruguière (n 89) 266.

[305]However, originality is not subject to quantitative or qualitative measurement. The notion of *l'unité de l'art* means that all works must be protected regardless of their artistic merit. It is noted that the protection of *petite monnaie* is itself an extension of this theory of *l'unité de l'art* that prevents a distinction from being made between creations that display a high degree of creativity and those that display a slight degree of creativity. *See* Lucas, Lucas-Schloetter and Bernault (n 5) 159.

[306]Benabou (n 47) 8. "[l]a vérité oblige à dire que l'on ne sait pas exactement en quoi consiste l'originalité'.' ('The truth obliges us to say that we do not exactly know what originality consists of.") (Translated into English by the author).

[307]Lucas, Lucas-Schloetter and Bernault (n 5) 127.

[308]Pollaud-Dulian (n 53) 157.

[309]ibid 271.

that is displayed through the form of the creation.[310] Lucas and Sirinelli opine that an original work is that in which the creator has been able to display a minimum of imagination (fantasy) inherent in all literary or artistic creations. They state that where there is room for arbitrariness, legal protection is acquired.[311] Edelman observes that creation is the product of a free intellectual effort, which expresses the personality of the creator and manifests it in an original form.[312] He emphasises the freedom enjoyed by the author in engaging in this intellectual effort as the key element of originality. Vivant and Bruguière are of the opinion that this element of freedom can be expressed through the choices made by the author in the creation of the work (which they point out is undoubtedly the view expressed by the CJEU).[313] Furthermore, Vivant and Bruguière observe that it is the creative activity that must be looked for in a work, in the sense that, the author's engagement in the creation process must involve a certain creative effort that manifests itself in the final work.[314] They proceed to elaborate that this doctrine accords with the personality theory of copyright law in the sense that, in order that a work manifests the creative activity of its author, it is necessary that the author has made a personal investment in the work.[315] This is confirmed by the opinion of Pollaud-Dulian who further notes that, the existence of a margin of creative freedom is indispensable to establish originality and to attribute the status of authorship to the creator of the work.[316] Thus, it appears that under the classical standard of originality, the author of a work must enjoy sufficient intellectual freedom within the creation process to make arbitrary choices and that in making those choices he must exercise sufficient creativity so as to allow his individuality to be displayed in the final work.

The notion of 'small change' (*petite monnaie*) extends the scope of copyright protection to works of a technical or utilitarian character such as a telephone directory, or the text of a patent[317] which cannot be considered to bear the stamp of their author's personality. As Lucas, et al. note, although the creation of these

[310] Pollaud-Dulian (n 303) 270–71.

[311] André Lucas and Pierre Sirinelli, 'L'originalité En Droit D'auteur' (1993) 23 La Semaine Juridique Edition Générale 10. "L'œuvre originale est celle dans laquelle le créateur a pu déployer le minimum de fantaisie inhérent à toute création littéraire ou artistique. Dès lors qu'il y a place pour l'arbitraire, la protection légale est acquise". ("An original work is one in which the creator was able to display a minimum of fantasy as is inherent in all literary or artistic creation. Where there is room for arbitrariness, legal protection is acquired".) (Translated into English by the author). *See contra* Pollaud-Dulian who notes that arbitrary choices that are not creative will not be sufficient to establish originality if those choices are not creative. (n 53) 163.

[312] Bernard Edelman, *La Propriété Littéraire et Artistique* (PUF 2008) 16, "la création est le produit d'un travail intellectuel libre, exprimant la personnalité du créateur, et s'incarnant dans une forme original". ("[c]reation is the product of free intellectual activity, expressing the personality of the creator, and embodying it in an original form".) (Translated into English by the author).

[313] Vivant and Bruguière (n 89) 268.

[314] ibid.

[315] ibid.

[316] Pollaud-Dulian (n 53) 203.

[317] Lucas, Lucas-Schloetter and Bernault (n 5) 131.

works requires the exercise of choice, these choices do not have a quality of arbitrariness and although they may demonstrate the author's know-how (which is an objective element), they do not reveal the author's personality. Thus, it becomes difficult to argue that these works carry the stamp of their authors' personality.[318] However, Lucas, et al. highlight that, in granting copyright protection to small change works, courts have often highlighted the necessity to consider the choices that have been made in the selection of the elements of the work and the order and method that has been employed in their presentation.[319] Thus, copyright protection has been granted to works, the elements of which have been drawn from existing works as those elements have been chosen with discernment, arranged in a new order and given a novel form.[320] However, as Pollaud-Dulian points out, even to qualify for copyright protection in the small-change category, it is necessary that some intellectual effort has been invested in the creation of the work and that this would not be the case where creation has been the result of a mechanical process or where the work is a servile copy of a pre-existing work.[321]

7.4.3.1.1 Objectification of the Classical Standard of Originality

In the decision delivered in the *Pachot*[322] case in 1986, the Supreme Court adjusted the classical originality standard and re-interpreted it as 'the mark of an intellectual creation of the author'. This re-interpretation was triggered by the enactment of the Law of 3rd July 1985 under which copyright protection was accorded to software programmes. As observed by Lucas, et al., it was left to the courts to exemplify a valid doctrinal basis upon which the copyright protection of software programmes could be justified. Thus, the extension of the notion of originality to utilitarian informational works tested the limits of the personality-based approach of the

---

[318]*Contra* Pollaud-Dulian (n 53) 271, "Dès lors, il n'y a rien d'absurde ou d'artificiel à déceler l'empreinte de la personnalité d'un auteur dans une oeuvre qui relève des arts appliqués ou de la petite monnaie, que l'ambition soit modeste, que les sujétions soient fortes n'êmpechent pas l'expression de la personnalité dans la création". ("Henceforth, there is nothing absurd or artificial in detecting the imprint of an author's personality in a work of applied art or small change, even if the ambition is modest and the constraints are strong these do not impede the expression of personality in the creation".) (Translated into English by the author).

[319]Lucas, Lucas-Schloetter and Bernault (n 5) 131 note 302, citing Cour de Cassation crim, 18 May 1938: Gaz Pal 1938 (2) 311 ("le choix, l'ordre et la méthode sous lesquels leur ensemble est présenté constituent incontestablement un travail de l'esprit de nature à donner naissance à un droit privatif de propriété") and Cour de Cassation crim, 27 November 1869: DP 1870 (1) 186 ("la protection du droit d'auteur s'étend aux ouvrages dont les éléments, bien qu'empruntés à des publications antérieurs, n'en sont pas moins choisis avec discernment, disposés dans un ordre nouveau, revêtus d'une forme nouvelle et appropriés avec l'intelligence à un usage plus ou moins général").

[320]ibid Cour de Cassation crim, 27 November 1869: DP 1870 (1) 186.

[321]Pollaud-Dulian (n 53) 271.

[322]Lucas, Lucas-Schloetter and Bernault (n 5) 138.

traditional notion of originality, and resulted in the classical notion of originality undergoing a process of objectification.[323]

Five years later, in the case of *Isermatic France,*[324] the Supreme Court upheld the originality of a computer programme because certain features of the programme (i.e., the content of the memory modules and tracking information) resulted from creative choices that demonstrated the author's personal contribution to the creation of the programme. More recently, in 2012, the Supreme Court affirmed that the originality of a software programme was to be established following a determination as to whether the choices made in the process of creating the software programme provided evidence of a specific intellectual effort and a personal contribution on the part of the author. The mere efficacy of the programme in providing a solution to an existing problem or fulfilling a practical need was considered irrelevant to the establishment of originality.[325]

In the 1989 case of *Harrap France v. Masson Editeur*[326] which involved the originality of a bilingual (English-French) information technology dictionary, the Court of Appeal of Paris held that, notwithstanding the technical nature of the dictionary, the choices made by the author (e.g., in the determining the entries that were to be included in the dictionary) involved an intellectual effort that bestowed the technical creation with originality to qualify it for copyright protection. However, the Court of Appeal distinguished the effort made by the author of the dictionary from a mere presentation of a list of words in alphabetical order, indicating that such a mechanical expenditure of labour would not qualify for copyright protection. Gervais and Judge interpret the decision as a rejection of the sweat of the brow or labour-based approach.[327] The rejection of a sweat of the brow approach to originality is also relied upon by the Supreme Court in the decision delivered in the case of *Coprosa.*[328] This case involved the copyright protection of an organisational chart of the world's leading car companies (in the form of lists of their managers and directors) published in an automobile newspaper. The Court of Appeal of Douai upheld the originality of the organisational chart based on the research effort that had been invested in assembling the data and the new composition through which they

[323]ibid.

[324]Cour de Cassation, Ch civ 1, 16 April 1991, 89-21071 – *Isermatic France.*

[325]Cour de cassation, Ch civ 1, 17 October 2012, 11-21641 – *Codix.*

[326]Cour d'Appel de Paris 4eme Ch, 21 March 1989, RIDA 156 (1989) 333 (*Harrap France c Masson Editeur*).

[327]Daniel J Gervais and Elizabeth F Judge, 'Of Silos and Constellations: Comparing Notions of Originality in Copyright Law' (2009) 27 Cardozo Arts & Entertainment Law Journal 375, 379.

[328]Cour de Cassation, Ch civ 1, 2 May 1989, 87-17657 – *Coprosa. See also* Cour d'Appel de Paris, 4eme Ch, 23 September 1992, RIDA 142 (1993) 224 (*Michel Lafon c Librarie Arthème Fayard*) where the Court of Appeal of Paris upheld the originality of a compilation of stories that had been derived from traditional folklore because although the stories emanated from a common resource, by selecting and narrating them in a manner which is particularly his own, and by arranging them in an order of his choice, the author gave the narrative a particular structure that transformed it into a creative work.

were presented. However, the Supreme Court overturned the decision made by the Court of Appeal on the grounds that the reasoning adopted by the Court of Appeal did not succeed in specifying how the graphic form of the publication could include an intellectual contribution by the author as would be necessary to characterise an original creation. In the 2005 decision delivered in the case of *Sawkins v Harmonia Mundi*[329] the Court of First Instance of Nanterre emphasised that, to be eligible for copyright protection, a work of the mind must bear the mark of the intellectual and personal contribution of the author. It determined that a restored edition of public domain music qualified for copyright protection because, during the restoration process, the author made personal and arbitrary artistic choices based on his personal interpretation.

Judge and Gervais explain that literary and artistic works are the result of one of more of three types of choices: technical choices that are essentially dictated by the technique used in the creation of the work, functional choices that are dictated by the function that a utilitarian work will serve, and creative choices that stem from the author himself.[330] They opine that the test of originality is focused upon the creative choices; the choices made by the author that were not guided by applicable standards, methods used to create the work, nor considerations of optimal functionality and efficiency, and which result from the author exercising his creative freedom.[331] Gervais defines a creative choice as a conscious human choice that is not dictated by the function of the work, the method or technique used, applicable standards or relevant good practice.[332] Gervais argues that, if function dictates the course to be followed, there is no room for creativity because from a copyright standpoint the result would be inevitable.[333] By way of illustrating the application of the proposed definition of 'creative choice' Gervais contends that technical choices made by a photographer such as the use of a filter, aperture, etc. that are usually dictated by good photographic practices would not lead to the creation of a literary or artistic work. Rather, it is the choices that are not-dictated by external considerations such as pose, angle, décor, lighting arrangements, etc. that would be relevant in determining the originality of a photograph.[334] This is also in accordance with Edelman's opinion that, while intellectual effort is the basis of all literary and artistic creation, the effort

[329]TGI Nanterre, Ch 1 A, 19 January 2005, JurisData 2005-279499 (*Sawkins c Société Harmonia Mundi*).

[330]Judge and Gervais (n 327) 377.

[331]ibid 379.

[332]Gervais presents this definition in an attempt to formulate a notion of 'creative choice' that would meet the requirements of international treaties and comply with the notions of creative choice in US and Canadian law, as well as civil law systems. Daniel J Gervais, 'Feist Goes Global: A Comparative Analysis of the Notion of Originality in Copyright Law' (2002) 49 Journal Copyright Society of the USA 949, 976–977.

[333]ibid 978.

[334]ibid 979, discussing the notion of 'creative choice' (n 332).

made must be free in the sense that it must have been furnished outside of all intrinsic constraints.[335]

Thus, even after the transformation of the classical originality standard following the *Pachot* and *Isermatic* cases, it appears that the exercise of creative choices by the creator of the work remains the operative element in the determination of originality in French law.[336] Hence, to satisfy the originality standard under French law, an intellectual effort that involves the exercise of creative as opposed to technical or functional choices is required. Skill and labour that has been expended in achieving technical or functional perfection in the production of a digitised version would not invest it with sufficient originality. Thus, it is argued here that, choices exercised by the producer of a digitised version of a rare document that are dictated by the functional consideration of reproducing an existing rare document in digital form with optimal accuracy and quality, would not allow it to satisfy the more objective originality standard of French law.

7.4.3.1.2 Know-How

French law makes an important distinction between originality and 'know-how' (*savoir-faire*). Thus, where the intellectual effort is merely aimed towards the implementation of a technique, this will not lead to the creation of a literary or artistic work that qualifies for copyright protection. Accordingly, a decision delivered by the Court of Appeal of Paris[337] determined that the director of an audio-visual work whose effort was limited to the sequencing of text and pictures with the assistance of two or three cameras, did not participate in the intellectual creation of the work for the reason that his achievement was nothing more than the implementation of a technique.

The determination delivered by the Court of Appeal of Aix-en-Provence in the *Deux Rougets*[338] case illustrates this point. The case involved a photograph that showed two red fish on a yellow platter. The photographer alleged that his photograph had been partially reproduced without his authorisation in a new photograph (i.e., a derivative work) that represented a collection of similar fish on a yellow platter, resulting in the infringement of his copyright. The Court of Appeal of Aix-en-Provence stated that originality referred to the reflection of the personality of the author or the revelation of a creative talent and that originality must not be confused with professional competence. The Court of Appeal noted that the photograph in its constituent elements did not display sufficient evidence of a creative activity that revealed the photographer's personality and that on a technical level it did not indicate any pursuit of aesthetic research as to appropriate lighting, background

[335]Edelman (n 312) 17.

[336]Gervais (n 332) 969, discussing the originality test in French law.

[337]Cour d'appel Paris, 4 March 1987, D 1988, 204, obs Colombet.

[338]Cour d'appel d'Aix-en-Provence, 6 May 2010 – *Deux Rougets*.

shading, shooting angles, etc. Thus, the Court of Appeal determined that, the photograph under review merely constituted a provision of technical services, resulting from 'know-how'. Hence, the photograph did not qualify as an original copyrightable work. On appeal to the Supreme Court,[339] the decision of the Court of Appeal was upheld. The Supreme Court approved of the reasoning adopted by the Court of Appeal that, in the absence of an indication of an aesthetic pursuit and a finding that the photograph was nothing more than a simple provision of technical services translating into 'know-how', the photograph could not qualify as an intellectual work. It is evident that the creation of a digitised version involves neither an aesthetic pursuit nor the exercise of creative choices. Thus, it is argued here that the creation of a digitised version represents an exercise of 'know-how' as opposed to an exercise of intellectual effort as would result in an original copyrightable work.

7.4.3.1.3 Originality of Reproductive Content

Lucas, et al. note that, in relation to works that are based upon existing works (i.e., derivative works) a relative notion of originality is adopted.[340] Accordingly, a work that reproduces an existing work could obtain copyright protection as a derivative work if it displays the stamp of the personality of the copyist.[341] Nonetheless, mere servile copies or works that do not express the personality of their author would not qualify for copyright protection, as they constitute simple reproductions as opposed to derivative works.[342] As Lucas, et al. note, everything depends on the margin of freedom that is afforded to the person making the copy.[343] Pollaud-Dulian[344] cites a decision delivered by the Court of Appeal[345] of Paris, where it was held that engravings that were based on an existing original drawing would qualify for copyright protection because the reproduction of the drawings in the form of an engraving resulted from the exercise of intelligence, experience and careful choices on the part of the engraver, as opposed to a purely mechanical process. The Court of Appeal determined that the engravings displayed the sensibilities of their author and were a personalised work which could be distinguished from a work created by

[339]Cour de Cassation, 1er ch Civ, 20 October 2011, 10-21251 – *Deux Rougets*.

[340]Lucas, Lucas-Schloetter and Bernault (n 5) 127, 147.

[341]Desbois notes for example that, a manually carried out reproduction of an artwork could qualify as a derivative work protected under copyright law, if the copyist's personality is reflected in the reproductive work. Henri Desbois, Le Droit D'auteur En France (3rd Edition Dalloz 1978) 76–77. Pollaud-Dulian (n 53) 205–206, confirms this view by stating that a manually executed reproduction of a work of art could itself be protected by copyright as a derivative work based on a relative notion of originality. *See also* Lucas, Lucas-Schloetter and Bernault (n 5) 156.

[342]Pollaud-Dulian (n 53) 206.

[343]Lucas, Lucas-Schloetter and Bernault (n 5) 156.

[344]Pollaud-Dulian (n 53) 207.

[345]Cour d'appel de Paris, 19 December 1962: D 1963, 609 (*Sté des bibliophiles v Crommelynck*).

another. Therefore, the engraver had created a personal creation which was original and had its own aesthetic value.

Pollaud-Dulian is of the view that the copyright protection of photographs of works of art that seek to reproduce those works of art as faithfully as possible (e.g., for publication in museum or exhibition catalogues or monographs) needs to be determined on a case by case basis and that it is not possible to systematically deny copyright protection to this genre of photographs on the sole pretext that the requirements of composition and fidelity make it a purely technical creation.[346]

In a 2001 decision, the Court of Appeal of Paris held that a series of photographic reproductions of Picasso's paintings that were published in a catalogue, qualified for copyright protection because of the deliberate choices made by the photographer as to the lighting, filters, framing and angle of shooting, which allowed his personality to be expressed in the photographs. However, this decision[347] is criticised by Caron, who notes that a photograph that seeks to faithfully reproduce a two dimensional work of art will not in normal circumstances qualify for copyright protection for the reason that the photographer does not enjoy a margin of freedom as would enable him to engage in the exercise of his own choice. Caron further argues that a servile photographic reproduction of a two-dimensional work of art would be the result of the exercise of know-how (*savoir-faire*) and would not usually grant its creator the status of an author.[348] Caron's argument is supported by case-law that establishes that the mere exercise of choice on the part of the photographer is in itself not sufficient; it must be further demonstrated that those choices were not merely determined by technical requirements. In the *Mirkine*[349] case, the Court of Appeal of Paris noted that a series of photographic stills of a film did not qualify for copyright protection on the grounds that, the choices made by the photographer as to the shooting angle was determined by technical constraints and did not testify to the exercise of any personal freedom on his part. Furthermore, in a 2013 decision[350] the Court of Appeal of Paris held that, photographic reproductions of three dimensional sculptures that were intended for publication in a monograph, while being of excellent technical quality, did not qualify for copyright protection for the reason that the choices made by the photographer in determining the frame of the photography and of the lighting were determined by the technical imperative of creating a faithful photographic reproduction, without any particular research as to its composition. The Court of Appeal concluded that the photographs were mere faithful

---

[346]Pollaud-Dulian (n 53) 207.

[347]Cour d'appel de Paris, 4eme Ch, 26 September 2001: 2001 Juris Data 159279 *(Réunion des Musées Nationaux v Wofsy) cited in* Christophe Caron, 'Protection des photographies de tableaux par le droit d'auteur' (2002) 7 La Semaine Juridique Entreprise et Affaires 321.

[348]ibid.

[349]Cour d'Appel de Paris, 15 October 2003 – *Mirkine. See also* Pierre Greffe, 'Appréciation de l'originalité d'une photographie de plateau' (2004) 5 Propriété industrielle 46.

[350]Cour d'appel de Paris, 1èrè Ch, 16 January 2013, 11-18788.

reproductions of the sculptures and only reflected the know-how of their creators while failing to express their personalities.

From the foregoing discussion, it is likely that the choices made by a human actor in the creation of a digitised version would be considered as being directed by the functional imperative of creating a faithful digital reproduction of a rare document. It is therefore highly probable that French courts would determine that the digitisation process does not afford sufficient freedom to the human actor as would enable him to exercise creative choices and to imprint his personality upon the digitised version.

7.4.3.2 Following CJEU Harmonisation

Vivant and Bruiguiére question whether the author's own intellectual creation standard will effect a change to the traditional originality standard in France. They note that, for a French lawyer, the author's own intellectual creation standard echoes the standard of originality that was adopted in the *Pachot* case, which resulted in an objectification of the classical standard of originality and a lowering of the threshold of originality by substituting personality with intellect.[351] They distinguish personality from intellect on the basis that, although for a work to be stamped with the author's personality, it is necessary that the author is totally present within his work, for a work to be the author's own intellectual creation, it is sufficient that the author has exercised his intelligence in the creation of the work. This element of intelligence can be demonstrated through the author's making of certain choices.[352] Vivant and Bruguière observe that, in spite of the reference to the stamp of the author's personality in the *Painer* case, the central criterion of the author's own intellectual creation test as interpreted in the *Painer* decision are the choices made by the author.[353] Therefore, Vivant and Bruguière argue that the *dictum* of the *Painer* case does not effect a significant change to the French test of originality for photographs because in any case, the choices made by an author form a central criterion of the French originality standard.[354]

Benabou argues that the *Premier League*[355] decision could be interpreted to mean that the exercise of know-how would be sufficient if it expresses originality in the choice or arrangement of the information.[356] Thus, Benabou observes that the *Premier League* decision can be construed to infer that the notion of choice no longer refers to the exercise of arbitrary preferences by the creator but to an effort

351 Vivant and Bruiguiére (n 89) 294.

352 Vivant and Bruiguiére (n 89) 293.

353 ibid 289, "Sans la moindre équivoque, et malgré le visa du "reflet" de la personnalité, le critère du choix, expressément mis en avant, est privilégié."

354 ibid 297.

355 Judgment of 4 October 2011, Football Association Premier League and Others, C-403/08 and C-429/08, EU:C:2011:631.

356 Benabou (n 47) 11.

made in the selection of data or to a display of expertise in their arrangement. Thus, she notes that, although the decision makes reference to the creative freedom of the author, it substantially reduces the artistic dimension that commonly lies at the core of that standard.[357] Hence, in Benabou's opinion it is possible to argue that the harmonised EU standard has the effect of lowering the French standard of originality to a more 'pedestrian' notion.[358]

However, French case-law does not demonstrate any material transformation on the standard of originality. Although courts allude to CJEU jurisprudence, in determining the originality of a work, they appear to proceed on the presumption that the author's own intellectual creation standard is identical to the traditional French standard of originality. At least, it is not possible to discern any significant changes in the way in which the stamp of the author's personality (*l'empreinte de la personnalité de l'auteur*) is being interpreted or applied following the introduction of the author's own intellectual creation standard. For instance, in the decision delivered in 2015 in the case of *Bowstir Ltd. v EgoTrade SARL*[359] (Jimmy Hendrix case), the High Court of First Instance (*Tribunal de Grande Instance*) of Paris citing the *Painer* case, determined that a photograph would be considered original if it bore the imprint of its author's personality, as a consequence of the choices made by the author. Similarly, the Supreme Court in a decision[360] delivered in 2015, held that a work is original only if it bears the imprint of its author's personality. Accordingly, the Supreme Court overturned a decision delivered by the Court of Appeal of Paris[361] that determined certain photographic works to be original merely from the fact that their creation required the making of choices, on the basis that the Court of Appeal's failure to explain how those choices disclosed the imprint of the author's personality upon the photographs made the decision bad in law.

Thus, it appears that no significant changes have been effected to the standard of originality applied by French courts following the introduction of the harmonised standard. Therefore, it can be concluded that a digitised version would not be able to obtain copyright protection under French law, following the introduction of the author's own intellectual creation standard as a harmonised standard of originality within the EU.

---

[357] ibid 12.

[358] ibid.

[359] TGI Paris, 3eme Ch 1, 21 May 2015 – *Bowstir Ltd, GM c. Egotrade SARL* (Jimmy Hendrix case).

[360] Cour de Cassation Ch civ, 15 May 2015, 13-27391 – *Glamour*.

[361] Cour d'Appel de Paris, 18 September 2013.

7.5 Summary and Conclusions

Both under the author's own intellectual creation standard of originality, as well as the traditional standards of originality in the copyright law frameworks of France and Germany, the author's ability to exercise creative choices and thereby to express his personality or individuality through the resulting work, forms the central criterion.

A production of a digitised version of a rare document requires the expenditure of an intellectual effort on the part of its creator. However, this intellectual effort is constrained by the functional requirement of ensuring that the visual elements of the digitised versions correspond faithfully to those of the original rare document. Therefore, the process of producing a digitised version does not provide the creator the freedom to express his personal creative or artistic choices in determining the final form of the digitised version.

Thus, it is concluded that, a digitised version will not obtain copyright protection either as an original photograph under Article 6 of the Term Directive or as a work in terms of the InfoSoc Directive, as it would not qualify as its author's own intellectual creation. Similarly, a digitised version would not obtain copyright protection under the traditional originality standards of France or Germany. It is likely that under French copyright law the creation of a digitised version would be categorised under as an exercise of know-how (*savoir-faire*) that does not give rise to an intellectual creation.

It is possible that in Germany, a digitised version may be able to obtain related rights protection as a non-creative photograph or a photographic image (*Lichtbild*) under section 72 of the German Copyright Act as the creation of a clear reproduction of a rare document devoid of distortions requires the expenditure of intellectual effort (*geistiger Leistung*). The requirement for such intellectual effort would be especially evident when the rare document that is subject to the digitisation process is faded or damaged in such a way that the need for the exercise of human intellect becomes more pronounced. However, the protection of a digitised version as a non-creative photograph (*Lichtbild*) would have to be determined on a case by case basis, considering the specific choices that have been made by the human actor in the creation of each individual digitised version (or a series of digitised versions when they have been created *en masse* under identical conditions). This renders the protection offered under the *Lichtbild* regime an inefficient means of regulating digitised versions, especially in terms of the uncertainty it can create for producers and users.

In comparison with France and Germany, the standard of originality in the UK that needs to be fulfilled by a digitised version to obtain copyright protection in the UK, is difficult to discern. However, an examination of case-law and scholarly opinion suggests that digitised versions would not qualify for copyright protection in the UK for the reason that the functional requirement of replicating an existing rare document as exactly as possible, minimises the ability of the human actor to exercise free and creative choices, which is considered to be a central criterion of the originality test following the introduction of the harmonised EU standard of originality.

Thus, the copyright law framework as it exists within the EU is not capable of granting protection to digitised versions of rare documents. Hence, there is a need to explore an alternative mechanism that would be able to protect and regulate the use and exploitation of digitised versions within the EU.

Chapter 8
Why Are Related Rights the Best Mechanism?

As observed in Chap. 6, of the available mechanisms for the protection of digitised versions of rare documents, copyright law provides an established legal framework aimed at balancing the interests of copyright owners and users of copyright protected content. However, as demonstrated in Chap. 7, a digitised version would not fulfil the required standard of originality to qualify for copyright protection within the existing EU law framework. Thus, it is necessary to find a suitable alternative mechanism for the regulation of digitised versions that would be able to achieve an effective balance between the competing interests of users and producers. It is argued that the best strategy would be to bring the regulation of digitised versions under the related rights framework that exists within EU law.

This chapter analyses the suitability of protecting digitised versions under a related rights regime. The following chapter presents a proposal for the practical formulation of a regulatory regime based on related rights that could be introduced within the EU for the protection of digitised versions of rare documents.

8.1 What Are Related Rights?

Related rights are based on a concept that primarily developed within the Continental copyright law (authors' rights) tradition. In its essence, related rights (also referred to as 'neighbouring rights') protect achievements that, although not giving rise to the creation of an original copyrightable work, nevertheless contribute to the interpretation, communication, or dissemination of a creation.[1] Such contributions are considered to hold sufficient social value that justify their protection by law. In

[1] As Pollaud-Dulian notes, related rights, are neighbouring to copyright in that they revolve around the creation, because its right-holders contribute in making the creation known by interpreting it, financing it or communicating it. Frédéric Pollaud-Dulian, *Le Droit D'Auteur* (2nd Ed, Economica 2014) 1494.

S. Mendis, *A Copyright Gambit*, Munich Studies on Innovation and Competition 11,
https://doi.org/10.1007/978-3-662-59454-4_8

one sense, related rights are 'related to copyright' in that they are inspired by and resemble copyright (i.e., the rights of authors) in terms of structure and modes of protection.[2] Meanwhile, they could also be seen as 'related to copyright' as some of holders of related rights, although not engaging in intellectual creation, engage in acts which are auxiliary to intellectual creation in terms of producing, diffusing or executing the creations of others.[3]

As Lucas points out, related rights do not constitute a homogenous category of rights.[4] The inherent flexibility of the concept is evidenced by its ability to accommodate within its scope a diverse array of interests, such as a creative investment made by a performing artist that is contrasted with the financial, technological and entrepreneurial investment made by the producer of a phonogram or a broadcasting organisation.[5] The following discussion will focus upon related rights in its character as a legal mechanism that grants protection to achievements that involve the investment of financial, entrepreneurial or technological resources as opposed to achievements that involve creative or intellectual investment.[6] It is noted that the production of a digitised version of a rare document shares many similarities with the production of a phonogram. As discussed in Chap. 7 it requires financial investment, technological expertise in using the scanning equipment and software to create the digital image and entrepreneurial skill in distributing and making available the digitised version to the public. Thus, it is argued here that, related rights protection is the mechanism that is best suited for the protection of the non-creative investment that has been made in the production of a digitised version.

---

[2]ibid 1494. *See also* André Lucas, *Propriété Littéraire et Artistique* (5th Edition, Dalloz 2015) 135.

[3]Pollaud-Dulian (n 1) 1494–1495. For example, a musician who performs a musical score, thereby executing the musical work in a way that it could be perceived by the public, is granted a related right over his performance. Similarly, the producer of phonogram (i.e., sound recording) that fixates upon that musical performance in such a way that it can be reproduced and distributed to the public is granted a related right over the phonogram recording.

[4]André Lucas, Agnès Lucas-Schloetter and Carine Bernault, *Traité de la propriété littéraire et artistique* (5th edn, Lexis Nexis 2017) 1013.

[5]World Intellectual Property Organization, *Neighboring Rights': Guide to the Rome Convention and to the Phonograms Convention* (WIPO 1981) 12. "[T]he purist may complain that, notwithstanding the skill and talent of a recording engineer or a broadcast producer, the making of a record or of a broadcast is, after all, an essentially industrial act, whereas the performances of artistes are of their nature acts of spiritual creation."

[6]It is noted that the right granted to performing artists constitutes a special case within the related rights regime that is primarily focused on protecting entrepreneurial investment against acts of unfair competition, as opposed to a personal creative investment. *See* Herman Cohen Jehoram, 'The Nature of Neighboring Rights of Performing Artists, Phonogram Producers and Broadcasting Organizations' (1990) 15 Columbia VLA Journal of Law & the Arts 76.

8.1.1 International Landscape

The term related rights is an abbreviation of 'rights related to copyright'. The origins of the concept of related rights protection can be traced to the 1948 Brussels Diplomatic Conference for the Revision of the Berne Convention where the term 'neighbouring rights' first appeared in a resolution relating to the protection of performing artists.[7] The Conference expressed the wish that governments of the countries of the union should study means by which to ensure the protection of performers, manufacturers of instruments that mechanically reproduce musical works and transmissions made by radio broadcasting institutions.[8] Bodenhausen notes that, although protection of the subject-matter referred to had already been introduced by statute in some countries and in other jurisdictions courts were in the practice of deriving protective consequences from general statutory provisions such as those against torts or unfair competition, it was widely felt that protection could not be permanently left to very general legal provisions.[9] It was further considered that protection could not be merely left to be developed through case-law for the reason that the delimitation of the protection to be awarded to the subject-matter under review was (because of the public interest and the interplay of private interests concerned) an extremely delicate task which could not be satisfactorily performed by the courts.[10]

The International Convention for the Protection of Performers, Producers of Phonograms and Broadcasting Organizations, adopted in 1961[11] (hereinafter referred to as the 'Rome Convention' as it was agreed upon in Rome, Italy), set out minimum requirements of protection to be granted by the contracting states to performers concerning their performances, to producers of phonograms concerning phonograms (i.e., sound recordings) and to broadcasting organisations concerning broadcasts. Although the term 'related right' or 'neighbouring right' was not used in the text of the Convention, since then these terms have been used interchangeably in designating the rights conferred upon performers, producers of phonograms and broadcasters by the Rome Convention.[12] The 1981 Guide to the Rome Convention published by the World Intellectual Property Organization (WIPO) refers to these protections as neighbouring rights.[13] However, the EU law framework uses the term

---

[7]ibid 75.

[8]George Bodenhausen, 'Protection of "Neighboring Rights"' (1954) 19 Law and Contemporary Problems 156, 157.

[9]ibid 158.

[10]ibid.

[11]International Convention for the Protection of Performers, Producers of Phonograms and Broadcasting Organizations, 26 October, 1961, 496 U.N.T.S. 43. The Convention came into effect in 1964.

[12]Cohen Jehoram (n 6) 76.

[13]WIPO Guide to Rome Convention (n 5) 7, "For ease of reference, the expression 'neighboring rights' will be used here to cover the rights granted by the Rome Convention to performers,

'related rights' in referring to the rights granted by the *acquis communautaire* to performers, broadcasters and producers of films and phonograms.[14] For the purpose of this discussion, the term 'related rights' is used in referring to this protection mechanism.

The TRIPS Agreement of 1994[15] also included provisions for the protection of performers, producers of phonograms and broadcasting organisations.[16] Two years later, the WIPO Performances and Phonograms Treaty ('WPPT') which was adopted in 1996[17], sought to further develop and expand the scope of this protection without derogating from the existing obligations of contracting parties under the Rome Convention, considering the economic and technological realities of the new digital environment.[18] The WPPT thereby widened the scope of protection granted under related rights than that which had been accorded under the Rome Convention and the TRIPS Agreement.[19] Thus, related rights are at present an ingrained feature of international intellectual property law.[20] As the EU is a signatory of the TRIPS[21]

producers of phonograms and broadcasting organizations (without prejudging the question whether or not these are in truth neighbors to the copyright of authors)".

[14]*See* Article 1(1) of Directive 2001/29/EC of the European Parliament and of the Council of 22 May 2001 on the harmonisation of certain aspects of copyright and related rights in the information society [2001] OJ L167/10 (InfoSoc Directive). *See also* Article 1 of Directive 2014/26/EU of the European parliament and of the council of 26 February 2014 on collective management of copyright and related rights and multi-territorial licensing of rights in musical works for online use in the internal market [2014] OJ L 84/72; Article 5 of Directive 93/83/EEC of 27 September 1993 on the coordination of certain rules concerning copyright and rights related to copyright applicable to satellite broadcasting and cable retransmission [1993] OJ L 248/15.

[15]Agreement on Trade-Related Aspects of Intellectual Property Rights, Apr. 15, 1994, Marrakesh Agreement Establishing the World Trade Organization, Annex 1C, Legal Instruments – Results of the Uruguay Round vol 31; 33 ILM 81 (1994) (TRIPS Agreement).

[16]TRIPS Agreement Article 14.

[17]WIPO Performances and Phonograms Treaty, Apr. 12, 1997, S. Treaty Doc. No. 105-17 36 ILM 76 (1997) (WPPT). The WPPT came into effect in 2002.

[18]WPPT Article 1(1).

[19]For example, in the case of producers of phonograms, the Rome Convention granted a right of reproduction (Article 10) and a single right to equitable remuneration for publication of the phonogram for commercial purposes or reproduction for the direct broadcast or communication to the public of the phonogram (Article 12). The TRIPS Agreement preserved the right of reproduction [Article 14 (2)] but also introduced a right to authorise or prohibit the commercial rental of originals or copies of phonograms [Article 14(4)]. The WPPT further expanded upon these instruments by also granting to phonogram producers the right to making available by wire or wireless means. For a comprehensive evaluation of the progress achieved by the WPPT *see* Jörg Reinbothe and Silke von Lewinski, *The WIPO Treaties on Copyright: A Commentary on the WCT, the WPPT and the BTAP* (2nd Edition, Oxford University Press 2015) 597–606.

[20]Also of relevance is the Convention for the Protection of Producers of Phonograms Against Unauthorized Duplication of their Phonograms (1971) and the Beijing Treaty on Audiovisual Performances (2012).

[21]The EU adopted the TRIPS Agreement by Council Decision 94/800/EC of 22 December 1994 concerning the conclusion on behalf of the European Community, on matters within its competence, of the agreements reached in the Uruguay Round multilateral negotiations (1986–1994) [1994] OJ L 336/1.

Agreement and the WPPT[22], related rights also form an integral aspect of EU law, as will be discussed below.

8.1.2 Related Rights Within the EU Law Framework

Continental copyright law systems traditionally distinguish between copyright (authors' rights) and related rights, and these are treated as distinct regimes of protection. In Germany, related rights are referred to as *verwandten Schutzrechten* and *Leistungsschutzrechte*. These are understood as exclusive rights granted for the protection of cultural achievements which, although not qualifying as the personal intellectual creations of their authors, have a decisive importance in relation to the creation of a work of authorship and/or, because of their character as immaterial goods, are protected in a manner similar to copyright.[23] In France, related rights are referred to as *droits voisins*. Desbois distinguishes related rights (*droits voisins*) from copyright (*droit d'auteur*) as related rights contribute to the diffusion as opposed to the creation of literary and artistic works.[24]

Related rights protection is also an accepted doctrine within the common law jurisdictions of the UK and Ireland.[25] In the UK, protection granted to sound recordings and broadcasts is informally distinguished as belonging to the category of 'entrepreneurial copyright'.[26] Macqueen, et al. note that, although UK legislation does not formally distinguish between authorial and other works, that distinction still underlies a good part of the assumptions on which the legal framework is built.[27] Accordingly Macqueen, et al. observe that while authors' rights are understood to refer to the works created by authors such as books, music, art, etc., related rights (also referred to as entrepreneurial rights or media rights) protect the investment

---

[22]The EU signed the WPPT in 2000. *See* Council Decision of 16 March 2000 on the approval, on behalf of the European Community, of the WIPO Copyright Treaty and the WIPO Performances and Phonograms Treaty, [2000] OJ L 89/6. The EU ratified the WPPT in 2009.

[23]Thomas Dreier in Thomas Dreier, Gernot Schulze and Louisa Specht (eds), *Urheberrechtsgesetz: Urheberrechtswahrnehmungsgesetz, Kunsturhebergesetz Kommentar* (5th Edition, CH Beck 2015) §§70ff para 1.

[24]Henri Desbois, *Le Droit D'auteur En France* (3rd Edition Dalloz 1978) 193.

[25]Hugh Laddie, Peter Prescott and Mary Vitoria, *The Modern Law of Copyright and Designs* (LexisNexis, 4th Ed, 2011) 385–87. The Copyright Related Rights Act No. 28 of 2000 of Ireland, protects sound recordings, broadcasts and typographical arrangements under copyright law [s 17 (2)], rights of performers are separately dealt with under Chapter III and IV of the Act.

[26]Lionel Bently and Brad Sherman, *Intellectual Property Law* (4th Edition, Oxford University Press 2014) 32. *See also* Cornish who notes that in the English common law tradition, these are considered entrepreneurial copyright that give protection to entrepreneurial skills in an aesthetic field. WR Cornish, *Intellectual Property* (2nd Edition, Sweet & Maxwell 1989) 265.

[27]Hector L MacQueen, Charlotte Waelde and T Laurie Gaeme, *Contemporary Intellectual Property: Law and Policy* (Oxford University Press 2008) 229.

made in the technical or organisational skill rather than the creative effort.[28] In the UK, sound recordings were granted protection under copyright law by the Copyright Act of 1911.[29] Cornish notes that, although the right granted to producers of sound recordings was indiscriminately labelled as copyright, "[i]t was (. . .) not an author's right at all, but something which continental theory would scrupulously distinguish as a [related] right".[30] The 1956 Copyright Act added to the expansion of entrepreneurial copyright by introducing protection for cinematographic films,[31] television and sound broadcasts[32], as well as typographical arrangements of published editions[33]. These subject-matter together with sound recordings, were grouped together under Part II of the Act, separated from the classical literary, dramatic, musical and artistic works protected under copyright law which were dealt with in Part I of the Act. As Cornish argues, this difference in grouping seems to indicate a conscious recognition of the differences between the two regimes of protection, i.e., the original intellectual effort that is protected by classical copyright and the entrepreneurial skills protected by the new entrepreneurial copyright.[34] It is to be noted that the current Copyright Designs and Patent Act (CDPA)[35] of 1988 does not make a distinction between classical and entrepreneurial copyright in the grouping of subject-matter. Nevertheless, the differences between classical copyright and entrepreneurial copyright is maintained by the absence of the requirement of originality as a pre-condition for the protection of entrepreneurial works.

Related rights protection has been the subject of harmonisation within the EU legal framework. The Rental and Lending Rights Directive of 1992[36] was the first effort to harmonise related rights within the EU. The differences in legal protection among Member States, their negative impact on intra-community trade and the functioning of the Internal Market and the resulting distortions to competition were provided as justifications for the harmonisation of related rights.[37] The Directive *inter alia* granted the exclusive right to prohibit rental and lending; to performers in respect of fixations of their performances, to phonogram producers in respect of

---

[28]ibid.

[29]Copyright Act 1911 (1&2 Geo 5 Ch 46) s 19 (1), 'Copyright shall subsist in records, perforated rolls, and other contrivances by means of which sounds may be mechanically reproduced, in like manner as if such contrivances were musical works (. . .).'

[30]Cornish (n 26) 299–300.

[31]s 13 of the Copyright Act 1956 (UK).

[32]s 14 Copyright Act 1956 (UK).

[33]s 15 Copyright Act 1956 (UK).

[34]Cornish (n 26) 265.

[35]Copyright, Designs and Patents Act 1988 (UK).

[36]Council Directive 92/100/EEC of 19 November 1992 on rental right and lending right and on certain rights related to copyright in the field of intellectual property [1992] OJ L346/61. *See also* Sylvie Nerisson, 'The Rental and Lending Rights Directive' in Irini Stamatoudi and Paul Torremans (eds), *EU Copyright Law: A Commentary* (Edward Elgar 2014) 1103.

[37]Michael Walter and Silke von Lewinski, *European Copyright Law: A Commentary* (Oxford University Press 2010) 255.

their phonograms and to film producers in respect of the first fixation of a film. This directive was repealed and replaced by a homonymous Directive enacted in 2006[38], which is currently in force and preserves the fundamental substance of the 1992 Directive and the protections granted under it while incorporating amendments to preserve its relevance to the new digital environment[39] and the EU's international obligations[40].

By its decision of 16 March 2000, the European Council approved the EU's signing of the WPPT.[41] The InfoSoc Directive of 2001[42] was enacted *inter alia* to implement the EU's obligations under the WPPT.[43] Article 3(2) of the InfoSoc Directive provides the exclusive right to authorise or prohibit the making available to the public; for performers in respect of fixations of their performances, phonogram producers in respect of their phonograms, film producers in respect to their films and broadcasting organisations in respect of their broadcasts. The Directive also harmonises exceptions and limitations that must or may be introduced by Member States to their related rights frameworks[44] and makes the application of these exceptions and limitations subject to the three-step-test[45] introduced by the TRIPS Agreement.

Thus, as Pila and Torremans observe, EU law provides a two-tier system for the protection of expressive and informational subject-matter involving copyright for authorial works and related rights for their non-authorial counterparts.[46] Hence, protection under related rights is a well-entrenched concept within the EU law framework that could be used for the protection of subject-matter that, although not qualifying as a work of authorship, represents a financial, technological, or entrepreneurial investment that merits protection.

---

[38]Directive 2006/115/EC of the European Parliament and of the Council of 12 December 2006 on rental right and lending right and on certain rights related to copyright in the field of intellectual property [2006] OJ L 376/28 (Rental and Lending Rights Directive).

[39]Recital 4 of the Rental and Lending Rights Directive.

[40]Recital 7 of the Rental and Lending Rights Directive.

[41]Council Decision of 16 March 2000 (n 22).

[42]InfoSoc Directive (n 14).

[43]Recital 13 of the InfoSoc Directive. *See also* IViR Report on the implementation of the InfoSoc Directive which observes that, "one of the principal objectives behind the adoption of the Information Society Directive was to transpose into Community law the main international obligations arising from the WIPO Internet Treaties". Lucie Guibault and others, 'Study on the Implementation and Effect in Member States' Laws of Directive 2001/29/EC on the Harmonisation of Certain Aspects of Copyright and Related Rights in the Information Society.' (IViR2007) 70 <https://papers.ssrn.com/sol3/papers.cfm?abstract_id=2006358> accessed 31 January 2019.

[44]Article 5(3) and (4) of the InfoSoc Directive.

[45]Article 5(5) of the InfoSoc Directive. The three-step test was introduced in Article 13 of the TRIPS Agreement (n 15) and is as follows, "[m]embers shall confine limitations or exceptions to exclusive rights to certain special cases which do not conflict with a normal exploitation of the work and do not unreasonably prejudice the legitimate interests of the right holder".

[46]Justine Pila and Paul Torremans, *European Intellectual Property Law* (Oxford University Press 2016) 246.

8.1.3 Salient Features of the Concept of Related Rights

As observed in the preceding discussion, related rights are primarily focused upon the economic value embodied by the protected subject-matter.[47] Thus, in its essence, it is a system of economic rights that protect economic, organisational and technical investments[48] made by individuals and entities in the development and dissemination of copyright protected works.

Bently and Sherman observe that, related rights are typically derivative in the sense that they; use or develop existing authorial works, are a product of technical and organisational skill rather than authorial skill, grant rights not to the human creator but to the body or person that was financially and organisationally responsible for the production of the material.[49] For example, while the lyric writer and the composer of the melody would be considered the 'authors' of a song and be granted copyright over it, the singer who performs the song and the producer of the phonogram who fixates the singer's performance will be granted related rights over the respective performance and fixation of that performance. The related right enables the singer to protect the economic interests in the creative skill invested by him in communicating the song to the public through his performance. Similarly, the related right enables the producer of the phonogram to protect the financial, technical and entrepreneurial investment made by him in capturing and fixating the singer's particular performance and distributing it to the public. Thus, the related right grants to the performer and producer of the phonogram an exclusive right that is enforceable *erga omnes* which allows them to prevent any other person or entity from free-riding upon the investment made by them in communicating a work of authorship to the public. As Cohen Jehoram observes, related rights provide strengthened protection against certain acts of unfair competition which can be very loosely associated with copyright infringements.[50] A similar opinion is expressed by Dreier, who notes that, as far as investment protection is their central focus, related rights can be understood as a regime of exclusive rights that seek to prevent anti-competitive free-riding.[51] The related right therefore assists in preserving the incentives of the performer and phonogram producer to continue to engage in the performance and fixation of future works of authorship.

---

[47]Andreas Rahmatian, 'Originality in UK Copyright Law: The Old "Skill and Labour" Doctrine Under Pressure' (2013) 44 IIC 4, 60.

[48]*See* Dreier (n 23) 1223, "[i]nsoweit bezweckt der Schutz die Absicherung der in der wirtschaftlichen, organisatorischen und technischen getatigen Investition". ("To this extent, the purpose of protection is to safeguard the investment made in the economic, organisational, and technical aspects"). (Translated into English by the author).

[49]Bently and Sherman (n 26) 32.

[50]Cohen Jehoram (n 6) 76.

[51]Dreier (n 23) §§70ff para 2, "[s]oweit dieser Investitionsschutz im Zentrum steht, lassen sich die verwandten Schutzrechte als ein zu Ausschliesslichkeitsrechten verdichteter wettbewerbsrechtlicher Nachahmungsschutz (. . .) verstehen".

Related rights can also arise independently, in the absence of a copyright protected work. A good example is section 72 of the German Copyright Act which grants a related right (*Leistungsschutzrecht*) to the creator of a non-creative photograph (*Lichtbild*).[52] As discussed in the preceding Chap. 7, this related right is granted in respect of a photograph which does not fulfil the requisite originality standard for copyright (authors' rights) protection, but nevertheless involves the investment of a certain degree of skill and labour on the part of the photographer. Another example is the exclusive right granted to creators of non-original databases under the Database Directive[53] which aims to protect the substantial investment made by a creator of a database in the obtaining, verification or presentation of its contents.[54] This exclusive right is independent of copyright protection and while it may co-exist with copyright protection, where the database concerned fulfils the requirements for copyright protection, it can also arise when copyright protection is absent. The Database Directive refers to this exclusive right as a *sui generis* right, as opposed to a related right. However, it is argued here that, in its nature and scope the *sui generis* right is similar to a related right in terms of its objective of protecting the economic investment made by producers of non-original databases. Thus, the *sui generis* database right aims to provide incentives for the production of a subject-matter which although not fulfilling the requisites for copyright protection, nevertheless constitutes, "a vital tool in the development of an information market".[55]

An examination of the historical evolution of related rights demonstrates their character as a legal innovation that was conceived of as a response to technological changes and the challenges posed by these changes to the protection of the economic interests of performers, phonogram producers, and broadcasting organisations.[56] In

---

[52]*See* Sect. 7.4.2.1.2 for a full discussion.

[53]Article 7 of the Directive 96/9/EC of the European Parliament and of the Council of the European Union of 11 March 1996 on the legal protection of databases [1996] OJ L 77/20 (Database Directive).

[54]Pila and Torremans (n 46) 246 observe that:

> EU law requires the recognition and protection by Member States of related rights in respect of a closed list of non-authorial expressive subject-matter, including broadcasts, phonograms, fixation of films and performances, and certain databases (...). Thus, copyright subsists in databases as authorial works (...), whereas the *sui generis* database right subsists in databases the contents of which are the product of substantial commercial investment, and confers more limited rights focused on the protection of those contents and that investment.

[55]Database Directive (n 53) Recital 9.

[56]Paul Goldstein, *International Copyright: Principles, Law and Practice* (Oxford University Press 2001).

See also Cohen Jehoram (n 6) 77 who states that:

> [B]efore and during most of the nineteenth century, performers did not feel any need for protection along the lines of copyright; their performances could not be fixed on any recording or be reproduced, (...). The picture changed radically with the inventions of professional sound recordings, films, radio, television, cable-retransmission and all sorts of equipment for private recording. This technological revolution made performers as vulnerable as traditional authors to unauthorized exploitation by third parties.

the absence of a possibility to grant protection to these entities under the copyright law regime, policy makers devised the concept of related rights as an alternative means of protecting what was seen to be the legitimate interests of persons and entities who fulfilled an socially important function in securing the improved availability and accessibility of creative and informational content to the public.[57]

It appears therefore, that the concept of related rights presents a perfect-fit for the protection of digitised versions of rare documents. Its underlying conceptual framework appears to be eminently suited to the task of protecting the investment made by private sector entities in the production of digitised versions. Similar to the producer of a phonogram who invests finances, technological skills and entrepreneurship in recording a musical performance and making it available to the public, the creation of a digitised version also involves the investment of finances and technological skills and expertise in the creation of a digital reproduction of an existing rare document and making it available to the public. The creation of a digitised version constitutes an act that creates social value by means of improving the accessibility of knowledge and information. Therefore, the investment made by the creator of a digitised version merits protection on an equal level with the investment made by a producer of a phonogram. The flexibility of the concept of related rights to adapt and respond to new technological innovation was discussed above. As will be demonstrated in the following discussion, the introduction of a related right over a digitised version would not require any radical upheaval of the existing legal doctrine or the re-interpretation or reformulation of existing legal concepts.

8.2 Why a Related Rights Regime?

We consider why the introduction of a related right would be an improvement on the *status quo* as regards the regulation of digitised versions?

8.2.1 Provide for Legislation to Replace the Current Regime of Private Ordering

The current regulation of digitised versions is largely based on private ordering.[58] This is evidenced by the use of contractual provisions and the application of digital-

[57]Vivant and Brugière note that, the appearance of related rights *(droits voisins)* in the French copyright law system originated with technologies that enabled the fixation and reproduction of sounds. Michel Vivant and Jean-Michel Bruguière, *Le Droit d'auteur et Droits Voisins* (3rd Edition, Dalloz 2016) 1029.

[58]The term 'private ordering' as used here refers to decentralised processes of rule-making through which private entities create their own rules to substitute the default rules provided by legislation or case law. Branislav Hazucha, 'Intellectual Property, Private Ordering and Legal Certainty' in Mark

rights-management (DRM) systems as a means of controlling the access and use of digitised versions. The application of a system of private ordering in the regulation of digitised versions gives rise to many inequities and inefficiencies.

Firstly, it results in the regulatory system being heavily weighted in favour of the interests of the producer as against those of the user. Where contract is used as an instrument to control the access and use of digitised versions, users are required to agree to certain contractual terms and conditions as a pre-condition to accessing or using the content. These contractual provisions are usually standard-form contracts that set out uniform, non-negotiable terms and conditions which are determined according to the will of the producer of the digitised version, and often in a manner that is designed to further the producer's interests.

The use of private ordering as opposed to statutory regulation is often justified on the basis that it allows for greater autonomy and freedom for the parties involved to determine the terms and conditions upon which they agree to be governed. Thus, it has been argued that, under the tenets of liberal political theory, this model of deliberative rule-making carries greater legitimacy than the imposition of a system of rules through a centralised governmental model.[59] However, this argument rests upon the assumption that the private ordering model that is employed does in fact grant equal autonomy to both parties to determine the terms and conditions of use and access. In contrast, if the bargaining power of the contracting parties is not equal or at least comparable, private ordering can lead to a completely reverse outcome.[60]

The presumption of the equality of bargaining power between the parties assumes that both parties are able to negotiate the terms of contract in such a way as to optimise their individual interests. However, in the context of digitised versions, the equal autonomy and equitable distribution of bargaining power between the producer and user is reduced to a mere fiction. The rarity of the materials that are digitised means that in the majority of instances the producer of the digitised version will be the sole source of that material in digital form. Thus, the bargaining power of the user is reduced to a minimum and it becomes possible for the producer to use standard-form contracts that are offered to a user on 'take-it or leave-it' terms, negating the presumption that the contractual terms reflect a fair balance of the competing interests of the parties.[61] As observed by Dinwoodie:

> [C]opyright law notwithstanding public choice concerns that have made recent legislative activity unattractive to some scholars, is devised through a democratic system that confers a degree of legitimacy on the norms that are applied by courts. Private ordering lacks that

---

Fenwick and Stefan Wrbka (eds), *Legal Certainty in a Contemporary Context* (Springer 2016) 34. Elkin-Koren differentiates private ordering from public ordering based on the process through which rules are generated; public ordering models being based on centralised institutions that formulate rules such as the legislature and the courts, in contrast to which private ordering processes is decentralised and spread among various social agents. Niva Elkin-Koren, 'Copyrights in Cyberspace – Rights without Laws?' (1998) 73 Chicago Kent Law Review 1155, 1161.

[59] Elkin-Koren (n 58) 1172.

[60] Hazucha (n 58) 34.

[61] Elkin-Koren (n 58) 1180–1182.

> legitimacy. Proponents of private ordering thus rest their claim of legitimacy on the nominally limited reach of that ordering, namely the parties to the transaction.[62]

Dinwoodie further argues that such a notion of legitimacy is fanciful given that 'users' as parties to the transaction are largely powerless to influence the terms of the deal.[63] In fact, the current legal framework allows producers almost unfettered freedom in determining the contractual terms and conditions of access, use, and re-use of digitised versions. The same is true in the case of the use of DRM systems that can be tailored according to the needs of the producer.[64] Thus, legislative intervention is required to remedy the significant imbalance of power between users and producers within the existing framework that is largely based on private ordering.

Furthermore, private ordering is also justified upon the basis that it could lead to greater efficiency in the distribution of works by allowing the supplier (or producer) the flexibility to tailor the distribution process according to the individual needs of user groups through the employment of mechanisms such as price-discrimination.[65] However, the ability to use a variety of economic models that cater to the needs of different categories of users is not solely limited to the domain of private ordering. While acknowledging that private ordering mechanisms grant greater flexibility in the application of such economic models it is also possible to apply them with a comparable degree of effectiveness within a copyright or related rights framework. For example, in the context of digitised versions price discrimination could be exercised within a related rights framework by means of licensing the use of different (quality) versions of the same product under a variety of schemes. A non-commercial use licence can be offered for the use of a low-resolution copy at a certain price while a license for commercial use can be offered over the same product in a high resolution format at a higher price. Locating such economic models within a legislative framework means that there is the added advantage that these models operate within a system that includes adequate limitations and exceptions to the exclusive right that are aimed at protecting the legitimate interests of the user.

Furthermore, a regulatory framework based on private ordering gives rise to diverse standards of protection. Certain producers would allow some uses that other producers forbid. Thus, to determine his rights in relation to a particular digitised version a user is required to examine the terms and conditions of the particular contract attached to it. Considering the heavy legalese in which many of these contracts are formulated, obtaining a correct and comprehensive understanding

---

[62] Graeme B Dinwoodie, 'Private Ordering and the Creation of International Copyright Norms: The Role of Public Structuring' (2004) 1 Journal of Institutional and Theoretical Economics 160, 168.

[63] ibid.

[64] Although the InfoSoc Directive requires the application of DRM to be subject to certain specified limitation and exceptions, as already discussed in Chap. 6, Sect. 6.1, this provision can be overridden by private arrangements and is not adequate for bringing about a balance between the interests of producers and users.

[65] Dinwoodie (n 62) 167.

of the terms and conditions of use may not be within the grasp of an average-user. Under such uncertainty a user may (exercising an abundance of caution) either opt to forgo making certain uses of the digitised version or in the alternative feel compelled to communicate with the rights holder to clarify that the intended use is permitted under the terms of the contract, thereby increasing the transaction costs associated with the use of the digitised version. Thus, uncertainty as to terms of use could detract from the social value that is gained through the availability of a work in digitised form, and result in inefficiencies in the use and exploitation of these digitised versions. Bringing digitised versions within a legislative framework based on related rights could resolve this uncertainty to a large extent, by introducing a uniform standard of protection.

8.2.2 Provide for a Period of Protection That Is Limited in Time

The protection granted under contract law or implemented through DRM systems is not limited in time. Rather, the producer is able to secure exclusivity over an indefinite period. A key feature of copyright and related rights protection is that the enjoyment of exclusivity by the rightholders is limited in duration. According to Benabou and Dusollier, at the beginning of the copyright era the concept of the limitation of intellectual property rights in time was designed with the object of preserving a public domain where contents could be used freely by members of the public. Thus, it aimed at achieving a balance between proprietary protection and public availability, thus creating two separate domains, constituted by the passing of time.[66]

The limited duration of the exclusive right provides rightholders the opportunity to obtain a return on their investment within the period of protection, while guaranteeing to the public that the work will become freely available once the period of protection expires. Thus, bringing the protection of digitised versions of rare documents within a legal framework based on related rights enables the maintaining of a balance between user and producer interests.

Furthermore, unlike copyright law that fixes a uniform term of protection, the related rights regime allows the legislator the flexibility to calibrate the duration of protection to achieve an adequate balance between user and producer interests. For example, as of 1993, the duration of related rights of performers, phonogram producers, film producers, and broadcasting organisations within the EU is set at

[66] Valérie-Laure Benabou and Séverine Dusollier, 'Draw Me a Public Domain', in Paul Torremans (ed), *Copyright Law: A Handbook of Contemporary Research* (Edward Elgar 2007) 164.

50 years.[67] The term of protection for posthumous publications is 25 years.[68] The *sui generis* right over non-original databases lasts for a period of 15 years.[69] This demonstrates the possibility granted under the related rights framework to adjust the period of protection to suit the particular interests of producers and users of a particular subject-matter. As will be discussed further in the following chapter (Sect. 9.2), it is proposed that the duration of the related right over digitised versions of rare documents should fixed at a considerably shorter duration of 7 years.

8.2.3 Achieving a Balance of Interests Through Exceptions and Limitations

Exceptions and limitations are a primary mechanism through which copyright law attempts to maintain a balance between the interests of authors and users. They restrict the ability of the rights-holders to exclude persons from certain types of uses that are either deemed to be in the public interest or not considered likely to cause substantial prejudice to the rightholder.

The area that is covered by exceptions and limitations has been compared to a type of public domain, in the sense that it creates a reservoir of information that can be used by the public for certain pre-defined purposes without the rightholder being able to determine the terms of such use. Hence, it shifts the ability to determine the nature and purpose of the use from the rightholder to the public.[70] As noted by Benabou and Dusollier, "the freedom to copy entailed by the public domain occurs at different places within the copyright regime, not only outside its scope of protection but also within the rules of the protection itself, namely in the gaps between the exclusive rights and the exceptions".[71]

Thus, locating the regulation of digitised versions within the related rights framework would enable the application of standard exceptions and limitations to the exclusive rights granted over digitised versions. Although the existing EU legal framework demonstrates many weaknesses in its ability to safeguard statutorily introduced exceptions and limitations from being overridden through the use of

---

[67] Article 3 of the Council Directive 93/98/EEC of 29 October 1993 harmonising the term of protection of copyright and certain related rights [1993] OJ L 290/9, replaced by Article 3 of Directive 2006/116/EC of the European Parliament and of the Council of 12 December 2006 on the term of protection of copyright and certain related rights [2006] OJ L372/12 (Term Directive).

[68] ibid Article 4.

[69] Database Directive (n 53) Article 10 (1).

[70] For further discussion on this point *see* Julie E Cohen, 'Copyright, Commodification and Culture: Locating the Public Domain' in P Bernt Hugenholtz and Lucie Guibault (eds), *The Future of the Public Domain* (Kluwer Law International 2006). *See also* Jane C Ginsburg, 'Copyright, Common Law and Sui Generis Protection of Databases in the United States and Abroad' (1997) 66 University of Cincinnati Law Review 151.

[71] Benabou and Dusollier (n 66) 171.

contractual provisions and DRM systems, it is proposed that this could be remedied through the adoption of specific statutory provisions that effectively safeguard the ability of users to benefit from these exceptions and limitations. The national legal frameworks of several EU Member States already include such provisions.[72] Nevertheless, the general legal position within the EU law framework on the ability to override exceptions and limitations to copyright and related rights through the use of contract remains uncertain.[73]

Therefore, it is argued here that, the proposed related rights regime for the protection of digitised versions should incorporate a comprehensive list of exceptions and limitations that are designed to authorise socially valuable uses of digitised versions without causing substantial prejudice to the ability of the producer to obtain a reasonable return on his investment. These exceptions and limitations should be reinforced by an explicit provision that prevents rightholders from using DRM systems and contractual provisions to override them.

8.2.4 Preference for a Related Right Over a sui generis *Regime*

It is argued that it makes better legislative sense to locate the protection of digitised versions within the classical framework of related rights as opposed to the introduction of a novel *sui generis* regime, such as the *sui generis* exclusive right that was introduced under the Database Directive.

The *sui generis* exclusive right is an innovation of European law that protects databases that can demonstrate a substantial investment in the obtaining, verification or presentation of its contents against the extraction and/or re-utilisation of the whole or substantial parts thereof.[74] It was created for providing protection to databases that would have attracted protection under the 'sweat of the brow' standard in British copyright law, but would have failed to qualify for protection under the harmonised standard of originality established under the Database Directive, that followed the relatively stricter standard of originality set out in the continental copyright (authors'

[72]Drexl and von Lewinski report that a survey of German law indicates that within the German legal framework, freedom of contract may prevail in principle but be subject to certain conditions imposed by general civil law relating in particular to standard form contracts. They further cite Cornish [WR Cornish, *Intellectual Property* (5th Edition, Sweet & Maxwell 2003)] for the view that the fair dealing exception in the UK law prevails over contract. Josef Drexl and Silke von Lewinski, 'The Digitising of Literary and Artistic Works' (2007) 11 Electronic Journal of Comparative Law 15 available at <www.ejcl.org/113/article113-19.pdf> accessed 31 January 2019.

[73]As observed by Drexl and von Lewinski, "it may seem astonishing that such a fundamental question in most countries is either hardly discussed, or is unclear or controversial". ibid.

[74]Article 7 of the Database Directive (n 53).

rights) system.[75] The Commission also believed that there was a need to protect investment against parasitic behaviour by those who seek to misappropriate the results of the financial and professional investment made in obtaining and collecting data and to find an appropriate balance between the legitimate interests of database authors/makers and users.[76]

However, the EU Commission's 2005 report on the evaluation of the Database Directive acknowledges that, interpreting the precise scope of the *sui generis* exclusive right has proven difficult, especially as no jurisdiction had a comparable legal instrument before the introduction of this new form of protection. The Commission notes that, consequently, the *sui generis* provisions have caused considerable legal uncertainty both at the EU and national level and that "the [CJEU] judgements have the merit of pointing to the serious difficulties raised by attempting to harmonize national laws by recourse to untested and ambiguous legal concepts".[77]

The introduction of a *sui generis* regime for the regulation of digitised versions means that both the courts and the stakeholders involved would require some time to fully understand the nature and scope of the regulatory regime and the legal concepts introduced by it. Until such time, the uncertainty surrounding the new *sui generis* regime would give rise to a certain amount of inefficiency in the application and enforcement of the legal regime. The advantage in adopting a related rights regime is that it would bring the regulation of digitised versions within an established legal framework, the scope and nature of which is better defined than a *sui generis* regime.

8.3 Examples of Subject-Matter Protected Under Related Rights

Within the legal framework of the EU, it is possible to identify several interesting instances where related rights protection has been creatively and strategically used to provide protection to diverse subject-matter that would otherwise have been left unprotected. These protection regimes could act as a precedent for the introduction of a related right for the protection of digitised versions of rare documents.

[75] EU Commission, 'DG Internal Market and Services Working Paper: First Evaluation of Directive 96/9/EC on the Legal Protection of Databases' (2005) 3.

[76] ibid 9.

[77] ibid 13.

8.3.1 Related Right for the Protection of Non-creative Photographs Under German Law

The exclusive right (*Leistungsschutzrecht*) provided to the producer of a non-creative photograph provides an interesting precedent as to how protection could be granted to photographic creations that do not involve the exercise of individual creative choices on the part of their producer. The protection granted under section 72 of the German Copyright Act[78] is justified based on the need to protect photographs produced with financial and technological investment (and sometimes using sophisticated technical knowledge and craftsmanship) against unauthorised access and use by third parties.[79] Thus section 72 employs related rights protection as a mechanism by which to protect the financial, technological and entrepreneurial investment that has gone into the production of non-creative photographs that would otherwise be left unprotected.[80] It is significant that only prototype images will obtain protection under section 72, and that protection will not extend to photographs that reproduce an existing photograph in an exclusively mechanical way.[81] As discussed in Chap. 7,[82] it is unclear whether a digitised version of a rare document that is produced through a process of scanning could qualify for protection under Article 72 (this issue has been shrouded in even more uncertainty following the decision delivered by the Regional Court of Berlin in the case of the *Reiss Engelhorn Museum*[83]). Nevertheless, section 72 acts as a precedent for the protection of the financial, technological and entrepreneurial investment that has been made in the creation of non-original photographs against unauthorised access and use by third parties.

8.3.2 Related Right for Posthumous Publications Under EU Law

Article 4 of the Term Directive provides an exclusive right to any person who lawfully publishes or communicates to the public a previously unpublished work in which copyright protection has already expired. The exclusive right is granted for

[78]Urheberrechtsgesetz 1965 BGBl. I S. 1273 (Copyright Act of Germany).

[79]Martin Vogel in Gerhard Schricker and Ulrich Löwenheim (eds), *Urheberrecht: Kommentar* (4th ed, CH Beck 2010) § 72 para 13.

[80]Thomas Dreier and Louisa Specht, 'Germany' in Reto M Hilty and Sylvie Nérisson (eds), *Balancing Copyright – A Survey of National Approaches* (Springer 2012) 431.

[81]*See* decisions delivered by the Federal Supreme Court of Germany in the cases, BGH, 08.11.1989 – I ZR 14/88, GRUR 1990, 669 – *Bibelreproduktion* and BGH, 07.12.2000 – I ZR 146/98, GRUR 2001, 755 – *Telefonkarte.*

[82]*See* Sect. 7.4.2.1.2.

[83]LG Berlin 3.05.2016, 15O 428/15 – *Reiss Engelhorn Museum.*

the duration of 25 years from the date when the work was lawfully published or communicated to the public. Thus, the exclusive right granted under Article 4 provides an incentive to invest in the publication or making available to the public of a previously unpublished posthumous work.[84] Once again, the subject matter of protection is the effort that has been expended upon the discovery, publication and communication of a work which otherwise would not have been available to the public. The related right granted to the publishers of posthumous works clearly supports the argument that efforts taken to enhance the availability and accessibility of public domain content which would otherwise not be easily accessible to members of the public, deserves legal protection.

8.3.3 Protection for Typographical Arrangements Under UK Law

Section 1(1)(c) of the CDPA[85] grants copyright protection to typographical arrangements of published editions for a period of 25 years.[86] Although protection is granted under copyright, it is evident that the exclusive right falls under the category of 'entrepreneurial copyright'. Originality is not a requirement for protection. However, similar to the protection of non-creative photographs under section 72 of the German Copyright Act, protection does not extend to mere reproductions of an existing typographical arrangement.[87] To obtain protection, the typographical arrangement is required to be a prototype arrangement. As noted in the decision delivered by the Court of Appeal in the case of *The Newspaper Licensing Agency v. Marks and Spencer plc.*,[88] the origins of protection lie partly in the need to prevent the appropriation of the skill and labour that has been invested in the creation of the typographical design by other publishers who could reproduce them in the form of facsimile copies.[89] According to Laddie, et al., the subject-matter of protection is the whole typographical layout, i.e., the choice of typeface, as well as other aspects of presentation such as juxtaposition of text, photographs and headlines, the width of

---

[84] Gemma Minero, 'The Term Directive' in Paul Torremans and Stamatoudi, Irini (eds), *EU Copyright Law: A Commentary* (Edward Elgar 2014) 248, 273.

[85] Copyright, Designs and Patents Act of 1988 (UK). Copyright protection for typographical arrangement was first introduced by the UK Copyright Act of 1956, s 15.

[86] ibid. Section 15 of the CDPA states that copyright in the typographical arrangement of a published edition expires at the end of the period of 25 years from the end of the calendar year in which the edition was first published. Bently and Sherman note that the protection granted to typographical arrangements largely remain a peculiarity of British and British-influenced copyright, and has no counterpart in other jurisdictions. Bently and Sherman (n 26) 90.

[87] ibid CDPA s 8(2).

[88] *The Newspaper Licensing Agency v Marks and Spencer plc* [2003] 1 AC 551, 558.

[89] ibid 555.

columns, the space between the margins, etc.[90] However, protection does not extend to the reproduction of the content of the published work, i.e., it does not prevent the reproduction of the same work under a different typographical arrangement.[91] Thus, on a typographical arrangement of a work that is in the public domain, the protection would not extend to the public domain content itself but merely to the layout and presentation of the typesetting of the text that reproduces the public domain content.[92] As Bently and Sherman observe, the subject-matter of protection is the publisher's skill and investment in typesetting, as well as the process of design and selection that is reflected in the appearance of the text.[93] Thus, an analogy can be drawn between the protection granted to a typographical arrangement under the CDPA and the protection of a digital reproduction of an existing rare document, where the protection would only serve to prevent the unauthorised reproduction of whole or parts of the digital image and would not prevent the reproduction or use of the public domain textual content that is reproduced by that image.

8.4 Determination of Ownership of the Related Right

On achievements that involve a personal creative input such as artistic performances, the related right is vested in the person who actually made that creative input. Thus, where a singer performs a song, ownership of the related right over that performance is vested in the singer.

However, where the related right is not concerned with the protection of a personal creative input but with the protection of a financial, technological or entrepreneurial investment made in the production of a particular subject-matter, the legislator has a wider discretion in determining the person or entity that should be granted ownership over the related right. For example, the related right in a sound recording does not vest in the engineer who created the fixation or representation of the sounds but in the legal or natural person who took the responsibility and initiative (i.e., economic, organisational, technical investment) for that fixation or representation.[94] The WIPO Guide to the Rome Convention makes it clear that, on the protection granted to phonogram producers for the first fixation of a sound in a phonogram, the accent is on an industrial as opposed to a personal activity. Thus, when an employee of a legal entity fixes the sounds during his employment, the

[90]Hugh Laddie, Peter Prescott and Mary Vitoria, *The Modern Law of Copyright and Designs* (LexisNexis, 4th Ed, 2011) 487.

[91]Bently and Sherman (n 26) 90.

[92]Laddie, et al. (n 90) 487 give the example of the typesetting of a Bach Cantata where the typesetting would be protected but not the musical work itself.

[93]Bently and Sherman (n 26) 90.

[94]WPPT (n 17) Article 2(d).

employer (legal entity), rather than the employee, is to be considered the producer.[95]

Therefore, in formulating a related right over digitised versions, the legislator has the ability to consider all different stakeholders that are involved in the creation of the digitised version, and to grant ownership of the related right to the person or entity that, in his opinion, is best placed to exercise that right in a manner which achieves an equilibrium between the competing interests of the producer and the user. For the reasons given in Sect. 4.9 above, it is proposed that the ownership of the related right over a digitised version should be granted to the entity that has ownership of the original analogue document, at the time the digitised version is produced.

8.5 How Would the PSI Directive Affect the Operation of the Related Right?

The Public Sector Information (PSI) Directive, first introduced in 2003[96] and codified in 2013[97], seeks to harmonise the rules and practices in EU Member States relating to the re-use and exploitation of public sector information.[98] With this objective in mind it establishes a minimum set of rules governing the re-use and the practical means of facilitating the re-use of existing documents held by public sector bodies.[99]

The question arises whether the introduction of a related right over digitised versions of rare documents held by public sector memory institutions would be affected by provisions of the PSI Directive and if so the nature and extent to which it would affect the introduction of a related right.[100]

While the PSI Directive of 2003 did not apply to museums, libraries and archives (i.e., cultural institutions), these have been brought within its scope by the revisions introduced in 2013.[101] Thus, any museum, library, or archive that is deemed a public sector body[102] under the Directive will fall within its purview.

As noted in Recital 15 of the Directive:

---

[95] WIPO Guide to Rome Convention (n 5) 23.

[96] Directive 2003/98/EC of the European Parliament and of the Council of 17 November 2003 on the re-use of public sector information [2003] OJ L345/90.

[97] Directive 2013/37/EU of the European Parliament and of the Council of 26 June 2013 amending Directive 2003/98/EC on the re-use of public sector information [2013] OJ L175/1 (PSI Directive).

[98] PSI Directive, Recital 2.

[99] PSI Directive, Article 1(1).

[100] Hereafter all references to the PSI Directive will refer to the 2013 Directive (n 97) unless otherwise explicitly stated.

[101] PSI Directive, Article 1(1)(iv).

[102] PSI Directive, Article 2(1) defines 'public sector body' to mean the State, regional or local authorities, bodies governed by public law or associations formed by one or several such bodies governed by public law. *See also* PSI Directive recital 14.

> Libraries, museums and archives hold a significant amount of valuable public sector information resources, in particular since digitisation projects have multiplied the amount of digital public domain material. These cultural heritage collections and related metadata are a potential base for digital content products and services and have a huge potential for innovative re-use in sectors such as learning and tourism.

The PSI Directive applies to 'documents'[103] that are defined under Article 2(3) as any content whatever its medium (written on paper or stored in electronic form or as a sound, visual or audio-visual recording) or any part of such content. However, the Directive makes a crucial distinction between documents that were collected, produced, reproduced, and disseminated in the process of performing its 'public task'[104] and documents the supply of which is an activity falling outside the scope of the 'public task'.[105] Accordingly documents that come within the 'public task' of the public sector body fall within the scope of the PSI Directive while documents that do not are excluded.

The 'public task' of a public sector body is described as its *raison d'être,* i.e., the functions for the performance of which the public body has been established.[106] In the context of public sector museums, libraries and archives whose mission *inter alia* involves the collection, preservation and making available of works of cultural heritage to the public at large, the rare documents in its possession would come within the definition of documents that have been collected in the process of performing its 'public task'. Furthermore, any reproductions of these documents, whether in digital or non-digital format, would qualify as public sector information for the purposes of the Directive, as the reproduction and dissemination of the material in its possession also comes within the 'public task' of such institutions.

8.5.1 Impact of the PSI Directive on the Introduction of an Exclusive Related Right Over Digitised Versions

It is interesting to note that, intellectual property protection for PSI has been considered as a possible mechanism for providing necessary incentives for investment in the production and distribution of PSI. As argued by Ricolfi, PSI being a classic public-good, it is to be expected that market mechanisms if left to their own devices would lead to the under-provision (or no provision) of the resource. Ricolfi observes that, intellectual property protection offers a device that may remedy the

[103] PSI Directive, Article 1(1).

[104] PSI Directive, Article 1(2)(a).

[105] PSI Directive, Article 2(4).

[106] EPSI Platform, 'Clarifying the Concept of Public-Task' (2010).

market failure induced by the public good character of PSI.[107] However, he acknowledges that relying on excludability to create an incentive to invest entails that primarily market demand, as opposed to social and public demand, will be considered in making decisions as to the production and distribution of the resource and of the products and services based on it.[108] It is noted that, the proposal for granting a related right over digitised versions is only intended to shift a portion of the burden of investment from public sector memory institutions (and consequently the tax-payers) to private sector for-profit entities. Memory institutions would be free to use their own resources, as well as resources obtained under not-for-profit models (e.g., sponsorships, fund-raising) for the digitisation of rare documents with a high social value but a low market demand that will not capture the interest of for-profit investors.

The PSI Directive does not pose an impediment to the introduction of an exclusive right over digitised versions of rare documents. Neither does it prevent a memory institution from entering into a public-private-partnership (PPP) agreement with a private sector for-profit entity that may grant that private sector entity certain exclusive rights and privileges over the exploitation of the digitised versions that are created within the PPP. Recital 30 to the PSI Directive acknowledges the social value of cooperation agreements entered into between memory institutions and private partners for the facilitation of worthwhile use of cultural collections and for accelerating public access to cultural heritage resources.[109] Recital 31 concedes that a certain period of exclusivity might be necessary to give the private partner the possibility to recoup the investment made by him in the digitisation of cultural resources, but emphasises that the duration of the exclusive right should be limited in time and as short as possible. Thus, as will be further discussed below, the PSI Directive does not prevent the introduction of a related right over digitised versions of rare documents that qualify as public sector documents under Article 2(3) of the Directive.

8.5.2 Impact of the PSI Directive on Exclusive Licences for Digitisation and the Commercial Exploitation of Digitised Versions

Under the related rights regime that is proposed by this study, when a private-sector for-profit partner enters into a contract with a public sector memory institution for the digitisation of rare documents and the subsequent commercial exploitation of the

[107] Marco Ricolfi, 'Public Sector Information as Open Data: Access, Re-Use and the Third Innovation Paradigm' in Dana Beldiman (ed), *Access to Information and Knowledge: 21st Century Challenges in Intellectual Property and Knowledge Governance* (Edward Elgar 2013) 46–49.

[108] ibid 50.

[109] PSI Directive, Recital 30.

digitised versions, it can give rise to two types of contractual arrangements between the parties.

Firstly, the parties could enter into a contractual arrangement whereby the memory institution grants to the private-sector partner a licence (usually an exclusive licence[110]) for the digitisation of the rare documents in its possession. Secondly the parties could also enter into a contractual arrangement whereby the memory institution as the holder of the related right over the digitised versions that are produced through the digitisation process, agree to grant a licence to the private-sector partner to exploit the digitised versions for commercial profit. Usually this licence will also be framed as an exclusive licence[111] that grants to the private-sector partner exclusive rights over the commercial and/or non-commercial exploitation of the digitised versions for the duration of the related right. It is worth exploring whether the PSI Directive would apply to these contractual arrangements and if so, the nature and degree of its influence upon them.

As noted in Recital 7 of the 2013 Directive, the 2003 Directive did not contain an obligation concerning access to documents or an obligation to allow re-use of documents. However, the 2013 amendments introduced a clear obligation to make all documents re-usable unless access is restricted or excluded under national rules or other exceptions that may be laid down in the Directive.[112] Article 3(1) of the PSI Directive lays down an obligation on Member States to ensure that documents (falling within the scope of the Directive) are made available for re-use for commercial or non-commercial purposes under the provisions of the Directive. Article 3 (2) enunciates a more specific obligation that applies to documents over which libraries (including university libraries) museums and archives hold intellectual property rights. It requires Members States to ensure that, '*where the re-use of such documents is allowed, these documents shall be re-usable* for commercial or non-commercial purposes under the conditions set out in Chapters III and IV'.[113]

A memory institution would not hold any copyright over the rare documents in its possession because the intellectual content that is recorded upon these documents belongs to the public domain. It is also unlikely that a memory institution would hold any other intellectual property right (e.g., trade mark rights) over these documents or

[110]It cannot be ruled out that the 'licence for digitisation' is a non-exclusive contract as it is possible that the memory institution decides to allow multiple entities to create digitised versions of a rare document. However, considering the tendency of private-sector investors to push for exclusive licences in relation to the digitisation of rare documents, and the fact that fragility and antiquity of most rare documents mean that, memory institutions are anxious, as much as possible, to limit the number of instances that they are made subject to digitisation, it is anticipated that most licences for digitisation will be exclusive licences.

[111]It is noted that in certain instances this licence may be framed as a non-exclusive license (e.g., the LIA programme of the TNA-UK grants to private-sector partners who digitise their documents, non-exclusive licences over the digitised versions). However, as noted before in Chap. 3, it is more usual for private-sector for-profit entities to insist upon exclusive rights for the exploitation of digitised version created by them.

[112]PSI Directive, Recital 8.

[113]PSI Directive, Article 3(2) (emphasis added).

the content recorded upon them.[114] Moreover, if a related right were granted over digitised versions of rare documents to the public sector library, museum or archive that has ownership of that rare document, those digitised versions would constitute documents over which the public sector library, museum or archive hold an intellectual property right. It is unclear how the phrase 'where the re-use of such documents is allowed' is to be interpreted. However, a common-sense interpretation would be to construe this phrase as referring to documents that are generally available for public re-use in the sense that they are not subject to conditions of confidentiality or privacy. If one were to accept this interpretation, it would appear that a digitised version that is distributed to the public over the Internet or by other means would fall within the scope of Article 3(2).

However, it is noted that the obligation set out in Article 3(2) only requires that the digitised versions shall be re-usable for either commercial or non-commercial purposes. It clearly allows the memory institution the choice to decide whether to allow re-use solely for non-commercial purposes or for both commercial and non-commercial purposes. Neither does it appear to prevent re-use being made subject to a licence, contract or any other regime that imposes restrictions on use such as a DRM system. This is reiterated in Article 8(1) (Chapter III) of the PSI Directive that enables public sector bodies to allow re-use subject to conditions, so long as those conditions do not unnecessarily restrict possibilities for re-use and are not used to restrict competition. Article 10(1) (Chapter IV) requires that, "[a]ny applicable conditions for the re-use of documents shall be non-discriminatory for comparable categories of re-use". Thus, Article 10(1) allows the imposition of different conditions of re-use with respect different categories of use, such as commercial and non-commercial use. It does not impede the application of price-discrimination schemes based on the type of re-use that is intended, so long as the conditions of re-use, comply with Article 8(1) in that, they do not unreasonably restrict possibilities for re-use, and are not designed to restrict competition.

Article 11(1) (Chapter IV) prohibits arrangements between public-sector bodies holding documents and third parties that grant to those third party entities exclusive rights over the re-use of the documents.[115] However, Article 11(2a) provides that the granting of exclusive rights will be allowed where it relates to the digitisation of cultural resources.[116] Thus, the PSI Directive does not prevent a public sector memory institution from granting an exclusive licence to a private-sector body for

---

[114]However, yet again this is not impossible. For example, the possibility cannot be ruled out that a memory institution uses an image contained in a painting or drawing as a logo and therefore obtains a trade mark right over it. However, this would be a rare and especial occurrence that is outside the scope of this study.

[115]Article 11(1) of the PSI Directive of 2003 (n 96) carried a similar prohibition upon contracts or other arrangements between public sector bodies holding documents and third parties, however Article 11(2) carried a proviso to the effect that such contracts or arrangements may be allowed where an exclusive right is necessary for the provision of a service in the public interest.

[116]The specific exception to the prohibition on exclusive arrangements in relation to the digitisation of cultural resources is an innovation introduced by the PSI Directive of 2013.

the digitisation of rare documents in its collection, or from granting an exclusive licence for the exploitation of the digitised versions. Article 11(2a) (1) states that the exclusive right shall in general not exceed 10 years, but allows for the duration of the exclusive right to be extended for an indeterminate period subject to periodical review.[117] Furthermore Article 11(2a)(3) requires that the exclusive right be granted subject to the public sector memory institution being provided with copies of the digitised versions free-of-charge which can be made available for re-use at the end of the period of exclusivity.

Legislation enacted by EU Member States upholds the ability of public sector entities to enter into exclusive arrangements with third parties in relation to the digitisation and exploitation of digitised versions of cultural materials held by them. For example, the Re-use of Public Sector Information Regulations[118] of the UK enacted in 2015, contain a general prohibition on exclusive arrangements between public sector bodies and any other person[119], but specifically allow public sector bodies to enter into exclusive arrangements in relation to the digitisation of cultural resources.[120] An exclusive arrangement is defined as a contract or other arrangement granting an exclusive right to re-use a document.[121] The European Communities (Re-use of Public Sector Information) (Amendment) Regulations (2015)[122] of Ireland that were enacted to amend the earlier European Communities (Re-Use of Public Sector Information) Regulations (2005)[123] carries an amendment that allows public sector bodies to enter into exclusive arrangements with a third party in relation to the digitisation of cultural resources.[124] Similarly, in Germany, the First Act amending the Re-use of Information Act (2015)[125] permits public sector bodies to enter into arrangements that grant third parties exclusive rights to the re-use of

---

[117]Article 11 (2a) (1) of the PSI Directive provides that where an exclusive right relates to the digitisation of cultural resources, "the period of exclusivity shall in general not exceed ten years" (emphasis added). Furthermore, it states that where the period of exclusivity exceeds ten years, its duration shall be subject to review during the eleventh year and, if applicable, every seven years thereafter.

[118]The Re-use of Public Sector Information Regulations n°1415 of 2015 (UK PSI Regulations).

[119]UK PSI Regulations, s 14(1).

[120]UK PSI Regulations, s 14(6) and s 14(7) state that the period of the exclusive arrangement should not normally exceed 10 years, but allows for the extension of the period of exclusive arrangements subject to periodic review as set out in the PSI Directive under s 14(8).

[121]UK PSI Regulations, s 14(13).

[122]The European Communities (Re-use of Public Sector Information) (Amendment) Regulations S.I. n° 525 of 2015 (Ireland Re-use of PSI Regulations).

[123]European Communities (Re-Use of Public Sector Information) Regulations S.I. n° 279 of 2005.

[124]Ireland Re-use of PSI Regulations, Regulation 9 (2A). The provision states the period of exclusivity shall in general not exceed 10 years and be subject to review during the eleventh year and, if applicable, every seven years thereafter.

[125]First Act amending the Re-use of Information Act of 8 July 2015 (German Re-use of Information Act). This Act was enacted to amend the Re-Use of Information Act of 13 December 2006 (Informationsweiterverwendungsgesetz) to implement the changes introduced by the PSI Directive of 2013.

public sector information, where the exclusive right relates to the digitisation of cultural resources.[126] In France, Article L325-3 of the French Code on the relations between the public and the administration (2017)[127] permits exclusive rights to be granted over the re-use of public sector information, when the exclusive right is necessary for achieving the digitisation of cultural resources.

8.5.3 Impact of PSI Directive upon the Maintenance of Confidentiality of the License for Digitisation

Article 11(2a)(2) of the PSI Directive (introduced by the 2013 revisions) requires that 'arrangements granting exclusive rights' on the digitisation of cultural resources should be transparent and be made public. This may pose a problem for private-sector for-profit partners who have an interest in keeping at least certain terms of the exclusive license contract for digitisation confidential. The market for digitisation is a competitive one and at present, the ability to keep certain terms of the license contract confidential allows the private-sector partner greater freedom in negotiating license contracts (partnership agreements) and in maintaining a competitive advantage in the market for digitisation.

At present, it is possible to maintain confidentiality of licensing contacts and public private partnership agreements by invoking specific national laws that protect commercially sensitive information from public disclosure. For example in the UK, the Freedom of Information Act (FOIA)[128] exempts the disclosure of information that can be shown to constitute a trade secret[129], as well as the disclosure of information which would be likely to prejudice the commercial interests of any person.[130] In 2011, two years before the introduction of the revised PSI Directive, these exemptions were successfully relied upon by the British Library in withholding certain clauses and schedules of the contract it had entered into with the private sector entity *BrightSolid,* to digitise its newspaper archive.[131] In this instance, the Commissioner of Information upheld the application of the above exemptions because the disclosure of the information under review would allow competitors of *BrightSolid* to bypass its negotiated trading advantage and thereby reduce the profitability of the contract to *BrightSolid.* Some of the information that was withheld related to the management of sub-contractors by *BrightSolid.* The

[126]German Re-use of Information Act, s 3a (3).

[127]Code on the Relations between the Public and the Administration, January 2017.

[128]The Freedom of Information Act 2000 (c36), the United Kingdom (UK Freedom of Information Act).

[129]UK Freedom of Information Act, s 43(1).

[130]UK Freedom of Information Act, s 43(2).

[131]Freedom of Information Act 2000 (FOIA) (UK) Decision notice, 14th September, 2011. Ref. FS50361862.

Commissioner accepted the argument that the disclosure of this information may compromise *BrightSolid's* negotiating position with these parties in the future because it would allow sub-contractors to know where the Company was unable to concede ground and thereby to leverage that knowledge to obtain better terms than they would otherwise have been able to obtain. Therefore, it was held that, the disclosure of such information would be prejudicial to the commercial interests of *BrightSolid* as it could harm its ability to maximise profits under the contract.

In reaching its decision in the above matter, the Commissioner weighed the public interest in the disclosure of the information as against the public interest in maintaining the exemption. The Commissioner concluded that, while there was a legitimate public interest in the complete disclosure of the terms of the contract in terms of providing greater transparency and accountability in relation to the spending of public money, on the specific facts of the case, there was a stronger public interest in maintaining these exemptions. In this regard, particular reference was made to the fact that the Private-Public Partnership agreement under review, whilst creating a commercial opportunity for a private company also assisted in improving public access to the British Library's newspaper archive. It was held that disclosure of such information would not only prevent *BrightSolid's* ability to successfully implement the digitisation project but that it would be likely to deter other contractors and providers of services from working with public sector bodies if they felt that their commercially sensitive information could be disclosed to the public. As the Commissioner stated, "[t]his would not be in the public interest as it would mean that public sector bodies would be forced to rely on less competitive and/or inferior products and services".[132] The Commissioner further noted that, any commercial opportunity for the British Library would ultimately benefit the taxpayer and accordingly held that, the public interest would not be served by the disclosure of information that would prevent the British Library from commercially exploiting the contract to the benefit of the taxpayer.

However, following the revisions introduced to the PSI Directive in 2013, it appears that national laws of EU Member States that could have hitherto been relied upon to preserve the confidentiality of exclusive arrangements between public sector bodies and private sector partners have now been overridden by Article 11 (2a)(2) of the PSI Directive. Accordingly, the Re-use of Public Sector Information Regulations of the UK introduced in 2015, explicitly require that any exclusive arrangement entered into by a public sector body for the digitisation of its cultural resources be published by the public sector body.[133]

However, because many of these exclusive arrangements contain commercially sensitive information that, if publicly disclosed, could prejudice the ability of a private sector entity to successfully compete in the market for digitisation (licensing market), it is proposed that Article 11(2a)(3) should be reviewed to allow private

---

[132]ibid para 33.

[133]UK PSI Regulations, s 14(9).

sector entities to withhold contractual terms and clauses that contain commercially sensitive information from public disclosure.

It is noted that, Article 1(2)(c) exempts commercially sensitive documents from the scope of the PSI Directive. Although this provision relates to public sector information, and not to exclusive arrangements that have been entered into between a public sector institution and a private partner for the digitisation of public sector information, it demonstrates an acknowledgement on the part of the legislator of the need to protect commercially sensitive information from public disclosure.

8.5.4 Impact of PSI Directive on Ability to Make Re-Use of Digitised Versions Subject to Payment

Although Article 6(1) of the PSI Directive requires that charges made for the re-use of documents be limited to the marginal costs incurred for their reproduction, libraries, museums and archives are exempted from this requirement under Article 6(2)(c). Thus, the PSI Directive allows the memory institutions or their licensees to charge fees for the re-use of digitised version that go beyond the marginal costs incurred in their reproduction and distribution.

However, Article 6(4) stipulates that, when fees are charged for the re-use of documents by libraries, museums and archives, the total income from supplying and allowing re-use of documents over the appropriate accounting period shall not exceed the costs of collection, production, reproduction, dissemination, preservation and rights clearance together with a reasonable return on the investment. It is interesting to consider the effect of Article 6(4) on the ability of a public or semi-public sector memory institution to commercially exploit a digitised version of a rare document. It is noted that Article 6(4) specifies this condition as being applicable to instances where charges are made by the specified public sector bodies, thus it may be possible to argue that Article 6(4) would not apply to situations where fees are charged by a private sector partner in respect of a digitised version of a rare document produced by that partner. In any event it is observed that, the vague manner in which Article 6(4) has been formulated, grants to the public sector institution or its private sector partner considerable latitude in determining the fee that should be charged from users of digitised versions. Thus, even if Article 6 (4) was construed to apply to private sector partners, it is unlikely that it would cause any substantial prejudice to their ability to commercially exploit a digitised version produced by them.

Meanwhile, it is observed that Article 6(4) provides a basis for introducing a formula that could be applied in determining the payment to be charged from users for the use and re-use of digitised versions either by a memory institution or its licensee(s). The introduction of a price regulation mechanism[134], which is based on a

[134] *See* proposed price regulation mechanism in Chap. 9, Sect. 9.2, Article 10 of the proposed model.

pricing formula, could be a useful way of ensuring the producer's ability to obtain a reasonable return on his investment while enabling users to use and re-use the digitised version at a fair price that corresponds to its cost of production and dissemination.

8.6 Summary and Conclusions

At present, related rights are an entrenched feature of the EU legal framework. Although originating in the continental copyright law tradition, related rights have been incorporated into the English copyright tradition as a form of 'entrepreneurial' copyright. The conceptual foundations of the related rights regime render it particularly suitable for the protection of digitised versions as it is focused on the protection of a financial, technical or entrepreneurial investment that has been made in the creation of a product against anti-competitive free-riding. However, related rights are usually employed for the protection of products or achievements that seek to secure the improved availability and accessibility of creative and informational content to the public. In both respects, the related rights regime presents a perfect-fit for the protection of digitised versions.

The introduction of a related right over digitised versions would be preferable to the existing regulatory framework that is largely based on private ordering, as it would serve to bring the protection of digitised versions within a legislative framework that provides a limited duration of protection and makes the exercise of exclusive rights subject to exceptions and limitations that are established by statute.

It is observed that the formulation of the related right should be carried out bearing in mind the amendments introduced to the PSI Directive in 2013 as rare documents held by public sector memory institutions and digitised versions thereof would come within the scope of the revised Directive. However, it is emphasised that the PSI Directive would not form an impediment to the introduction of an exclusive related right over digitised versions of rare documents.

Chapter 9
The Proposed Model

The proposed model set out in this chapter aims to describe the key features of a legal regime for the regulation of digitised versions of rare documents within the EU. In doing so, it attempts to answer the final limb of our third research question by presenting a regulatory framework that is able to achieve an adequate balance between the interests of users and producers of digitised versions of rare documents.[1]

As noted in Chap 2, Sect. 2.4 above, adequacy refers to the ability of the regulatory framework to provide sufficient incentives to producers to invest in the digitisation of rare documents, while at the same time enabling users to use and re-use the digitised versions as much as possible, without damaging the producer's incentive to invest.[2]

The proposed model identifies the key features and concepts of a regulatory framework based on related rights protection that could be introduced within the EU. However, it is not meant to propose a comprehensive regulatory framework which is fit for implementation.

9.1 Core Elements

The model proposes the introduction of a unitary EU related right (intellectual property right) over digitised versions of rare documents, granted under Article 118 of TFEU,[3] by means of a Regulation of the European Parliament and of the

[1] *See* Chap. 2, Sect. 2.4 above. The third research question sought to answer firstly, what legal/non-legal mechanism could be introduced within the EU to ensure the preservation of an adequate balance between the interests of users and producers and secondly, how that mechanism should be formulated.

[2] *See* Chap. 2, Sect. 2.4. *See also* definition of adequacy in Chap. 6, note 2.

[3] Consolidated version of the treaty on the functioning of the European Union (TFEU) [2012] OJ C326/47. Article 118 of the TFEU provides for the creation of European intellectual property rights

S. Mendis, *A Copyright Gambit*, Munich Studies on Innovation and Competition 11,
https://doi.org/10.1007/978-3-662-59454-4_9

Council. Obtaining protection under the related right is made subject to the fulfilment of formalities including a registration requirement.

The proposed regulatory framework is presented below, in the form of legal provisions and explanatory notes to those provisions. The regulatory framework consists of two main aspects:

(i) An exclusive right over digitised versions of rare documents (Articles 2–5 and Articles 11–16) that is subject to a list of mandatory exceptions and limitations (Article 17) and an enforceable right granted to users to benefit from those exceptions and limitations (Articles 18 and 19).
(ii) a Central European Database (CED) for the registration of digitised versions after the fulfilment of all necessary formalities (Articles 6–10).

Article 1: Definitions

(a) 'Digitised version' means a two dimensional prototype digital photographic image of an existing rare document that has been produced through the employment of a mechanism that enables a process of analogue to digital conversion.
(b) 'Prototype' means that the digital photographic image is a digital reproduction of a rare document that exists in analogue form, as opposed to a reproduction of an existing digital photographic image. A digital photographic image that reproduces an existing digital photographic image will not qualify as a prototype.
(c) 'Rare document' means a two dimensional (planar) physical surface upon which public domain content is recorded, predominantly in textual form, and of which there are no more than twenty-five original copies in existence in the world. 'Textual form' refers to the public domain content being recorded upon the rare document in the form of writing or in a mode akin to writing. 'Recorded' refers to the textual content being written, printed or inscribed upon the document or fixated upon the document by any equivalent method.
(d) 'Cultural institution' means any publicly accessible gallery, library, museum, archive or a film or audio heritage institution.
(e) 'Educational institution' means a school, university or any other institution the primary goal of which is to provide educational services.
(f) 'Institution engaged in scientific research' means a research institution or any other organization the primary goal of which is to conduct scientific research.
(g) 'Text and data mining' means any automated analytical technique that aims to analyse text and data in digital form in order to generate information such as patterns trends and correlations.
(h) 'Lawful user' means any legal or natural person who is legally entitled to use a digitised version or copy thereof and uses it in good faith.

---

to provide uniform protection of intellectual property rights throughout the Union and for the setting up of centralised Union-wide authorisation, coordination, and supervision arrangements.

(i) 'Lawful use' means any use of the digitised version that is made by a legal or natural person in accordance with (h) above.
(j) 'Technological measure' means any technology, device or component that, in the normal course of its operation is designed to protect the exclusive related right granted to any person over a digitised version.
(k) 'Thumbnail version' means a reduced-sized, lower-resolution version of a digitised version, the size of which does not exceed more than 30% of the size of the 'basic edition' as per Article 6(1)(a) and the resolution of which does not exceed 50% of the resolution of the 'basic edition'.
(l) 'Basic edition' means the master copy of the prototype digital photographic image that complies with the minimum technological standards specified by the Central European Database under Article 8 and which is attached to the application for registration under Article 6(1)(a). The basic edition should not incorporate any supplementary features such as value-added-features.
(m) 'Date of filing' refers to the date on which the application for registration of a digitised version is officially received by the Central European Database. The 'Date of filing' shall be the date that is specified on the receipt issued to the applicant by the Registry of the Central European Database under Article 6(3), confirming the receipt of the application for registration.

Explanation of Article 1

Article 1 defines several key terms that are used in the following provisions. The definitions provided under subsections (d)–(g) have been formulated based on the definitions provided in Article 2 subsections (1)–(4) of the proposed EU Directive on copyright in the digital single market.[4]

Article 1(a) defines a digitised version as a 'prototype' digital photographic image of an existing rare document. Article 1(b) defines a 'prototype' as the digital reproduction of a rare document as opposed to a mere reproduction of an existing digital image. This definition has been formulated with the objective of preventing the related right from being claimed over digital reproductions of an existing digitised version.[5] The related right is intended to protect the investment that has gone into converting an existing analogue document into digital form. Therefore, mere reproductions (duplications) of existing digital content are excluded from its scope of protection. In doing so, it reflects the protection granted to non-creative photographs *(Lichtbilder)* and to audio-recordings under German law.[6] The limitation of the scope of protection to prototype digital photographic images means that, following the expiration of the term of protection over a digitised version of a rare

[4]Proposal for a directive of the European Parliament and of the Council on copyright in the Digital Single Market, 14 September 2016, COM(2016) 593.

[5]The definition of a digitised version as a prototype image is inspired by the German law protection framework for *Lichtbilder* under Article 72 of the German Copyright Act. *See also* BGH, 08.11.1989 – I ZR 14/88, GRUR 1990, 669 – *Bibelreproduktion.*

[6]Article 85(1) of German Copyright Act on audio-recordings. *See* discussion in Chap. 7, Sect. 7.4.2.1.2 above.

document, a producer would be compelled to create a new digitised version of that rare document to be able to claim a related right over the digitised version. In producing this new digitised version of the rare document, the producer would be required to comply with the revised (usually more sophisticated) technology standards declared by the Central European Database (CED) under Article 8 that are applicable at that particular time, thereby making available to users a higher quality digitised version of the rare document as opposed to a mere digital reproduction of the initial digitised version.

Article 1(c) defines a 'rare document' as a document of which no more than twenty-five original copies exist in the world. This arbitrary criterion has been applied in limiting the protection provided under the proposed related right to digitised versions of documents that are not usually available to members of the public in their original form. At present, there is no universally accepted definition as to what constitutes a 'rare document'. While curators, archivists and antiquarians usually possess an intuitive understanding as to the criteria that would lead to a particular document being classified as a 'rare document',[7] these criteria have not been formalised in a manner that would enable their use in a legal context. As provided in Article 6(1)(b), the legal obligation of a person who makes an application for the registration of a digitised version in confirming that the underlying document qualifies as a 'rare document' under the definition provided in Article 1(c), is limited to a simple statement made in good faith to that effect in the application for registration.

Article 1(h) and (i) define the terms 'lawful user' and 'lawful use'. The term 'lawful user' is already employed in Articles 6, 8 and 9 of the Database Directive.[8] The Computer Programmes Directive[9] does not use the specific term 'lawful user' but refers to a 'lawful acquirer'[10] and 'person having right to use'.[11] According to Synodinou,[12] these terms should be regarded as being identical to that of the 'lawful user' used in the Database directive. However, neither the Database Directive nor the Computer Programmes Directive provides a definition of the term, which lacuna is sought to be resolved here. The recognition of a specific legal person who is entitled to benefit from exceptions and limitations to the related right would be useful in the enforcement of the rights granted to users to benefit from these exceptions and

[7] Sunimal Mendis, 'Rare Documents' in Marie Cornu, Fabienne Orsi and Judith Rochfeld (eds), *Dictionnaire des Bien Communs* (PUF 2017).

[8] Article 3(1) of the Directive 96/9/EC of the European Parliament and of the Council of the European Union of 11 March 1996 on the legal protection of databases [1996] OJ L 77/20 (Database Directive).

[9] Directive 2009/24/EC of The European Parliament and of the Council of 23 April 2009 on the legal protection of computer programmes [2009] OJ L 111/16 (Computer Programmes Directive).

[10] Database Directive, Article 5(1).

[11] Computer Programmes Directive, Articles 5(2) and 6(1)(a) use the term, 'person having right to use computer programme'.

[12] Tatiana-Elena Synodinou, 'The Lawful User and a Balancing of Interests in European Copyright Law' [2010] 41 IIC 819, 824.

limitations under Article 18. The definition of a lawful user has been formulated having reference to the proposals made by Synodinou. Synodinou opines that the existence of a contract and the lawful acquisition of a work or a copy thereof should be considered the principal grounds for lawful use and that these criteria could be invoked either cumulatively or individually for the user to qualify as a lawful user.[13] In comparison, the present Regulation adopts a broader notion of a 'lawful user' by defining it as any person who is 'legally entitled to use a digitised version or copy thereof' which is intended to cover any person having a legal entitlement to use as may arise through a sale, a 'bare' license or contractual license, lending, rental and inheritance.[14] This definition has been formulated having regard to the opinion expressed by the EU Commission in their Report[15] on the implementation and effects of the Computer Programmes Directive that the term 'lawful acquirer' used in Article 5(1) of the Computer Programmes Directive and 'lawful user' used in Articles 6, 8 and 9 of the Database Directive, is intended to have a broad scope encompassing purchasers, licensees, renters or even persons authorised to use the program on behalf of anyone of the above.[16] Accordingly, under the present Regulation a person who is legally authorised to use the digitised version or copy thereof on behalf of the person who lawfully acquired it, would be considered a 'lawful user'. The inclusion of the standard of good faith prevents persons from using lawfully acquired digitised versions in ways that are prejudicial to the legitimate interests of the rightholders or any other person who may have an exclusive right over the digitised version (e.g., persons who hold exclusive rights over the software applied to value-added features that are included in the digitised versions).[17] As Synodinou proposes, the standard of good faith included in the definition should be interpreted as an objective standard of reasonableness as opposed to a subjective evaluation that considers the personal inner beliefs of the user.[18]

The definition of 'technological measure' in Article 1(j) is based on the definition provided in Article 6(3) of the InfoSoc Directive,[19] but with a further limitation to its scope, by defining a technological measure as a technology, device or component that is designed to protect the related right granted over a digitised version. Thus,

---

[13]ibid 831.

[14]ibid 831–34.

[15]'Report from the Commission to the Council, the European Parliament and the Economic and Social Committee on the Implementation and Effects of Directive 91/250/EEC on the Legal Protection of Computer Programmes', 10 April 2000, COM (2000) 199 final.

[16]ibid 12.

[17]In Synodinou's opinion interpreting the concept of a lawful user, considering elements of natural justice, such as good faith, attributes a dynamic character to the concept and could also function as criteria to judge whether a particular use is really lawful and remains lawful. Synodinou (n 12) 837. *See also* obligations of lawful users set out in Article 20 of the proposed model.

[18]Synodinou (n 12) 835–36.

[19]Directive 2001/29/EC of the European Parliament and of the Council of 22 May 2001 on the harmonisation of certain aspects of copyright and related rights in the information society [2001] OJ L167/10 (InfoSoc Directive).

unlike Article 6(3) of the InfoSoc Directive, the definition in Article 1(j) has the effect of explicitly limiting the protection granted to technological measures to instances where an act of circumvention results in the infringement of an exclusive right granted under Articles 11–16.

The definition of a 'thumbnail version' in Article 1(h) has been formulated, based on the definition provided by the Court of Appeals of the United States in the decision delivered in the case of *Perfect 10 v Google*.[20] It is argued here that, limiting the size of a thumbnail image to not more than 30% of the basic edition of the digital image as defined in Article 6(1)(a) and its resolution to not more than 50% of the basic edition, enables the thumbnails to be used for indexing and facilitating online searchability by a search engine as permitted under Article 18(4)(e) but prevent them from being viable substitutes to the actual digitised version.

Article 2: Unitary related right

A digitised version which has been registered in accordance with this Regulation shall convey to its rightholder a unitary right, which shall provide uniform protection and have equal effect throughout the Union. It shall not be registered, transferred or surrendered or be the subject of a decision revoking the rights of the proprietor or declaring it invalid, nor shall its use be prohibited, save in respect of the whole Union. This principle shall apply unless otherwise provided for in this Regulation.

Explanation of Article 2

Article 2 makes the related right contingent upon the completion of a formal process of registration. At present, EU law provides unitary EU-wide protection for trademarks,[21] patents[22] and design rights[23] subject to a formal process of registration. Article 5(2) of the Berne Convention posits that the exercise and enjoyment of the rights laid down by the Berne Convention shall not be subject to any formality.[24] However, this prohibition on formalities applies only with respect to 'works' protected under the Berne Convention.[25] Thus, it does not preclude making the

[20] *Perfect 10 Inc v Google Inc* [2007] 508 F3d 1146 (9th Circuit) 1155.

[21] Council Directive 2015/2436 of the European Parliament and of the Council of 16 December 2015 to approximate the laws of the Member States relating to trade marks [2015] OJ L336/1, Article 1 and Chapter 3.

[22] Regulation (EU) 1257/2012 of 17 December 2012 implementing enhanced cooperation in the area of the creation of unitary patent protection [2012] OJ L361/1, Article 3.

[23] Council Regulation (EC) 6/2002 of 12 December 2001 on Community designs [2002] OJ L3/1, Article 12. The Regulation also provides protection to unregistered designs under Article 11.

[24] Berne Convention for the Protection of Literary and Artistic Works S. Treaty Doc. No. 99-27 (1986) 1161 UNTS 3.

[25] Berne Convention, Article 5(1) read with Article 5(2).

exercise and enforcement of the related right over a digitised version subject to a registration requirement and the fulfilment of formalities.[26]

Furthermore, the Rome Convention[27] provides a precedence for the possibility to make protection under a related rights regime subject to the fulfilment of formalities. Article 11 of the Rome Convention states that, if the domestic law of a Contracting State makes the protection provided to phonogram producers and performers with respect to phonograms, subject to compliance with formalities, these formalities shall be considered as fulfilled if all the copies in commerce of the published phonogram (or their containers) bear a notice consisting of the symbol (P), accompanied by the date and year of the first publication that is placed in such a manner as to give reasonable notice of the claim of protection along with the names of the owners of the related rights.

The reasons for making the related right contingent upon the completion of a registration procedure are as follows. Firstly, in accordance with Article 6(1)(a) and Article 8(2) of the proposed regulatory framework, it would require persons who wish to claim the related right to comply with minimum technological and quality standards. This would ensure that the digital surrogates of rare documents that profit from protection under the related right fulfil minimum quality standards and technological standards that facilitate their interoperability[28] and long-term digital preservation.[29] Secondly, it would require each potential rightholder to deposit a master copy of the digitised version (i.e., 'basic edition') with the Central European Database that can be made available to the public free-of-charge and free of restrictions once the term of protection has expired. Thirdly, it would create more openness and certainty as to the protection that is granted to a particular digitised version. For example, the requirement under Article 7(2) that rightholders should make the registration information of each digitised version (including the date on which the protection period expires) available to users each time a digitised version is distributed or communicated to the public means that users would be able to easily identify digitised versions over which the protection period has expired or is about to expire. This would be useful in preventing 'copyfraud'.[30]

---

[26]As van Gompel observes, the prohibition on formalities imposed by Article 5(2) would not even extend to the 'Berne-plus' provisions of the TRIPS Agreement. Stef Van Gompel, *Formalities in Copyright Law: An Analysis of Their History, Rationales and Possible Future* (Kluwer Law International 2011) 165.

[27]International Convention for the Protection of Performers, Producers of Phonograms and Broadcasting Organizations, 26 October, 1961, 496 U.N.T.S. 43. The Convention came into effect in 1964 (Rome Convention).

[28]Interoperability refers to the ability to access, use, and distribute a particular digitised version within a range of different electronic devices. The adoption of common technical standards that lead to the use of commons formats and software tools in the production of digitised versions could improve their interoperability.

[29]For further discussion on the importance of standardisation for interoperability and digital preservation, *see* the discussion in Sect. 9.4.2 below.

[30]Copyfraud refers to the act of falsely claiming a copyright in a public domain work. Jason Mazzone, *Copyfraud and Other Abuses of Intellectual Property Law* (Stanford University Press 2011) 2. *See* Chap. 1, Sect. 1.4 for a discussion on the notion of copyfraud.

Article 3: Subject-matter of protection

(1) The subject-matter of protection shall be the basic edition of the digitised version that has been registered under Article 6 and which fulfils the formalities specified by Article 7. Higher-resolution versions of the basic edition that have been registered under Article 6(2) and which fulfil the formalities specified by Article 7 are also protected.
(2) The right granted under Article 2 shall not give rise to a new right over the rare document that is the object of digitisation, nor shall it change the public domain status of the content recorded upon the rare document in any way.
(3) Value-added-features that are applied to a digitised version will not obtain protection under Article 2. However, any rights that may independently attach to those features, will not be affected.

Explanation of Article 3
Article 3 has been introduced with the purpose of emphasising that the related right granted over the digitised version will only apply to that particular digitised version and any registered higher-resolution copies thereof, and will not affect the public domain status of the rare document or the content recorded upon it. It also emphasises that value-added-features (e.g., zoom-in and page-turner) shall not obtain protection under the related right.

Article 4: Ownership of related right

(1) The legal or natural person who is the owner of the rare document on the date of filing as specified in Article 6(3) shall, in the absence of any subsequent amendments made to the application for registration by the original applicant under Article 6(3), hold title in the right granted under Article 2.
(2) Title in the right granted under Article 2 shall be separate from any rights held over the underlying rare document. Changes to the ownership of the underlying rare document shall not affect title in the right granted under Article 2.

Explanation of Article 4
The legal or natural person who has ownership of the rare document at the date on which the application for registration of the digitised version is officially received by the Central European Database i.e., the date of filing as defined in Article 1(m), shall obtain title in the related right for the reasons discussed in Sect. 4.9 above.

Title in the related right over the digitised version shall be separate and independent of any proprietary or personal rights that may exist in relation to the underlying rare document. In the event that a change in ownership of the underlying rare document takes place after the date of filing but before the registration of the digitised version being issued, it would be possible for the original applicant (i.e., owner at the date of filing) to request an amendment to the application under Article 6 (3) to reflect the change in ownership. Where such an amendment is carried out, the new owner of the underlying rare document shall be granted title in the right over the digitised version.

However, changes to the ownership of the underlying rare document that may take place after the registration has been issued, will not affect ownership of the related right over the digitised version. This provision has been introduced with the objective of preventing confusion as to the ownership of rights over the digitised version that may arise following changes to the ownership of rare the documents once the registration process has been issued and the protection period has commenced.

Article 5: Duration of protection

(1) The right granted under Article 2 shall expire 7 years after the date on which the registration of the digitised version has been issued by the central European database under Article 6(5)(c).
(2) The period of 7 years shall be calculated from the first day of January of the year following the date of registration.

Explanation of Article 5

Calculating the optimal duration of related rights is an extremely difficult task. Digitised versions of rare documents being heterogeneous goods, it is not possible to calculate a uniform duration of protection that would in all cases enable the achievement of an optimal balance between user and producer interests.

Subparagraph 1 of Article 11(2)(a) of the PSI Directive,[31] specifies a duration of 10 years (without the requirement for review) for exclusive arrangements (i.e., license contracts) relating to the digitisation of cultural resources, but allows for exclusive arrangements to continue for a longer period subject to periodic review.[32]

The Comité des Sages recommends that a period of preferential commercial exploitation over digitised versions of public domain material should not exceed 7 years.[33] It appears that the period of 7 years was determined upon by the Comité based on the minimum duration of protection that would be capable of preserving the incentives of private sector entities to invest in the digitisation process.

According to Elisabeth Niggemann, the Director of the German National Library and a member of the Comité des Sages:

> Following extensive consultations with both private sector investors and public sector memory institutions, the Comité des Sages decided that the duration for preferential use (or preferential commercial exploitation) of public domain material digitised as a result of public-private partnerships should be set at a maximum of seven years. The duration of seven years was determined upon the understanding gleaned by the Comité des Sages during

[31]Directive 2013/37/EU of the European Parliament and of the Council of 26 June 2013 amending Directive 2003/98/EC on the re-use of public sector information [2013] OJ L175/1 (PSI Directive).

[32]PSI Directive, Article 11(2)(a)(1).

[33]Elisabeth Niggemann, Jacques De Decker and Maurice Lévy, *The New Renaissance: Report of the Comité des Sages on Bringing Europe's Cultural Heritage Online* (European Commission 2011) 48. <https://ec.europa.eu/digital-single-market/sites/digital-agenda/files/final_report_cds_0.pdf> accessed 31 January 2019. The recommendation of the Comité des Sages has been incorporated in Annex I para 2 of the European Commission Recommendation of 27 October 2011 on the digitisation and online accessibility of cultural material and digital preservation [2011] OJ L283/39.

> the consultation process that, private sector investors would not be willing to accept a duration of preferential use that would be less than seven years. Thus, the Comité decided to set the maximum duration for preferential use at the minimum period that they perceived would be acceptable to private sector investors. However, this period was not determined upon following any mathematical or economic calculation as to the period of protection that would optimize the interests of all stakeholders, nor based on any other empirical data (for example, cost data or revenue data).[34]

The proposed model adopts the 7-year duration proposed by the Comité des Sages as the duration of the related right over digitised versions. It is argued here that, granting a duration of protection that is less than the minimal period, which private-sector investors consider acceptable, may fail to provide sufficient incentives for private-sector investment in the digitisation process. In the absence of an economic model or statistical data that would allow for the calculation of a period of protection capable of optimising the competing interests of producers and users, it is proposed that the adoption of the 7-year period proposed by the Comité des Sages following extensive consultation with private-sector investors and public-sector memory institutions is the most sensible option available to legislators.

9.2 Central European Database

The model proposes the setting up of a Central European Database (CED) that is to be launched and administered by the EU Commission and operated under a non-profit model.

The CED will be entrusted with following tasks:

(i) Creating and maintaining an online platform that can be accessed by the public free-of-charge through which members of the public may access the databases indicated in (ii) and (iv) below.

(ii) Receiving applications for registration and issuing registrations of digitised versions through its 'Registry' and for maintaining records of registered digitised versions. The Registry shall also be responsible for the maintenance of a searchable database of data relating to digitised versions registered by it, including the information specified in Article 6(5) that will be made available to the public free-of-charge.

(iii) As per Article 9(1) maintaining a database of the basic editions and master copies of higher-resolution versions that have been registered by the CED which will not be accessible to members of the public.

[34]Opinion expressed by Dr. Elisabeth Niggemann, Director of the German National Library and member of the Comité des Sages during an interview carried out with the author (via email) on 13 January 2014. (Interview transcript in possession of the author).

(iv) As per Article 9(4) maintaining a searchable database of basic editions and master copies of higher-resolution versions of digitised versions that have entered the public domain which will be made available to members of the public free-of-charge.

It is proposed that The Europeana Foundation[35] that owns and manages *Europeana* (Europe's Digital Library) could be authorised to manage the CED, with the assistance and under the supervision of the EU Commission. It is argued here that, vesting the task of managing the CED with the Europeana Foundation would allow for master copies of digitised versions over which related rights protection has expired to be made available to the public through the existing *Europeana* platform, and thereby avoid the need to create a new distribution channel for their dissemination.

Article 6: Registration of digitised version

(1) Any person who is the owner of a rare document as per Article 1(c) may make an application to the Registry of the Central European Database for the registration of a prototype digital photographic image of that rare document which qualifies as a digitised version under Article 1(a). The application for registration shall be accompanied by the following data:

(a) a basic edition of the digitised version in electronic form, in respect of which registration is sought, that complies with the minimum technological standards specified under Article 8. The basic edition shall not incorporate any supplementary features such as value-added-features. This basic-edition shall be deposited in the database of digitised versions maintained by the central European database in accordance with Article 9,

(b) a statement made in good-faith by the owner of the document that is reproduced by the digitised version, that the document qualifies as a rare document under Article 1(c). The Central European database shall be free of any obligation to investigate whether the underlying document falls within the definition of a rare document under Article 1(c). The burden of proving that the document does not come within the definition of a rare document under Article 1(c), shall be on the party challenging protection under the right granted under Article 2 in a judicial proceeding. Subsequent evidence establishing that the document did not qualify as a rare document at the time the application was made, will not expose the owner of the document to any liability, unless it is determined in the course of a judicial proceeding that the statement was made by the owner in bad-faith and with

[35]The Europeana Foundation is a private, non-profit entity incorporated in the Netherlands as a *Stichting* (foundation), and housed within the Koninklijke Bibliothek in The Hague. Europeana is mainly funded by grants from the European Commission, thereby making it a rare example of an informational commons that is financially supported by the European Union. *See also* Sunimal Mendis, 'Europeana' in Marie Cornu, Fabienne Orsi and Judith Rochfeld (eds), *Dictionnaire des Biens communs* (PUF 2017).

the intention of misleading the Central European Database, in which case the owner shall be liable for punitive damages.

(c) the name of the owner of the rare document who shall obtain title in the exclusive right granted under Article 2 and who shall henceforth be referred to as 'the rightholder'. The Central European database shall be free of any obligation to verify ownership of the rare document. Where it is determined, in the course of a judicial proceeding that the claim of ownership has been made by the person submitting the application for registration, in bad-faith and with the intention of misleading the Central European Database, he shall be liable for restitutionary and punitive damages.

(d) information as to how the rightholder, his representative or authorized agent can be contacted for the purpose of Article 19(3),

(e) the name or designation by which the rightholder wishes to be identified for the purpose of Article 20(3), and

(f) the maximum sale price that can be charged for the sale of the basic-edition as per Article 10, and the cost data that has been used in the calculation and determination of the maximum sale price.

(2) The application for registration may also include master copies of higher-resolution versions of the basic edition provided in accordance with subsection 1(a) of this Article, which fulfil higher technological standards in comparison with the basic edition. These master copies of higher-resolution versions of the basic edition shall not incorporate any supplementary features such as value-added-features. Where master copies of higher-resolution versions are attached to the application, these shall be duly deposited in the database of digitised versions maintained by the Central European Database in accordance with Article 9, and registered as higher-resolution copies of the digitised version.

(3) Upon receipt of an application for the registration of a digitised version, the Registry of the Central European Database shall forthwith issue a receipt to the applicant which shall include the date on which the application for registration was received by the Central European Database. This date shall constitute the date of filing as defined in Article 1(m). As specified in Article 4(1) the person or entity who has ownership of the rare document at the date of filing shall hold title in the right granted under Article 2. Where the ownership of the rare document undergoes change before the registration of the digitised version has been issued, it shall be possible for the applicant to request that the application be amended in order to include the name of the new owner of the rare document. In such an event, title in the right granted under Article 2 shall vest in the new owner of the rare document as specified in the amended application.

(4) Unless an amendment is made to the application under subsection (3) of this Article, the person who has ownership of the rare document at the date of filing shall hold title in the right granted under Article 2.

(5) Having verified that all information specified in subsection (1) of this Article, has been received, and that the requirements for protection of the digitised version under Article 2(1) have been fulfilled, the Registry of the Central European Database shall register the basic edition of the digitised version provided in accordance with subsection (1)(a) above and any higher-quality copies thereof that may be attached to that application under subsection (2) of this Article, in a register maintained by it, along with the following information:

(a) the serial number issued to the digitised version upon registration,
(b) the date of filing as specified in subsection (3),
(c) the date on which the registration has been issued,
(d) date on which the term of protection expires,
(e) the name or designation by which the rightholder wishes to be identified for the purpose of Article 20(3) and information as to how the rightholder, his representative or authorized agent can be contacted by a user of the digitised version for the purpose of Article 19(3),
(f) the catalogue number (if any) by which the original rare document that has been digitised is identified by the person or entity who has custody of that document at the date of filing and/or other information that could facilitate the identification of the rare document and its location, and
(g) the maximum sale price of the basic-edition.

(6) When any of the information provided under subsection 5 (e) and (f) undergoes change the rightholder shall either directly or through his representative or authorized agent inform the Registry of the Central European Database of such change and provide the Registry with the correct information, no later than 28 days from the change taking place. The registry shall accordingly amend the information recorded in its register with a minimum of delay. The failure on the part of the rightholder to inform the Registry of any changes as specified under this subsection shall prevent the rightholder from asserting the exclusive rights set out in Articles 11–17 in a legal action brought against a third party for the infringement of one or more of these exclusive rights.
(7) When ownership in title over the right granted under Article 2, undergoes change through sale, inheritance or by any other means, the person or entity who obtains the new ownership in title shall make an application to the Registry for the amendment of information recorded in the register of the Central European Database, no later than 28 days from such change taking place. Such application for amendment shall include information under subsection 5(e) and (f). The Registry shall accordingly amend the information recorded in its register with a minimum of delay. The failure on the part of the new owner in title to inform the Registry as specified under this subsection shall prevent the new owner from asserting the exclusive rights set out in Articles 11–17 in a legal action brought against a third party for the infringement of one or more of these exclusive rights.
(8) If any person who holds title in the ownership of the right granted under Article 2 dedicates the digitised version to the public domain, it may inform the

Registry of the Central European Database of such dedication in writing. Following which, the Central European Database shall make the basic edition of the digitised version and any higher-resolution versions of master copies thereof, provided under subsection 2 of this Article, available on its online database in accordance with Article 9(4) specifying that the digitised version has been dedicated to the public domain.

(9) When title over the right granted under Article 2 is revoked or invalidated through a judicial proceeding, that decision shall be conveyed to the Registry of the Central European Database by the court or judicial body responsible for delivering that decision. Upon receipt of that decision, the Registry shall forthwith cancel the registration of the digitised version and with a minimum of delay make the basic edition of that digitised version and any master copies of higher-resolution versions thereof, provided under subsection 2 of this Article, available on its online database in accordance with Article 9(4), with an accompanying statement announcing the revocation or invalidity of registration and specifying the date on which the registration has been cancelled.

(10) The symbol 'D' that stands for 'digitised', shall be used to indicate to the public that a digitised version or any copy thereof is protected by the related right granted under Article 2.

(11) Where higher-resolution copies of the basic edition are attached to the application for registration in accordance with subsection 2 of this Article, each higher-resolution copy shall obtain the same registration serial number as given to the basic edition with the suffix 'HQ' denoting its status as a higher-resolution copy, and an additional number that allows each higher-resolution copy to be separately identified from the others.

(12) It shall be possible for the rightholder, his representative or authorised agent to register additional higher-resolution copies of the basic edition, at any time during term of protection of the registered basic edition. However, the protection granted to any of these higher-resolution copies shall expire on the date on which the protection granted to the registered basic edition expires. At no time shall the duration of protection granted to a higher-resolution copy subsist once the term of protection of the registered basic edition has expired.

(13) Any higher-resolution version that has not been registered as a copy of the registered basic edition shall not obtain protection under this Regulation.

Explanation of Article 6

Article 6 outlines the process under which a digitised version should be registered for claiming the related right granted under Article 2. It requires *inter alia* that the basic edition of the digitised version that is attached to the application for registration should comply with minimum technological and quality standards.

This 'basic edition' shall be subject to a maximum sale price that shall be determined according to the price regulation formula published by the CED under Article 10. It is noted that, the maximum sale price shall only apply to instances where electronic copies of the basic edition of a digitised version is distributed to the public by sale or any other transfer of ownership. Transactions such as rental and lending which do not result in a transfer of ownership will not be subject to the maximum sale price under Article 10. The rightholder is also permitted to register master copies that have a higher image resolution than the 'basic edition'. These higher-resolution versions shall be registered as 'copies' of the registered digitised version (i.e., the basic edition) and their sale will not be subject to price regulation. The maximum sale price will also not apply to instances when the basic edition is being sold in combination with other features or services that enhance its value to the user (i.e., value-added-features). However, under Article 19, within 14 days of the date of registration of the digitised version, the rightholder shall have an obligation to offer the basic edition of the digitised version for sale to the public.

Subsection 1(b) releases the owner of a document reproduced in a digitised version from a legal obligation to verify that the document comes within the definition of a rare document in Article 1(c). Most importantly, this releases the legal or natural person who owns the underlying rare document from having to investigate whether more than twenty-five original copies of that document exist in the world. As noted in the explanation of Article 1 above, most curators and archivists have a general understanding as to how many original copies exist of documents that are classified by them as 'rare'. However, it may be impossible to make an affirmation to that effect with complete certainty. Thus, for the purposes of registration, a statement made in good faith by the owner that the underlying document comes within the definition of a rare document in Article 1(c) is adequate. The burden of proving that more than twenty-five original copies thereof exist will be on the person who wishes to challenge that the underlying document reproduced by a digitised version registered under this Regulation comes within the definition of Article 1(c).

Subsection 1(c) releases the Central European Database of a legal duty to verify the ownership of the underlying rare document. However, the subsection provides for sanctions to be imposed in the case of false claims of ownership that has been made in bad-faith and with the intention of misleading the Central European Database.

Article 6 also includes provisions that enable the amendment of the record maintained by the registry of the CED in the event of a change of ownership in the related right (subsection 7), when the digitised version is dedicated to the public domain by the rightholder (subsection 8) or when the related right granted under Article 2 is revoked or invalidated through a judicial proceeding for any reason (subsection 9). The related right over a digitised version could become invalidated or revoked through a judicial proceeding which determines that the requirements for protection under Article 2 have not been met; for example, if the underlying document that has been digitised is established as not coming within the definition of a 'rare document' or if the digitised version is established not to be a prototype image of an existing analogue document.[36]

[36]It is noted that a detailed discussion on the grounds for revocation or invalidation of the related right, the procedure to be followed in an action for revocation or invalidation, and the consequences of the revocation or invalidation, is not within the scope of this study.

Article 7: Formalities

(1) During each act of distribution, communication and making available to the public of the digitised version or any copy thereof, including higher-resolution copies, the symbol D referred to in Article 6(10) and the registration serial number provided under Article 6(5)(a) and Article 6(11) must be attached to the digitised version in such a manner that makes them easily discernible to a user.
(2) All other information provided under Article 6(5) subsections (b)–(g) shall be made available free-of-charge to any lawful user of the digitised version or any copy thereof, including lawful users of higher-resolution copies, in such a manner that the information is easily discernible to the user.
(3) Where the digitised version that is distributed, communicated or made available to the public is not a basic edition as defined by Article (l), the rightholder shall also provide to any lawful user of that digitised version or copy thereof, including higher-resolution copies, information as to how the basic edition could be purchased by the user. This information shall be provided free-of-charge and in a manner that makes it easily accessible to the user.
(4) A digitised version or any copy thereof, including higher-resolution copies, shall not be imprinted with any visible trade mark, logo, insignia or marking of any kind. However, tracking software and digital-rights-management software can be applied to the digitised version or any copy thereof subject to the provisions of Article 16.

Explanation of Article 7

The formalities set out in subsections (1)–(4) of Article 7 have been introduced with the following objectives.

- Facilitating a user to identify a digitised version that is protected under a related right.
- Facilitating licence clearance procedures by providing information relating to the period of protection, the name of the rightholder and the means by which the rightholder could be contacted.
- Facilitating use and exploitation of the digitised version by members of the public and preventing copyfraud by informing users of the date on which related rights protection expires.
- Informing users as to the maximum sale price of the digitised version and as to how the 'basic edition' could be purchased under the maximum sale price.
- Providing information as to how the original analogue rare document that is reproduced by the digitised version could be located within the memory institution which holds it.
- Preventing digitised versions from being imprinted with a visible marking of any kind, including trademarks that may detract from its value for research and education and its overall utility to users.[37]

[37] *See* detailed discussion on the application of trademarks and other visible markings to digitised versions in Chap. 6, Sect. 6.2.1.

Article 8: Declaration of technological and quality standards

(1) The Central European Database shall be authorized to fix minimum technological and quality standards that must be met by the basic edition of a digitised version under Article 6(1)(a).
(2) Any application for registration that does not include a basic edition that complies with the technological and quality standards specified by the Central European Database, shall be refused.
(3) The Central European Database may periodically revise the technological and quality standards specified by it, for the purpose of being up-to-date with advancements in digitisation technology. Each revised version of the technology and quality standards shall come into force 6 months from the date on which it has been published on the official website of the central European database.
(4) Any digitised version in respect of which a registration has been issued under Article 6(5) prior to the coming into effect of the revised technology and quality standards, shall not lose protection under the related right granted under Article 2 by reason of not complying with the revised technological and quality standards that came into effect after the registration was issued.
(5) Any digitised version in respect of which, the date of filing the application for registration is on the same date or prior to the coming into effect of revised technological and quality standards, shall not be refused registration on the grounds of its failure to comply with the revised technological and quality standards if, it complies with the technological and quality standards that were in force immediately prior to the coming into force of the revised standards.
(6) Any application for registration of a digitised version which, as per its date of filing, is made 18 months after coming into effect of the technological or quality standards applicable at the date of filing, shall not be refused registration on the grounds of its failure to comply with the prevailing technological and quality standards if, following the examination of any documentary evidence provided to that effect, the Registry is satisfied that the digitised version has been produced before the prevailing technological and quality standards came into effect. In this case, the eligibility of the digitised version to obtain a registration under Article 6 shall be determined based on the technological and quality standards that were applicable immediately before the coming into effect of the prevailing technological and quality standards.

Explanation of Article 8

The minimum technological and quality standards have been proposed to achieve the following objectives:

- To ensure that a digitised version that obtains protection under the related right (especially the basic edition that is subject to price regulation) is of a quality that enables it to function as a satisfactory digital surrogate of the underlying rare document reproduced by it.

- To ensure that digitised versions that obtain protection under the related right comply with uniformly applicable standards that facilitate their interoperability and long-term digital preservation.

The period of 18 months provided under subsection (4) functions as a grace period[38] that provides additional time to producers of digitised versions, the production of which has commenced prior to the coming into effect of revised technological standards. It is intended to minimise the prejudice that could otherwise be caused to producers as a result of the periodic revision of technological standards under Article 8.

Article 9: Database of digitised versions

(1) The Central European Database shall maintain a database of basic editions of digitised versions and master copies of higher-resolution versions, that have been registered under Article 6.
(2) Each basic edition as well as any higher-resolution copies thereof, shall be included in the database along with the information specified under Article 6(5).
(3) The basic edition or master copies of higher-resolution versions thereof, shall not be distributed, communicated or otherwise made available to any person other than the rightholder, his representative or authorized agent during the term of protection of the digitised version, except in accordance with Article 19.
(4) Following the expiration of the term of protection, the Central European Database shall make the basic edition and any higher-resolution copies thereof available to the public together with the information specified under Article 6(5), through its online database, free-of-charge and free of restrictions or controls.

Explanation of Article 9

The maintenance of a database of digitised versions, whereby digitised versions can be made available to the public free-of-charge and free of restrictions once the period of related rights protection has expired, is one of the key features of the regulatory framework. It seeks to facilitate the achievement of one of the overarching objectives of introducing a related right over digitised versions that is limited in duration, that is, to secure the enhanced availability and unrestricted use and exploitation of digitised versions of rare documents in the long-term. The CED shall be responsible for the preservation of the digitised versions included in its database and for the maintenance of a distribution channel and infrastructure that facilitates their access, use, and re-use by the public.

[38] A 'grace-period' is defined as, "Additional time scheduled or allocated to complete a task, such as complying with a regulation, meeting an obligation, or obtaining an agreement". (The Law Dictionary 2018) <https://thelawdictionary.org/grace-period/> accessed 31 January 2019.

Article 10: Price regulation

(1) The Central European Database shall be authorized to publish a formula that shall be used to calculate the maximum sale price of the basic edition of a digitised version.
(2) Digitised versions other than the basic edition, including higher-resolution copies and copies that incorporate additional elements such as value-added features shall not be subject to the maximum sale price. Digitised versions that are incorporated in a tangible medium shall also be exempted from the maximum sale price.
(3) The maximum sale price shall only apply to instances where electronic copies of the basic edition of a digitised version is distributed to the public by sale or any other transfer of ownership.

Explanation of Article 10

The introduction of the price regulation formula according to which the maximum sale price of a basic edition should be calculated is intended to ensure that the basic edition is available for purchase by members of the public at a fair price. It thereby seeks to prevent rightholders from abusing their position as the sole source of a rare document in digital form in order to obtain exorbitant profits from the sale of basic editions that comply with minimal technological and quality standards. It is also expected that the regulation of the sale price of basic editions would act as an incentive to rightholders to make available higher quality copies of digitised versions and to introduce value-added-features to the digitised versions sold by them to maximise their profits, which in turn would enhance the user experience and increase the overall utility of digitised versions of rare documents.

The maximum sale price will only apply to transactions that result in a permanent transfer of ownership in the electronic copy of a basic edition of a digitised version that has not been incorporated in a tangible medium. As per the decision delivered by the CJEU in the *UsedSoft v Oracle International*[39] case, any licensing contract concluded between the rightholder and a user that allows the user to download a copy of a basic-edition in return for the payment of a fee and to use the basic-edition for an unlimited period would be deemed as a sale.

It is proposed that the price regulation formula under which the maximum sale price of a digitised version is to be calculated should be designed to allow the following factors to be considered.

(i) The fixed costs of producing the digitised version.
(ii) The costs of creating and distributing copies thereof to the public (including costs of maintaining distribution channels, etc.).
(iii) Adjustment for inflation that allows users to periodically increase the maximum sale price by a pre-defined percentage.
(iv) The ability of the investor to recoup a reasonable return[40] on his investment.

[39]Judgment of 3 July 2012, *UsedSoft*, C-128/11, EU:C:2012:407.

[40]The determination as to what constitues a 'reasonable return' is beyond the scope of this study. It is proposed that this should be determined in consultation with private sector for-profit entities that are active in the licensing market within the EU.

9.3 Scope of Related Right

Article 11: Right to reproduction

The right granted over a digitised version under Article 2 shall confer upon its proprietor the exclusive right to authorize or prohibit the direct or indirect, temporary or permanent, reproduction of the digitised version or copies thereof, by any means and in any form, in whole or in part.

Explanation of Article 11

Article 11 is based on Article 2 of the InfoSoc Directive. Article 11 includes both acts that reproduce the digitised version directly onto a digital or non-digital medium (i.e., 'direct' reproduction), as well as acts of reproduction, that are done via an intermediate stage (i.e., 'indirect' reproduction),[41] such as for example, the reproduction of a digitised version by means of scanning the pages of a book on which it has been reproduced. Article 11 brings within its scope both permanent and temporary reproductions. However, Article 17(1) provides for an exception as regards transient or incidental acts of reproduction.

Article 12: Right of distribution to the public

(1) The right granted over a digitised version under Article 2 shall confer upon its proprietor the exclusive right to authorize or prohibit any form of distribution to the public of the digitised version or copies thereof by sale or otherwise.
(2) The first sale in the Community of a digitised version or copy thereof in electronic or non-electronic form that is incorporated in a tangible medium shall exhaust the distribution right within the Community of the digitised version or its copy that is incorporated in the tangible medium. The exhaustion of the distribution right shall not result in the exhaustion of the rental and lending right provided under Article 14.

Explanation of Article 12

Subsection (1) is based on Article 4(1) of the InfoSoc Directive and is intended to have the same meaning and effect. As per the determination delivered by the CJEU in the case of *Peek & Cloppenburg*,[42] the exclusive right to distribution provided under Article 4(1) of the InfoSoc Directive should be interpreted as being limited to acts that entail a transfer of ownership in the protected subject matter or a copy thereof.[43] Article 12(1) of the present Regulation is to be interpreted in the same way

[41] *See* discussion relating to the meaning of direct and indirect reproduction in Proposal for a European Parliament and Council Directive on the harmonisation of certain aspects of copyright and related rights in the Information Society COM (97) 628 final, Brussels, 10 December 1997, 24 (discussion on 'Article 2: Reproduction Right', paragraph 3), available at, <ec.europa.eu/transparency/regdoc/rep/1/2002/EN/1-2002-414-EN-F1-1.Pdf> accessed 31 January 2019.

[42] Judgment of 17 April 2008, *Peek & Cloppenburg*, C-456/06, EU:C:2008:232.

[43] ibid para 33–36.

and the term 'or otherwise' should be interpreted as referring to acts which entail a transfer of ownership in a digitised version or a copy thereof.

Subsection (2) that deals with the exhaustion of the distribution right within the EU, limits exhaustion to the sale within the EU of digitised versions or copies thereof that have been incorporated in a tangible medium. The term tangible medium refers to a digitised version being sold subsequent to its incorporation in a physical object, for example a digitised version that has been recorded upon a CD-ROM or printed upon a paper.

The limitation of exhaustion of the distribution right to digitised versions incorporated in a tangible medium is by way of a reaction to the decision of the CJEU in the *UsedSoft*[44] case. It is anticipated that the distribution of electronic copies over the Internet would constitute the main channel of distribution and account for a major portion of the revenue obtained by the commercial exploitation of digitised versions while the revenue obtained from the distribution of digitised versions incorporated in CD-ROMs, etc. would be comparatively smaller. Therefore, it is argued here that, to enable producers of digitised versions to optimise the financial return that could be obtained through the commercial exploitation of a digitised version, it is necessary to prevent digitised versions from being distributed over the Internet by competitors.

Exhaustion of the distribution right is limited to the EU in order to enable the separation of the EU market and international markets, and to facilitate the exercise of price-discrimination, especially regarding markets in developing countries.

Article 13: Right of communication and making available to the public

The right granted over a digitised version under Article 2 shall confer upon its proprietor the exclusive right to authorize or prohibit any communication to the public of the digitised version or copies thereof, by wire or wireless means, including the making available to the public of the digitised version or copies thereof in such a way that members of the public may access them from a place and at a time individually chosen by them.

Explanation of Article 13

Article 13 is based on Article 3(1) of the InfoSoc Directive. The right of communication to the public is defined as the right to communicate the digitised version to the public in such a way that the persons forming the public may access it: what matters being that the work has been put in a position so that it may be potentially accessed by the public at large.[45]

The making available right covers instances of unauthorised acts of intervention that put the work at the disposal of users in such a way that it could enjoyed at a place and time individually chosen by them, regardless of whether they actually have

[44]Judgment of 3 July 2012, *UsedSoft*, C-128/11, EU:C:2012:407.

[45]Emanuela Arezzo, 'Hyperlinks and Making Available Right in the European Union-What Future for the Internet After Svensson' [2014] 45 IIC 524, 532–33, citing Judgment of 2 June 2005, *Mediakabel*, C-89/04, EU:C:2005:348, para 30 and Judgment of 14 July 2005, *Lagardère Active Broadcast*, C-192/04, EU:C:2005:475, para 31.

access to it.[46] As Arezzo notes, the main difference between the right of communication to the public and the right of making available to the public ultimately lies in the fact that in the case of the making available right, the actual transmission of the work takes place through an individual communication as the digital content is transmitted to the user in the precise moment chosen by the user.[47]

The exclusive right to communicate and to make available the digitised version to the public is provided to the rightholder to enable him to prevent users from accessing the digitised version from unauthorised alternative sources, thereby possibly by-passing the terms and conditions of access imposed by the rightholder under Article 15.

Thus, the exclusive right to communicate and to make available, enables the rightholder to limit access of the digitised versions only to authorised users (e.g., those who have paid a subscription fee to access digitised versions). Furthermore, the ability to be the sole source from which the digitised version could be accessed can create additional value to the rightholder in terms of preserving its position as the origin of a particular digitised version and in ensuring that potential users of a digitised version are directed to the rightholder's own webpage which would, for example, enhance the value of the webpage as a platform for online advertising.

Article 14: Rental and lending right

(1) The right granted over a digitised version under Article 2 shall confer upon its proprietor the exclusive right to authorize or prohibit the rental and lending of the digitised versions and copies thereof both in electronic and non-electronic form. For the purpose of this provision:

  (a) 'rental' means making available for use, for a limited period of time and for direct and indirect economic or commercial advantage,
  (b) 'lending' means making available for use, for a limited period of time and not for direct or indirect economic or commercial advantage.

(2) The exclusive right referred to in subsection (1) shall not be exhausted through the exhaustion of the distribution right in accordance with Article 12(2).

Explanation of Article 14

Article 14 is based on Article 1 and Article 2(1)(a) and (b) of the Rental and Lending Rights Directive.[48] As per the determination delivered by the CJEU in the case of *Vereniging Openbare Bibliotheken (VOB)*[49] the concept of 'lending' within the meaning of Article 2(1)(a) of the Rental and Lending Rights Directive includes the

[46] Arezzo (n 45) 533.

[47] ibid.

[48] Directive 2006/115/EC of the European Parliament and of the Council of 12 December 2006 on rental right and lending right and on certain rights related to copyright in the field of intellectual property [2006] OJ L 376/28 (Rental and Lending Rights Directive).

[49] Judgment of 10 November 2016, *Vereniging Openbare Bibliotheken*, C-174/15, EU:C:2016:856.

lending of digital copies and of intangible objects[50] and therefore encompasses the phenomenon of electronic lending (e-lending) as well. For the present Regulation, both concepts of 'rental' and 'lending' are defined so as encompass the rental and lending of digitised versions both in electronic form, as well as when they are fixed in a tangible medium, so that acts of e-lending come within its scope.

Article 14 has been formulated to allow the rightholder to commercially exploit the digitised version to an optimal level in the market for the rental and lending of digitised versions. Article 17(3)(a) provides an exception to the exclusive right in favour of cultural and educational institutions and institutions engaged in scientific research, to facilitate rental and lending which is not for direct commercial purposes and are aimed towards the advancement of culture and education.

As noted in the explanation to Article 12 above, the distribution right provided under Article 12 of the present Regulation is based on Article 4(1) of the InfoSoc Directive. Thus, as per the determination delivered by the CJEU in the *Peek & Cloppenburg*[51] case, the exclusive right to distribution granted under Article 12 of the present regulation will not apply to acts of rental and lending which, as made evident by their definitions in Article 14(1)(a) and (b), do not entail a transfer of ownership of a digitised version or a copy thereof. Accordingly, the exhaustion of the distribution right will not automatically bring about the exhaustion of the exclusive rental and lending right provided under Article 14 of the present Regulation. Therefore, Article 14(2) may seem superfluous. Nevertheless, it has been included in this Regulation to clarify and emphasise that the exhaustion of the distribution right under Article 12 will not result in the exhaustion of the rental and lending right provided for in Article 14.

Article 15: Right to make access subject to terms and conditions

(1) The right granted over a digitised version under Article 2 shall confer upon the proprietor of the related right the right to make access to the digitised version subject to terms and conditions determined by the rightholder.
(2) The application and enforcement of these terms and conditions shall be subject to the exceptions set out in Articles 17 and the provisions of Articles 18 and 19.

Explanation of Article 15

EU law does not explicitly grant to the holder of a copyright or related right an exclusive right to authorise or prevent access to protected content. However, Heide argues that, such a right becomes implicit in the protection granted to technological measures that control access to copyright and related rights protected content under Article 6(1) of the InfoSoc Directive.[52]

The ability to restrict and limit the ways in which a digitised version could be accessed by the public becomes especially vital, following the decision delivered by

[50]ibid para 44.

[51]Judgment of 17 April 2008, *Peek & Cloppenburg*, C-456/06, EU:C:2008:232.

[52]Thomas Heide, 'Copyright in the EU and US: What "Access-Right"?' (2001) 48 Journal of the Copyright Society of the USA 363, 375.

the CJEU in the *Svensson*[53] case. In this decision, the CJEU determined that the provision of clickable links to a protected work would not be considered an infringement of a rightholder's exclusive right to communicate the work to the public, unless access to the protected work had been restricted to certain groups of authorised users.

Thus, Article 15 of the present Regulation provides the rightholder an exclusive right to prevent access of a digitised version or a copy thereof in violation of the terms and conditions imposed by the rightholder. This access right affords the rightholder a right *in rem* to control access to a digitised version or a copy thereof, regardless as to whether a contractual relationship exists between the rightholder and the party accessing the digitised version. It is noted that, the exercise of the right to control access is subject to exceptions and limitations set out in Article 17 and the rights granted to users of digitised versions under Articles 18 and 19.

The introduction of an explicit access right provides additional strength to the protection of technological measures applied to digitised versions against circumvention under Article 6 of the InfoSoc Directive. However, the access right introduced by the present Regulation exists independently of the protection provided against the circumvention of technological measures under the InfoSoc Directive.

It is emphasised that what is granted under Article 15 is a right to control access, by determining the terms and conditions of such access[54] as opposed to a right to prevent access. Article 15 does not enable a rightholder to deny access to any person who acts under the terms and conditions of access imposed by him.[55] As noted in Article 19, users have a right to access the basic edition of a digitised version by purchasing it under the terms and conditions imposed by the rightholder. Furthermore, Article 19 imposes an obligation upon the rightholder to make the basic edition of a digitised version available for purchase by members of the public within 14 days of its registration.

Article 16: Technological measures

(1) The proprietor of the related right shall have the right to apply technological measures in order to safeguard and enforce the rights granted under Articles 11–16.

---

[53] Judgment of 13 February 2014, *Svensson*, C-466/12, EU:C:2014:76.

[54] Ginsburg defines an access right as a right to control the manner in which members of the public apprehend a work. Thus, the access right is distinguished from the right to reproduction or communication to the public to the extent that, although a work may be communicated or distributed to a user, the user may not 'open' (i.e., access) the work unless he acquires the 'key' to the work that is required by the technological protection measures. Jane C Ginsburg, 'Essay: From Having Copies to Experiencing Works: The Development of an Access Right in U.S. Copyright Law' (2003) 50 Journal of the Copyright Society of the USA 113, 120.

[55] Thus, the definition of the contours of the right to control access under Article 14 diverges from the definition of the access-right provided by Efroni under which a person comes under Hohfeldian duties of abstention unless a rightholder's authorisation to access is granted. Zohar Efroni, *Access-Right: The Future of Digital Copyright Law* (Oxford University Press 2011) 144–47.

(2) The use of these technological measures shall be subject to the exceptions set out in Article 17 and shall be proportionate for the purpose of safeguarding the exclusive rights provided by Articles 11–16 above.
(3) Effective technological measures applied to digitised versions in accordance with subsections (1) and (2) above, shall be protected against acts carried out by any person, for the purpose of enabling or facilitating without the rightholder's authority, the circumvention of those technological measures for the commission of any act that infringes upon the exclusive rights of the proprietor granted under Articles 11 and 16, with the knowledge or with reasonable grounds to know that he is pursuing that objective.

Explanation of Article 16

Article 16 is based on Article 6 of the InfoSoc Directive. It grants rightholders with a positive and explicit right to use technological measures to safeguard their exclusive rights. On the one hand, Article 16 read with Article 15 improves upon the strength of protection granted to rightholders under Article 6 of the InfoSoc Directive, by granting them a positive right to use technological measures in enforcing terms of conditions of access imposed by them, and for safeguarding their exclusive rights over the digitised version. On the other hand, it explicitly circumscribes the application of technological measures for the purpose of safeguarding and enforcing rights granted under Articles 11–16, and requires the application of technological measures to be proportionate to that purpose. In doing so, it follows the decision delivered by the CJEU in the *Nintendo v PC Box*[56] case, where the CJEU held that technological measures must be suitable for achieving the objective of preventing or eliminating acts that are not authorised by the rightholder and must not go beyond what is necessary for this purpose.[57]

Subsection (3) is based on Article 6(1) of the InfoSoc Directive and grants protection against circumvention to 'effective' technological measures. Article 6 (3) of the InfoSoc Directive deems a technological measure as being effective where the access control, copy control mechanism or protection process achieves the protection objective. The term 'effective' has been construed as a reflection of the legislator's intention to avoid granting protection to obsolete devices or devices in relation to which circumvention is too easy, accidental or simply possible.[58] It has also been interpreted to mean that the technological measure must be proportionate to the objective of protecting the exclusive rights of the rightholder.[59] It is noted that, unlike Article 6(1) the protection granted under subsection (3) is limited to acts of circumvention that have the effect of infringing upon the exclusive rights of the

[56]Judgment of 23 January 2014, *Nintendo and Others,* C-355/12, EU:C:2014:25.

[57]ibid para 31.

[58]Lucie Guibault and others, 'Study on the Implementation and Effect in Member States' Laws of Directive 2001/29/EC on the Harmonisation of Certain Aspects of Copyright and Related Rights in the Information Society' (IViR 2007) 75 <https://papers.ssrn.com/sol3/papers.cfm?abstract_id=2006358> accessed 31 January 2019.

[59]ibid.

rightholder granted under Articles 11–16. Thus, acts of circumvention that do not have the effect of infringing upon one or more of these exclusive rights will not result in an infringement of the present Article.

Article 17: limitations and exceptions

(1) Temporary acts of reproduction made by a lawful user which are transient or incidental and an integral and essential part of a technological process and whose sole purpose is to enable,

(a) the transmission in a network between third parties by an intermediary,
(b) the lawful use, of a digitised version or a copy thereof to be made, and which have no independent economic significance shall be exempted from the reproduction right provided for in Article 10.

Explanation to Article 17(1)

Article 17(1) is based on Article 5(1) of the InfoSoc Directive. It authorises acts of reproduction that are integral to a technological process and made for the sole purpose of executing another act of exploitation, but which have no economic significance of their own.[60]

(2) The following exceptions and limitation shall apply to the exclusive right provided for in Article 11:

(a) Reproduction in non-electronic form of a digitised version or a copy thereof, by a lawful user, for private use and for ends that are neither directly nor indirectly commercial.

Explanation to Article 17(2)(a)

This provision is based on Article 5(2)(a) and (b) of the InfoSoc Directive. It authorises lawful users of a digitised version (including higher-resolution versions) to make an unlimited number of reproductions in a non-electronic format (e.g., a paper print) for private non-commercial purposes.

However, Article 17(2)(a) dispenses with the optional requirement introduced by the InfoSoc Directive that the reproduction should be made subject to fair compensation paid to the rightholder. It is observed that reproductions made in a non-electronic format for private non-commercial purposes by a lawful user is unlikely to cause significant prejudice to a rightholder's ability to commercially exploit the digitised version so as to obtain a reasonable return on his investment. In comparison with reproductions made in electronic form, reproductions in non-electronic format are less likely to be abused and to lead to large-scale piracy or unauthorised distribution (e.g., by being shared over peer-to-peer networks). Therefore, it is considered that the requirement for fair compensation is unnecessary and would merely increase the transaction costs incurred by a user in benefitting from the exception.

---

[60] *See* discussion on Article 5(1) of EU Commission proposal for InfoSoc Directive, 10th December 1997 (n 41), 29 (discussion on 'Article 5', paragraph 3).

However, as per the decision delivered by the CJEU in the *ACI Adam*[61] case, where it was held that the private copy exception under Article 5(2)(b) of the InfoSoc Directive cannot be interpreted to extend to private copies made from unlawful sources, the scope of the present Article 17(2)(a) is limited to acts of reproduction carried out by a lawful user of a digitised version, which means that it would only cover reproductions made in good faith by a person who is legally entitled to use the particular digitised version or copy.

(b) A maximum of no more than three reproductions of a digitised version or a copy thereof, by a lawful user in electronic form, for the purpose set out in (a) above.

Explanation to Article 17(2)(b)
This provision restricts the number of reproductions that could be made of a digitised version in electronic (digital) form for private non-commercial purposes to no more than three. As noted in the explanation to Article 17(2)(a) above, the ability to make an unlimited number of reproductions in electronic format has a high possibility of being abused and unless subject to strict regulation, can damage the ability of a producer of a digitised version to obtain a reasonable return on his investment. It is observed that the restriction imposed on the number of copies could be enforced through the application of DRM systems.

(c) Reproduction by a lawful user in non-electronic form for the sole purpose of illustration for teaching or scientific research, for ends that are not directly commercial and to the extent justified by the non-commercial purpose.

Explanation to Article 17(2)(c)
This provision is based on the Article 5(3)(a) of the InfoSoc Directive. It permits the creation of an unlimited number of reproductions in non-electronic (tangible) form for illustration in teaching and scientific research for ends that are not directly commercial.

(d) reproduction and extraction by a lawful user of digitised versions or copies thereof in order to carry out text and data mining for the purposes of scientific research and to the extent justified by that purpose.

Explanation Article 17(2)(d)
This provision is based on Article 3(1) of the EU Commission proposal for a Directive on copyright in the digital single market.[62] The term 'text and data mining' is defined in Article 1(g) of the present Regulation.

The exception does not distinguish between scientific research that is aimed at commercial and non-commercial purposes. It is argued here that, the reproduction of a digitised version to extract the public domain content recorded upon it for scientific research is unlikely to cause economic damage to rightholders, especially as the

---

[61] Judgment of 10 April 2014, *ACI Adam and Others*, C-435/12, EU:C:2014:254.

[62] Article 3(1) of the Proposal for a directive of the European Parliament and of the Council on copyright in the Digital Single Market, 14 September 2016, COM(2016) 593.

exception is limited to instances of reproduction and extraction carried out by a lawful user who is legally entitled the use the digitised version.

(3) The following exceptions and limitations shall apply to the exclusive rights provided for in Articles 11–14.

(a) Lawful use of a digitised version or a copy thereof for the sole purpose of illustration for teaching, scientific research or cultural discourse, for ends that are not directly commercial and to the extent justified by the non-commercial purpose, provided that the use takes place on the premises of a cultural or educational institution or an institution engaged in scientific research, and through a secure electronic network accessible only by the teaching staff, students and other persons who have been specifically authorised by the institution to access the electronic network.

Explanation to Article 17(3)(a)

This provision is based on Article 4(1) of the EU Commission proposal for a Directive on copyright in the digital single market.[63] The scope of Article 4(1) of the proposed directive has been expanded to include illustrations for cultural discourse carried out by educational, cultural institutions or institutions engaged in scientific research. The exception has been inspired by the discussion on the social planning theory in Chap. 5[64] and is intended to secure the broad availability of cultural and informational content for educational and cultural contemplation and deliberation.

(b) Use by a lawful user of a digitised version or a copy thereof either in whole or in part, in the creation of a new work that is original in the sense that it is its author's own intellectual creation and which, in its visual aspects, demonstrates a distinguishable variation to the underlying digitised version(s).

Explanation to Article 17(3)(b)

This provision, seeks to authorise the use of digitised versions in the creation, reproduction, distribution, communication and making available to the public, and the rental and lending of derivative works that qualify for copyright protection under the author's own intellectual creation standard of EU copyright law.[65]

It has been formulated with the objective of encouraging and facilitating the creation of new original works that are based on existing digitised versions by lawful users. As per the author's own intellectual creation standard, this exception would only apply to acts of creation where the creator of the new derivative content has exercised his creative abilities in an original manner by making free and creative choices.[66]

---

[63] ibid Article 4(1).

[64] *See* Chap. 5, Sect. 5.4.2.

[65] *See* Chap. 5, Sect. 7.3.1.

[66] *See* decisions delivered by the CJEU in the cases of Judgment of 16 July 2009, *Infopaq International*, C-5/08, EU:C:2009:465; Judgment of 4 October 2011, *Football Association Premier League and Others*, C-403/08 and C-429/08, EU:C:2011:631 and Judgment of 1 March 2012, *Football Dataco v Yahoo! UK Ltd*, C-604/10, EU:C:2012:115.

The requirement that the derivative work demonstrates a distinguishable to the visual aspects of the underlying digitised version or versions, is inspired by UK copyright law relating to the originality of a reproductive work. In the *Interlego*[67] case, the Privy Council held that, to obtain copyright protection, a new creation that reproduces a pre-existing work must effect a transformation of visual significance to that pre-existing work.[68] Furthermore, in the *Bridgeman I*[69] decision, Judge Kaplan held that the colour transparencies in issue could not obtain copyright protection under the law of the UK, as they did not demonstrate any distinguishable variation that could set them apart from the pre-existing art works.[70] The requirement for a distinguishable variation has been included in the present provision to ensure that the exception would not lead to the creation of reproductions that could act as substitutes to the original digitised versions on which they are based. It is argued here that, where a distinguishable variation has been effected to the visual aspects through the exercise of free and creative choices, it is unlikely that the resulting work would be able to serve as a substitute to the digitised version on which it is based.[71]

(c) Use by a lawful user of a digitised version or copy thereof for the benefit of people with a disability, which are directly related to the disability and of a non-commercial nature, to the extent required by the specific disability.

Explanation of Article 17(3)(c)
This provision is based on Article 5(3)(b) of the InfoSoc Directive.

(d) Use of an amount that is no more than 15% of the total digitised version by Internet search engines and online services for the purposes of providing snippets or by a lawful user for the purpose of criticism, commentary or review.

Explanation of Article 17(3)(d)
The ability of a user to browse through snippet views of digitised versions that contain keywords and search terms can facilitate the user's ability to search through

---

[67] *Interlego v Tyco* [1989] AC 217.

[68] ibid 266.

[69] *Bridgeman Art Library Ltd., v Corel Corporation* [1998] 25 F Supp 2d 421 (SDNY) [hereinafter referred to as 'First hearing – *Bridgeman I*'].

[70] ibid para 6.

[71] It is noted that the requirement of a 'distinguishable variation' can be compared to the concept of 'transformative use' in the 'fair-use' doctrine of US Copyright law [Copyright Act of 1976 (USA) 17 United States Code s. 107], which is granted a high degree of weight in the 'fair-use' analysis. As noted in the case of *Campbell v Acuff-Rose,* the more transformative a new work, the less will be the significance of other factors, like commercialism, that may weigh against a finding of 'fair-use'. *Campbell, et al. v Acuff-Rose Music Inc* [1994] 510 US 569, 579. However, it is noted that the concept of 'transformative use' does not require a distinguishable variation to the underlying work but that, as noted in the *Perfect 10* case, the new work, 'adds something new with a further purpose or different character, altering the first with new expression, meaning or message'. *Perfect 10 Inc v Google Inc* [2007] 508 F3d 1146 (9th Circuit) 1155, 1164. In this sense, the standard introduced in Article 17(3)(b) is much stricter than the concept of 'transformative use' in US law.

different rare documents to discover texts that hold particular relevance to his specific purpose or interest. It also enhances the searchability of digitised versions by allowing users to browse through a wide array of databases with considerable ease. Further, considering the significance of many of these rare documents in understanding modern culture, politics and sciences, and their character as cultural heritage material, members of the public have a legitimate interest in using portions of the digitised versions of these documents for commentary, criticism, and review.

It is observed that, the existence of a related right would not preclude any person or entity from reproducing a transcribed version of the public domain content recorded upon the digitised version. Thus, Internet search engines, as well as ordinary users, would have the ability to reproduce portions of the transcribed content as snippets (in Internet searches) or as citations (for commentary, criticism and review). However, the present provision is based upon the conviction that the ability to use a portion of a digitised version carries value in terms of the greater authenticity it gives to textual content that is reproduced by it.

The creation and display of snippets of content under copyright or related rights protection has been a contentious issue within the EU.[72] Thus, it is felt that an explicit exception that permits the creation and display of snippets is necessary in relation to digitised versions.

Moreover, an exact specification of the maximum amount that could be legitimately reproduced in a snippet would provide reassurance to search engines and to users as to the extent of a digitised version that could be legitimately used by them under this exception without exposing themselves to legal sanction.

It is noted that the use of a portion that is less than 15% of the total digitised version would not cause economic prejudice to rightholders. On the contrary, it is expected that the display of snippet views by Internet search engines and online services would benefit rightholders by facilitating the discovery of digitised versions by users.

As per the decision delivered by the CJEU in the *Svensson*[73] case, the provision of a hyperlink to a copyright protected work would not constitute an infringement of copyright, if the work has been made available to the public by the rightholder without the imposition of restrictive measures as to its access. It can be surmised, that most digitised versions produced by private sector for-profit entities would be made available to the public subject to access restrictions. Thus, no exception is provided concerning the provision of hyperlinks.

(e) Creation and use of a thumbnail version of a digitised version in electronic form by an internet search engine for the purposes of indexing and facilitating

[72]For example, in its decision in the case of *Google Inc v Copiepresse SCRL, et al.*, Cour d'appel de Bruxelles, Ch 9, 5 mai 2011. the Court of Appeal of Belgium held that, Google Inc.'s online free service 'Google News' which produced snippet views of newspaper articles infringed the copyright over the articles. *See also* Phillipe Laurent, 'Copiepresse SCRL and All v Google Inc' (2011) 27 Computer Law and Security Review 542.

[73]Judgment of 13 February 2014, *Svensson*, C-466/12, EU:C:2014:76.

searchability. This exception shall not be applicable where the creation and use of the thumbnail has been carried out through the circumvention of effective technological measures that have been applied by the rightholder to prevent the creation and use of thumbnail images of the digitised version without the rightholder's authorization.

Explanation of Article 17(3)(e)

A thumbnail version is defined in Article 1(k) as a reduced-sized, lower-resolution version of a digitised version, the size of which does not exceed more than 30% of the size of the 'basic edition', and the resolution of which does not exceed 50% of the resolution of the 'basic edition'.

It is argued here that, the creation and use of thumbnail images by search engines would facilitate users in finding digitised versions online and thereby enhance public accessibility to digitised images that are made available by different websites.[74] It is noted that the improvement of the public availability and accessibility of rare documents in digital form is a key objective in the introduction of the exclusive related right. Nevertheless, especially in the context of digitised versions that record textual content, it is unlikely that a thumbnail version could constitute a substitute to the actual digitised version as the textual content displayed in a thumbnail version would be very difficult to read.

Furthermore, as Leistner observes, the use of a thumbnail image by a search engine's image search function would not conflict with the normal use and exploitation of a digitised version by the rightholder, as their normal use of a digitised version will typically not cover indexing use in a search engine.[75] Therefore, Leistner argues that an unreasonable prejudice to the legitimate interests of the rightholder cannot be established based on the use of thumbnail versions of images by a search engine.[76]

Under US law, the use of thumbnail versions of copyright protected photographs by search engines have been determined to constitute a fair-use under s. 107 of the US Copyright Act. In the determinations delivered in the cases of *Kelly v Arribasoft*[77] and *Perfect10*[78] it was held that, although the use of thumbnail images by search engines could amount to a commercial use, it would still qualify as a fair-use for the reason that the use of a thumbnail version as a pointer (i.e., a link)

---

[74]Leistner correctly points out that to give the user an idea of the image's relevance for the search, it is necessary that he is able to see the image in its entirety. It is argued here that, merely allowing search engines to present snippets of a digitised version or transcribed extracts of the public domain content recorded upon them may not be sufficient for allowing users to appreciate the relevance of an image. Matthias Leistner, 'The German Federal Supreme Court's Judgement on Google's Image Search – a Topical Example of the "Limitations" of the European Approach to Exceptions and Limitations' (2011) 42 IIC 417, 419.

[75]ibid 421.

[76]ibid.

[77]*Kelly v Arriba Soft Corporation* [2003] 336 F3d 811.

[78]*Perfect 10 Inc v Google Inc* [2007] 508 F3d 1146 (9th Circuit) 1155.

that improves access to information, amounts to a transformative use of the photograph that does not necessarily result in market substitution.[79] However, in the *Perfect 10 case* it was held that, notwithstanding the fact that the search engine's use of the thumbnail versions of the photographs constituted a commercial use (although the revenue made by the search engine from the use of thumbnails was not considered to be significant), this was outweighed by the significantly transformative nature of the use, particularly in light of its public benefit in improving access to information.

At present, EU law does not grant a statutory exemption as regards the use of thumbnail versions of images. In Germany, the creation and use of thumbnail versions of copyright protected images by search engines has been considered to amount to an infringement. Thus, in the *Vorschaubilder*[80] decision, the German Federal Supreme Court affirmed that the unauthorised use of thumbnail images by the Google search engine did in fact infringe copyright over the original images. However, in this case, the Supreme Court argued that Google's infringing use was justified as the copyright holder's act in uploading the images onto the Internet without taking any steps to block the image search function constituted an implied consent for the use of thumbnail versions of those images by Google. Thus, it is necessary to introduce an explicit exception in favour of the use of thumbnail images of digitised versions by search engines. However, this exception would not apply if the creation and use of the thumbnail image has been carried out through the circumvention of technological measures.

(f) Use of a thumbnail version by a lawful user, for the purpose of criticism, commentary or review, or in connection with the reporting of news or current events, to the extent required for that purpose.

Explanation of Article 17(3)(f)

From the reasons given in Articles 17(4)(c) and (d) above, the use of thumbnail versions is permitted for the purposes specified by the provision. It is reiterated that the use of a thumbnail version for the above purposes would not prejudice the ability of the rightholder to commercially exploit the digitised version.

(g) Use of a lawfully acquired digitised version or a copy thereof by a lawful user for the purpose of caricature, parody, or pastiche in a way that displays a distinguishable alteration with respect to the underlying digitised version.

Explanation of Article 17(3)(g)

As noted in Article 17(3)(d) members of the public have a legitimate interest in using the digitised versions of rare documents in cultural and social discourse. Caricature,

[79] In the *Perfect10* case, it was argued that the thumbnail images created by Google Inc. could serve as substitutes in the market for reduced-size versions of Perfect 10's photographs. However, the Court of Appeal rejected this argument because there was no evidence that Google's thumbnail images were in fact being used as a substitute for the reduced-size versions. ibid 11.

[80] BGH, 29.04.2010 – I ZR 69/08, GRUR 2010, 628 – *Vorschaubilder*.

parody and pastiche constitute particularly powerful and creative tools of such discourse.

This provision is based on, Article 5(3)(k) of the InfoSoc Directive, and the decision delivered by the CJEU in the *Deckmyn*[81] decision. The InfoSoc Directive does not provide any definition of the terms caricature, parody and pastiche. In the *Deckmyn* case, the CJEU held that, 'parody' is an autonomous concept of EU law and that, as the InfoSoc Directive does not provide any definition of the concept of parody, the meaning and scope of that term must be determined by considering its usual meaning in everyday language, while also considering the context in which it occurs and the purposes of the rules of which it is part.[82] Thus, the CJEU determined that the essential characteristics of parody are, first, to evoke an existing work while being noticeably different from it, and, secondly, to constitute an expression of humour or mockery.[83] However, the CJEU dispensed with the requirement that the parody should display an original character of its own.[84] It is argued here that this principle should be applied in defining the terms of caricature and pastiche as well. Thus, the requirement for a 'noticeable difference' established in the Deckmyn decision has been incorporated into the present provision through the term 'distinguishable alteration'.

(4) The exceptions and limitations provided for in paragraphs 1–4 shall only be applied in certain special cases which do not conflict with the normal exploitation of the digitised version and do not unreasonably prejudice the legitimate interests of the rightholder.

Explanation of Article 17(4)

The exceptions and limitations provided under Article 14 have been formulated keeping in mind the need to balance the interests of producers and users of digitised versions. It authorises uses that have been highlighted as being of particular importance in maintaining a robust social and cultural discourse,[85] but are nevertheless unlikely to cause substantial prejudice to the economic interests of the rightholder.

Article 17(4) is a verbatim reproduction of Article 5(5) of the InfoSoc Directive. It makes the exercise of exceptions and limitations to the related right subject to the three-step test initially introduced under Article 9bis of the Berne Convention. Thus, any incompatibility of an exercise of an exception or limitation with the criteria of the three-step test would render an ordinarily 'lawful use' of a digitised version unlawful.[86]

[81]Judgment of 3 September 2014, *Deckmyn*, C-201/13, EU:C:2014:2132.

[82]ibid para 19.

[83]ibid para 20.

[84]ibid para 21.

[85]*See* Chap. 5, Sect. 5.4.

[86]Synodinou (n 12) 840.

It is proposed that the application of the three-step test provided under Article 17 (4) should be carried out under the guidelines set out in the Declaration on a balanced interpretation of the three-step test in copyright law.[87] Thus, exceptions and limitations should not be interpreted narrowly and should always be interpreted in accordance with the objective and purpose for which they have been introduced,[88] namely to preserve an adequate balance between the interest of the rightholder in obtaining a reasonable return on his investment and the user's interest in using and re-using the digitised versions.

Article 18: User's right to benefit from exceptions and limitations

(1) Exceptions and limitations provided for in Article 17 cannot be overridden by contractual provisions. Any contractual provision contrary to an exception or limitation provided under Article 17 shall be null and void *ab initio*.
(2) Exceptions and limitations provided for in Article 17 cannot be overridden by the use of technological measures.
(3) Any lawful user of a digitised version shall have a positive and enforceable right to benefit from the exceptions and limitations provided under Article 17 as regards a digitised version or copy thereof that he is legally entitled to use.

Explanation of Article 18

As noted in Chap. 6, Sect. 6.1, one of the main challenges faced by copyright law at present is to prevent rightholders from overriding legally established exceptions and limitations to copyright using contractual provisions and technological measures.

In the preceding chapters, it was also concluded that Article 6(4) of the InfoSoc Directive that seeks to circumscribe the ability of rightholders to use technological measures to override exceptions and limitations is not adequate, as it contains numerous loopholes that could be used by rightholders to bypass its application.[89] Furthermore, Article 6(4) only prevents the overriding of exceptions and limitation through the application of technological measures, and does not address the use of contractual provisions in denying users the ability to benefit from exceptions and limitations to copyright. In providing access to digital informational goods, rightholders are increasingly relying on standard-form contracts that enhance the strength and scope of their exclusive rights beyond legally established limits. Thus, it is essential to introduce legal provisions that prevent rightholders of digitised versions from overriding the exceptions and limitations granted under Article 17 using contractual provisions and technological measures. Accordingly, subsections (1) and (2) of Article 18 impose a blanket restriction on the use of contractual

[87]Christophe Geiger, Jonathan Griffiths and Reto M Hilty, 'Declaration on a Balanced Interpretation of the "Three-Step Test" in Copyright Law' [2008] 39 IIC 707.

[88]ibid 711.

[89]*See* discussion in Chap. 5, Sect. 5.4.6 and Chap. 6, Sect. 6.1 above.

provisions or technological measures for overriding exceptions and limitations granted under Article 17.

It is noted that, Article 8 paragraph 2 of the Computer Programmes Directive[90] prevents contractual provisions from being used to override certain exceptions and limitations provided under that Directive by stating that any contractual provision contrary to those exceptions and limitations shall be null and void. Similarly, Article 15 of the Database Directive[91] contains a provision that deems any contractual provision that is contrary to the exceptions and limitations established by that Directive to be null and void. It is also interesting that Article 3(2) of the EU Commission proposal for a Directive on Copyright in the Digital Single Market prevents certain exceptions and limitations from being overridden by contract by stipulating that any such contractual provision shall be unenforceable. In subsection (1) we use the formulation employed by the Computer Programmes and Database Directives with the addition of the term *'ab intio'*. The addition of the term *'ab intio'* is intended to highlight that a contractual provision that overrides an exception or limitation provided under Article 17 is presumed to have never existed in the eyes of the law as opposed to merely being unenforceable.

Subsection (3) attempts to re-conceptualise limitations and exceptions as positive user rights by providing lawful users with an enforceable right to benefit from the exceptions and limitations provided under Article 17. It is argued that, at present, exceptions and limitations to copyright are formulated as a privilege[92] granted to the user, as opposed to being a legal right that could be enforced by the user against a rightholder or any third party, in a court of law.[93] Thus, a user may invoke an exception or limitation to a rightholder's exclusive right to defend his use of a protected work. However, the existing legal framework does not provide a user with the ability to go before court to invoke his entitlement to benefit from an exception or

---

[90] Directive 2009/24/EC of The European Parliament and of the Council of 23 April 2009 on the legal protection of computer programmes [2009] OJ L 111/16 (Computer Programmes Directive).

[91] Directive 96/9/EC of the European Parliament and of the Council of the European Union of 11 March 1996 on the legal protection of databases [1996] OJ L 77/20 (Database Directive).

[92] In the Hohfeldian scheme of jural relations, a privilege, is defined as the correlative of a no-right i.e., if A has a privilege to make a specific use of a digitised version, then the rightholder or any other person will not have a right to prevent A from engaging in that specific use. A right is defined as a correlative of duty i.e., if A has a right to make a specific use of a digitised version, then the rightholder or any other person will have a duty to not to interfere with that right. Wesley Newcomb Hohfeld, 'Some Fundamental Legal Conceptions as Applied in Judicial Reasoning' (1913) 23 The Yale Law Journal 16, 28–33. *See also* Arthur Corbin, 'Jural Relations and Their Classification' (1921) Yale Law School Faculty Scholarship Series: Paper 2873 <http://digitalcommons.law.yale.edu/cgi/viewcontent.cgi?article=3877&context=fss_papers> accessed 31 January 2019.

[93] Although Synodinou (n 12) 822–23, appears to interpret Article 9 of the Database Directive and Article 5 of the Computer Programmes Directive as granting 'rights' to lawful users in respect of certain specified exceptions and limitations established by those Directives, it is noted that these Directives do not frame the entitlement provided to a lawful user to benefit from the specified exceptions and limitations as a 'positive right'. Furthermore, the enforceability of these provisions by a user against any person who impedes such benefit is unclear.

limitation, when his ability to benefit from that exception or limitation is being impeded by the rightholder or any other person. Article 18 attempts to remedy this situation by granting a lawful user of a digitised version a positive and enforceable right to benefit from the exceptions and limitations provided under Article 17. Thus, when a lawful user is prevented from benefitting from any exception or limitation to the related right, he would be able to go before court and ask for a legal remedy.

Article 19: User's right to purchase basic edition

(1) The rightholder shall have an obligation to offer a basic edition of the digitised version in electronic form for sale to the public within a period of 14 days from the date of registration under Article 6. The distribution or making available of the basic edition in electronic form so that it could be accessed by members of the public shall be deemed to fulfil this requirement.
(2) Where a rightholder fails to fulfil the obligation under subsection (1) above, any user who wishes to access the basic edition shall have the right to lodge a formal complaint with the Central European Database.
(3) The Central European Database shall forthwith communicate the complaint to the rightholder in accordance with the contact information provided under Article 6(1)(e) above and request the rightholder to offer a basic edition of the digitised version for sale to the complainant.
(4) If the rightholder fails to comply with the request made by the Central European Database under subsection (3) above, within a period of 21 days, the Central European Database shall provide to the complainant a copy of the basic edition that has been deposited in its database in exchange for the payment of a sum determined by the Central European Database as being reasonable and which does not exceed the maximum sale price specified under Article 6(5)(g). The proceeds from the sale shall be retained by the Central European Database.
(5) The copy of the basic edition that is sold to the complainant in accordance with subsection (4) above shall be used subject to the provisions set out in Articles 11 to 18 and Article 20.

Explanation of Article 19

Article 19 has been introduced with the objective of preventing rightholders of digitised versions from denying users access to the basic edition that is subject to the maximum sale price, and seeking to maximise their profits by compelling users to purchase higher-resolution versions or value-added editions that are exempted from the maximum sale price.

Article 20: Obligations of lawful users

(1) A lawful user of a digitised version shall not perform acts that conflict with the normal exploitation of the digitised version or unreasonably prejudice the legitimate interests of the rightholder.
(2) A lawful user of a digitised version may not cause prejudice to the legitimate interests of a rightholder in respect of any subject-matter incorporated in or combined or associated with a digitised version.

(3) A lawful user who reproduces a digitised version either in whole or in part shall, whenever it is reasonably possible, indicate the name or designation of the rightholder as provided under Article 6(5)(e) in a manner that can be easily discerned by a user.
(4) Failure to fulfil any of the obligations set out in subsections (1)–(3) shall preclude any person from benefitting from the legal rights and privileges that accrue to a lawful user under Article 17 and 18.

Explanation of Article 20
Article 20 is inspired by Article 8 of the Database Directive. The objective of Article 20 is to impose a general obligation on users to engage in the access, use, and re-use of a digitised version under the provisions of the three-step test, even where legitimacy of the access, use, and re-use does not arise from an exception or limitation specified under Article 17. Subsection (2) also requires a lawful user to respect the rights of persons other than the holder of the related right granted under the Regulation, who may have rights over subject-matter that is incorporated or associated with the digitised version. For example, this would include persons who hold a copyright over the software that is used in a value-added-feature (such as the zoom-function) that is incorporated in a digitised version.

Subsection (3) has been introduced with the objective of facilitating members of the public to correctly identify the source of a digitised version when it is reproduced by a user. Unless a change of ownership in the title has taken place, the legal or natural person who is indicated as the rightholder under Article 6(5)(e) would usually be the owner of the underlying rare document. Thus, requiring lawful users who reproduce the digitised version or any portion thereof to acknowledge the rightholder, whenever doing so is reasonably possible, would serve to enhance the identifiability of the source of the underlying rare documents. This would in turn assist members of the public in identifying and locating the underlying rare documents and also facilitate memory institutions to maintain their relevance[94] and visibility as repositories of rare documents.

9.4 Administrative Guidelines

The introduction of uniform administrative guidelines that assist in harmonising practices and procedures currently followed by public and semi-public sector memory institutions in the digitisation of their collections of rare documents could be useful in achieving a balance between user and producer interests in the production, distribution and use of digitised versions.

[94] *See* discussion in Chap. 4, Sect. 4.4.3 on the importance of maintaining the relevance of memory institutions.

Administrative guidelines should be adopted by the governments of EU Member States and implemented through administrative circulars or through national legislation.

The following provides a brief outline of two aspects in relation to which the harmonisation of administrative practices could be useful. It further proposes certain specific rules that could be adopted in relation to these diverse aspects.

9.4.1 Tender Procedure

Most public and semi-public sector memory institutions are already bound by rules governing the tender procedures that need to be followed in granting a contracts to third parties for the digitisation of rare documents held by them.

For example, the Licensed Internet Associates (LIA)[95] programme of The National Archives of the UK (TNA-UK) follows a tender procedure that is controlled by an IFTS[96] accredited information fair trade scheme. The tender procedure is built around an evaluation matrix within which points are given for differently weighted criteria. The bidder who obtains the highest amount of points wins the contract for digitisation.[97]

It is proposed that a framework of rules and guidelines that aims to harmonise institutional procedures in relation to digitisation should place particular emphasis on the following aspects.

(1) Sophistication and reliability of the technology (hardware and software) that is used in the digitisation process.
(2) Skill and expertise of the staff who will be carrying out the digitisation, and the technical standards according to which the production, distribution, and preservation of digitised versions will be carried out.
(3) Estimated costs of digitisation, and distribution of digitised versions, (with cost efficiency to be given particular emphasis).
(4) Estimated timeframe within which the digitised versions will be made available to the public.

---

[95] *See* Chap. 3, Sect. 3.1, Example 3 for an overview of the LIA programme.

[96] Refers to the 'Information Fair Trader Scheme' (IFTS) that set and assessed standards for public sector bodies. Since 2017, the IFTS has been superseded by statutory arrangements put in place by the Re-use of Public Sector Information Regulations n°1415 of 2015 (UK PSI Regulations). For more information see The National Archives, 'Closure of the Information Fair Trader Scheme announced' <http://www.nationalarchives.gov.uk/about/news/closure-of-the-information-fair-trader-scheme-announced/> accessed 31 January 2019.

[97] This is based on a description of the tender procedure employed by the LIA programme provided by an Official of The National Archives, UK during an interview held with the author on 3 April, 2013. Participation in the interview was on grounds of anonymity (interview transcript in possession of author).

(5) Distribution channels through which the digitised versions will be made available and their capacity to make the digitised versions easily and widely accessible to the public.
(6) The terms and conditions of access that are to be adopted by the potential producer or distributor of digitised versions (i.e., the bidder).

9.4.2 Guidelines for Standardisation and Interoperability

In declaring the technological standards that must be fulfilled by the basic editions of digitised versions under Article 8, it is proposed that the Central European Database is *inter alia* guided by the objective of ensuring that digitised versions of rare documents comply with general technical standards that allow them to be widely accessible, portable and durable.[98]

It is further proposed that memory institutions within the EU should be encouraged to follow common technical standards in relation to the production, dissemination and preservation of digitised versions of rare documents in their collections. For instance, compliance with such common technical standards could form a component of the inquiry into 'technical standards' in evaluating potential bidders within the tender process described in above.

It is noted that, several such common technical standards have been formulated and proposed by various organisations who are working in the field of digitisation in Europe. Notable examples include the Minerva network[99] and the SUCCEED (Support Action Center of Competence in Digitisation) project.[100] Technical standards for interoperability refer to the use of common tools, formats and procedures that enable the achievement of uniformity and harmony in relation to the access, use, re-use and preservation of digitised versions. It is observed that the achievement of such uniformity and harmony could enhance user experience, facilitate the dissemination and exchange of digitised versions between different electronic devices and also ensure the preservation of digitised versions. The improvement effected to the way in which digitised versions could be accessed, used, and preserved through the adoption of common technical standards would assist in optimising the social value that could be gleaned by making rare documents available to the public in digital form.

---

[98]MINERVA, 'MINERVA EC – Technical Guidelines' <http://www.minervaeurope.org/technicalguidelines.htm> accessed 31 January 2019.

[99]Kate Fernie, Giuliana De Francesco and David Dawson, 'MINERVA Technical Guidelines for Digital Content Creation Programmemes: Version 2.0' (2008) <http://www.minervaeurope.org/publications/MINERVA%20TG%202.0.pdf> accessed 31 January 2019.

[100]For more information on proposals made for the adoption of common technical standards within the framework of the SUCCEED project *see* Sylvia Garcia, 'Succeed Interoperability Workshop Report' <https://www.digitisation.eu/succeed-interoperabily-workshop-report/> accessed 31 January 2019.

9.5 Implications for Users

It is argued here that, under the proposed regulatory framework, a member of the public who wishes to access a digitised version will be left at least as well-off as under a legal framework that prevents claims of exclusive rights from being made over digitised versions of rare documents.[101] Firstly, the incentive provided to private sector for-profit entities to invest in the digitisation process is expected to result in a quantitative increase in the number of rare documents that are available to members of the public in digital form. An increase in private sector for-profit investment would also serve to accelerate the pace of the digitisation of rare document collections within the EU, thereby making the digital surrogates of rare documents available to the public at an earlier time.[102] Secondly, the introduction of the proposed regulatory framework could only increase the utility of the user, as the existence of a digitised version of a rare document (notwithstanding the restrictions placed upon its access and use during the term of protection) provides the user with an extra option as to how the public domain content recorded upon that rare document can be accessed. It does not decrease the utility of the user because the option of accessing public domain content by consulting the rare document in its original analogue form is not interfered with in any way.

Users of rare documents can be categorised into two groups. The first group is composed of 'average-users' who are defined for the purpose of this discussion as users who reside in the city where the memory institution that holds the rare document is located. For example, regarding the *Codex Arundel* currently held by the British Library in London, a user who resides in London would be an 'average-user'. In accessing the rare document in its original analogue form, an 'average-user' would typically incur the cost of travelling to the memory institution where the rare document is located using ordinary means of transportation (usually public transport) and the fees or taxes that are charged by the memory institution (if applicable) for accessing the rare document. The second group is composed of 'non-average users' who are users who reside outside the city where the memory institution is located. For example, a user residing in India who wishes to access the *Codex Arundel* held by the British Library would be a 'non-average' user of that document. The costs incurred by a 'non-average' user in travelling to the memory institution would be typically higher than the costs incurred by an 'average-user'.

We assume that the expected value of accessing the public domain content by consulting the rare document in its original analogue form and by consulting the rare

[101] For brevity and simplicity, we consider only the perspective of access and not of use.

[102] For example, if X is a rare document that is kept in the dark archives of a memory institution, it is possible to assume that under a digitisation model that relies on public and not-for-profit sources of funding, a digitised version of X would be produced and distributed to the public at some point in the future. However, it is argued that the increase in private sector (for-profit) investment in the digitisation process under the proposed regulatory framework would result in a digitised version of X being produced and distributed to the public at an earlier time than could be achieved with public and other not-for-profit sources of funding.

document in digital form would be the same to an 'average-user', as well as a 'non-average' user.[103]

Thus, in this situation we assume that the following will happen:

(a) If the cost of accessing the rare document in digital form is *lower* than the transaction cost of accessing the rare document in its original analogue form, then the user will access the digitised version.
(b) If the cost of accessing the rare document in digital form is *equal* to the transaction cost of accessing the rare document in its original analogue form, then the user will be indifferent between accessing the original analogue document and the digitised version.
(c) If the cost of accessing the rare document in digital form is *higher* than the transaction cost of accessing the rare document in its original analogue form, then the user will access the original analogue document.

It is argued here that, especially in view of the price-regulation mechanism that applies to the basic-edition of a digitised version under the proposed model, the costs of accessing the basic-edition in digital form (especially for a 'non-average user') would be significantly lower than of accessing the rare document in its original analogue form. Thus, under the proposed regulatory framework a 'non-average user' would be left better-off, as he would be able to access the rare document in digital form at much lower costs.

For an 'average-user', if the cost of accessing the digitised version is higher than the costs of accessing the rare document in its original analogue form, he would still be left at least as well-off, as he would be able to travel to the memory institution and access the document in analogue form. Meanwhile, if the costs of accessing the digitised version are equal to the costs of accessing the analogue document, the 'average-user' would be left better-off as he would now have an extra-option as to the means in which the rare document could be accessed by him. Similarly, if the cost of accessing the digitised version is lower than the costs of accessing the analogue document, he would be left better-off.

Furthermore, once the period of protection expires (i.e., in the post-protection period following the expiration of the 7-year period of protection) both categories of users would be able to access the digitised version, through the Central European Database free-of-charge as public domain content.

We proceed to consider several hypothetical situations that could arise under the proposed regime to illustrate the above argument.

Hypothetical

Rutania is an EU Member State, located in Central Europe. The National Library of *Rutania* (NLR) is situated in its capital *Kaz*. The NLR has legal possession of

[103]This is despite the fact that the expected value of accessing the public domain content recorded upon the rare document in its original analogue form and in digital form can vary according to the subjective preferences of the user, as well as the purpose of the intended use. However, it is not possible to capture these preferences within the basic economic argument presented here.

Manuscript X. Manuscript X is an illuminated manuscript that records a ballad which recounts a battle that took place between the two main ethnic groups of *Rutania*; the majority *Majorcs* and the minority *Minorcs*, in the year 1150 A.D. The ballad glorifies the role of the *Majorcs* in the battle and highlights their racial superiority over the *Minorcs* in a manner that could be considered as hurtful to the sentiments of the *Minorcs* in the modern day. It also contains certain remarks that could be interpreted as being derogatory of the *Minorcs*. However, there is no obvious racist import and it is accepted that Manuscript X is an important source of *Rutanian* history. There is only one copy of this manuscript in existence. It is kept in a secure storage space located underneath the NLR building.

The NLR allows access to the original manuscript within the library premises in *Kaz* upon request. Access is granted free of charge. However, access, use, and re-use are subject to the following restrictions. The NLR justifies its ability to impose these conditions based upon its ownership rights over the tangible property of the manuscript.

(1) Access is granted only to persons authorised by the NLR and is subject to the establishment of a justifiable reason for accessing the manuscript.
(2) Re-use of the document and the content recorded upon it is allowed under the terms laid down by the PSI Directive.[104]
(3) Where a reproduction of the document is requested, the NLR requires the payment of a fee that is equal to the cost of reproducing the requested copy.

The NLR has also digitised Manuscript X under a partnership agreement with the private sector company *Trinillion*. The digitised version of Manuscript X is available for public access and use on the NLR website. The NLR claims exclusive rights over the digitised version for a period of 7 years during which time it *inter alia* requires the user to pay for access and reproduction of the digitised image. A payment of 10 EUR is charged for accessing the digitised version, and a further 10 EUR to download a low-resolution copy of Manuscript X.

Higher-resolution copies of the digitised version of Manuscript X can be obtained from the NLR upon request. The request can be made online. The copy will be supplied subject to a license. The terms of the license are to be negotiated between the user and the NLR.

User A

User A is a professor of ethnology at the University of Kaz. He wishes to access Manuscript X for writing a scholarly article that is to be published in an academic journal. He further wishes to reproduce an image of Manuscript X in his article. He has a choice between accessing the digitised version of Manuscript X or the original. He prefers to access the original document as he feels that it would be better to study the document first hand. In any case, the NLR is situated not too far away from the University. He first makes a written request to the NLR seeking access to Manuscript

[104](n 31).

X and a high-resolution reproduction of Manuscript X in paper form which will in turn be reproduced in his scholarly article.

Within 10 days he is granted permission. Transportation to the NLR costs him 5 EUR and the paper copy of the high definition reproduction he requested costs him another 12 EUR.

Thus, *User A* is left as well-off under the proposed regime.

User B

User B is a poet who lives in *Kaz*. His work is usually considered controversial because of its provocative nature. He posts his work on his personal blog that is made available to the public and which itself has been the subject of controversy in recent times because of the provocative content that has been posted on it.

Having seen a reproduction of Manuscript X in the academic article written by *User A*, he gets the idea of creating a satirical version of the ballad that would highlight the racial tensions between the *Majorcs* and the *Minorcs* in modern day *Rutania*. His object is to demonstrate that the tension between the two ethnic groups is at as high a point as during the battle in 1150 A.D., and that the attitude of the *Majorcs* towards their fellow *Minorcs* has not undergone substantial change, although it is expressed differently within the modern socio-political context. The intention of *User B* is to make people aware of the futility of racial prejudice and bigotry.

User B makes a written request to the NLR to provide him with a high-quality reproduction of Manuscript X which could be digitally altered to create the satirical work.

The NLR refuses to provide him with the requested reproduction as the proposed derivative work could hurt minority sentiments and be prejudicial to national security. The NLR also fears that providing *User B* with a reproduction of Manuscript X could make it the subject of controversy and possibly give rise to a backlash from members of the *Minorc* community.

User B then decides to access Manuscript X in digital form for 10 EUR and purchases a low-resolution reproduction for another 10 EUR online. He creates his derivative work. He proceeds to display it on his blog. Although the NLR does not approve of its display to the public, it cannot take any measures to prevent such use because it does not have an exclusive right over the creation of derivative works of the digital image nor the ability to determine the purpose for which the digital image can be used.

User B is strictly better off.

User C

User C is a student of medieval art who lives in New Delhi, India. He is completing his postgraduate research at a University in New Delhi. His research focuses upon a comparative study of medieval Indian and European manuscripts. He wishes to consult Manuscript X to study the illuminations contained therein. The cost of a return air ticket from *New Delhi* to *Kaz* is 550 EUR. Therefore, he decides to access the manuscript for 10 EUR in digitised format, and furthermore downloads a low-resolution version of the digital image for another 10 EUR, which he proceeds to use in a presentation of his work at an academic conference in India.

User C is strictly better off.

User D

User D is a Tourism Agency in Japan that organises tours to *Rutania*. It is searching for an image that would evoke the historical and cultural grandeur of *Rutania* which could be posted on its website for advertising purposes. The agency accesses the website of the NLR and browses through the thumbnail images of the illuminated manuscripts available in digital form. It is impressed by a particular portion of the illumination on Manuscript X. The agency directly communicates its interest in the re-use of that portion of the illumination to the NLR through the online form available for that purpose. The NLR agrees to provide a high resolution version of that portion of the image that is suitable for display on a website for a license fee of 200 EUR. The agency agrees and the license is concluded.

User D is strictly better off.

9.6 Summary and Conclusions

This chapter presents a legislative framework for the introduction of a related right over digitised versions of rare documents within the EU. The proposed framework is founded upon the reasoning that the introduction of a related right would leave users of rare documents at least as well-off, by providing them with an extra option as to the way in which the public domain content recorded upon a digitised version could be accessed. It is emphasised that their ability to consult the rare document in its original analogue form would be left undisturbed under the proposed regulatory framework.

The proposed framework presents a basic outline of the key concepts and features that could be introduced for the regulation of digitised versions of rare documents that record public domain content in textual form.

It is noted that, the formulation and implementation of an efficient regulatory framework for digitised versions requires the participation of and collaboration among a variety of key stakeholders (i.e., memory institutions, Central European Database, private-sector entities), and that by harnessing the different strengths and resources of these stakeholders into the regulatory framework, the social value that could be gleaned by the digitisation process could be optimised.

Chapter 10
Conclusion

As stated in Chap. 2, the goal of this study was to find means of achieving an adequate balance between the conflicting interests of producers and users of digitised versions of rare documents within the EU. In accordance with this goal, the study formulated a series of research questions. The answers provided to these questions through the research study are summarised below.

10.1 Question 1: *'Is There a Need to Preserve Exclusivity Over Digitised Versions of Rare Documents?'*

The study concludes that there is a need to preserve exclusivity over digitised versions of rare documents that record public domain content in textual form.

Data collected from memory institutions from five EU Member States during the empirical survey indicate the existence of an underproduction problem as regards digitised versions of rare documents within the EU. Thus, it is argued that there is a need to achieve a quantitative increase of documents that are available to the public in digital form.

The main cause of underproduction is the inadequacy of the funding (especially the financial investment) that is currently available for digitisation. It is noted that the best means of enhancing the funding available for digitisation is by providing stronger incentives for private sector for-profit entities to invest in the digitisation process.

Digitised versions are informational goods that hold public good characteristics and are particularly susceptible to piracy and free-riding. Thus, in order to obtain a reasonable return on the investment that has been made in their production, it is necessary that the producer is able to restrict and limit the ways in which the digitised versions are used and accessed by members of the public. It is argued that such

S. Mendis, *A Copyright Gambit*, Munich Studies on Innovation and Competition 11,
https://doi.org/10.1007/978-3-662-59454-4_10

maintenance of control essentially translates into an exercise of exclusivity over the digitised versions.[1]

To strengthen the incentives of private sector for-profit entities to invest in the digitisation process, it is necessary to afford them the ability of obtaining a reasonable return on their investment through the commercial exploitation of the resulting digitised versions. Thus, it is concluded that the preservation of exclusivity over digitised versions is necessary to sustain and strengthen the incentives of private sector for-profit entities to invest in the digitisation process.

Additionally, the ability to exercise exclusivity over digitised versions would also serve the long-term sustainability of the digitisation process, as the revenue generated from the successful commercial exploitation of digitised versions could be re-invested in the creation of further digitised versions, thereby strengthening the economic viability of the digitisation process.

It is noted that, the incentive theory of copyright law provides an economic justification for the preservation of exclusivity over digitised versions of rare documents, while the social planning theory of copyright law provides a normative framework that can be applied in determining the strength and scope of the exclusivity that is required for achieving an adequate balance between the competing interests of users and producers.

10.2 Question 2: *'Are Current Legal and Non-legal Mechanisms Sufficient Either Alone or in Combination (with or Without Modification) to Preserve an Adequate Balance Between the Interests of Users and Producers of Digitised Versions?'*

The study concludes that, legal and non-legal mechanisms that are currently used for the maintenance of exclusivity over digitised versions of rare documents are not able to preserve an adequate balance between the interests of users and producers of digitised versions.

An analysis of mechanisms that are commonly used to maintain exclusivity over digitised versions and of mechanisms that have the potential to be used for that purpose demonstrates that none of these have the capacity to balance the competing interests of users and producers by providing sufficient incentives for investment in the digitisation process, while at the same time, providing sufficient protection for user interests.

It is observed that, of the available mechanisms, copyright law holds the most potential for effecting an adequate equilibrium between user and producer interests, but that its capacity to achieve an adequate equilibrium is marred by the existing EU

[1] *See* Chap. 4, Sect. 4.5.

law framework's inability to prevent contractual provisions and technological measures from being used to extend the strength and scope of copyright protection beyond legally sanctioned limits.

Nonetheless, it is concluded that a digitised version of a rare document would not qualify for copyright protection within the EU law framework, as the functional requirement of creating an exact and faithful digital photographic reproduction of an existing document prevents it from fulfilling the requisite standard of originality needed to obtain copyright protection within the EU.

10.3 Question 3: *'What Legal/Non-legal Mechanisms Could Be Introduced Within the EU, in Order to Ensure the Preservation of an Adequate Balance Between the Interests of Users and Producers? How Should They Be Formulated?'*

It is argued that related rights protection offers a suitable alternative regime to achieve an optimal balance between producer and user interests regarding the access, use, and re-use of digitised versions. In fact, the related rights framework is even better suited for the regulation of digitised versions than copyright law because it is a legal regime that has been specifically formulated for the protection of achievements that reflect an economic, organisational, or technical investment as opposed to a creative or intellectual investment. Thus, the conceptual basis of the related rights regime accords with the investment protection objective that motivates the introduction of an exclusive right over digitised versions.

At present, related rights is an entrenched legal doctrine within the EU law framework and is recognised by both common law and civil law copyright systems. It allows for the regulation of digitised versions to be brought within a legislative framework and, in addition, has an inbuilt system of limitations and exceptions that is invaluable in effecting a balance between the interests of producers and users.

Following the identification of related rights as the preferred mechanism for the protection of digitised versions, the study presents a proposal for a legal framework that could be introduced within the EU for the regulation of digitised versions.

The proposed regulatory framework is based on the economic reasoning that the introduction of a related right over digitised versions would leave users of rare documents at least as well-off by providing them with an extra option as to how the public domain content recorded upon a digitised version could be accessed. Key features of the proposed framework include a unitary right that shall have equal effect throughout the EU (under Article 118 of the TFEU) granted by means of an EU Regulation, a registration requirement for claiming related rights protection over a digitised version, the establishment of a Central European Database that would be responsible for making the digitised versions available to the public as public domain content once the duration of protection has expired, a list of exceptions and limitations to the exclusive right that are aimed at facilitating the use of digitised versions in socially valuable ways, and a protection period that lasts for seven years.

The ultimate objective of the proposed framework is to create and sustain better incentives for private sector for-profit investment which is expected to lead to a quantitative increase in the number of rare documents that are available to the public in digital form. It is envisioned that the short-term social costs that arise through the exercise of exclusive rights by producers and distributors of digitised versions would be off-set by the enhanced availability of rare documents that record public domain content and the social benefits that would accrue in the long-term from the use, re-use, and commercial exploitation of this content.

The EU, as the repository of a substantial amount of invaluable rare documents that record public domain content, has a responsibility, not only towards its citizens but to humanity at large, to make the cultural and historical heritage preserved in its memory institutions widely accessible and available. The technology required to achieve this purpose already exists. What is needed now is the political will and legislative resolve to put into place mechanisms that could facilitate the achievement of this goal. The European renaissance of the fourteenth and fifteenth centuries opened a new chapter in the saga of human civilisation. Our generation has been bestowed with the tools to initiate a new digital renaissance. It is our responsibility to use these tools efficiently and creatively in order to optimise the social value that could be gleaned from them.

The creation of a robust digitisation strategy within the EU, which does not require the maintenance of exclusivity over digitised versions of rare documents that record public domain content, is an ideal that we must all strive towards. However, until we succeed in obtaining the resources and infrastructure necessary to support such a digitisation initiative, it is imperative to make intelligent and strategic use of the resources and institutional capabilities available to us in fostering a new European digital renaissance.

Annex

Empirical Survey: Objectives, Design and Methodology

I. Objectives

The survey was carried out with the objective of eliciting quantitative and qualitative information on the following aspects of the digitisation of rare public domain textual materials in Europe.

- The reasons for digitisation from the perspective of the memory institution (i.e., their interests and priorities).
- The challenges faced by the memory institution in the digitisation of their collections of rare public domain textual material.
- The way in which memory institutions view the final digitised product (e.g., as a commercially exploitable resource or as the common heritage of humankind) and particularly, their views regarding the ownership of the digitised product.

II. Design

In accordance with the above objectives, the following survey design was adopted.

a. Main Sample: Memory Institutions

A sample of 14 memory institutions was drawn from the following EU Member States.

S. Mendis, *A Copyright Gambit*, Munich Studies on Innovation and Competition 11,
https://doi.org/10.1007/978-3-662-59454-4

- The United Kingdom
- France
- Germany
- Spain
- Italy

These Member States were selected based on the high quantum and qualitative richness of rare public domain textual materials held by them, and the diverse copyright law traditions represented by them (i.e., the British common law tradition and the monistic and dualistic models of the Continental civil law tradition).

A stratified purposeful sample of memory institutions was formulated, primarily based on information that was gathered on the digitisation initiatives of different memory institutions through an Internet search.

The following factors were given especial consideration in the construction of the sample.

- Sample should be representative of memory institutions that operate under different ownership models (i.e., institutions belonging to the public, semi-public and private sectors).
- Sample should represent different-sized collections of rare public domain textual materials (i.e., small, medium and large).
- Sample should represent memory institutions that pursue different objectives and reflect a diversity of mission statements (e.g., libraries, archives and museums; institutions that function for public benefit; institutions that exist for the primary benefit of a closed group of persons but may be accessible to the public for limited purposes).
- Sample should represent the variety of business models that are currently employed in the digitisation of rare public domain textual material (e.g., self-funded, funded by a private sector non-profit entity, funded by a private sector for-profit entity etc.)

The response from memory institutions to the invitation to participate in the survey was very encouraging. The final sample was composed of the following memory institutions.

	Memory institution	Country	Date completed	Resource person/s
1.	*Bayerische Staatsbibliothek*	Munich, Germany	November 15, 2012	Confidential
2.	*Biblioteca Nacional de España*	Madrid, Spain	April 04, 2013	Confidential
3.	*Bibliothèque Sainte-Geneviève*	Paris, France	February 04, 2014	Confidential
4.	*Biblioteca nazionale centrale di Roma*	Rome, Italy	May 28, 2014	Confidential
5.	Bodleian Libraries	Oxford, UK	September 02, 2013	Mr. Michael Popham—Head of Digital Initiatives, *and* Dr. Christine Madsen—Manager, Infrastructure and Innovation

(continued)

	Memory institution	Country	Date completed	Resource person/s
6.	British Library	London, UK	February 14, 2014	Confidential
7.	Deutsches Literaturarchiv	Marbach, Germany	April 09, 2013	Confidential
8.	Middle Temple Library	London, UK	April 02, 2013	Ms. Renae Satterley—Senior Librarian
9.	*Musée des Lettres et Manuscrits*	Paris, France	April 02, 2014	Mr. Jean-Pierre Guéno—Director of Culture
10.	Museo Galileo	Florence, Italy	February 01, 2014	Mr. Stefano Casati—Digital Library
11.	The National Archives (UK)	Richmond, UK	April 03, 2013	Confidential
12.	*Universitäts- und Stadtbibliothek Köln.*	Cologne, Germany	January 28, 2014	Mr. André Welters—Member
13.	University of Salamanca Library	Salamanca, Spain	April 25, 2013	Ms. Margarita Becedas González—Director, Biblioteca General Histórica, *and* Ms. Tránsito Ferreras—Technical Co-ordinator, GREDOS Repository (Digital Library)
14.	'One of the Largest French Libraries with a rare public domain works collection.' (Name Withheld)	France	May 07, 2014	Confidential

Apart from this, an effort was made to obtain information from several private and public sector stakeholders involved in the digitisation process. It was hoped that this information would serve to complement the information obtained from memory institutions and assist in obtaining a more balanced view of the interests of producers and distributors of digitised versions of rare public domain textual material.

The response from these stakeholders was not encouraging. The following institutions participated in the survey.

	Institution	Category	Date completed	Resource person
1.	The Public Domain Review	Private non-profit	June 28, 2013	Confidential
2.	ProQuest LLC	Private for-profit	February 06, 2014	Confidential
3.	Europeana	Public non-profit	August 09, 2014	Confidential

b. Data Collection

The selected institutions were sent an invitation to participate in the survey, which included a brief outline of the objectives of the survey, as well as the particular aspects of digitisation on which the survey would focus.

Accordingly, each institution was requested to nominate a resource person/s who would represent the institution in the survey.

With regard to the main sample of memory institutions, the survey was designed to proceed in two stages.

Stage 1: Questionnaire (sent via post or email).
Stage 2: Interview (carried out via email, telephone or in person).

The questionnaire and interviews were in English, although in several instances, translations of the questionnaire were provided in the national languages of the resource person/s. It is noted with much appreciation that few resource persons even provided themselves with interpreters during the interview to ensure the accuracy of their responses.

Timeframe
The timeline of the survey was flexible and was capable of being adjusted to suit the needs of the individual resource persons. Thus, the period of the survey lasted from November 2012 to August 2014 (21 months). It is felt that the flexibility of the timeframe helped in securing a higher response rate.

III. Methodology

Main Sample: Memory Institutions

Stage 1: Questionnaire
The questionnaire was employed to gather both quantitative (i.e., facts and figures), as well as qualitative data (e.g., attitudes and perceptions).

The formulation of each questionnaire was carried out following an online research on the memory institution and the digitisation projects it has undertaken. Thus, each questionnaire contained a set of questions that were specific to the particular memory institution, as well as a set of general questions that were put forward to every participant in common.

The questions were drafted in multiple choice format (closed form), but the participants were always provided with the opportunity to indicate any response or opinion that was not included in the multiple choice options provided in the questionnaire. They were also encouraged to provide general comments and to elaborate upon their ideas and opinions in relation to the issues raised by the questionnaire.

Altogether, 14 completed questionnaires were collected.

Stage 2: Interview
Following the completion of the questionnaire, an interview was held with the resource person/s with the objective of following up on the responses provided in the questionnaire and with a view to discuss certain aspects of the digitisation projects in greater detail.

Interviews were held with thirteen participants (one participant was not available for an interview), usually over the telephone, while some interviews were carried out via email or in person. An average interview had a length of 30–40 minutes.

a. Secondary Sample: Stakeholders

These institutions were directly invited to participate in an interview (without being provided with a questionnaire). All interviews were conducted via email.

Bibliography

Books and Articles

Abramowicz, Michael. 2012. 'Privatizing the Public Domain.' In *Perspectives on Commercializing Innovation,* edited by F. Scott Kieff and Troy A. Paredes. Cambridge: Cambridge University Press.

Arezzo, Emanuela. 2014. 'Hyperlinks and Making Available Right in the European Union-What Future for the Internet After Svensson.' *IIC* 45: 524.

Arrow, Kenneth. 1962. 'Economic Welfare and the Allocation of Resources for Invention.' In *The Rate and Direction of Inventive Activity: Economic and Social Factors,* edited by Committee on Economic Growth of the Social Science Research Council, Universities-National Bureau Committee for Economic Research. New Jersey: Princeton University Press.

Balganesh, Shyamkrishna. 2009. 'Debunking Blackstonian Copyright (Reviewing Neil Weinstock Netanel, Copyright's Paradox (2008)).' *Yale Law Journal* 118: 1126.

Barbieri, C., A. Omizzolo and F. Rampazzi. 2003. 'Digitisation of the Archive of Plates of the Asiago Observatory and of the Specola Vaticana.' *Memorie della Società Astronomica Italiana* 74: 430.

Bechtold, S. 2004. 'Digital Rights Management in the United States and Europe.' *The American Journal of Comparative Law* 52: 323.

Becker, Lawrence. 1993. 'Deserving to Own Intellectual Property.' *Chicago-Kent Law Review* 68: 609.

Belleflamme, Paul. 2016. 'The Economics of Digital Goods: A Progress Report.' *Review of Economic Research on Copyright* 13: 1.

Benabou, Valérie Laure. 2009. 'Jurisprudence Infopaq : Que Reste-t-Il Au Juge National Pour Dire Le Droit d'auteur.' *Revue du Droit des Technologies de l'Information* 37: 71.

Benabou, Valérie Laure. 2014. 'Originalité ? Vous Avez Dit Originalités.' *LEGICOM* 53: 5.

Benabou, Valérie Laure and Séverine Dusollier. 2007. 'Draw Me a Public Domain.' In *Copyright Law: A Handbook of Contemporary Research*, edited by Paul Torremans. Edward Elgar.

Benkler, Yochai. 1999. 'Free as the Air to Common Use: First Amendment Constraints on Enclosure of the Public Domain.' *New York University Law Review* 74: 354.

Bentham, Jeremy. 1838. 'The Works of Jeremy Bentham.' In *The Works of Jeremy Bentham*, edited by John Bowring. Edinburgh: William Tait.

Bently, Lionel and Brad Sherman. 2009. *Intellectual Property Law*, 3rd ed., Oxford: Oxford University Press.

S. Mendis, *A Copyright Gambit*, Munich Studies on Innovation and Competition 11,
https://doi.org/10.1007/978-3-662-59454-4

Bently, Lionel and Brad Sherman. 2014. *Intellectual Property Law* 4th ed., Oxford: Oxford University Press.

Bodenhausen, George. 1954. 'Protection of "Related Rights"' *Law and Contemporary Problems* 19: 156.

Bollier, David. 2004. 'Why We Must Talk about the Information Commons Law.' *Law Library Journal* 96: 267.

Bollinger, Lee. 2004. 'Book Review: Protect This Work of Expression: Clarifying the Unique Economics of Intellectual Property Rights.' *Santa Clara Law Review* 44: 1287.

Boyle, James. 2003. 'The Second Enclosure Movement and the Construction of the Public Domain.' *Law and Contemporary Problems* 66: 33.

Brennan, David. 2005. 'What Is Equitable Remuneration for Intellectual Property Use?' Seminar Paper presented at Oxford Intellectual Property Research Centre. Available at <www.oiprc.ox.ac.uk/EJWP105.pdf.> accessed 31 January 2019.

Caron, Christophe. 2002. 'Protection des photographies des tableaux par le droit d'auteur.' *La Semaine Juridique Entreprise et Affaires* 7: 321.

Carson, Cindy. 1995. 'Raiders of the Lost Scrolls: The Right of Scholarly Access to the Content of Historic Documents.' *Michigan Journal of International Law* 16: 298.

Chander, Anupam and Madhavi Sunder. 2004. 'The Romance of the Public Domain.' *California Law Review* 92: 1331.

Cohen, Julie E. 2006. 'Copyright, Commodification and Culture: Locating the Public Domain.' In *The Future of the Public Domain,* edited by P Bernt Hugenholtz and Lucie Guibault. The Netherlands: Kluwer Law International.

Cohen Jehoram, Herman. 1990. 'The Nature of Related Rights of Performing Artists, Phonogram Producers and Broadcasting Organizations.' *Columbia VLA Journal of Law & the Arts* 15: 75.

Coombe, Rosemary. 1991. 'Objects of Property and Subjects of Politics: Intellectual Property Laws and Democratic Dialogue.' *Texas Law Review* 69: 1853.

Corbin, Arthur. 1921. 'Jural Relations and Their Classification.' Yale Law School Faculty Scholarship Series: Paper Number 2873. Available at <http://digitalcommons.law.yale.edu/cgi/viewcontent.cgi?article=3877&context=fss_papers> accessed 31 January 2019.

Cornish, William and David Llewelyn. 2007. *Intellectual Property: Patents, Copyright, Trade Marks and Allied Rights,* 6th ed., London: Sweet & Maxwell.

Cornish, William. 1989. *Intellectual Property*, 2nd ed., London: Sweet & Maxwell.

Cornish, William. 2003. *Intellectual Property*, 5th ed., London: Sweet & Maxwell.

Craig, Carys. 2011. *Copyright, Communication and Culture: Towards a Relational Theory of Copyright Law.* Cheltenham: Edward Elgar Publishing.

Derclaye, Estelle. 2010. 'Wonderful or Worrisome? The Impact of the ECJ Ruling in Infopaq on UK Copyright Law.' *European Intellectual Property Review* 32: 247.

Derclaye, Estelle. 2014. 'Assessing the Impact and Reception of the Court of Justice of the European Union Case Law on UK Copyright Law: What Does the Future Hold?' *Revue International de Droit d'Auteur* 5: 240.

Desbois, Henri. 1978. *Le Droit d'auteur En France,* 3rd ed., Paris: Dalloz.

Dibble, William. 1994. 'Justifying Intellectual Property.' *UCL Jurisprudence Review* 59: 74.

Dinwoodie, Graeme. 2004. 'Private Ordering and the Creation of International Copyright Norms: The Role of Public Structuring.' *Journal of Institutional and Theoretical Economics* 1: 160.

Drassinower, Abraham. 2003. 'Sweat of the Brow, Creativity, and Authorship: On Originality in Canadian Copyright Law.' *University of Ottawa Law & Technology Journal* 1: 105.

Dreier, Thomas, Gernot Schulze, and Louisa Specht. 2015. *Urheberrechtsgesetz: Kommentar,* 5th ed., Munich: CH Beck.

Dreier, Thomas and Louisa Specht. 2012. 'Germany' In *Balancing Copyright – A Survey of National Approaches,* edited by Reto M Hilty and Sylvie Nérisson. Heidelberg ; New York: Springer.

Drexl, Josef, and von Lewinski, Silke. 2007. 'The Digitising of Literary and Artistic Works.' *Electronic Journal of Comparative Law* 11. Available at <www.ejcl.org/113/article113-19.pdf> accessed 31 January 2019.

Dupuit, Jules. 1861. 'Du Principe de Propriété: Le Juste-l'utile.' *Journal des Economistes* 30:28.

Dusollier, Séverine. 2003. 'Tipping the Scale in Favour of the Right Holder: The European Anti-Circumvention Provisions.' In *Digital Rights Management: Technological, Economic, Legal and Political Aspects,* edited by Eberhard Becker, Willms Buhse, Dirk Günnewig and Neils Rump. Heidelberg ; New York: Springer.

Dusollier, Séverine. 2011. 'Scoping Study on Copyright and the Related Rights and the Public Domain.' WIPO CDIP/7/INF/2. Available at <http://www.wipo.int/edocs/mdocs/mdocs/en/cdip_7/cdip_7_inf_2.pdf> accessed 31 January 2019.

Dusollier, Séverine. 2016. 'Common Vocabulary and Definition of Inclusivity.' ERC INCLUSIVE Report 1. Paris: Sciences Po. [Unpublished]

Edelman, Bernard. 2008. *La Propriété Littéraire et Artistique*. Paris: PUF.

Edmondson, Ray. 2002. 'Memory of the World: General Guidelines to Safeguard Documentary Heritage.' CII-95/WS-11rev. Available at <http://unesdoc.unesco.org/images/0012/001256/125637e.pdf> accessed 31 January 2019.

Efroni, Zohar. 2011. *Access-Right: The Future of Digital Copyright Law*. Oxford: Oxford University Press.

Elkin-Koren, Niva. 1995. 'Copyright and Social Dialogue on the Information Super Highway: The Case Against Copyright Liability of Bulletin Board Operators.' *Cardozo Arts & Entertainment Law Journal* 13: 346.

Elkin-Koren, Niva. 1998. 'Copyrights in Cyberspace – Rights without Laws?' *Chicago-Kent Law Review* 73: 1155.

Fernie, Kate, De Francesco, Giuliana, and Dawson, David. 2008. 'MINERVA Technical Guidelines for Digital Content Creation Programmes: Version 2.0'. Available at <http://www.minervaeurope.org/publications/MINERVA%20TG%202.0.pdf> accessed 31 January 2019.

Fichte, Johann Gottlieb. 1793. 'Proof of the Unlawfulness of Reprinting: A Rationale and a Parable' (translated by Martha Woodmansee). In *Primary Sources on Copyright (1450-1900)*, edited by L. Bently and M. Kretschmer. Available at <www.copyrighthistory.org/cam/tools/request/showRecord.php?id=record_d_1793> accessed 31 January 2019.

Fisher, William. 1988. 'Reconstructing the Fair Use Doctrine.' *Harvard Law Review* 101: 1744.

Fisher, William. 2001. 'Theories of Intellectual Property.' In *New Essays in the Legal and Political Theory of Property,* edited by Stephen R. Munzer. Cambridge: Cambridge University Press.

Foster, Jonathan. 2013. 'Valorising the Cultural Content of the Commodity: On Immaterial Labour and New Forms of Informational Work.' In *Consumer Information Systems and Relationship Management: Design, Implementation and Use*, edited by Angela Lin, Jonathan Foster and Paul Scifleet. Pennsylvania: IGI Global. DOI: https://doi.org/10.4018/978-1-4666-4082-5.ch011.

Frischmann, Brett M. 2007. 'Evaluating the Demsetzian Trend in Copyright Law.' *Review of Law and Economics* 3: 649.

Garnett, Kevin, Gillian Davies and Gwilym Harbottle. 2005. *Copinger and Skone James on Copyright*, 15th ed., London: Sweet & Maxwell.

Geiger, Christophe, Franciska Schönherr, Irini Stamatoudi and Paul Torremans. 2014. 'The Information Society Directive.' In *EU Copyright Law: A Commentary*, edited by Irini Stamatoudi and Paul Torremans. Cheltenham: Edward Elgar.

Geiger, Christophe, Griffiths, Jonathan, and Hilty, Reto M. 2008. 'Declaration on a Balanced Interpretation of the "Three-Step-Test" in Copyright Law.' *IIC* 39: 707.

Gervais, Daniel J. 2002. 'Feist Goes Global: A Comparative Analysis of the Notion of Originality in Copyright Law.' *Journal-Copyright Society of the USA* 49: 949.

Gervais, Daniel, and Elizabeth Judge. 2009. 'Of Silos and Constellations: Comparing Notions of Originality in Copyright Law.' *Cardozo Arts & Entertainment Law Journal* 27: 375.

Ginsburg, Jane. 1995. 'Putting Cars on the "Information Superhighway": Authors, Exploiters and Copyright in Cyberspace.' *Columbia Law Review* 95: 1466.

Ginsburg, Jane. 1997. 'Copyright, Common Law and Sui Generis Protection of Databases in the United States and Abroad.' *University of Cincinnati Law Review* 66: 151.

Ginsburg, Jane. 2003. 'Essay: From Having Copies to Experiencing Works: The Development of an Access Right in U.S. Copyright Law.' *Journal-Copyright Society of the USA* 50: 113.

Goldstein, Paul. 2001. *International Copyright: Principles, Law and Practice.* Oxford: Oxford University Press.

Goldstein, Paul. 2003. *Copyright's Highway: From Gutenberg to the Celestial Jukebox*, revised ed., Stanford: Stanford University Press.

Gordon, Wendy. 1982. 'Fair Use as Market Failure: A Structural and Economic Analysis of the Betamax Case and Its Predecessors.' *Columbia Law Review* 82: 1600.

Gordon, Wendy. 1992. 'On Owning Information: Intellectual Property and the Restitutionary Impulse.' *Virginia Law Review* 78: 149.

Gordon, Wendy. 1993. 'A Property Right in Self-Expression: Equality and Individualism in the Natural Law of Intellectual Property.' *Yale Law Journal* 102: 1533.

Greffe, Pierre. 2004. 'Appréciation de l'originalité d'une photographie de plateau.' *Propriété industrielle* 5: 46.

Griffiths, Jonathan. 2011. 'Infopaq, BSA and the "Europeanisation" of United Kingdom Copyright Law.' *Media & Arts Law Review.* Available at <https://papers.ssrn.com/sol3/papers2.cfm?abstract_id=1777027> accessed 31 January 2019.

Griffiths, Jonathan. 2013. 'Dematerialization, Pragmatism and the European Copyright Revolution.' *Oxford Journal of Legal Studies* 33: 767.

Griffiths, Jonathan. 2014. 'The Role of the Court of Justice in the Development of European Union Copyright Law.' In *EU Copyright Law: A Commentary*, edited by Irini Stamatoudi and Paul Torremans. Cheltenham: Edward Elgar.

Guibault, Lucie, and others. 2007. 'Study on the Implementation and Effect in Member States' Laws of Directive 2001/29/EC on the Harmonisation of Certain Aspects of Copyright and Related Rights in the Information Society.' Institute for Information Law (IViR). Available at 2017 <https://papers.ssrn.com/sol3/papers.cfm?abstract_id=2006358> accessed 31 January 2019.

Hadfield, Gillian. 1988. 'The Economics of Copyright: An Historical Perspective.' *Copyright Law Symposium* 38: 1.

Handig, Christian. 2009. 'The Copyright Term "Work"- European Harmonisation at an Unknown Level.' *International Review of Intellectual Property and Competition Law* 40: 665.

Hazucha, Branislav. 2016. 'Intellectual Property, Private Ordering and Legal Certainty.' In *Legal Certainty in a Contemporary Context,* edited by Mark Fenwick and Stefan Wrbka. Heidelberg; New York: Springer.

Heckmann, Jörn. 2011. *Die Retrospektive Digitalisierung von Printpublikationen.* Frankfurt: Peter Lang.

Hegel, G.W.F. 1896. *The Philosophy of Right* (translated by SW Dyde). London: G Bell.

Heide, Thomas. 2001. 'Copyright in the EU and US: What "Access-Right"?' *Journal-Copyright Society of the USA.* Available at <https://papers.ssrn.com/sol3/papers.cfm?abstract_id=270861> accessed 31 January 2019.

Hilty, Reto M., and Nerisson Sylvie. 2012. *Balancing Copyright – A Survey of National Approaches.* Heidelberg; New York: Springer.

Hirtle, Peter. 2003. 'Archives or Assets?' *The American Archivist* 66: 235.

Hohfeld, Wesley Newcomb. 1913. 'Some Fundamental Legal Conceptions as Applied in Judicial Reasoning.' *The Yale Law Journal* 23: 16.

Höppner, Thomas. 2011. 'Reproduction in Part of Online Articles in the Aftermath of Infopaq (C-5/08): Newspaper Licensing Agency Ltd v Meltwater Holdings BV.' *European Intellectual Property Review* 33: 331.

Hughes, Justin. 1988. 'The Philosophy of Intellectual Property.' *The Georgetown Law Journal* 77: 287.

James, Steven, and Ruth Arkley. 2013.'European Jurisprudence and Its Impact on Copyright Protection.' *E-commerce Law & Policy.* Available at <https://www.lw.com/thoughtLeadership/impact-on-copyright-protection> accessed 31 January 2019.

Jeanneney, Jean-Noël. 2006. *Google and the Myth of Universal Knowledge: A View from Europe* (translated by Teresa Lavender Fagan). Chicago: University of Chicago Press.

JISC. 2005. 'Digitisation in the UK: The Case for a UK Framework.' Available at <https://www.rluk.ac.uk/wp-content/uploads/2014/02/Digitisation_in_the_UK.pdf> accessed 31 January 2019.

Kant, Immanuel. 1887. *The Philosophy of Law* (translated by W Hastie). Edinburgh: T & T Clark.

Klijn, Edwin. 2008. 'The Current State of Art in Newspaper Digitisation: A Market Perspective.' 14 D-Lib Magazine. Available at <http://www.dlib.org/dlib/january08/klijn/01klijn.html#1> accessed 31 January 2019.

Kretschmer, Michael, Estelle Derclaye, Marcella Favale and Richard Watt. 2010. 'The Relationship between Copyright and Contract Law.' Strategic Advisory Board for Intellectual Property and Policy (SABIP). Available at <http://eprints.bournemouth.ac.uk/16091/1/_contractlaw-report.pdf> accessed 31 January 2019.

Laddie, Hugh, Peter Prescott and Mary Vitoria. 2000. *The Modern Law of Copyright and Designs*, 3rd ed., London: Butterworths.

Laddie, Hugh, Peter Prescott and Mary Vitoria. 2011. *The Modern Law of Copyright and Designs*. 4th ed., New York: LexisNexis.

Lallement, Jérôme. 2011. 'La Propriété Intellectuelle Selon Walras : Entre Monautopole et Majorat Littéraire'. *Oeconomia* 1: 393.

Lambrecht, Maxime. 2015. 'Droit d'auteur et Ouverture de l'environnement Numérique : Responsabilité Sociale Contre Législation ?' Université catholique de Louvain. Available at <https://dial.uclouvain.be/pr/boreal/fr/object/boreal%3A157582> accessed 31 January 2019.

Lambrecht, Maxime. 2017. 'The Time Limit on Copyright: An Unlikely Tragedy of the Intellectual Commons.' *European Journal of Law and Economics* 43: 475.

Landes, William M., and Posner, Richard A. 2003. *The Economic Structure of Intellectual Property Law*. Massachusetts: Harvard University Press.

Laurent, Phillipe. 2011. 'Copiepresse SCRL and All v Google Inc.' *Computer Law and Security Review* 27: 542.

Lee, Stuart. 2001. *Digital Imaging: A Practical Handbook,* 1st ed., Chicago: Neal-Schuman Publishers.

Leistner, Matthias. 2011. 'The German Federal Supreme Court's Judgement on Google's Image Search – a Topical Example of the "Limitations" of the European Approach to Exceptions and Limitations.' *IIC* 42: 417.

Lemley, Mark A. 2004. 'Ex Ante versus Ex Post Justifications for Intellectual Property'. *The University of Chicago Law Review* 79:129.

Litman, Jessica. 1990. 'The Public Domain' *Emory Law Journal* 39: 965.

Locke, John. 1823. 'Second Treatise of Government', *The Works of John Locke*, revised ed., Thomas Tegg. Available at <http://socserv2.socsci.mcmaster.ca/econ/ugcm/3ll3/locke/government.pdf> accessed 31 January 2019.

Löwenheim, Ulrich, and others. 2010. *Schricker/Löwenheim Urheberrecht: Kommentar*, 4th ed., Munich: CH Beck.

Lucas, André and Sirinelli, Pierre. 1993. 'L'originalité En Droit d'auteur' La Semaine Juridique Edition Générale. Available at <http://www.lexisnexis.com/fr/droit/auth/bridge.do?rand=0.8097504848385858> accessed 31 January 2019.

Lucas, André. 2015. *Propriété Liitéraire et Artistique,* 5th ed., Paris: Dalloz.

Lucas, André, Lucas-Schloetter, Agnès and Bernault, Carine. 2017. *Traité de La Propriété Littéraire et Artistique,* 5th ed., New York: Lexis Nexis.

Lunney, Glynn. 1996. 'Reexamining Copyright's Incentives-Access Paradigm.' *Vanderbilt Law Review* 49: 483.

Lunney, Glynn. 2008. 'Copyright's Price Discrimination Panacea.' *Harvard Journal of Law and Technology* 21: 387.

MacQueen, Hector Lewis. 2014. 'Copyright Law and the Dead Sea Scrolls: A British Perspective' Edinburgh School of Law Research Paper Number 2014/25. Available at <https://papers.ssrn.com/abstract=2430794> accessed 31 January 2019.

MacQueen, Hector Lewis, Charlotte Waelde and Graeme Laurie. 2008. *Contemporary Intellectual Property: Law and Policy*. Oxford: Oxford University Press.

Madow, Michael. 1993. 'Private Ownership of Public Image: Popular Culture and Publicity Rights.' *California Law Review* 81: 125.

Marciano, Alain, and Nathalie Moreau. 2016. 'Museums, Property Rights, and Photographs of Works of Art. Why Reproduction through Photograph Should Be Free.' *Review of Economic Research on Copyright Issues* 13: 1.

Margoni, Thomas. 2014. 'The Digitisation of Cultural Heritage: Originality, Derivative Works and (Non) Original Photographs.' IVIR University of Amsterdam. Available at <https://papers.ssrn.com/sol3/papers.cfm?abstract_id=2573104> accessed 31 January 2019.

Margoni, Thomas. 2016. 'The Harmonisation of EU Copyright Law: The Originality Standard.' In *Global Governance of Intellectual Property in the 21st Century*, edited by Mark Perry. Switzerland: Springer International Publishing.

Maron, Nancy L. 2011. 'The National Archives (UK): Digitisation with Commercial Partnerships via the Licensed Internet Associates Programme.' Ithaka S+R. Available at <http://www.sr.ithaka.org/sites/default/files/reports/SCA_IthakaSR_CaseStudies_TNA_2011.pdf> accessed 31 January 2019.

Mazziotti, Giuseppe. 2008. *EU Digital Copyright Law and the End-User*. Heidelberg; Berlin: Springer.

Mazzone, Jason. 2011. *Copyfraud and Other Abuses of Intellectual Property Law*. Stanford: Stanford University Press.

McKenzie, Richard and Dwight Lee. 2008. *In Defense of Monopoly*. Michigan: University of Michigan Press.

Merges, Robert P. 1993. 'Are You Making Fun of Me? Notes on Market Failure and the Parody Defense in Copyright.' *AIPLA Quarterly Journal* 21: 305.

Michaux, Benoît. 2009. 'L'originalité En Droit d'auteur, Une Notion Davantage Communautaire Après l'arrêt Infopaq'. *Auteurs & Media* 5: 473.

Minero, Gemma. 2014. 'The Term Directive.' In *EU Copyright Law: A Commentary*, edited by Paul Torremans and Stamatoudi, Irini Cheltenham: Edward Elgar.

Morrison, Alan, Michael Popham and Karen Wikander. 1999. *Creating and Documenting Electronic Texts: A Guide to Good Practice*. Arts and Humanities Data Service (AHDS). Available at <https://ota.ox.ac.uk/documents/creating/cdet/chap3.html#2> accessed 31 January 2019.

Nerisson, Sylvie. 2014. 'The Rental and Lending Rights Directive.' In *EU Copyright Law: A Commentary* Irini Stamatoudi and Paul Torremans. Cheltenham: Edward Elgar.

Netanel, Neil Weinstock. 1996. 'Copyright and a Democratic Civil Society' *Yale Law Journal* 106: 283.

Nimmer, Melville and Paul Geller. 1998. *International Copyright Law and Practice*. New York: Matthew Bender & Co.

Norman, Helen. 2014. *Intellectual Property Law: Directions*, 2nd ed., Oxford: Oxford University Press.

Nozick, Robert. 1974. *Anarchy, State and Utopia*. New York: Basic Books.

Ochoa, Tyler T. 2002. 'Origins and Meanings of the Public Domain.' *University of Dayton Law Review* 28: 215.

Ottolia, Andrea. 2004. 'Preserving User's Rights in DRM: Dealing with "Judicial Particularism" in the Information Society.' *IIC* 35: 491.

Peifer, Karl-Nikolaus. 2014. '"Individualität" or Originality? Core Concepts in German Copyright Law.' *GRUR International* 12: 1100.

Pila, Justine and Paul Torremans. 2016. *European Intellectual Property Law*. Oxford: Oxford University Press.

Pollaud-Dulian, Frédéric. 2000. 'O. Lalignant, La Véritable Condition d'application Du Droit d'auteur: Originalité Ou Création?' *Revue internationale de droit comparé* 52: 270.

Pollaud-Dulian, Frédéric. 2014. *Le Droit D'Auteur*, 2nd ed., Paris: Economica.

Posner, Richard A., and William M. Landes. 2003. 'Indefinitely Renewable Copyright.' *University of Chicago Law Review* 70: 471.

Puglia, S., and E. Rhodes. 2007. 'Digital Imaging-How Far Have We Come and What Still Needs to Be Done.' *RLG DigiNews*. Available at <http://worldcat.org/arcviewer/2/OCC/2009/07/29/H1248893457622/viewer/file2.html#pubinfo> accessed 31 January 2019.

Radin, Margaret Jane. 1982. 'Property and Personhood.' *Stanford Law Review* 34: 957.

Rahmatian, Andreas. 2013. 'Originality in UK Copyright Law: The Old "Skill and Labour" Doctrine Under Pressure.' *IIC* 44: 4.

Rayna, Thierry. 2008. 'Understanding the Challenges of the Digital Economy: The Nature of Digital Goods.' *Communications & Strategies* 71: 13.

Reinbothe, Jörg, and Silke von Lewinski. 2015. *The WIPO Treaties on Copyright: A Commentary on the WCT, the WPPT and the BTAP*, 2nd ed., Oxford: Oxford University Press.

Ricketson, Sam. 1991. 'The Concept of Originality in Anglo-Australian Copyright Law.' *Journal-Copyright Society of the USA* 39: 265.

Ricolfi, Marco. 2013. 'Public Sector Information as Open Data: Access, Re-Use and the Third Innovation Paradigm.' In *Access to Information and Knowledge: 21st Century Challenges in Intellectual Property and Knowledge Governance*, edited by Dana Beldiman. Cheltenham: Edward Elgar.

Ricolfi, Marco. 2015. 'The New Paradigm of Creativity and Innovation and Its Corollaries for the Law of Obligations.' In *Kritika: Essays on Intellectual Property* edited by, Peter Drahos, Gustavo Ghidini and Hans Ullrich. Cheltenham: Edward Elgar.

Rosati Eleonora. 2010. 'Originality in US and UK Copyright Experiences as a Springboard for an EU-Wide Reform Debate.' *IIC* 5: 524.

Rosati Eleonora. 2011. 'Originality in a Work, or a Work of Originality: The Effects of the Infopaq Decision'. *Journal-Copyright Society of the USA* 58: 795.

Rosati Eleonora. 2013. *Originality in EU Copyright Full Harmonization through Case Law*. Cheltenham: Edward Elgar.

Salokannel, Marjut. 1997. *Ownership of Rights in Audiovisual Productions: A Comparative Study*. Netherlands: Martinus Nijhoff Publishers.

Samuelson, Pamela. 2006. 'Challenges in Mapping the Public Domain'. In *The Future of the Public Domain* edited by, Lucie Guibault and P. Bernt Hugenholtz. The Netherlands: Kluwer Law International.

Sherman, Brad and Lionel Bently. 2008. *The Making of Modern Intellectual Property Law. The British Experience*. Cambridge: Cambridge University Press.

Skone James, EP and others. 1991. *Copinger and Skone James on Copyright* 13th ed., London: Sweet & Maxwell.

Steinhauer, Eric W. 2012. 'Informationskompetenz Und Recht'. In *Handbuch Informationskompetenz*, edited by Wilfried Sühl-Strohmenger. Berlin: Walter de Gruyter.

Sterk, Stewart E. 1996. 'Rhetoric and Reality in Copyright Law.' *Michigan Law Review* 94: 1197.

Synodinou, Tatiana-Elena. 2010. 'The Lawful User and a Balancing of Interests in European Copyright Law' *IIC* 41: 819.

Talke, Armin. 2010. 'Lichtbildschutz Für Digitale Bilder von Zweidimensionalen Vorlagen' *Zeitschrift für Urheber- und Medienrecht* 11: 846.

Toft, Kirsten. 2014. 'Case Comment: Suzy Taylor v Alison Maguire.' *Entertainment Law Review* 25: 154.

Torremans, Paul. 2009. 'Legal Issues Pertaining to the Restoration and Reconstitution of Manuscripts, Sheet Music, Paintings and Films for Marketing Purposes.' In *Copyright Law: A Handbook of Contemporary Research,* edited by Paul Torremans. Cheltenham: Edward Elgar.

Torremans, Paul. 2016. *Holyoak and Torremans: Intellectual Property Law*, 8th ed., Oxford: Oxford University Press.

Toula, Christopher M. and Gregory C. Lisby. 2014. 'Towards an Affirmative Public Domain.' *Cultural Studies* 28: 997.

Towse, Ruth, Christian Handke and Paul Stepan. 2008. 'The Economics of Copyright Law: A Stocktake of the Literature.' *Review of Economic Research on Copyright Issues* 5: 1.

Ulmer, E. 1980. *Urheber-Und Verlagsrecht,* 3rd ed., Heidelberg; Berlin: Springer.

Van Eechoud, Mireille. 2012. 'Along the Road to Uniformity-Diverse Readings of the Court of Justice Judgements on Copyright Work.' *JIPITEC* 3: 60.

Van Gompel, Stef. 2011. *Formalities in Copyright Law: An Analysis of Their History, Rationales and Possible Future.* The Netherlands: Kluwer Law International.

Van Gompel, Stef and Erlend Lavik. 2013. 'Quality, Merit Aesthetics and Purpose: An Inquiry into EU Copyright Law's Eschewal of Other Criteria than Originality.' *Revue International du Droit d'Auteur* 236: 100.

Vivant, Michel and Jean-Michel Bruguière. 2016. *Le Droit d'auteur et Droits Voisins,* 3rd ed., Paris: Dalloz.

von Lewinski, Silke. 2014. 'Introduction: The Notion of a Work under EU Law.' *GRUR International* 63: 1098.

Vousden, Stephen. 2010. 'Infopaq and the Europeanization of Copyright Law.' *The WIPO Journal* 1: 197

Waisman, Agustin. 2009. 'Revisiting Originality.' *European Intellectual Property Review* 31: 370.

Walras, Léon. 1859. 'De La Propriété Intellectuelle.' *Journal des économistes* 24: 392.

Walter, Michael, and Silke von Lewinski. 2010. *European Copyright Law: A Commentary*. Oxford: Oxford University Press.

World Intellectual Property Organization. 1981. *'Related Rights': Guide to the Rome Convention and to the Phonograms Convention.* Geneva: WIPO.

Reports and Submissions

EU Commission. 2000. *Report from the Commission to the Council, the European Parliament and the Economic and Social Committee on the Implementation and Effects of Directive 91/250/EEC on the Legal Protection of Computer Programmes.* 10 April 2000. COM (2000) 199 Final.

EU Commission. 2005. *DG Internal Market and Services Working Paper: First Evaluation of Directive 96/9/EC on the Legal Protection of Databases.* 12 December 2005. Available at <http://ec.europa.eu/internal_market/copyright/docs/databases/evaluation_report_en.pdf> accessed 31 January 2019.

Garcia, S. *Succeed Interoperability Workshop Report.* Impact Centre of Competence. Available at <https://www.digitisation.eu/succeed-interoperabily-workshop-report/> accessed 31 January 2019.

High Level Expert Group on Digital Libraries. 2008. *Final Report on Public Private Partnerships for the Digitisation and Online Accessibility of Europe's Cultural Heritage.* i2010 European Digital Libraries Initiative.

High Level Expert Group on Digital Libraries. 2009. *Final Report: "Digital Libraries: Recommendations and Challenges for the Future".* i2010 European Digital Libraries Initiative. Available at <www.dlorg.eu/uploads/External%20Publications/HLG%20Final%20Report%202009%20clean.pdf> accessed 31 January 2019.

Niggemann, Elisabeth, Jacques De Decker and Maurice Lévy,. 2011. *The New Renaissance: Report of the Comité des Sages on Bringing Europe's Cultural Heritage Online.* Available at <https://ec.europa.eu/digital-single-market/sites/digital-agenda/files/final_report_cds_0.pdf> accessed 31 January 2019.

Rappaport, Edward B. 1998. *Copyright Term Extension: Estimating the Economic Values.* CRS Report for Congress. Congressional Research Service (USA).

Renda, Andrea and others. 2015. *The Implementation, Application and Effects of the EU Directive on Copyright in the Information Society.* Centre for European Policy Studies.

Tomkins, David. 2009. *Electronic Ephemera: Digitised Selections from the John Johnson Collection.* JISC.

News Articles and Blog Articles

Aigrain, Phillipe. 'Nous Devons Empêcher La Privatisation Du Domaine Public'. 16 January 2013. *Communs.* Accessed 31 January 2019 <http://paigrain.debatpublic.net/?p=6333>

'British Library and Brightsolid Partnership to Digitise Upto 40 Million Pages of Historic Newspapers'. 19 May 2010. *British Library.* Accessed 31 January 2019 <http://pressandpolicy.bl.uk/Press-Releases/British-Library-and- brightsolid-partnership-to-digitise-up-to-40-million-pages-of-historic-newspapers-271.aspx>

Cellan-Jones, Rory. 'Wikipedia Painting Row Escalates'. 17 July 2009. *BBC News.* Accessed 31 January 2019 <http://news.bbc.co.uk/2/hi/technology/8156268.stm>

Filippetti, Aurélie, Gallois, Louis, and Racine, Bruno. 'Investing in the Future: Two Major Partnerships Have Been Concluded to Digitise and Make Available Collections Held by the BnF'. *BnF* (Bibliothèque nationale de France). Accessed 31 January 2019 <http://www.bnf.fr/documents/cp_accords_proquest-believe_eng.pdf>

Gómez, Pablo Uceda, and Keller, Paul. 'The Missing Decades: The 20th Century Black Hole in Europeana'. 13 November 2015. *Europeana.* Accessed 31 January 2019 <http://pro.europeana.eu/blogpost/the-missing-decades-the-20th-century-black-hole-in-europeana>

Lenssen, Philipp. 'Freeing Google Books'. 10 January 2007. *blogoscoped.* Accessed 31 January 2019 <http://blogoscoped.com/archive/2007-01-10-n14.html>

martijnd, 'Music Movies, Books...Museums Next'. Comment. 17 July 2009. *Slashdot.* Accessed 31 January 2019 <https://news.slashdot.org/comments.pl?sid=1305967&cid=28728209>

Moeller, Erik. 'Protecting the Public Domain and Sharing Our Cultural Heritage' 16 July 2009. *Wikimedia Blog.* Accessed 31 January 2019 <https://blog.wikimedia.org/2009/07/16/protecting-the-public-domain-and-sharing-our-cultural-heritage/>

Montilly, Juliette. 'Guillaume, Jeté Du Louvre Pour Avoir Pris Des Photos : "C'est Un Mépris Du Visiteur"' 10 March 2017. *Rue89-Le Nouvel Observateur.* Accessed 31 January 2019 <http://tempsreel.nouvelobs.com/rue89/20170310.OBS6400/guillaume-jete-du-louvre-pour-avoir-pris-des-photos-c-est-un-mepris-du-visiteur.html>

'NPG and BAPLA at War with Wikipedia'. 22 July 2009. *The British Journal of Photography* Accessed 31 January 2019 <https://web.archive.org/web/20090805101606/http://www.bjp-online.com/public/showPage.html?page=866109>

Sullivan, Danny. 'Authorama: Testing If Google Can Restrict Public Domain Books It Offers For Download'. January 10 2007. *Search Engine Land.* Accessed 31 January 2019 <http://searchengineland.com/authorama-testing-if-google-can-restrict-public-domain-books-it-offers-for-download-10232>

Patry, William. 'Photographs and Derivative Works'. *The Patry Copyright Blog.* 5 February 2008. Accessed 31 January 2019 <http://williampatry.blogspot.com/2008/02/photographs-and-derivative-works.html>

'Press Release: Google and the Italian Ministry of Cultural Heritage Reach Agreement to Digitise Works from Italian Libraries' 10 March 2010. *pressatgoogle.* Accessed 31 January 2019 <https://sites.google.com/a/pressatgoogle.com/italianlibraries/press-release-and-or-googlegram>

Gary, Nicholas. 'Refuser La Privatisation Du Domaine Public Par La BnF'. 20 January 2013. *ActuaLitté* Accessed 31 January 2019 <https://www.actualitte.com/usages/refuser-la-privatisation-du-domaine-public-par-la-bnf-39680.htm>

'U.K. National Portrait Gallery Threatens U.S. Citizen with Legal Action over Wikimedia Images'. 14 July 2009. *Wikinews.* Accessed 31 January 2019 <https://en.wikinews.org/wiki/U.K._National_Portrait_Gallery_threatens_U.S._citizen_with_legal_action_over_Wikimedia_images>

Legal Dictionaries and Encyclopaedias

Cornu, Gérard. 2016. *Vocabulaire juridique,* 11th ed.,PUF.

Lehmann, Jeffrey, and Shirelle Phelps. 2008. *West's encyclopedia of American law*, 2nd ed.,The Gale Group. Accessed 31 January 2019 <http://legal-dictionary.thefreedictionary.com/exclusive>

Mendis, Sunimal. 2017. 'Europeana'. In *Dictionnaire des Biens communs* edited by, Marie Cornu, Fabienne Orsi and Judith Rochfeld. Paris: PUF.

Mendis, Sunimal. 2017. 'Manifeste Pour Le Domaine Public'. In *Dictionnaire des Biens communs* edited by, Marie Cornu, Fabienne Orsi and Judith Rochfeld. Paris: PUF.

Other Documents and Resources

Communia. 2010.'The Public Domain Manifesto'. Accessed 31 January 2019 <www.publicdomainmanifesto.org/manifesto>

'Cooperative Agreement between Google Inc and the University of Michigan/University Library'. Accessed 31 January 2019 <www.lib.umich.edu/files/services/mdp/um-google-cooperative-agreement.pdf>

'Copyright Notice: Digital Images, Photographs and the Internet 1/2014'. November 2015 (updated version). *Intellectual Property Office (UK).* Accessed 31 January 2019 <www.gov.uk/government/uploads/system/uploads/attachment_data/file/481194/c-notice-201401.pdf>

Cornell University Library/Research Department, 'Moving Theory into Practice: Digital Imaging Tutorial'. Accessed 31 January 2019 <http://preservationtutorial.library.cornell.edu/contents.html>

'Digital Rights Management'. *encoding.com*. Accessed 31 January 2019 <www.encoding.com/digital-rights-management-drm/>

EPSI Platform. 2010. 'Clarifying the Concept of Public-Task'. Fact Sheet.

Europeana. 2010. 'The Europeana Public Domain Charter'. Accessed 31 January 2019 <http://pro.europeana.eu/files/Europeana_Professional/Publications/Public%20Domain%20Charter%20-%20EN.pdf>

'Guidelines for Digitisation of Archival Material', edited by Dipti S. Tripathi. Accessed 31 January 2019 <https://namami.gov.in/downloads>

'Guidelines for Digitisation of Manuscripts'. Accessed 31 January 2019 <https://fr.scribd.com/document/376803180/Guidelines-for-Digitization-of-Manuscripts>

JISC Digital Media, 'Guide: File Formats and Compression'. Accessed 31 January 2019 <https://edu.hioa.no/ark2200/h18/pensum/jisc/infokit/file_formats/redundancy-and-irrelevancy.html>

Museo Galileo. 'Ancient Mathematics'. Accessed 31 January 2019 <www.museogalileo.it/en/explore/libraries/digitallibrary/digitalcollections/en-802.html>

Museo Galileo. 'Digital Reproduction'. Accessed 31 January 2019 <http://www.museogalileo.it/en/explore/libraries/library/services/digitalreproduction.html>

National Endowment for the Humanities, US, *Digitizing Illuminated Manuscripts at the Walters Art Museum, Maryland* <www.youtube.com/watch?v=umOc5nXmO_U> accessed 22 February 2017 (Video)

Puglia S, Reed J and Rhodes E, 'Technical Guidelines for Digitizing Archival Materials for Electronic Access: Creation of Production Master Files-Raster Images'. Accessed 31 January 2019 <www.archives.gov/files/preservation/technical/guidelines.pdf>

The British Newspaper Archive, 'Terms and Conditions: How You Can Use Our Service'. Accessed 31 January 2019 <www.britishnewspaperarchive.co.uk/content/terms_and_conditions>

The National Archives, 'Information Fair Trader Scheme (IFTS) and Regulation'. Accessed 31 January 2019 <www.nationalarchives.gov.uk/information-management/re-using-public-sector-information/ifts-and-regulation/>

Andrea, N Maria Teresa. Tempera, 'MINERVA EC – Technical Guidelines' Accessed 31 January 2019 <www.minervaeurope.org/technicalguidelines.htm>

Woodford, C. 2016. 'Digital Cameras', *Explain That Stuff.* Accessed 31 January 2019 <www.explainthatstuff.com/digitalcameras.html>

Ottewill, Matt. 'How Do Audio Analogue to Digital Converters Work?' *Planet of tunes.* Accessed 31 January 2019 <www.planetoftunes.com/digital-audio/how-do-analogueue-to-digital-converters-work.html#.WHyiEU0zXIW>

Peter, Hirtle. 'Archives or Assets?'. Presentation at 67th Annual Meeting of the Society of American Archivists, Los Angeles, USA, 21 August 2003. Accessed 31 January 2019 <https://core.ac.uk/download/pdf/4900558.pdf>

Wikipedia, 'National Portrait Gallery and Wikimedia Foundation Copyright Dispute' Accessed 31 January 2019 <https://en.wikipedia.org/wiki/National_Portrait_Gallery_and_Wikimedia_Foundation_copyright_dispute>

Cases: Austria

O (Peter) v F KG [2006] ECDR 9

Cases: Belgium

Artessuto v B&T Textilia [2012] SC C1101018 N

Cour d'appel de Bruxelles, *Google Inc v Copiepresse SCRL et al,* Ch 9, 5 mai 2011

M-Design Benelux SPRL [2013] SC C120263 N/1

Cases: Canada

The Law Society of Upper Canada v CCH Canadian Ltd [2004] SCC 13

Cases: Court of Justice of the European Union

Case C-435/12 *ACI Adam BV and Others v Stichting de Thuiskopie* [2014] ECDR 13

Case C-393/09 *Bezpečnostní softwarová asociace – Svaz softwarové ochrany v Ministerstvo kultury* [2011] ECR I-13971

Case C-201/13 *Deckmyn v Vandersteen* [2014] ECDR 21

Case C-604/10 *Football Dataco v Yahoo! UK Ltd* [2010] 2 CMLR 24

Cases C-403/08 and 429/08 *Football Association Premier League Ltd et al v QC Leisure et al* [2011] ECR I – 09083 (joined cases)

Case C-5/08 *Infopaq International A/S v Danske Dagblades Forening* [2009] ECR – 6569

Case C-89/04 *Mediakabel BV v Commissariaat voor de Media* [2005] ECR I 4891
Case C-466/12 *Nils Svensson, Sten Sjögren, Madelaine Sahlman, Pia Gadd v Retriever Sverige AB* [2014] ECDR 9
Case C-355/12 *Nintendo Co Ltd v PC Box Srl* [2014] ECDR 6
Case C-145/10 *Painer v Standard Verlags GmbH et al* [2012] ECR I -12533
Case C-406/10 *SAS Institute Inc v World Programming Ltd,* [2012] 3 CMLR 4
Case C-203/02 *The British Horseracing Board Ltd and Others v William Hill Organization Ltd* [2004] ECR I-10415
Case C-128/11 *UsedSoft GmbH v Oracle International Corp* [2012] [2012] ECDR 19

Cases: France

Cour de Cassation crim, 27 novembre 1869: DP 1870 (1) 186
Cour de Cassation crim, 18 mai 1938: Gaz Pal 1938 (2) 311
Cour d'appel de Paris, 19 déc 1962, D, 1963 609 *[Sté des bibliophiles c Crommelynck]*
Cour d'Appel de Paris 4eme Ch, 21 mars 1989, RIDA 156 (1989) 333 *[Harrap France c Masson Editeur]*
Cour de Cassation, Ch civ 1, 2 mai 1989, 87-17657 *[Coprosa]*
Cour de Cassation, Ch civ 1, 16 avril 1991, 89-21071 *[Isermatic France]*
Cour d'Appel de Paris, 4eme Ch, 23 septembre 1992, RIDA 142 (1993) 224 *[Michel Lafon c Librarie Arthème Fayard]*
Cour d'Appel de Paris, 15 octobre 2003; Propriété industrielle (Ed. du Juris-classeur), 2004, n° 5, mai, commentaires, § 46 *[Mirkine]*
TGI Nanterre, Ch 1 A, 19 Janvier 2005 JurisData 2005-279499 *[Sawkins c Société Harmonia Mundi]*
Cour d'appel d'Aix-en-Provence, 6 mai 2010 *[Deux Rougets]*
Cour de Cassation, 1er ch Civ, 20 oct 2011, 10-21251 *[Deux Rougets]*
Cour de cassation, Ch civ 1, 17 octobre 2012, 11-21641 *[Codix]*
Cour d'appel de Paris, 1èrè Ch, 16 janvier 2013, *11-18788*
Cour de Cassation Ch civ, 15 mai 2015, 13-27391 [Glamour]
TGI Paris, 3eme Ch 1, 21 mai 2015 *[Bowstir Ltd, GM c Egotrade SARL]*

Cases: Germany

BGH 09.05.1985 – I ZR 52/83, GRUR [1985] 1041 – *Inkasso Programm*
BGH, 08.11.1989 – I ZR 14/88, GRUR [1990] 669 – *Bibelreproduktion*
OLG Düsseldorf 13.02.1996 – 20 U 115/95, GRUR [1997] 49 – *Beuys-Fotografien*
BGH, 28.05.1998 – I ZR 81/96, GRUR [1998] 916 – *Stadtplanwerk*
BGH, 03.11.1999 – I ZR 55/97, GRUR [2000] 317 – *Werbefotos.*
BGH, 07.12.2000 – I ZR 146/98, GRUR [2001] 755 – *Telefonkarte*
BGH, 29.04.2010 – I ZR 69/08, GRUR [2010] 628 – *Vorschaubilder*
BGH, 12.05.2011 – I ZR 53/10, GRUR [2012] 58 – *Seilzirkus*
LG Köln 12.12.2013, 14 O 613/12 – *Rote Couch*
BGH, 13.11.2013 – I ZR 143/12, GRUR [2014] 175 – *Geburtstagszug*
LG Berlin 03.05.2016, 15 O 428/15 – *Reiss Engelhorn Museum I*
LG Stuttgart 27.09.2016, 17 O 690/15 – *Reiss Engelhorn Museum II*
OLG Stuttgart 31.05.2017, 4 U 204/16 – *Reiss Engelhorn Museum II (Appeal)*

Cases: Israel

Eisenmann v Qimron, 54[3] PD 817

Cases: United Kingdom

Antiquesportfolio.com v Rodney Fitch [2001] FSR 345
Fredrick Emerson v Chas Davies [1843] 3 Story Under Section Rep 708
GA Cramp Sons Ltd v Frank Smythson Ltd [1944] AC 329
Graves case [1869] LR 4 QB 715
Interlego v Tyco [1989] AC 217
Ladbroke (Football) Ltd v William Hill (Football) Ltd [1964] 1 WLR 273
LB (Plastics) Ltd v Swish Products Limited [1979] RPC 551 (Ch)
Macmillan and Company Ltd v K and J Cooper [1924] 26 BOMLR 292
Powell v Head [1879] 12 Ch D 686
Reject Shop Plc v Robert Manners [1995] FSR 870
Rose Plastics GmbH v William Beckett & Co (Plastics) Ltd [1989] FSR 113 (Ch)
SAS Institute Inc v World Programmeming Ltd [2015] ECDR 17
Sawkins v Hyperion [2005] 1 WLR 3281
Taylor v Maguire [2013] EWHC 3804 (IPEC)
Temple Island Collections Ltd v New English Teas Ltd [2011] EWPCC 21
The Newspaper Licensing Agency and others v Meltwater Holding BV and others [2010] EWHC 3099 (High Court of Justice Chancery Division)
The Newspaper Licensing Agency and others v Meltwater Holding BV and others [2011] EWCA Civ 890 (Court of Appeal)
The Newspaper Licensing Agency v Marks and Spencer plc [2003] 1 AC 551 558
Ultra Marketing(UK)Ltd v Universal Components Ltd [2004] EWHC 468 (Ch)
University of London Press v University Tutorial Press [1916] 2 Ch 601
Walter and Another v Lane [1900] AC 539

Cases: United States

Bridgeman Art Library Ltd, v Corel Corporation [1998] 25 F Supp 2d 421 (SDNY)
Bridgeman Art Library Ltd, v Corel Corporation [1999] 36 F Supp 2d 191 (SDNY) (Rehearing)
Campbell et al v Acuff-Rose Music Inc [1994] 510 US 569
Durham Industries, Inc v Tomy Corp [1980] 630 F2d 905 (2d Cir)
Feist Publications, Inc, v Rural Telephone Service Co [1991] 499 US 340
Kelly v Arriba Soft Corporation [2003] 336 F3d 811
L Batlin & Son, Inc v Snyder [1976] 536 F2d 486
Perfect 10 Inc v Google Inc [2007] 508 F3d 1146
SHL Imaging Inc v Artisan House Inc [2000] 117 F Supp 2d 301 (SDNY)

Legislation and Pre-enactment Material: European Union

Amended proposal for a European Parliament and Council Directive on the harmonisation of certain aspects of copyright and related rights in the information society [1999] OJ C180/6
Completing the Internal Market: White paper to the Commission from the European Council 1985 COM (85) 310 final
Council Decision 94/800/EC of 22 December 1994 concerning the conclusion on behalf of the European Community, with regard to matters within its competence, of the agreements reached in the Uruguay Round multilateral negotiations (1986-1994) [1994] OJ L 336/1
Council Decision of 16 March 2000 on the approval, on behalf of the European Community, of the WIPO Copyright Treaty and the WIPO Performances and Phonograms Treaty, [2000] O JL 89/6
Council Directive 92/100/EEC of 19 November 1992 on rental right and lending right and on certain rights related to copyright in the field of intellectual property [1992] OJ L 346/61
Council Directive 93/98/EEC of 29th October 1993 harmonizing the term of protection of copyright and related rights [1993] OJ L 290/9
Council Directive 2015/2436 of the European Parliament and of the Council of 16 December 2015 to approximate the laws of the Member States relating to trade marks [2015] OJ L 336/1
Council Regulation (EC) 6/2002 of 12 December 2001 on Community designs [2002] OJ L 3/1
Directive 96/9/EC of the European Parliament and of the Council of the European Union of 11 March 1996 on the legal protection of databases [1996] OJ L 77/20
Directive 2001/29/EC of the European Parliament and of the Council of 22 May 2001 on the harmonisation of certain aspects of copyright and related rights in the information society [2001] OJ L 167/10
Directive 2003/98/EC of the European Parliament and of the Council of 17 November 2003 on the re-use of public sector information [2003] OJ L 345/90
Directive 2006/115/EC of the European Parliament and of the Council of 12 December 2006 on rental right and lending right and on certain rights related to copyright in the field of intellectual property [2006] OJ L 376/28 [2006] OJ L 376/28
Directive 2006/116/EC of the European Parliament and of the Council of 12 December 2006 on the term of protection of copyright and certain related rights 2006 OJ L 372/12
Directive 2006/116/EC of the European Parliament and of the Council of 12 December 2006 on the term of protection of copyright and certain related rights [2006] OJ L 372/12
Directive 2009/24/EC of The European Parliament and of the Council of 23 April 2009 on the legal protection of computer programmes [2009] OJ L 116/16
Directive 2013/37/EU of the European Parliament and of the Council of 26 June 2013 amending Directive 2003/98/EC on the re-use of public sector information [2013] OJ L 175/1
European Commission Recommendation of 27 October 2011 on the digitisation and online accessibility of cultural material and digital preservation [2011] OJ L 283/39
Proposal for a directive of the European Parliament and of the Council on copyright in the Digital Single Market, 14 September 2016, COM (2016) 593
Proposal for a European Parliament and Council Directive on the Harmonization of Certain Aspects of Copyright and Related Rights in the Information Society, 10 December 1997, COM (1997) 628
Proposal for a European Parliament and Council Directive on the harmonization of certain aspects of copyright and related rights in the Information Society [1998] OJ C 108/03
Recommendation 2006/585/EC of the European Commission of 24 August 2006 on the digitisation and online accessibility of cultural material and digital preservation [2006] OJ L 236/28
Recommendation 2011/711/EU of the European Commission of 27 October 2011 on the digitisation and online accessibility of cultural material and digital preservation [2011] OJ L 283/39
Regulation (EU) 1257/2012 of 17 December 2012 implementing enhanced cooperation in the area of the creation of unitary patent protection [2012] OJ L 361/1

Legislation and Pre-enactment Material: France

Intellectual Property Code (1992), consolidated version, 2018.
Code on the Relations between the Public and the Administration, consolidated version, 2017
Loi n° 2012-287 du 1er mars 2012 relative à l'exploitation numérique des livres indisponibles du XXe siècle, JORF n°0060 10 mars 2012 4424

Legislation and Pre-enactment Material: Germany

First Act amending the Re-use of Information Act of 8 July 2015
Re-Use of Public-Sector Information Act of 13 December 2006
German Copyright Act 1965 BGBl. I S. 1273

Legislation and Pre-enactment Material: Ireland

Copyright and Related Rights Act n°28 of 2000
European Communities (Re-Use of Public Sector Information) Regulations S.I. n° 279 of 2005
The European Communities (Re-use of Public Sector Information) (Amendment) Regulations S.I. n° 525 of 2015

Legislation and Pre-enactment Material: United Kingdom

Copyright Act 1911 (1&2 Geo 5 Ch 46)
Copyright, Designs and Patents Act 1988
The Re-use of Public Sector Information Regulations n°1415 (2015)

Legislation and Pre-enactment Material: United States

Copyright Act (1976), 17 United States Code

Treaties and Conventions

Consolidated version of the treaty on the functioning of the European Union [2012] OJ C 326/47
Agreement on Trade-Related Aspects of Intellectual Property Rights, Apr. 15, 1994, Marrakesh Agreement Establishing the World Trade Organization, Annex 1C, Legal Instruments -- Results of the Uruguay Round vol. 31; 33 I.L.M. 81 (1994)
Beijing Treaty on Audiovisual Performances (2012)
Berne Convention for the Protection of Literary and Artistic Works S. Treaty Doc. No. 99-27 (1986) 1161 U.N.T.S. 3

Convention for the Protection of Producers of Phonograms Against Unauthorized Duplication of their Phonograms (1971)
International Convention for the Protection of Performers, Producers of Phonograms and Broadcasting Organizations, Oct. 26, 1961, 496 U.N.T.S. 43
The Copyrights and Related Rights Regulations 1996 (S.I. 1996/2967)
WIPO Copyright Treaty Apr. 12, 1997, S. Treaty Doc. No. 105-17 36 ILM 65 (1997) (entry into force March 6, 2002)
WIPO Performances and Phonograms Treaty, Apr. 12, 1997, S. Treaty Doc. No. 105-17 36 ILM 76 (1997) (entry into force May 20, 2002)

FSC
www.fsc.org
MIX
Papier | Fördert gute Waldnutzung
FSC® C083411

Kolibri 360 GmbH
Ferdinand-Jühlke-Straße 7
99095 Erfurt, Deutschland
produktsicherheit@kolibri360.de